The History of New Thought

Swedenborg Studies No. 21

The History of New Thought

*From Mind Cure to Positive Thinking
and the Prosperity Gospel*

John S. Haller Jr.
Foreword by Robert C. Fuller

Swedenborg Foundation Press
West Chester, Pennsylvania

Swedenborg Studies is a scholarly series published by the Swedenborg Foundation. The primary purpose of the series is to make materials available for understanding the life and thought of Emanuel Swedenborg (1688–1772) and the impact his thought has had on others. The Foundation undertakes to publish original studies, English translations of such studies, and primary sources that are otherwise difficult to access. Proposals should be sent to: Editor, Swedenborg Foundation, 320 North Church Street, West Chester, PA 19380.

Library of Congress Cataloging-in-Publication Data
Haller, John S.
    The history of New Thought : from mind cure to positive thinking and the prosperity gospel / John S. Haller, Jr. ; foreword by Robert C. Fuller.
    p. cm. — (Swedenborg studies ; 21)
   Includes bibliographical references and index.
   isbn 978-0-87785-348-0 (alk. paper)
1. New Thought. 2. Mind and body. I. Title.
   bf639.h4195 2012
   299′.93—dc23
                        2012018465

29.95

Edited by Morgan Beard
Index by Robin Haller
Design and typesetting by Karen Connor

Printed in the United States of America

Swedenborg Foundation Press
320 North Church Street
West Chester, PA 19380
www.swedenborg.com

Contents

Foreword

An unknown Australian author took the American reading public by storm in 2006. Rhonda Byrne's *The Secret* rapidly climbed to the top of the *New York Times* best-seller list, where it remained for 146 consecutive weeks (selling over twenty-one million copies). The book's commercial success was hardly owing to its literary merits or conceptual clarity. It offered little more than a rehashing of simplistic aphorisms first formulated by an American "positive thinker" a full century earlier. Yet Byrne's bold confidence in the power of disciplined thinking resonated with some of the most enduring themes in American religious and cultural life. The same can be said of James Redfield's *The Celestine Prophecy,* which performed a similar commercial feat a decade earlier (spending 165 weeks on the *New York Times* best-seller list en route to sales of over twenty million). Mixing axioms drawn from nineteenth-century metaphysics and contemporary self-help psychology, Redfield pointed readers to the powerful energies lying deep within themselves. As these two stunning examples suggest, the general reading public often imbues a book with a meaning or significance that far surpasses the book's actual content. Certain philosophical conceptions persist in a culture, enabling people to make connections between ideas that aren't always explicit in the ideas themselves. There is an important story here that needs to be told.

Neither journalists nor academic scholars seemed comfortable trying to explain the public's avid interest in these books. Although these best sellers were surely inspirational and even spiritual, they had no overt connection to biblical religion. They explored themes that were clearly psychological, yet they had no overt connection to academic psychology. Some commentators depicted the books' idealism as naïve and magical. Others decried their narcissistic focus on the inner self. Almost no one was attentive to the subtleties of their message. Even those who knew that the books' major themes were linked with the New Thought movement didn't really know what this meant or how this helped place the books in a broader theological and cultural context.

John Haller provides the perceptive eye we need to make judicious sense of America's long-standing interest in the power of mind and thought. He reminds us that New Thought is not fundamentally about cultivating a willful ego as so many of its critics have mistaken it to be. New Thought instead expresses a nuanced and surprisingly sophisticated metaphysical vision. It rests on an ontological conviction born of its adherents' numinous experiences. These experiences seem to reveal that mind in any single human is an individuated expression of a grander cosmic reality. Whether phrased in monistic, pantheistic, or panpsychic theological terms, New Thought coheres around its experiential conviction that the human mind is intimately connected with a much vaster spiritual universe. It is true that New Thoughters insist that "all creation is mental" and believe in "the power of positive thinking." But they are not simply subscribing to some hyper version of rugged American individualism. They are testifying to their metaphysical conviction that humans are potentially continuous with the "final" or "ultimate" causal force in the universe: God.

The History of New Thought traces the origin and subsequent development of these beliefs beginning with Ralph Waldo Emerson and the transcendentalists. Many of the individuals who figure into Haller's story are well-known creatures and creators of American thought. Mary Baker Eddy, William James, Norman Vincent Peale, Dale Carnegie, and Deepak Chopra find their way into many religious and cultural histories. Yet Haller finds that lesser-known thinkers such as Phineas Parkhurst Quimby, Warren Felt Evans, Napoleon Hill, Henry Wood, Orison Swett Marden, and Emma Curtis Hopkins have equally contributed to this enduring strain of American piety. True, most New Thoughters (with the obvious exceptions of Emerson and James) have not been original thinkers. Their genius has been in synthesizing various strands of unchurched American spirituality and restating it in the idioms of the day. Their only philosophical test has been that ideas in some way enrich the lives of those who embrace them. As William James observed, "the plain fact remains that the spread of the movement has been due to practical fruits, and the extremely practical turn of character of the American people has never been better shown than by the fact that this, their only decidedly original contribution to the systematic philosophy of life, should be so intimately knit up with concrete therapeutics."

Haller shows us how these spiritual and psychological ideas came together to create an enduring cluster of cultural metaphors that to this day connect otherwise disparate ideas. He does this in a way that clarifies concepts and meanings that lurk just beneath the surface of so much of modern spiritual and psychological writings. There have, of course, been about a dozen previous efforts to illuminate this somewhat amorphous cluster of beliefs and practices.[1] Yet none has succeeded so well at articulating the movement's principal tenets and demonstrating their connection with wider currents in modern intellectual and social life. In 1963, Charles Braden published the first comprehensive account of the rise of New Thought since the early histories written by Julius and Horatio Dresser, who were partisan participants in the very movement they sought to explain. Haller updates the best features of Braden's work in that his primary purpose is to explain rather than to critique the movement. Yet Haller's grasp of the wider social and intellectual sweep of American history takes us well past Braden's narrower descriptions. His account explains why William James considered New Thought to be the quintessential expression of "The Religion of Healthy-Mindedness" in his epochal *The Varieties of Religious Experience*. Haller similarly expands on the works of historians Catherine Albanese and Sydney Ahlstrom, who have shown that New Thought constitutes a "harmonial" approach to religion in which spiritual composure, physical health, and even economic well-being are understood to flow from a person's inner connection with the ultimate source of things. He explains how New Thought's emphasis on meditative practices such as "entering the silence," its interest in the power of suggestion, and its deliberate schemes for cultivating optimistic attitudes all stem from the movement's faith in an immanent spiritual power.

Not all historians have been sympathetic to New Thought's theological and psychological beliefs. While himself a central figure in the movement, William James conceded that the movement had a tendency to naïve or magical thinking and noted that some New Thought publications were "so moonstruck with optimism and so vaguely expressed that an academically trained intellect finds it almost impossible to read at all." A more pointed critique was advanced by Donald Meyer. Meyer noted that New Thought exemplifies Americans' penchant for ignoring the brute realities of social class and economic conflict. Later joined by Gail Thain Parker and Barbara Ehrenreich, this critical assessment of New Thought faults it for desensitizing Americans to the real social and economic forces affecting our collective well-being. By directing us to pay attention only to our own inner thoughts, New Thought risks perpetuating the status quo. Its self-help regimens often lure weak people into imagining themselves to be strong while fating them to remain weak and without the skills to engender meaningful change in their lives. Haller incorporates these criticisms into his narrative, striving to balance his account of what he describes as the movement's "youthful aspirations, its preoccupation with healthy-mindedness, its spirit of self-sufficiency, and its varying degrees of passivity to life's distasteful edges."

The History of New Thought builds on these previous works and becomes our most sensitive account of this countervailing—yet surprisingly pervasive—form of personal spirituality. Haller shows us how works like *The Secret, The Celestine Prophecy,* or Norman Vincent Peale's *The Power of Positive Thinking* didn't simply burst onto the scene out of nowhere. They are instead living expressions of what he describes as "an intricately interwoven philosophy of practical idealism" anchored in an enduring cultural heritage. This practical idealism cuts across all traditional denominational lines or boundaries. Americans from every walk of life assimilate at least bits of the New Thought outlook into the stock of ideas with which they take their bearings on life. New Thought remains vital even in the twenty-first century. True, New Thought occupies an unusual place in our cultural landscape. It doesn't connect with the "old thought" found either in our existing churches or in those forms of science that lack curiosity about the final or ultimate source of the universe. Yet New Thought encourages its adherents to incorporate both a suitably expanded science and a suitably expanded spirituality into a practical philosophy for daily living. We are fortunate that John Haller has given us such a fresh and intelligent account of Americans' only decidedly original contribution to the systematic philosophy of life.

Robert C. Fuller
Bradley University

Acknowledgments

Those to whom I am indebted include Director Joanna Hill, Managing Editor Morgan Beard, Art Director Karen Connor, and Marketing Assistant Carol Urbanc at the Swedenborg Foundation in West Chester, Pennsylvania, for their support and wise counsel. In particular, I want to acknowledge Morgan for her unstinting commitment to the project, her meticulous reading of the drafts, and her gentle prodding in those areas that required clarification or deeper analysis. To her I remain deeply appreciative. I also wish to express my personal thanks to Robert C. Fuller, professor of religious studies at Bradley University, for his generous comments in the book's foreword. His own works, which have been an inspiration to me for many years, include *Spiritual, But Not Religious: Understanding Unchurched America* (2001), *Alternative Medicine and American Religious Life* (1989), *Americans and the Unconscious* (1986), and *Mesmerism and the American Cure of Souls* (1982). Others to whom I am indebted include James F. Lawrence, dean of the Swedenborgian House of Studies at the Pacific School of Religion; Kevin K. Baxter, pastor of the Swedenborg Chapel in Cambridge, Massachusetts; Eugene Taylor, professor of the history and philosophy of psychology at Saybrook University and lecturer at Harvard Medical School; and those anonymous reviewers of the manuscript who supported its publication. Others include the librarians and staff of Morris Library of Southern Illinois University Carbondale; the Southern Illinois University School of Medicine, Springfield, Illinois; Boston Medical Library; Harvard College Library; the Francis A. Countway Library of Medicine, Harvard Medical School; the Swedenborgian House of Studies Library and Archives, Pacific School of Religion; the John Crerar Library of

Chicago; the New York Academy of Medicine Library; New York Public Library; Northwestern University; Stanford University Library; University of Illinois Library at Champaign-Urbana; University of Wisconsin Library; University of Kansas Library; University of Michigan Library; Yale University Cushing/Whitney Medical Library; JSTOR; and Google Books.

As always, I am grateful to my wife, Robin, who offered inspiration, encouragement, criticism, and substantial assistance, including the reading of numerous drafts and indexing the finished manuscript. Those errors of fact or interpretation that remain are mine alone, and for them I take full responsibility.

The History of New Thought

Introduction

The metaphysical movement known as New Thought has long been a conspicuous force in American culture, articulating a set of ideas and practices that remain to this day at the forefront of our contemporary religious and secular scene. The pioneers of this movement found their initial voice in the lecture halls of the nineteenth-century lyceum. Exploiting that forum, a handful of spiritually minded entrepreneurs attracted to the recently discovered "sciences" of neurology, mesmerism, and phrenology sought to graft them to a mixture of liberal Christianity, transcendentalism, Spiritualism, and Swedenborgianism. In doing so, they marked a path religious in content, middle class in character, focused on healing in the broadest sense of the word, and anxious to illuminate the more practical side of human nature. These revelators spoke of a harmony unfolding within the individual, God, and society that would eventually permeate American culture and become a creed for its distinctive brand of individualism, self-reliance, and healthy-mindedness. The outcome of their collective efforts was a hybrid philosophy simultaneously religious, synoptic, idealistic, optimistic, transformative, and eclectic.

Believing that the mental world was the only true reality and the material world its creation, these practitioners of the soul felt they could utilize their newly found sciences to free the human body of its material impediments, including sickness and disease. Only by discovering the personal freedom and individuality within one's inner or spiritual nature, and merging that individuality with God or the One, could the individual find lasting health and happiness. Through affirmation, advocacy, prayer, and visualization of a "Christ Science," they set out to transform mental thought into a dynamic power with which to counter the body's material and spiritual failings. In doing so, they replaced the angry God of the Old Testament with a Creator whose powers were checked by the imposition of rational laws and embraced a worldview where disease was a physical event, not an expression of divine purpose or retribution. Unlike dogma-bound Christians who dwelt on humankind's fall from grace and the need to expiate themselves from sin and darkness, the practitioners who explored these new sciences chose to celebrate life by identifying the spark of divinity in humanity's inner nature. The presumption of humanity's total depravity and of predestination fell before a benevolent Deity operating through known laws, where the intellect alone was free. All that a person was and could be lay within human power that, by inference, was received through an influx of life from the Divine. One of the paths that these new metaphysical philosophers forged would eventually become known as New Thought.

The transition from Calvinism to New Thought followed a path struck by the self-made philosopher and mental healer Phineas Parkhurst Quimby (1802–66) of Belfast, Maine, whose gospel of healthy-mindedness captured the attention of several generations of mental healers in search of a new "Christ Science." The common denominator for Quimby and his devotees was the proposition that illness resulted from erroneous belief. Drawing from the magnetic theories of German physician Franz Anton Mesmer (1734–1815) and the revelatory writings of Swedish scientist and philosopher Emanuel Swedenborg (1688–1772), Quimby's followers set themselves to building a whole new mental framework for humanity. For them, not all knowledge was scientific in the same sense as chemistry and physics, since much additional understanding could be gained if one relied on extrasensory channels found in séances, clairvoyance, and other paranormal experiences. As a consequence, New Thought's healing practices oscillated between the inflationary scope of the sciences and the hegemony claimed by the revelatory side of religion.

New Thought represented a temper of mind that ranked emotions and intuition as equal to reason and experience. Building on concepts rooted in idealism and celebrated in transcendentalism, it held strongly to the principle that the human mind was capable of knowing the very essence of things. This evoked a particular mood of incorrigible optimism and a faith in individuality that rebelled against authoritarianism of all kinds, particularly cold and formalized creeds. This was nowhere more succinctly stated than in Ralph Waldo Emerson's essay "Nature," published in 1836 and reprinted numerous times in the succeeding decades. "In the woods," Emerson wrote, "I feel that nothing can befall me in life,—no disgrace, no calamity, (leaving me my eyes,) which nature cannot repair. Standing on the bare ground,—my head bathed by the blithe air, and uplifted into infinite space,—all mean egotism vanishes. I become a transparent eyeball. I am nothing. I see all. The currents of the Universal Being circulate through me; I am part or particle of God."[1]

New Thought relied heavily on Emerson, whose thoughts and observations were repeatedly quoted in their oral and written communications. His occasional mysticism, his sweep of imagination, and the stretch of his wit and good sense provided exceptional insight into the passions and judgments of the age. The movement borrowed his terms for God, including the interchangeable use of *Father, Spirit, Supreme Being, Soul,* and *Over-Soul.* They also borrowed his ideas: God was incarnate in nature and in human beings, with the earth and heavenly bodies as the visible retinue of his spirit. Nature was not God but a garment used to express his constant emanation.

New Thought was also laced heavily with the wisdom and metaphysics of Swedenborg, whose writings, inspired by his visionary experiences of heaven and hell, shaped many thinkers' views on the spirit world. Others picked up on his law of correspondences, which held that everything in the physical world is a representation of a spiritual counterpart; the rejection of ecclesiasticism and theological dogmatism; the emphasis on the inner (spiritual) and outer (sense-based or "natural") person; matter as a condition of spiritual substance made visible for divine purposes; and closure to a host of questions left unanswered in the writings of the church fathers. Swedenborg's concept of the Universal Human—that all of the spiritual universe was in the shape of a human being, and that its individual parts were composed of communities of angels, who in turn were once human beings—captured the fellowship of spirituality in a way that elevated human nature into the divine image without the Calvinist underpinning of sin and corruption. Building on Swedenborg's assertion that love is the sum and substance of the Divine Being, New Thought preached a gospel of good tidings that made the universe appear as an organism whose origin and substance remained unknowable but whose attributes were forever changing for the better.

In a broad range of publications that included motivational literature, philosophical and religious texts, and even occasional novels, nineteenth-century New Thought writers exposed the speculative aspects of their world with a temperament of curiosity mixed with optimism. Like Emerson and Swedenborg, they had only contempt for those who dwelled on tragedy or fatalism. Arguably the most philosophical movement in American culture, New Thought represented a form of applied idealism that resonated across the religious and secular landscape, offering a purposive life filled with optimism, practicality, healthy-mindedness, and economic well-being. Religious scholar Sydney E. Ahlstrom included New Thought in the tradition of transcendentalism, Spiritualism, and Theosophy as a diffuse "harmonial religion" that cut across sects, cults, and denominations offering a spiritual message that drew its sustenance from the individual's inner rapport with the energies flowing from the universe. To the extent that the individual shaped his or her outer self with these cosmic forces, the individual better enjoyed the riches of the world.[2]

New Thought found numerous avenues of expression, some of which came by way of its many church affiliations—both denominational and nondenominational—while others surfaced in the form of unchurched thought and inspiring self-discoveries. Whether viewing themselves as theologians, healers, philosophers, publishers, or marketers, the expositors of New Thought taught a reverence for both the sciences and extrasensory knowledge that far exceeded their acceptance of Scripture and religious dogma, neither of which seemed to carry as much recognition as before. Their reading of Swedenborg—whose compelling vision of the spiritual realms was laced with unflinching criticism of the church doctrine of his day—gave them a feeling that orthodox Christianity had not only failed but, in the process, lost much of its legitimacy. Theological vapors dissolved in the presence of New Thought; so, too, did the ecclesiastical subtleties and dogmatic paradoxes that contrived to separate the individual from God. Taking a cue from Swedenborg's Universal Human, they viewed humankind as a collective spiritual being whose individual souls were submerged in a fellowship of redeemed beings formed around infinite and creative Love. They believed that an individual in him- or herself, apart from the collective spiritual being, was nothingness, that is, a soul without compass or direction.

While New Thought's proponents revered Emerson and Swedenborg, these two thinkers were by no means their sole approach to spiritual life; New Thought drew as well from classical literature, science, non-Western religion and philosophy, and poetry. New Thought literature resolved to carry its passions into the moment, embellished with quotable sayings from the ancient and recent past. Inspired to return Christianity to its original teachings and practices, New Thought writers made a great show of bringing American society to reason through their revulsion against abstractions, an undeclared war on systematic theology, eloquence concerning the soul, and outright insistence on the possibility of living in harmony with the universe. Their vocabulary contained such magical words as *will, wisdom, love,* and *consciousness,* all of which prefigured the future course of intellect. The written and spoken word was the most powerful idiom at hand, and New Thought proponents were masters of both.

Except for the Christian Scientists, with whom they had an unusually bifurcated relationship, the proponents of New Thought felt no pressing need to engage their critics, since there was a sufficiently wide field of knowledge on which they could demonstrate the truths of their intuitive reasoning. Far from being dismayed over differences of opinion among themselves or between themselves and other sects and denominations, they took courage from their interpretations of Scripture, in the certainty of their own convictions, and from revelation when it suited them. In carrying out their resolve, they formulated an amalgam of beliefs that resulted in a set of newly formed churches (i.e., Unity Church, Church of Divine Science, Religious Science, and Home of Truth), schools (i.e., Unity Institute, Emerson Theological Institute), and associations (i.e., the International New Thought Alliance and the School of Applied Metaphysics) as well as a concordance of mainline Protestant churches willing to express its ideals. Loosely organized, they represented groups of like-minded thinkers whose goal was to teach the Christianity of Jesus without dogma, sects, or denominations, and the acceptance of an inner voice as the source of inspiration, health, power, and prosperity. While indifferent to the minutia of ceremony and ecclesiastical government, they still felt bound by Scripture, from which they eagerly sought warrants for their actions and the purposes of Jesus's life.

The New Thought movement focused its initial energies on the application of mental science to health through a combination of the physical sciences, romantic idealism, Spiritualism, mysticism, Emersonianism, and Swedenborgianism. By the early twentieth century, these supports would be replaced with a universal law of evolution governing both natural and human history, and a synthetic philosophy of cosmic progression revealing a pattern of ever-unfolding new forms. Disclaiming any potential dysteleology, its devotees chose to celebrate humanity's position as the principal species in the universe with powers revealed through the incarnation of Christ. As taught by the new quantum physics, the whole of nature quivered with vibrations that pointed to humanity's destiny as co-creator. The starting point of their universe was God the creator; its terminus was God revealed. While some were willing to consider elements of irregularity, indeterminacy, and chance among the byproducts of evolution (particularly those who insisted that Darwin's theory of natural selection best fit the process of evolution), few were willing to take the theory to its logical consequences by considering the human species as the product of natural selection and, as with every other species, subject to extinction. Instead, they chose to find a more agreeable teleology amid the chaos of cosmic debris. New Thought's theistic evolutionists saw the world as a progression from the material to the immaterial; from the primitive human being to modern humans' co-divinity; and from the mind/body dualism associated with French philosopher and mathematician René Descartes (1596–1650) to the organismic path to body/soul spirituality found in the writings of Jesuit priest and philosopher Pierre Teilhard de Chardin (1881–1955). Within this scheme of things New Thought thrived, offering a mind-over-body formula of positive thinking, visualization, and self-affirmation to achieve health and prosperity. Rather than accept the possibility of the extinction of the human species, they insisted that the essential purpose behind humanity's creation precluded a destiny reduced to chance. Teleology was openly accepted, and promised an organic scheme of evolution that was every bit religious. Science remained in constant support of a divine mind whose design transcended rational interpretation. In spite of false creeds and dogmas, religious truths still formed the bedrock of evolutionary progress.

While cynics viewed New Thought as little more than a confused mixture of grand illusion and autosuggestion, no form of Christianity was as revealing in its accommodation to the broader society. By rejecting the tragic sense of life and viewing humanity as moving ever forward in a linear progression, New Thought exhibited a preoccupation with positive thinking that brooked no reference to pessimism. It openly confessed to a teleology that joined the intelligible universe with the birth of human thought and its role, albeit limited, in the cosmic process. Using a combination of Emerson's Over-Soul and Swedenborg's metaphysics, its proponents clothed natural history in spiritual garments, suggesting a more purposeful and directive pattern of cause and effect. Just as members of the Swedenborg-inspired Church of the New Jerusalem believed his writings portended a new dawn for humanity's relationship with the Divine, so New Thought viewed human nature as having a progression from savagery to divine nature. A new age had come, one in which human beings were privileged to hear the voice of God through silent prayer and inward illumination. No longer corrupt, human nature became the means through which God unfolded his plan, molded by natural forces and the revelations of science. The encounter of God, nature, and mind openly announced the commencement of a great and glorious new age made fruitful by the labors of each participating soul. In this new age, God united humanity with itself by revealing a spiritual philosophy that connected faith in the cosmic order with New Thought.

While New Thought can be viewed as an outgrowth of the past, it also represents a break from the past. It emerged at a time when American popular culture was attempting to strike a balance between the power of its institutional denominations and what sociologist Robert Bellah termed "civil religion," whose creed was drawn from the nation's presumed destiny under God and its perfection within a democratic society.[3] It was within the tension created by these two phenomena that New Thought was able to find secure footing, offering both a churched and unchurched route to self-fulfillment and transcendence. Within both its churched and unchurched communities of followers, the prevailing philosophy leveled out to what can best be described as consensus principles, namely, those principles that could be accepted without serious dispute. It is worth noting, for example, that the principles of the church communities within New Thought remain surprisingly similar to those of its unchurched members.

The origin of the term New Thought remains elusive in part because of modifications made during its journey through the late nineteenth and early twentieth centuries. Tracing boundaries and fixing location remains a challenge since its ideas run in so many different directions. Some attribute to Emerson and Margaret Fuller (1810–1850, an American journalist, women's rights activist, and transcendentalist) the earliest use of the term, since both referred to transcendentalist philosophy as "this new thought." Yet even William Ellery Channing (1780–1842), one of the early founders of Unitarianism, sometimes described his ideas as "new thought."[4]

In 1879, Emerson perhaps anticipated New Thought when he explained in an address to graduates of the Cambridge divinity school:

> We are born too late for the old and too early for the new faith. I see in those classes and those persons in whom I am accustomed to look for tendency and progress, for what is most positive and most rich in human nature. . . . I see in them character but skepticism. . . . They have insight and truthfulness; they will not

mask their convictions; they hate cant; but more than this I do not readily find. The gracious notions of the soul—piety, adoration—I do not find. That religious submission and abandonment which give man a new element and being, and make him sublime—it is not in churches, it is not in houses. I see movement. I hear aspirations, but I see not how the great God prepares to satisfy the heart in the new order of things.[5]

In 1889, homeopath and Swedenborgian William Holcombe, MD, capitalized "New Thought" in his *Condensed Thoughts about Christian Science* to express his preference for what he saw as a whole new teaching in mental science. "New Thought always excites combat in the mind with old thought, which refuses to retire," he remarked. When, in 1894, *New Thought* became the title of a magazine published in Melrose, Massachusetts, it acquired a collective meaning appropriate to a more ecumenical expression of commonly held principles. A year later, it was adopted by the Metaphysical Club of Boston and subsequently incorporated into the titles of *New Thought Essays* (1899) and *What is the New Thought* (1901) written by Charles Brodie Patterson; Sidney Flower's *New Thought Magazine* (1901); Ella Wheeler Wilcox's *The Heart of the New Thought* (1902); and Henry Wood's *New Thought Simplified* (1903).[6]

New Thought represents a remarkable exhibition of nondenominational Christianity. Even on the eve of World War I, it remained a marvel that so many could unite in a form of pseudoscientific Christian thinking while differing in so many other areas. Perhaps this helps to explain why New Thought was so prescient in predicting that the lines of denominational demarcation would grow indistinct over time as the word of God was interpreted by what some would see as common sense. In looking at the world and consulting its universal interests, provinciality seemed to fade away almost effortlessly. New Thought found strength in this diversity, allowing it to not only survive but prosper. Here was the great alternative to mainstream Protestantism. While ministers in the principal denominations continued to rule in matters of theological dispute, the organizations espousing New Thought left much to individual choice as there remained elements of equivocation that pleaded for compromise. As historian Stow Persons explained in *Free Religion: An American Faith* (1963), Americans chose not to leave their doctrines for the clergy to explain or defend, but took it upon themselves to restate their faith in the language of a more secular and academically based philosophy.[7]

As New Thought broke into the twentieth century, it advocated a new religious pluralism that applied not only to the major Protestant denominations but to Catholics, Jews, and other world religions. With minds open to cosmic consciousness, they all searched for truth about life both inside and outside the normative institutions of their day. Drawing upon Emerson's "Over-Soul," Walt Whitman's *Leaves of Grass* (1855), the Hindu sacred texts of the Bhagavad Gita and the Upanishads, and Confucius's maxims, among others, they introduced an Oriental flavor to American thought and culture. It was not the Emerson of "The American Scholar" or "Self-Reliance," but the Emerson of the poems "Brahma" and "Maya" that carried forward into the new age. Other progenitors of New Thought's second generation of writers were Swedenborg's spiritualistic readings of the Bible; Helena Blavatsky's brotherhood of Mahatmas; the clairvoyant Edgar Cayce (1877–1945), who promoted reincarnation; the mystic visions recounted in William James's *The Varieties of Religious Experience* (1902); the spiritual works of Indian leader Swami Vivekananda (1863–1902) and his American Vedanta Society; and the Self-Realization Fellowship of yoga master Paramhansa Yogananda (1893–1952).

With views widely shared across its many churches and unchurched social centers, associations, and publishing houses, the numbers of New Thought supporters swelled into the millions. The power of thought in the form of suggestion—popularized by Émile Coué ("Day by day, in every way, I am getting better and better") in the 1920s—gave a whole new meaning to applied psychology and, by inference, to the plentitude of New Thought books and periodicals.[8] While the issues remained philosophical, theological, and, at times, political, the climate of opinion had changed. What before had been judged a mind-cure movement now conflated those same images of spirit and matter into an unapologetic system of high-powered personal magnetism for exalting material success. With this change, what was left of Emerson's Over-Soul and Swedenborg's law of correspondences disappeared in the rhetorical flourishes of writers whose notions of positive thinking, visualization, and affirmation percolated into the general culture. The mind, once firmly in the domain of divine influx, became a distant echo, drowned out by the kinetic energy of free-market capitalism.

By the 1930s, millions of people were participating in some form of mind-power exercises. A large part of this newfound popularity stemmed from a change in focus from health to prosperity as evidenced by Charles B. Newcomb's *All's Right With the World* (1900); William Walker Atkinson's *Thought-Force in Business and Everyday Life* (1900) and *The Secret of Success* (1907); Orison Swett Marden's *He Can Who Thinks He Can* (1908); Wallace D. Wattles's *The Science of Getting Rich* (1910); Paul Ellsworth's *Mind Magnet: How to Unify and Intensify Your Natural Faculties for Efficiency, Health, and Success* (1924); and Napoleon Hill's *Think and Grow Rich*. Exemplary of the popularity of these books, estimates for Hill's *Think and Grow Rich* range from fifteen to seventy million copies sold since its original publication in 1937.[9]

Decades later, these same themes would continue with books such as Norman Vincent Peale's *The Power of Positive Thinking* (1952); Robert H. Schuller's *Move Ahead with Possibility Thinking* (1967); and more recently, Deepak Chopra's *Creating Affluence: Wealth Consciousness in the Field of All Possibilities* (1993) and *Unconventional Life: Discovering the Power to Fulfill Your Dreams* (1992). Thought-as-power became a route to happiness made possible through the creation of numerous New Thought business enterprises intent on marketing the power of the spirit.

Saul Bellow once remarked that "what Americans want to learn from their writers is how to live."[10] New Thoughters' reading was performed in isolation as well as in social networks of family, friends, and informal groups of educated and upwardly mobile people. In these books, they discovered values, secrets, and moral guidance that resonated with their needs. In time, a canonical positioning of New Thought literature emerged whose profitability was based on ever-widening circles of readers and careful marketing of the product. As ads complemented reviews and verbal endorsements, both printed and communicated orally, New Thought books enjoyed a popularity that few could emulate, surviving long after their initial publication in reprints, thus leading to a continually expanding audience. Added to this was the weighted endorsements that came by way of the *New York Times Book Review, The New Yorker, Commentary, Saturday Review, Harpers, Atlantic Monthly, Reader's Digest,* and *Woman's Home Companion* that kept their message alive, circulated, and discussed as part of the broad cultural agenda. In many ways, these periodicals served as welcoming gatekeepers for New Thought literature, building networks of readers, publishers, and reviewers—all benefiting from the marketplace.

Looking at the history of the movement through a modern lens, some commentators believe that New Thought represents a modification or reformulation of the Protestant ethic. Richard Huber in *The American Idea of Success* (1971) expressed it best when he suggested that the nation's ethic had changed over time from one of *character* to one of *personality,* a change explained by the American public's choice of Dale Carnegie's *How to Win Friends and Influence People* (1936) over the Calvinist values imbedded in William H. McGuffey's widely read readers (first published in 1836).[11]

New Thought did not break with Protestantism, nor did it escape the issues that had long troubled the American psyche. However, many of the judgments made by the proponents of New Thought were conclusive "only to the one who is easily overawed by assertion or is already at the start more than ready to believe," admitted New Thought author Henry C. Sheldon. It assumed "a list of indubitable inductions . . . identical with its own premises." With few of its spokespeople schooled in philosophy, most tended to borrow from each other, perhaps thinking that there was truth in numbers.[12] Over the course of its history, New Thought's latter-day spokespeople chose quick therapeutic fixes to tragedy and evil—a gospel of positive thinking as the antidote to serious moral and economic issues. As Barbara Ehrenreich rightly pointed out in *Bright-Sided: How the Relentless Promotion of Positive Thinking Has Undermined America* (2009), this overconfidence was based on a combination of bad science and a disregard for "vigilant realism."[13]

Any history of New Thought will require an extensive inventory of the literature before achieving any meaningful sense of its scope, purpose, players, strengths, weaknesses, and manner of contribution. Admittedly, much of this literature has been deservedly forgotten because of its duplicative and repetitive character. When dusted off and brought to light, however, the literature shows clearly that New Thought played an important role in defining the social, political, and religious parameters of American life and culture. Thinking and writing about New Thought brings one to the very roots of the American psyche. It exemplifies characteristics and motives derived from Reformation Protestantism, the Enlightenment, the early Federal period, and Romanticism before hitting its stride in late-nineteenth-century evolutionary theory. In essence, it has been a weather vane of middle-class values and remains to this day one of the major expressions of American thought and culture.

* * *

As a historian, my research into New Thought paralleled my study of similar healing systems whose origins in vitalistic philosophies competed with the rationalist-empiricist underpinnings of medical orthodoxy derived from Bacon and invigorated by Newton and Locke. In my examination of New Thought literature, I was impressed with its creativity, its eagerness to incorporate the sciences, and the extent to which Swedenborg's metaphysics became such an integral part of its early framework. As a secular humanist, I have long admired the drama of the mind in its search for meaning and the pathways to self-inquiry that dominate the canon of Western philosophical, religious, and medical traditions. For that reason, my purpose in writing this book was to better understand the phenomenon of New Thought through the philosophy, theology, science, and medicine that constituted its gospel of healthy-mindedness. By itself, this proved to be a wholesome task, because New Thought writings have been earnestly felt and deeply satisfying to millions of believers—then and now—and also because the intellectual origins of its metaphysics extend back in time to include many great historical movements and personages. In that spirit of inquiry, it seemed to me that New Thought had forged a remarkable and intricately interwoven connection between physical healing and what it perceived were the higher spiritual agencies.

The further my examination took me, however, the more dismayed I became with the countervailing voices that pulled this Swedenborgian-inspired belief system toward a more secular ideology of success and prosperity. Although New Thought began as a bridge of practical idealism linking nineteenth-century transcendentalist thinking with the emerging philosophy of pragmatism, it devolved into an unapologetic and shameless commercialism whose spokespeople wandered far from their roots. For a good number of New Thought's representative thinkers past and present, individual access to "revelation," "cosmic consciousness," "regeneration," "prosperity," "realization," "self-healing," and "unfoldment" lay along a path sentineled by a series of toll booths for which cash has become the price of admission. As critic Clifford Howard noted as early as 1910, when shorn of their "embroidery," many of New Thought's inspirational writers, speakers, and publishing houses behaved like patent-medicine vendors "marketing the power of God."[14]

This study of New Thought focuses principally on the history of the idea rather than on the accomplishments of any one individual, group, church, or organization. My attempt has been to broaden our understanding of its impact, underscoring its diaspora from a small handful of early nineteenth-century healers to a multitude of writers, entrepreneurs, ministries, groups, and organizations across the nineteenth, twentieth, and twenty-first centuries. While most studies of New Thought have chosen to emphasize its churches and affiliated organizations, I have sought to balance that aspect of its history with the equally if not more influential secular side, namely, the myriad of self-healing, self-help, positive thinking, and prosperity advocates using the printed word and the electronic media rather than the pulpit to communicate their message. Accordingly, I have tried not to frame this broader perspective within some myopic lens or wire-drawn metaphysics, but underscore its youthful aspirations, its preoccupation with healthy-mindedness, its spirit of self-sufficiency, and its varying degrees of passivity to life's distasteful edges.

Those differences in motivation that exist today within New Thought's global tent have not diminished its long-standing critique of the West's rationalist-empiricist tradition. By seeking a rapport between the individual and the unseen, this Swedenborgian-inspired worldview, enhanced with elements from Emerson and Eastern philosophy, has motivated the metaphysical yearnings of countless millions to interpret the physical and mental dimensions of humankind in ways that unlock the soul's capacity for limitless possibilities. As seen against the broader fabric of American thought and culture, this belief in the interconnectedness between the physical and spiritual has served as an engine for inspiring confidence in life's benevolent and progressive tendencies. From that perspective, it has much of which to be proud.

1

New Beginnings

*There are new lands, new men, new
thoughts. Let us demand our own
works and laws and worship.*

—Ralph Waldo Emerson, "Nature"

The first half of the nineteenth century was a period of experimentation for American society, particularly in the areas of religion, government, and medicine. It was a time for rejecting the cold and ritualized orderliness of the Christian church, the prejudices of elite rule in the body politic, and the heroic drenchings that defined medical therapeutics. Those who journeyed toward some form of political alternative formulated a people's government marked by political parties, machine politics, and patronage. In religion, Americans turned away from their preoccupation with a wrathful God to find belief in God's immanence and discourse in spirituality. Beginning with the earliest waves of antinomianism in the American colonies, the experience of direct communion with God and its identification with sanctification and regeneration filled sober Protestants with thoughts of perfectionism, contempt for negative thinking, and a sense of special purpose. And those patients seeking health beyond the limitations of orthodox medicine chose, in increasing numbers, a therapeutic environment marked by milder regimens and vitalistic philosophies whose ambitious maps of the body and mind displaced the older humoral pathologies for the newer sciences of phrenology and mesmerism.

Making a Social Democracy

As memories of their revolution receded, Americans entered the nineteenth century with two national political parties taking shape around the competing forces of internal improvements, protectionism, nationalism, sectionalism, and expansionism. Americans of every age and class expressed pride in their newly won freedoms, believing that the land had been divinely bequeathed for their exclusive use. Their collective sense of self-worth made them contemptuous of Old World monarchies, manners, and mores. Fashioned from a combination of republicanism and democracy, and augmented by a constant stream of immigrants, Northerners busied themselves transforming their land-scape with roads, turnpikes, canals, mills, public buildings, and factory villages. By contrast, Southerners went about their lives seemingly averse to change. Defending a slave-labor system that faced increased criticism at home and abroad, they chose to isolate themselves and, cloaked in their beliefs, set out to fiercely protect their way of life. The prairie lands of the Middle West, peopled by immigrant farmers from Western Europe, pioneer stock from New England, and the younger sons of Southern planters, reflected both the cultures of its tenants and the challenges of the environment. Demanding better and more efficient transportation to facilitate settlement and ensure Eastern markets, insisting upon improved machinery to create fencing and break up the tough prairie sod, and claiming popular sovereignty ("squatter sovereignty") as a matter of right, they learned quickly the value of their votes amid the give and take of sectional politics. The combination of cheap land, labor, and transport ensured that by 1850, with a population of roughly twenty-three million, this nation of dreamers was poised to embark on great new adventures.

Along with economic growth and geographic expansion were other currents—spiritual, intellectual, social, and scientific—influencing the American psyche. In New England, the once harsh code of Calvinism mellowed under the growing influence of Arminian tendencies and the skepticism emerging out of the Enlightenment. Elsewhere, Protestantism held its ground by building on traditions of independence and decentralization. Nevertheless, the idea of perfectionism, first evident among the Methodists and Presbyterians, brought individuals and even whole communities into self-professed states of purification and sanctification. These beliefs found safe harbor among the myriad of religious secular enthusiasts moving west across New York via the Erie Canal and into the Great Lakes and Middle West. From the "voices" heard by Mother Ann Lee (1736–84) of the Shakers, Ellen G. White (1827–1915) of the Adventists, and Johann George Rapp (1757–1847) of the Harmonists to the agrarian ideas of social radical George Henry Evans (1805–56), the rash of communitarian experiments designed around the socialist visions of Welsh reformer Robert Owen (1771–1858) and French utopian Charles Fourier (1772–1837), to the first free homestead bill introduced into Congress in 1846, efforts were underway to preserve Jefferson's ideal of a simple agrarian society amid the emergence of a new industrial order.

Those same forces that had quickened the pace of life by extending domestic markets and fortifying the factory system also contributed to social experimentation and free inquiry. These included the benefits of public education, mechanics' institutes, libraries, museums, and lectures on literary and scientific curiosities. Education, which heretofore had been relegated to private benevolence, gained importance as cities in the Northeast grew in population and as proceeds from the sale of public lands in the newer states created educational opportunities in the form of free public schools. Signs of this change came with the founding of *The American Journal of Education* in 1826, the appointment of Horace Mann (1796–1859) to the Massachusetts Board of Education in 1837, and the establishment of the first school for training teachers at Lexington, Massachusetts, in 1839. A *Report the State of Public Instruction in Prussia*, written by French philosopher and proponent of Scottish common-sense realism Victor Cousin, was translated and widely read by aspiring educators. It became became the working manual out of which much of the nation's educational system was framed.[1]

As with primary education, German universities provided the inspirational model for higher education in America. Acolytes such as educator and author George Ticknor (1791–1871), Harvard president

Edward Everett (1794–1865), librarian Joseph G. Cogswell (1786–1871), and historian and statesman George Bancroft (1800–91) returned from Europe with boundless admiration for the German educational system, including its love of efficiency, its Teutonic thoroughness, and its rigorous defense of academic freedom. Each of these men reinforced key elements of German education in their careers, including the securing of a valued place for the lecture method of instruction, a vigorous defense of scholarship, and an appreciation for the Romance and Germanic languages.

The same phenomena explain the founding of several hundred denominational colleges and universities by 1860. Entrusted with the souls of their students, trustees empowered professors to teach Greek, chemistry, physics, metaphysics, and math; provide wholesome reminders of their Christian obligations through daily chapel attendance and recitations from devout literature; and cultivate manliness through literary and debating societies, collecting minerals, stuffing birds, and playing hard at sports. While Oberlin College in Ohio would break tradition by offering coeducation as early as 1833, few schools were tempted to follow suit.

In literature, a new generation of New England writers sought to plumb the soul of the nation's psyche, capturing the essence of democratic thinking, individualism, and self-reliance. The flowering of this Concord school of letters—including Ralph Waldo Emerson, Nathaniel Hawthorne, Henry David Thoreau, Walt Whitman, Oliver Wendell Holmes, Bronson and Louisa May Alcott, Margaret Fuller, and Henry Wadsworth Longfellow—exerted a formidable influence on America's cultural life, feeding the appetites of those seeking new inspiration, form, and content. Their belief in individual access to God as opposed to dependence on the intermediary role of the priesthood was what made their ideas so passionately desirable. Echoes of the divine-human encounter reverberated through their writings with the same exuberance that had formerly been expressed in the writings of the Puritan and post-Puritan divines.

In this environment, the educational aspirations of the adult population were not neglected as cities and towns organized mechanics' institutes, vocational courses, and night schools as a means of producing better farmers, mechanics, and merchants. Complementing these efforts was the establishment of the lyceum, which offered the public a smorgasbord of lectures, demonstrations, debates, and entertainment. Begun in 1839 by the Lowell Institute in Boston and mimicked by countless public-spirited organizations, the lyceum reached into the hinterland, bringing science, politics, spirituality, literature, philosophy, and natural history to communities of eager learners. Dedicated to the advancement of public education, the lyceum movement blossomed as anxious learners sought amusement, knowledge, and moral improvement—probably in that order. With the word "practical" interspersed through popular lectures, Americans enlightened themselves by attending lectures and public demonstrations on a wide assortment of topics, thus widening the franchise on general literacy and improving public education for all classes.[2]

Among the favorites of the lyceum circuit was Ralph Waldo Emerson (1803–82), America's prophet, philosopher, and diviner of individualism, whose views on humanity and nature were interspersed with poignant symbols drawn from religion, poetry, philosophy, and the arts. He transformed the moral truths of his time into powerful imagery, drawing connections between human beings and their spiritual improvement. Emerson, who much preferred the freedom of the essay or lecture platform to that of the pulpit, influenced others far more than he was influenced by them. As a seer and poet who imagined himself as a "transparent eyeball," explained biographer Oliver Wendell Holmes, Emerson believed in the doctrine of spiritual influx from God "as sincerely as any Calvinist or Swedenborgian." He fused the best elements of New England's past by celebrating a belief in self that he expressed best in the essay "Self-Reliance"—a belief in the inalienable worth of his fellow human beings, and in reason as the expositor of the Divine Mind. Emerson's concept of self-reliance was not only the definition of the autonomous individual but a precondition for personal growth. It was a quality inherited from the nation's Puritan ancestors and remained a continuous tradition of American culture. Self-reliance *was* God-reliance operating through intuition. For Emerson, intuition gave insight into the soul, where true character was always known and where justice was instant and complete. Through it, the individual knew him- or herself. These ideas found broad acceptance among countrymen who viewed humanity as identical with the soul of the world—a mir- ror of the Eternal One. Emerson's confidence in the right of individuals to make their own judgments and his refusal to be tied down by dogma left him with a feeling that all religions, especially those that raised the spirit, were co-owners of a single great religion. Placing Jesus on the same level as Socrates, he anticipated society's revulsion from doctrinal absolutes in its transformative journey to human-reliance.[3]

In his "Divinity School Address" delivered at Harvard on July 15, 1838, Emerson spoke of the religious sentiment that sat at the heart of the conversion process, that moment of spiritual sentiment when the individual became conscious of the True or the Good. Unlike the pious Puritan whose conversion drama came from a sense of sin and despair, Emerson drew from a sense of willful harmony or unity of being. Emer- son turned away from historical Christianity in his discussion of conver- sion, confronting the power of the self as someone in full possession of Jesus's temporal purpose, namely, understanding how the natural man finds himself in the Christ. For Emerson, the outcome of historical Christianity's religious conversion and the realization of "self-reliance" were one and the same, namely, the passionate experience of the self finding repose in the One.[4]

More than any other American, the Concord Sage captured the sense of God's immanence in humanity's spirit and the feeling of hav- ing arrived at a singularly important moment in history. The Puritan past was no longer a dark spot on the nation's compass but a source of ideas to be rummaged for meaning. Emerson's fingerprints were quite metaphorically everywhere as generations of Americans read his essays and were kindled by his imagination. They adopted his words and borrowed his ideas to construct their spiritual lessons, confident that in doing so they were expressing a most authentic Americanism. As a representative philosopher of American democracy, he cultivated a love of independence, contempt for tradition, and a celebration of self-reliance that taught admirers to see themselves in an eclectic but highly individualistic light. Each of his utterances came as a revela- tion from the core of the American psyche. His was a combination of constructive idealism, Yankee sobriety, and poetic imagination—all served up as an expression of the new free spirit in humanity. Beneath his strong sense of self-reliance and individualism was a corresponding sense of the unity of life, an awareness that bordered on mysticism and that swept all of nature into an endless stream of energy in which human beings participated. For Emerson, humanity was living in a condition of perpetual youth where the "new" was replacing the "old," where nothing remained stationary, and where reality was where you knew you ought to be.[5] His message told men and women how to be great in their own special way. In each instance that he described the inner life of humanity as being a conscious part of the Universal Soul, he likewise disclosed it as the epitome of individualism. He pleaded for recognition of the divine presence in each, but he did not urge people to lose themselves in blissful contemplation. Each had the responsibility for playing one's part in the world. Every person had the obligation to be oneself and to celebrate one's own worth.[6]

Healing: Secular and Spiritual

The nation's medical schools, many patterned after Edinburgh, Exeter, and Liverpool, fared poorly in the vastness of the American landscape. They suffered from inadequate student preparation, limited texts and equipment, a repetitive two-course program, a shortened apprenticeship, and the ever-increasing demand for doctors. Out of this toxic mix emerged the proprietary school model, a joint-stock company operated for profit by doctors hoping to augment their meager incomes with the sale of lecture tickets. These schools overtook the slower-growing, university-based medical colleges by exploiting the nation's confidence in the common person. However, they offered little more than amateur therapeutics in a cultist environment where, in the absence of clinical teaching and sound medical philosophy, each instructor became his own *imperium in imperio*. In the overall confusion as to what defined a medical doctor and in the absence of any licensing or regulatory control, medical education deteriorated in both substance and form, giving rise to irregular schools seeking to legitimize their own idiosyncratic modes of treatment. Pathological theories multiplied as botanics, eclectics, homeopaths, Thomsonians, physio-medicals, hydropaths, and other irregulars challenged prevailing beliefs and practices. Given the combination of a free-market mentality, entrepreneurial aspirations, and the overuse of heroic therapeutics, patients not surprisingly turned to these alternative systems, whose healing modalities promised a more kindly regimen for their diseases and illnesses.[7]

In seeking to legitimize their practices, many of the nation's unconventional healers looked to thinkers like the Swiss physician and alchemist Theophrastus Paracelsus (1493–1541), chemist Jan Baptista van Helmont (1579–1644), physician Robert Fludd (1574–1637), Scottish physician William Maxwell (1581–1641), and Hungarian astronomer Maximilian Hell (1720–92), whose ideas were still popular among those interested in the occult. From them they learned that celestial bodies magnetically influenced terrestrial bodies, and that these same forces also applied to the relationship between living bodies. For example, van Helmont claimed that magnetic powers residing in human beings could affect others, including curing another's illnesses; and from Maxwell, author of *De Medicina Magnetica* (1679), they discovered that the universe contained a spirit or fluid connecting all bodies.

However, it was the Swabian physician Franz Anton Mesmer who stirred the most interest. His method involved rendering paper, silk, stones, glass, trees, fountains, and other substances into media for the cosmic force he called "animal magnetism," which he conveyed through an iron rod or wand into the patient's body. Organizing his claims into twenty-seven specific principles, he carried his healing system into Swabia and Switzerland, and then, in 1778, into Paris, where he won the fashionable world of the French court over to his novel healing practices.[8]

Using an oak tub or *baquet* filled with powdered glass, iron filings, and "magnetized" water to give the appearance of a gigantic galvanic cell, Mesmer conducted group treatments that resembled a séance more than a medical examination. His patients assembled around the *baquet,* each holding a rod that projected from the tub to that part of their body thought to be diseased, and held hands to form yet another magnetic field. Mesmer would then pass a wand over each patient, suggesting that the magnetic currents emanating from himself and from the *baquet* brought balance to energies in and about each individual. Patients undergoing this process experienced stages of hysterical laughter, tears, and even convulsions before lapsing into states of insensibility and cure.[9]

Mesmer befriended Charles d'Eslon (1750–86), a prominent physician and medical adviser to the Count d'Artois. Fascinated by the new healing technique, d'Eslon presented Mesmer's theories before the Faculty of Medicine of the University of Paris, requesting that a full investigation be undertaken to compare animal magnetism with orthodox therapeutics. The faculty rejected the proposal, but Mesmer's reputation continued to take root—so much so, in fact, that he was offered a lifetime pension provided he establish a school and make public the secrets of his methods. Mesmer refused the offer, choosing to treat his healing methods in a proprietary manner. Those who joined his Society for Universal Harmony and purchased a course of lectures were required to sign a document swearing to the secrecy of his healing techniques and agreeing to share half of their practitioner fees with Mesmer.[10]

In 1784, the French government appointed two commissions to investigate Mesmer's claims. The first consisted of members of the Faculty of Medicine and the Academy of Sciences, including Benjamin Franklin (1706–90), astronomer Jean-Sylvain Bailly (1736–93), and chemists Antoine-Laurent Lavoisier (1743–94) and Jean Darcet (1724–1801); the second consisted of members of the Royal Society of Medicine. Both produced reports critical of Mesmer's claims. While the commissions confirmed some of the alleged cures, they denied the necessity of assuming the cause to be animal magnetism. Instead, they concluded that imagination—not magnetism—accounted for Mesmer's results.[11]

Mesmer's extravagancies were soon supplanted by more practiced disciples whose scientific training and commonsense approach concentrated less on the existence of a universal or cosmic medium and more on the role of the healer. Such were the modifications put in place by naturalist Joseph Philippe François Deluze (1753–1835), who pursued a more materialistic explanation for the manifestations. His two-volume *Histoire critique du magnétisme animal* (A critical history of animal magnetism, 1813–19) focused principally on the therapeutic value of animal magnetism. His book, along with the publication of several journals devoted to animal magnetism, led to the topic being discussed widely across Europe, including among prominent members of the medical and scientific communities.[12]

Following Mesmer's death in 1815, his cause was taken up by many vocal disciples, including the Marquis de Puységur (1751–1825) whose assistant, a young man named Victor, exhibited telepathic and clairvoyant attributes when magnetized. Rather than employ Mesmer's *baquet* with its accompaniment of hysteria and crises, the marquis chose to magnetize his patients, a method he called *artificial somnambulism,* and to proceed from there to treat their illnesses through suggestion.[13] Another to take up the cause was Abbé José Custodio de Faria (1746–1819), a Goan Catholic monk who traveled from India to Paris to give public exhibitions of hypnosis. In debunking the fluidic theory, he demonstrated by experiment that the mesmeric state (which he called "Farism") did not require a magnetic fluid to achieve its purpose. One only had to induce a trancelike state in the subject, a process that was not dependent on any external cosmic force. Faria's conclusions were later reinforced in the work of Alexandre Jacques François Bertrand (1795–1831) and François Joseph Noizet (1792–1885), whose experiments at the Hôtel-Dieu hospital in Paris stressed the importance of suggestion.[14]

Initially, animal magnetism found few adherents in Great Britain, perhaps due to its French imprimatur and the historical enmity between the two countries. Nevertheless, several early French forays were made by Dr. John Bell, professor of animal magnetism and member of the Society for Universal Harmony of Paris, and by John Benoit de Mainauduc (d. 1797), a pupil of d'Eslon—both in the 1780s. These efforts died out after a few years and it was not until 1828 that interest was again aroused with demonstrations given in London by Richard Chenevix (1774–1830), and five years later by John Campbell Colquhoun (1803–70). The next significant French influence among members of the British medical profession occurred with the work of the Baron Jules Denis du Potet de Sennevoy (1796–1881), who employed mesmeric sleep on several patients of Dr. John Elliotson (1791–1868) at University College Hospital.[15] Elliotson claimed to have carried out 250 painless operations, including the removal of tumors, amputations, extirpation of an eyeball, lithotomy, breast removal, and nail removal.[16] However, opposition to his experiments led to his separation from the hospital in 1838. The hospital's objections were not altogether misguided; like Mesmer and d'Eslon, he had embarked on dubious experimenting with substances such as gold, nickel, silver, platinum, and water to enhance the virtues of mesmerism and the transposition of disease to the body's surface.[17]

Although the experiments undertaken by Dr. Elliotson made little splash among members of the British medical profession, his efforts were followed by Chauncy Hare Townshend (1798–1868) and William Scoresby (1789–1857), whose publications sought to encourage further investigation of the subject. In 1841, the work of Swiss magnetizer Charles Lafontaine (1803–92) attracted the interest of James Esdaile (1808–59) and James Braid (1795–1860) at Manchester, whose modus operandi was to induce a profound sleep in their patients. It was Braid who coined the term "hypnotism" (sometimes called "Braidism") to describe his painless operation. He touted having restored lost sight, improved the condition of paralyzed patients, and cured patients suffering from rheumatism. Significantly, Braid questioned the occult aspects of animal magnetism, preferring to focus instead on the acuteness of the senses to suggestion.[18]

Except for a few curious physicians, medical science kept its distance from mesmerism, believing it to be little more than a trickster's ploy for instant fame. The hundreds of experiments conducted by Braid failed to elicit support from peers as medical prejudice bore down heavily on his work. To complicate matters, the introduction in 1847 of chloroform as an anesthetic brought an end to hypnosis as a tool in surgical operations.[19] Not until twenty years later would experimenters advance the scientific value of hypnotism from the standpoint of psychology, pathology, and therapeutics. Among those who stood in prominence was Ambroise Auguste Liébeault (1823–1904), head of the School of Nancy, whose *Du sommeil et des etats analogues* (Sleep and similar states, 1866) represented one of the earliest methodical studies in the power of suggestion in both waking and hypnotic states. Another was Jean-Martin Charcot (1825–93) at Salpêtrière hospital, who researched the states of catalepsy, lethargy, and somnambulism using the power of suggestion. He, along with his disciples Alfred Binet (1857–1911) and Charles Féré (1852–1907), added much to the canon of literature on the subject.[20]

Much like the French, the German magnetizers Eberhardt Gmelin (1751–1808), Arnold Wienholt (1749–1804), Christoph Wilhelm von Hufeland (1762–1836), Karl Alexander Ferdinand Kluge (1782–1844), and Dietrich Georg von Kieser (1779–1862) were interested in using animal magnetism for healing purposes. In the course of their experiments, they claimed that they had the ability to identify light streaming from the fingers of the operator, that different metals could proportionally influence a somnambulant, and that thought-transference and clairvoyance represented a branch of the physical sciences rather than a mystical interpretation of the universe. Despite their rejection of a Spiritualist point of view, they agreed that in certain higher-level trances and in clairvoyance at a distance, the soul seemed to free itself of space and time.[21]

A medical doctor and later professor of political economy at the Universities of Marburg and Heidelberg, Johann Heinrich Jung (1740–1817), better known as Jung-Stilling, found that mesmerism had much in common with earlier Christian mystics and with the spiritual cosmology of the scientist and philosopher Emanuel Swedenborg. His *Theorie der Geister-Kunde* (Theory of the character of spirit, 1808) gave a thoroughly Christian explanation for the manifestations observed by way of somnambulism. He advanced fifty-five propositions, several of which are worth noting:

1. Animal magnetism undeniably proves that we have an inward man, a soul, which is constituted of the divine spark, the immortal spirit possessing reason and will, and of a luminous body that is inseparable from it.

2. Light, electric, magnetic, galvanic matter, and ether appear to be all one and the same body under different modifications. This light-substance or ether is the element which connects body and soul, and the spiritual and material world together.

3. When the inward man, the human soul, forsakes the inward sphere, where the senses operate and merely continues the vital functions, the body falls into an entranced state, or a profound sleep, during which the soul acts more freely, powerfully, and actively. All its faculties are elevated.

4. The more the soul is divested of the body, the more extensive, free, and powerful is its inward sphere of operation. It has, therefore, no need whatever of the body in order to live and exist. The latter is rather a hindrance to it.

5. The whole of these propositions are sure and certain inferences, which I have drawn from experiments in Animal Magnetism. These most important experiments undeniably show that the soul does not require the organs of sense in order to be able to see, hear, smell, taste, and feel in a much more perfect state.

6. The boundless ether that fills the space of our solar system is the element of spirits in which they live and move. The atmosphere that surrounds our earth, down to its centre, and particularly the night, is the abode of fallen angels, and of such human souls as die in an unconverted state.[22]

Mesmerism also made headway through the research of Baron Karl von Reichenbach (1788–1869), a German chemist and metallurgist who theorized that within the ether was an *aura* or *odylic force* analogous to the *animas* spirits or nervous fluid identified by previous physiologists. This was the medium through which the mind acted upon matter and constituted the boundary between the spiritual and natural worlds. Beyond the aura lay the lowest sphere of the spiritual world, which was organized in a system of many concentric circles.[23] The individuals on whom he experimented were highly susceptible to the influence of magnets and other substances—each substance having its own species of light that radiated from it. By discerning the particular radiant glow or luminous vapor hovering over the substance, and studying the gradations of its strength and color, he thought it possible to "feel" and "see" the type, quality, strength, and capacity of the substance—whether organic or inorganic.[24] Reichenbach was also enamored with magnets and their power to produce effects on the body. Like Mesmer, he held that the magnetic forces radiating from ordinary water, trees, crystals, drugs, and other material items possessed a force over patients similar to an ordinary magnet. These effects were also noticeable among *sensitives,* whose constitutions could sometimes be thrown into convulsive fits by the magnet's power. Reichenbach observed that magnets created a light or luminous vapor at their poles that increased or diminished with the power of the magnet. This same luminous appearance was visible in individuals and varied in intensity with their health or infirmity. The flame, which he claimed rose eight inches or more above an individual, was verification of a force that was conductible through bodies and communicated either by directly charging them or by dispersion. He concluded from this that the human hand acted like the pole of a magnet and could conduct energy through the body, giving credence to Mesmer's magnetic *baquet,* which had often been ridiculed by orthodox medicine as the height of charlatanism.[25]

In 1807, almost a generation after Mesmer's triumph in Paris, Viennese physician Franz Joseph Gall (1758–1828) arrived in the French capital to unveil his discovery of a system he called *craniology.* Author of the four-volume *Anatomy and Physiology of the Nervous System in General, and of the Brain in Particular* (1810–19), he offered the prospect of understanding the character, intellectual capability, and psychological tendencies of an individual by measuring the size, shape, and proportionality of the cranium. He asserted that the brain was a fleshy substance consisting of twenty-seven separate and independent organs, and that it was responsible for a person's moral and mental propensities. Gall attracted numerous disciples, who saw in his science the possibilities of a behavioral approach to the study of human beings. The prevailing opinion at the time treated the mind as a nonmaterial, unitary substance inserted into the body at birth by the Creator and removed at death.[26]

Gall originally gave the name *craniology,* or science of skulls, to his study of the forms and functions of the brain, and *cranioscopy* or *organology* to the science or art of manually surveying the head to estimate its capacities. When Johann Gaspar Spurzheim (1776–1832), Gall's dissectionist and assistant, substituted the term *phrenology,* or science of mind, as a more comprehensive descriptor, he gave full recognition to the mind as the subject of their combined investigations and regarded the brain and cranium as ancillary in their importance.[27]

Building upon the work of his mentor, Spurzheim wrote *Phrenology: In Connexion with the Study of Physiognomy* (1826), laying the groundwork for its acceptance with a lecture tour in 1814 and 1815 of the British Isles. In 1832, he began a similar but ill-fated tour through the United States, a visit brought short by his sudden death. George Combe's (1788–1858) successful visit six years later completed what Spurzheim had intended. Combe, a Scottish phrenologist, moral philosopher, and author of the popular *Constitution of Man* (1828), won many converts, including New York publishers Orson Squire Fowler (1809–87), Lorenzo Niles Fowler (1811–96), and Samuel Robert Wells (1820–75). Together, they helped transform the empirically based science into a practical and secular social philosophy for personal, social, and political improvement.[28]

With criticisms against phrenology mounting in the late 1830s and early 1840s, its advocates moved to identify areas of commonality with mesmerism and construct platforms on which both could build a more defensible system. It was claimed, for example, that when the somnambulant's head was touched by the hand or finger of a mesmerist, the action prompted a specific characteristic in the organs identified by Gall and Spurzheim. The subsequent combination of the two systems lent strength to their legitimacy and tended to deflect the arguments of skeptics. Evidence of this merger came in the form of Spencer T. Hall's monthly *Phreno-Magnet* (1843) and the publication of *The Zoist, A Journal of Cerebral Physiology and Mesmerism* (1843–56) by Drs. John Elliotson and W. C. Engledue. Both journals helped introduce the combined science to British and American readers.[29]

The Swedish Seer

Coinciding with the emerging sciences of mesmerism and phrenology, both products of analytical and synthetic propositions drawn from post-Enlightenment thinking, there loomed the published works of Emanuel Swedenborg, whose intellectual labors were intended to serve the greater glory of God. As a child of the Enlightenment, his critical and skeptical attitudes focused not on faith but on superstition, not on religion but on the Church, accusing the latter of having hindered intellectual progress and failing to establish a genuine morality and just social order. Sorting through the polemics of his age, Swedenborg sought always to use the tools of science and close observation to find the proof and seal of divinity. His view of the world began with the curiosity of an Enlightenment-era scientist forged by the cosmology of René Descartes and the mathematics of Isaac Newton (1642–1727). As he grew more spiritual and mystical in his later years, teleological conceptions took precedence over mechanical explanations. For Swedenborg, the origin, design, distribution, and hierarchy of nature were controlled by divine influx. In coming to this conclusion, he plumbed the wisdom of Aristotle and Plato as well as Europe's most renowned scientists and philosophers, studied the writings of the best anatomists of Europe, recorded and interpreted his dreams, and experienced psychic visions. His solution to Descartes's insistence on the duality of body and soul was to postulate a body whose respiration drew into the blood vessels the spirit-pulse of the universe, thus creating a body/soul nexus that involved both the natural and spiritual worlds. This spiritual influx from the Divine gave individuals life and enabled them to follow God's commands. Working through the recesses of the cortical glands, the soul, whose existence was at a level beyond mechanics and geometry, served as the instrument of God's purposes.[30]

Swedenborg's cosmographic views were sweeping in their breadth, pointing to the creation of a universe that derived from centers or points of energy, which eventually led, in increasing orders of magnitude, to the emergence of the sun, stars, and planets. Also moving outward from these elementary particles of energy—all under the guidance of divine influx—were the different animal, vegetable, and mineral spheres. Everything in the material world depended ultimately on a corresponding cause in the spiritual world, and nothing occurred that did not serve a final purpose. The human soul, being part of the individual but separate from and greater than the physical body, was of the same substance as the cosmic elements in the universe, and its influence on the conscious mind was the vibrations of divine influx. The cortical matter in the brain, which attracted the purest spirits from the blood before transmitting them into the fibers, became the locus for the universal forces breathed in by the lungs, which in turn served as the exchange center between the soul and the body, the infinite and finite. Swedenborg iden-

tified the cortical substance as the principal agent in bodily functions but the substance, he believed, was determined by the spirituous fluid that flowed into the body. This spirituous fluid represented the highest form of thought and the medium for the divine influx.[31]

Following a spiritual crisis lasting from 1743 to 1745, which included conversations with angels from the spirit world, Swedenborg began a journey into biblical revelation documented in twenty-five published volumes and many other unpublished ones. Besides clarifying the language of the Bible, he addressed such topics as heaven and hell, regeneration (a process of spiritual rebirth), correspondences (the connections between the spiritual and physical worlds), faith, charity, marriage, the nature of God and divine providence, and free will. Many of his meditations morphed into waking visions, allowing him special insight beyond the strict empiricism he knew as a scientist. Much of what he wrote in this phase of his life was published anonymously. Eventually, however, his writings became the cornerstone of the New Church, or Church of the New Jerusalem, begun by his followers.[32]

By the 1840s, the brilliance of Swedenborg's scientific accomplishments had been trumped by stories of his conversations with beings from the spirit world and his detailed revelations of heaven and hell, both of which laid the groundwork for America's journey into Spiritualism. His writings and revelatory remarks gave sustenance to countless mediums and their supporters seeking validation of their communications with the spirit world. Beginning as separate movements, mesmerism, phrenology, Spiritualism, and Swedenborgianism became intertwined during the so-called "enthusiasms" of the 1840s, when numerous secular and religious leaders propounded the reconstruction of society using a combination of pseudoscience, revelation, clairvoyance, and other wonders. Such was the popularity of the cultural phenomenon known as Spiritualism by the middle of the nineteenth century that no less a celebrity than the religious and social reformer Theodore Parker (1810–60) comfortably asserted that it had a greater chance of becoming the predominant religion of America than Christianity once had of becoming the official religion of the Roman Empire. Clearly, the séance and its prospect of communication with otherworldly spirits offered comfort to a generation buffeted by a myriad of new sciences and the awesome possibilities wrought by electricity.[33]

American Healers

In the hands of America's unconventional healers, the secular sciences of mesmerism and phrenology found common ground in the spiritual discoveries of Swedenborg to lend a distinctive character to their respective healing practices. Much of it was the outgrowth of a visit to the United States in 1836 by the French mesmerizer Charles Poyen (d. 1844), whose public appearances in the New England region made a strong impression on the popular imagination.[34] As it turned out, his experiments with magnetic power exercised over a sleeping subject startled audiences and led to a number of native imitators, who presented pseudoscientific and pseudo-religious theories as explanations for the phenomenon. Unlike the situation in England, where Dr. John Elliotson and his circle of friends became the spokespeople for mesmerism's scientific standing, there was no one person or persons in America to claim this role. Instead, the mesmeric trance became the property of scores of lecturers, medical doctors, and preachers—each with his own idiosyncratic view and claim of authorship. These lecturers, all of whom were popularly received in towns and cities across the country, claimed to have discovered the true nature of this "fluid" and schemed to capture fame and fortune by giving it their own special acronym.

Cures were reported as early as 1837 in Wrentham, Massachusetts, where Dr. E. Larkin, a practicing physician, conducted a series of tests using magnetism as his healing agent. By 1844, he would claim success in developing clairvoyant abilities in a patient who acquired a remarkable diagnostic capacity while in magnetic sleep. These experiments were accompanied by loud "rappings" or "knockings" attributed to various spirits and, not surprisingly, resulted in a series of resolutions and bans from nearby churches.[35]

Methodist minister and mental healer James Monroe Buckley (1836–1920) recalled seeing his first public demonstration of animal magnetism in 1849 when a visiting "professor" demonstrated its entertaining effects before an attentive audience. He recalled as well the excitement that stirred within the medical profession, some of whom chose to use it to treat paralysis and extract teeth. Later, in the 1850s, he reported seeing it displayed as a healing technique among the perfectionists at John Humphrey Noyes's Oneida Community, among the Millerites in Connecticut, and in the "cures" of Dr. James Rogers Newton (1810–83) of Boston, who documented his successes in *The Modern Bethesda, Or, the Gift of Healing Restored* (1879).[36]

One of the more popular mental healers at this time was New York philosopher and minister John Bovee Dods (1795–1872), author of *Six Lectures on the Philosophy of Mesmerism* (1847) and *The Philosophy of Electrical Psychology* (1870). Dods interpreted electricity as God's transfer agent connecting the human mind with its body and the physical and chemical forces of the world with the divine spirit. He gave his system the name *vital electricity,* reflecting his view of electricity as a rarified form of matter ("primeval and eternal matter") capable of being moved by the mind. This concept would be adopted by later New Thought writers such as William Walker Atkinson, who understood mental states as connected to electromagnetism and the neural processes.

Another popular mental healer was Dr. James Stanley Grimes (1807–1903) of Castleton Medical College in Vermont, who invented the term *electro-biology* to describe the subtle fluids through which the trance-state currents operated. Dr. Grimes suggested that the atmospheric force he called the *etherium* brought about the trancelike behavior.[37]

In the Middle West, one of the most influential mental healers was Joseph Rodes Buchanan (1814–99), a lecturer and phrenologist from Louisville. He was a former student of Dr. Charles Caldwell (1772–1853), who had published the earliest book in the United States on the subject of phrenology. Buchanan claimed discovery of *phrenomagnetism,* or the ability to touch with one's fingers the different phrenological regions on the surface of the cranium and cause a heightened degree of mental function in a corresponding organ in the brain. He also invented the terms *psychometry* and *sarcognomy.* He used the former to describe the ability of highly sensitive individuals to "read" the "outflow" of force from both living and nonliving matter and, in doing so, discern their psychohistory and character. The term sarcognomy referred to tracing the correspondence between the body and brain in much the same manner that phreno-magnetism had done for the brain and surface of the skull. Buchanan served as dean of the Eclectic Medical Institute of Cincinnati (1850–56), founded the *Journal of Man* (1849–56; 1887–90), and authored numerous books, including *Outlines of Lectures on the Neurological System of Anthropology* (1854); *Moral Education: Its Laws and Methods* (1882); *Manual of Psychometry: Dawn of a New Civilization* (1885); *Therapeutic Sarcognomy* (1891); and *Primitive Christianity* (1897).[38]

Buchanan's ideas on the faculties of the soul, brain, and body, and of their relationship to the spiritual world, were remarkably similar to those of Swedenborg. Like the Swedish seer, he employed the law of correspondences to show that "every function of the eternal or spiritual man, whether intellectual, emotional, or physiological, has its special apparatus in the nervous structure of the brain." Similarly, every function and organ of the brain had "a corporal correspondence or region of the body with which it is in close sympathy."[39] Healers' knowledge of these localities enabled a better understanding of disease and improved their ability to operate upon the mind through the body, or upon the body through the mind.[40] "When we understand clearly that life is located in the brain and its subordinate spinal and ganglionic structures," explained Buchanan, "we may inquire whether it *originates* there, or comes by influx and is replenished from the limitless ocean of unembodied life which is invisible—whether the over-soul of the universe does by any intelligible species of influx sustain and develop the life of individuals, which seems to be a fragment of the Divine nature." With these remarks, he expressed a deep and abiding debt to both Emerson and Swedenborg. Questioned whether and to what extent this influx originated from the spirit world, or indirectly from "an influx of ideas and emotions from the wise organization, order, beauty, and benevolence of the visible world," Buchanan answered that it came from both sources, with the latter subordinate to the former.[41] He did not regard discussion of spiritual life as distinct from practical science. Since life was immaterial and spiritual, it had to have entered matter from the spiritual world, which he called the Divine. These mysteries existed beyond the instruments of science, but they did not lie beyond the reach of psychometry.[42]

Buchanan dabbled extensively in Spiritualism (his first wife participated in numerous séances and his second wife was a prominent medium) and claimed to have carried on conversations with numerous individuals (including both wives and a father-in-law) who had passed to the spirit world. Just as Swedenborg claimed to have visited the heavenly spheres and met spirits of the departed, both famous and obscure, from unnamed men and women to Jesus himself, Buchanan revealed his own access to the "heavenly mansions" where he found Jesus in a "celestial plane" and generating magnetic forces that dispersed through the heavens before streaming downward into the worlds inhabited by living souls. These magnetic forces became "the light that lightens the pathway of progress for advanced minds." Like Swedenborg's conversations with angels, Buchanan recounted conversations with the apostles to correct biblical fictions and introduce his readers to a more accurate accounting of the life and character of Jesus. One of the surprising "facts" he related was that the apostles had often held séances with Jesus, during which light illuminated the room and prophecies and spiritual instructions were given. In Buchanan's book *Primitive Christianity* (1897), he sought to address the credibility of Scripture, demolish the false conceptions left by the Roman church and its descendants, and bring forth the lost gospels of the Apostles through the use of his psychometric powers.[43]

There was also the Methodist and revivalist preacher La Roy Sunderland (1804–85), whose sermons and ministerial performances often resulted in group hysteria. Offering a form of phreno-mesmerism he called *pathetism*, he observed that the key to the relationship between operator and subject was one of suggestion. As publisher and editor of the monthly *Magnet* (1842–44), and the weekly Spiritualist periodical *Spiritual Philosopher* (1851), he was a firm believer in communication with the spirit world. Following the public sensation caused by the announcement of spirit-rappings in the home of the Fox sisters in 1848—the story of alleged communication with the dead that launched the Spiritualist movement in the United States—Sunderland joined the ranks of the Spiritualists, for whom mesmerism had become an avenue for mediums ("angel guides") to communicate with those who had passed on to the spirit world. Within a decade, thousands of psychics and mediums were touting communications similar to the Fox sisters and, in the process, capturing the attention of millions of believers across America and Europe in their search for ways to connect the mind with the auric world of spheres and spirits.[44]

Yet another of the nation's unconventional healers was the clairvoyant Andrew Jackson Davis (1826–1910) who earned the title "Poughkeepsie Seer." Apprenticed in his youth to a shoemaker, Davis had been fascinated with a series of lectures on animal magnetism given by Professor J. Stanley Grimes in 1843. Following Grimes's visit, numerous members of the community began experimenting with the practice of magnetism (or mesmerism), including William Levingston, a local tailor, who successfully magnetized the fifteen-year-old Davis. During these experiments, Davis supposedly acquired the clairvoyant ability to diagnose and prescribe treatment for various illnesses. Recognizing a budding career as magnetic healers, Davis and Levingston took their newfound science on the road, demonstrating their healing before public and private audiences. By the time he was eighteen, Davis had left Levingston and, having acquired a circle of supporters, proceeded to dictate a series of trance-lectures later published as *The Principles of Nature, Her Divine Revelations, and a Voice to Mankind* (1847), and followed by *The Great Harmonia* (1850–61), *The Penetralia* (1856), and *The Present Age and Inner Life* (1870). Heavily influenced by the Fox sisters and other "spirit rappers" of the day, Davis combined his clairvoyant abilities with those of mesmerism and mediumship to treat patients' maladies and carry trance revelations from the spirit world to worried individuals who had lost spouses, children, friends, or relatives.[45]

In his *The Principles of Nature, Her Divine Revelations, and a Voice to Mankind*, Davis laid out his grand harmonial philosophy. The book borrowed extensively from Swedenborg's *The Economy of the Animal Kingdom* (1740–41; also known as *Dynamics of the Soul's Domain*)—without attribution.[46] In his book, Davis traced the origin of the universe, the process of differentiation that led to a vast solar system of suns moving in concentric circles, and the Great Eternal Center from which emanated the divine power. From these cosmic beginnings, he proceeded to account for the planets (based on his own planetary travels), the first appearance of living organisms, and the communion of humans through a system of correspondences or analogies with the spirit world. Finally, Davis's grand vision included a scheme for organizing society into phalanxes and cooperatives that combined utopian and socialist philosophies such as Owenism and Fourierism with a reinterpreted view of Swedenborg's Universal Human.[47] Accused of plagiarism, Davis responded by claiming to have gained his insight into Swedenborg's ideas through his clairvoyant trance states. This ratiocination provided temporary cover until Dr. George Bush (1796–1859), a Swedenborgian minister and professor of Hebrew at the University of New York, vouched for the authenticity of his spirit communications and of his ability to "acquire" his information clairvoyantly rather than by reading Swedenborg's works. Bush would later revise his opinion, warning readers in a pamphlet titled "Davis' Revelations Revealed" (1847) that the Poughkeepsie Seer's revelations were less than honest.[48]

After disappearing from the Spiritualist movement in the early 1880s, Davis went on to earn a medical degree from the eclectic New York Medical College and opened an office in Boston where he practiced for several years. Unlike conventional practitioners, he relied upon clairvoyance to diagnose disease.[49]

Psychical Research

Following the emergence of modern Spiritualism in 1848, mustered in by the Fox sisters and their many imitators, Americans and Europeans found themselves host to any number of paranormal phenomena (rappings, table-tippings, hauntings, apparitions, materializations, levitations, etc.) intended as forms of communication between the material and spirit worlds. Over time, however, much of what posed as real communication turned out to be fraud. As early as 1850, Edward White Benson (1829–96) organized a "Ghost Society" to investigate claims of mediumship. In carrying out their work, the society's members observed numerous séances, gathering data and building a canon of information concerning psychical claims of life continuing beyond mortal death. Before long, psychical research into hypnotism, mediumship, clairvoyance, and subconscious mental states became a quest that captured a generation or more of psychopathologists, who sought a means of determining scientifically whether life existed after bodily death. Although suspect in the world of professional science, individuals such as Sir Oliver Lodge (1851–1940), Sir William Crookes (1832–1919), John William Strutt (1842–1919), and professors Enrico Morselli (1852–1929) and Cesare Lombroso (1835–1909) became willing investigators into the phenomena.[50]

The work of the Ghost Society laid the groundwork for the London Dialectical Society, founded in 1869; the presentation of a paper read in 1876 by Professor W. F. Barrett before the British Association for the Advancement of Science on "Some Phenomena Associated with Abnormal Conditions of Mind"; and the establishment in 1882 of the Society for Psychical Research, whose investigative committees often detected fraud. Its areas of inquiry included whether or not one mind can influence another, hypnotism and mesmeric trance, the existence of Reichenbach's sensitives, ghosts and hauntings, and Spiritualism in general.[51] In studying hypnotism, the society was not so much interested in demonstrating its therapeutic value as it was in discovering if thought could be communicated from one mind to another by way of clairvoyance or thought transference without passing through ordinary channels of communication. The society's report, written by Edmund Gurney with the assistance of a Mr. Myers and Frank Podmore, and published in 1884, supported the theory that thoughts, feelings, and images could be transferred from one mind to another.[52]

The American Society for Psychical Research was founded in 1885 with astronomer Simon Newcomb as its first president. Like its English cousin, it had numerous distinguished members, including Episcopal Bishop Phillips Brooks, publisher Henry Holt, author Andrew Dickson White, Edward Pickering of the Harvard College Observatory, Dr. Henry Bowditch of Harvard Medical School, and professors William James, Josiah Royce, and Joseph Jastrow. Although it became a branch of the English society in 1889, it reorganized independently in 1906, taking a predominantly anti-spiritualistic and pro-telepathy tone under the leadership of Professor James Hervey Hyslop (1854–1920), a Columbia University professor of logic and ethics.

* * *

There is reason to believe that the idea of spheres of spiritual existence, including communication with spirits, received "official" standing in part because of Swedenborg's trance experiences and revelations. American Spiritualists, including Buchanan and Davis, found comfort in his accounts of heaven and hell. This connection, considered by Swedenborg's followers as a gift extended only to the seer himself, would now be claimed by numerous nineteenth-century mediums and clairvoyants, assisted by the spread of Spiritualist cosmology, séance circles, and prophetic messaging. Some Swedenborgians took heart from these eventful occurrences, believing that persons who had been mesmerized had experienced a mental state of impressibility and spiritual influx that had allowed them glimpses into the spirit world. Others condemned Spiritualism and refused to have any part in it.

Despite naysayers, by the late 1840s and 1850s, the devotees of Spiritualism felt at home in both mesmerism and Swedenborgianism, considering them to be essential steps in the soul's journey into spiritual growth and healthy-mindedness. Spiritual healing became a common characteristic of nineteenth-century American culture, savored at first by the Shakers, Mormons, Millerites, Oneidans, and other perfectionists and evangelicals operating on the fringes of the major denominations, and later among members of the broader society, including mainstream ministers, who gave willing testimony to its claims. It also became the common currency of the nation's unconventional healers seeking an alternative to what they considered to be the failures of medical orthodoxy. No longer viewed as a privilege extended only to Swedenborg, spirit communication became the democratic common ground of American Spiritualism and medical heterodoxy in the decades to follow.

Without an understanding of these early examples of mind cure, one can misjudge the intellectual origins of New Thought, thinking that its early emphasis on mental healing was tied wholly to an effort to resurrect the healing powers of Jesus and his apostles. While the desire to resurrect the healing abilities reportedly present in the early Christian church became a key element in New Thought, its more immediate lineage was to the sciences and pseudosciences emerging in the late eighteenth and early nineteenth centuries when traveling mesmerists and phrenologists catered to long-held yearnings, awakening thoughts of self and salvation that came from outside the normal channels of divine guidance. In lyceum-style gatherings at churches and public meeting halls, audiences gained insight from the new sciences, using the visions and prophesies of their interpreters to replace the Calvinistic sense of sin and abasement with more agreeable feelings. In these gatherings, the morphology of Protestant evangelical conversion was replaced by the power of the human mind and the comfort and responsibility that accompanied free will. Individuals such as Sunderland, Buchanan, and Davis were openly experimental, throwing off the unsettling and offensive doctrines of Calvinism and, utilizing the novel psychologies found in phrenology, mesmerism, phreno-magnetism, sarcognomy, and mediumship, helped struggling believers construct new understandings of self, justification, immanence, and sanctification. Rather than replace faith, these scientific psychologies sustained it by mapping brain/spirit correspondences from the head to all parts of the body.[53]

As will become evident in later chapters, the emergence of New Thought as a movement was not something cast onto American shores from an anonymous ship or unknown continent but an intricately interwoven philosophy of practical idealism drawn from eclectic elements— both native and foreign—of physical healing and the higher mental, spiritual, and even angelic planes. A mélange of the world's great philosophies, religions, and heterodox healing systems were combined with the intent of restoring harmony to the nation's physical and spiritual well-being. As Emerson noted, America was a land of new people and new thoughts that demanded "our own works and laws and worship."[54]

2

Christ Science

I believe there was one person who . . . I give all the credit of introducing this truth into the world, and that was Jesus. . . . He was the embodiment of a higher Wisdom, more so than any man who has ever lived

—Phineas P. Quimby, *The Quimby Manuscripts*

Despite the more secular approach to mental healing that predominated in Europe in the late eighteenth and early nineteenth centuries, Americans were unsurpassed in their effort to adapt the elements of mental healing to Christian belief. This explains the influence of Phineas Parkhurst Quimby (1802–66), whose independent opinions were given equal measure with those schooled in academe. In fact, it was Quimby's inquisitive and introspective experiences that challenged and made intelligible much of what passed as commonsense knowledge. Although only moderately educated, he drew from years of personal experience with patients of all types to deconstruct and then reconstruct a system of mental healing that laid the groundwork for later discussion and change. Unlike contemporaries who made the circuit of lecture venues using the more popular method of hypnotic treatment, Quimby broke from the prevailing practice to trace the outlines of the healing experience, question his own methods, and substitute new knowledge and practices for those he could no longer accept.

Quimby's intellectual journey began as an adherent of regular medicine, and from there he became a practitioner of mesmerism, a participant in séances, a believer in clairvoyance, and finally expressed his faith in the ability of each individual to access science (by which he meant achieving the understanding that would lead to good health) through the divine presence of Christ. Quimby conducted a lengthy investigation of mental phenomena that led him to develop his own unique healing method. At the core of his healing process was the idea that all people have an inner spiritual nature that could be reached through what he called the "silent method." Having found these keys to the mind and body, he proceeded to connect them to Christ's teachings in a system he called the "Science of Health."[1] What was largely unspoken in Quimby's life and work was the origin of his ideas. Some were arguably borrowed from the writings of Emanuel Swedenborg, but this was neither disclosed nor admitted by Quimby, as was the case with other contemporary healers whose writings showed similar ancestry.

Early Years

Born in 1802 in Lebanon, New Hampshire, Quimby was one of seven siblings and the son of a blacksmith. In 1804, he moved with his family to Belfast, Maine, where he was raised and spent his young adulthood. Neither his ancestry nor his education suggests anything other than an ordinary individual with an inquisitive mind. He attended school, but only for a short time, as the family's resources were too meager to provide opportunities beyond the bare rudiments of a country school education. This left him with a limited vocabulary and a lifelong difficulty with misspelled words. He was known by friends and neighbors as "Park" and went forth in life judged to be "honest, upright, dedicated to practical pursuits, and by no means peculiar."[2]

Showing an early interest in mechanical things, he apprenticed to a clockmaker and obtained patents for several devices of a mechanical nature.[3] These inventive and creative qualities would eventually migrate from mechanics to an intense desire to understand belief systems and to test theories for himself. He concluded early in life that true knowledge did not come through books, which consisted of other people's opinions, but through practical experience and what his own perceptive faculties could discern. "Truths" were to be tested.

Quimby had piercing black eyes; a high, broad forehead; a prominent nose; and black hair and whiskers. Of medium height and weighing all of 125 pounds, he projected what his generation called a nervous temperament or constitution. Sickly in his youth, he was once diagnosed with the "wasting away" disease of consumption. "I believed all this from the fact that I had all the symptoms and could not resist the opinions of the physician while having the proof with me," he admitted. Moreover, he claimed to have taken so much calomel (mercurous chloride) to treat his disease that he lost several teeth from its deleterious effects.[4]

Quimby had no specific religious affiliation, inclined as he was to be skeptical. Nor had his family been especially religious-minded, if one defined religion in terms of a specific creed. Neither he nor his family had membership in any denomination or sect. Nevertheless, he was always curious to understand the opinions of others, including the religious beliefs of Unitarians and Universalists, whose services he sometimes attended and, later, those of his patients. In this latter sense, Quimby was indeed religious, which manifested later when he looked to the historical Jesus as the founder of spiritual science.[5]

Mesmeric Period

When the Frenchman Charles Poyen visited Maine in 1836 as part of a lecture tour to introduce mesmerism into the United States, followed two years later by the visit of British physician Robert H. Collyer (1814–91), a former student of phrenologist Johann Gaspar Spurzheim and a self-described professor of mesmerism, Quimby decided to educate himself on the subject. His "awakening" came not from books, but from the public demonstrations of Poyen and Collyer. By 1838, Quimby had acquired sufficient knowledge to begin giving his own demonstrations, placing people into hypnotic trances or what was known at the time as "mesmeric sleep." His lectures and demonstrations represented the beginning of a lifetime of investigation into the subject of the mind and healing.[6]

In the course of his public presentations, Quimby met seventeen-year-old Lucius Burkmar, who, like Poughkeepsie seer Andrew Jackson Davis, exhibited astonishing powers of clairvoyance when placed in a hypnotic state. Before long, Quimby was working with Burkmar almost exclusively. He would sit opposite him, hold both hands in his own and, while looking intently into his eyes, cause Burkmar to enter a state of mesmeric sleep that Quimby controlled. As their experiments progressed, Burkmar seemed to be able to receive Quimby's instructions mentally without a word spoken between them. With this as their modus operandi, the two men plied the lecture circuit through Maine and neighboring areas of Canada, where they gave public demonstrations of their clairvoyant powers over a period of four years.[7]

As their exhibitions continued, the demonstrations evolved from simple entertainment to serious efforts at healing. This latter component originated after they received numerous requests to examine sick persons and diagnose their ills. Quimby discovered in fulfilling these requests that Burkmar was able to provide diagnoses of patients' conditions and prescribe cures that were remarkably successful. This apparent clairvoyant ability suggested to Quimby a whole new method of healing distinct from regular medicine's materialistic approach to disease. Numerous testimonials published in the local papers used the terms "mesmerism," "fluid," and "animal magnetism" to describe Quimby's power, giving an air of authenticity and legitimacy to his ability to use clairvoyance in treating disease. Often the terms were used interchangeably, and as their meanings were vague, they conveyed the idea of powers that put Quimby in the same class as other spiritists, mesmerists, magnetizers, and clairvoyants of the day.[8]

Burkmar kept a diary from 1843 through 1845 in which he recounted their circuit of neighboring towns and villages. He reported that they usually remained in one place no more than two days, giving public exhibitions as well as treating patients in private rooms before moving on to the next location. Typically, they stayed the night in a tavern, hotel, temperance house, or private home, and gave their exhibitions the following day in a church meeting room, concert hall, courthouse, or other available buildings. On an average evening, Burkmar would stand at the front door selling admission tickets and then, when the program was about to begin, proceed to Quimby's side to be mesmerized. Not including private patients, their normal income for an evening's work averaged $11, with the most they ever received being $22 from a crowded hall of three hundred people.[9]

Over time, Quimby observed that the cures prescribed by Burkmar varied widely both in quantity and strength. He noted, for example, that on some occasions Burkmar prescribed a totally benign herb tea that "cured" the patient of a serious illness while a regular physician obtained a similar result using a totally different stratagem. In one particular instance, Burkmar informed a young man that his lungs "looked like a honeycomb, and his liver was covered with ulcers."[10] Convinced that the mesmerized Burkmar had really not "seen" the diseased liver and that his prescribed "cure" had accomplished little or nothing in itself, Quimby came up with the novel thesis that his patients were suffering from no disease except their own misguided and erroneous thinking. Quimby felt that he could accomplish the same level of healing by correcting the patient's error in thinking, and that changes in the mind of the patient would lead the patient to recover his health. This conviction led Quimby to dismiss Burkmar and set out on his own using a new healing method that he called *psychotherapy*.[11]

As he put his ideas into practice, Quimby continued to introspectively question his own methodology. On those occasions when he mesmerized a patient, he sat in a chair opposite the subject, "willing" the person to sleep. The assumption he made at the time was that a "fluid" or "electricity" passed from his own body to the subject, and that he had the power to will the patient to sleep provided that his own fluid was stronger. On reflection, Quimby speculated that the results would have been the same without hypnosis, provided the subject knew what was expected to bring about cure. In effect, the entire process was mental and neither drug, spirit, touch, image, thought-reading, nor any other therapeutic regimen had anything to do with the result. The ability to cure was the result of mind acting on mind and nothing more.[12]

Quimby next reasoned that if it was possible to affect the thought of another with mesmerism, perhaps it could be done without it as well. If one mind could influence another in sleep, why not in a perfectly conscious state through a process of suggestion? If this was possible, then there was no reason to believe that mesmerism, clairvoyance, electric fluid, or any other fancied medium passed from one body to another. If disease was a state of mind, the cause of which existed in a particular form of belief, the patient's confidence in the healer's suggestion would be sufficient to bring about the cure. Disease could be cured with or without a particular medicine.[13]

As he developed this line of thought, Quimby made less use of hypnotic sleep and eventually discarded it altogether as a remedial agent. On occasion, however, he used physical manipulation on his patients, particularly if they came to him with lameness or sprains. In such instances, he would rub the limbs and even the head of the patient, wetting them with water as he proceeded. Quimby did this to instill the patient with confidence in his healing abilities, since otherwise his only obvious method of healing consisted of conversation. In either case, he insisted that his healing abilities owed nothing to any body manipulations, mesmeric trance, Spiritualism, or mediumistic powers. It was the patient's mind that underwent change from error or false belief to one of truth. Thus, Quimby progressed from being a mesmerist and clairvoyant in the tradition of La Roy Sunderland and Andrew Jackson Davis to a healer who employed the power of an active and inquiring mind. Instead of mesmerizing the patient, he sat in silence by the patient's side and, after using clairvoyance to understand the malady, explained to the patient the cure that lay within his or her own being. Through suggestion and subtle argument, he taught patients to think themselves healthy, certain that their malady would disappear with the inspired conviction of a healthy mind. "My practice is unlike all medical practice," he insisted. "I give no medicine, and make no outward applications. I tell the patient his troubles, and what he thinks is his disease; and my explanation is the cure. If I succeed in correcting his errors, I change the fluids of the system and establish the truth, or health. The truth is the cure."[14]

As he put his ideas to the test in the minds of his patients, Quimby came to believe that the medical profession had been largely responsible for creating and perpetuating erroneous beliefs about disease and false justification for various drugs and appliances. It was the doctor's belief that made the disease and, deceived by its supposed "truth," the patient acquired the effects. When the doctor prescribed bleeding, purging, or a simple herb tea and the patient recovered, both the doctor and patient believed that the specific regimen caused the cure, i.e., *post hoc, propter hoc*. Having created the patient's belief in the disease, the doctor was then able to change the mind of the patient through the application of a specific medicine.

Quimby believed that diseases and their cures were real for patients, but they carried no spiritual truths. "I never make war with medicine, but with opinions," he explained. "I never try to convince a patient that his trouble arises from calomel or any other poison, but the poison of the doctor's opinion in admitting a disease."[15] Quimby thus turned away from all traditional schools of medicine.

When asked his opinion of phrenology, Quimby called it "mere humbug [and] . . . a polite way of pointing out the soft spots of a man's vanity." He also denied that he was in any way a Spiritualist, medium, or clairvoyant in the manner of the Fox sisters with their so-called "rappings." Having personally attended numerous séances, he did not doubt the honest intent of the sisters and their imitators, but he considered Spiritualists to be misguided in their claim of exercising mediumship powers over otherworldly spirits. Instead, Quimby claimed belief in the "spirits of the living," by which he meant belief in the powers that existed independently of the natural senses and that provided access to "true knowledge." This other state of Spiritualism, he believed, had been manifested in all ages and enabled individuals to communicate outside the normal sense channels. Instead of receiving his knowledge from dead spirits, Quimby claimed the ability to acquire all essential information directly from the patients themselves. "I found that I had the power of not only feeling their aches and pains, but the state of their mind," he wrote, adding that by absorbing the aura or vapor that surrounded patients' nervous systems, he was able to identify the troubles that had caused these conditions.[16] In this manner, explained one of his disciples, "Mr. Quimby believed as thoroughly as any Quaker that he would be led by the Spirit." Quimby's objective was to establish a science whose principles were as certain as mathematics and thus could be adopted by anyone.[17]

Quimby acknowledged that mesmerists, Spiritualists, and mediums had made a highly remunerative business from their healing techniques. Making their patients believe they were sick with scrofula or some other illness, these false healers were able to prescribe an appropriate herb or spirit provided there was sufficient money in the transaction. All this proved, however, was that the human mind was open to suggestion. There was the power of one mind to control another and this, not mesmerism, priestcraft, mediumship, allopathy, spiritism, or magnetism, did the work of healing. The results produced in treating the sick depended upon securing the attention of the patient in favor of a certain diagnosis and the proper medicine. Remedies affected the body through the mind, a situation that required the patient to believe in the medicine and the intended result.[18]

"Science of Health"

Quimby could easily have spent his entire career treating patients using mesmerism. That he chose to depart from this practice and develop another theory of mental healing implied a quality in him that differed markedly from other healers in his day. During his mesmeric period, from 1843 through 1847, Quimby was in no way different than the myriad of "magnetic healers" whose circuits of the cities and towns had brought them in contact with patients anxious for the healing touch. This was certainly the manner in which John Bovee Dods, James Stanley Grimes, La Roy Sunderland, Joseph Rodes Buchanan, and others operated. Quimby followed the activities of each of these early healers and their "discoveries," commenting upon them in his writings. However, Quimby's mesmeric period was followed by an intermediate period between 1847 and 1859 when he developed a method of treatment that he called his "Science of Health."[19]

Quimby's intermediate period was understandably less noticed by contemporary observers, since it did not involve any public demonstrations. Instead, he sat silently beside his patients and depended upon his impressions and intuitions to discern each person's particular malady. The key was making an intuitive diagnosis and then moving on to suggestion—not through conversing with the patient, as in his earlier mode of healing, but by thought transference. To accomplish this, he allowed himself to be receptive to the patient's feelings, which sometimes gave patients the sense that he was taking on their troubles. "I take upon myself your infirmities that I may lead you to health, for health to you is heaven," he wrote. "The love for health prompts you to come. My love for you prompts me to lead you to health. This I do by teaching you the errors of your belief and showing you where you have been deceived." So difficult and overwhelming were his sympathies for patients that Quimby frequently took leave of his practice, presumably to rest from his ordeal. Eventually, however, he claimed to have transitioned through this period by learning to call on God's power to keep a portion of his spirit free. This led him to conclude that in every individual there was a portion of the spirit that was never sick and that never sinned. This he called the "scientific man," that is, the part of a human being that is divine, and the development of this concept marked the beginning of his effort to "learn the way of the Christ."[20]

When making a diagnosis, a process that Quimby called "the silence" or the "silent method," he deliberately absented his mind of everything but the impressions made by the patient, which he said created a "daguerreotype" on his mind. "When I sit by a patient," wrote Quimby, "their feelings affect me and the sensation I receive from the mind is independent of the senses, for they [the senses] do not know that they communicate any intelligence to me. This I feel, and it contains the cause of the trouble, and my Wisdom explains the trouble, and the explanation is the cure." Convinced that the daguerreotype was a "shadow of a false idea," he chose not to fear it but rather to send a daguerreotype of health and strength back to the mind of the patient through words of encouragement, explaining what he thought was the person's disease. Quimby then discussed the circumstances that caused the disease, how the patient fell victim to the error that made the disease possible, and how the patient's suffering could be corrected and health restored. When that happened, the patient's feelings worked in sympathy with his own and "the shadow grows dim, and finally the light takes its place, and there is nothing left of the disease." All this was accomplished without the patient saying a word.[21]

While oral instruction constituted a critical element in a healer's work, according to Quimby, it was not the most important component, as many cures were accomplished with little or no oral communication. He believed this was the strength of his method. Yet the technique was not hypnotic; there was no effort to force the patient's will into a condition of unconsciousness. The healer simply held in his mind an image of what the patient should be, and this image, through thought transference, was impressed upon the patient's mind. The change was accomplished by the two wills working in harmony.[22]

Once Quimby had connected the idea of an inner "scientific man" with Jesus as the original manifestation of this divine element on earth, he devoted more and more time to learning about the works, sayings, and gospels of Jesus. Unlike European medical practitioners who had undertaken the process of transforming mesmerism into a secular and scientifically grounded treatment, Quimby turned his psychotherapeutic method toward religion, declaring that its "truths" were consistent with the teachings of Jesus and the healings he and his apostles performed during the early years of the Christian church. Quimby concluded that Jesus's true mission had been to treat the sick.[23] As explained by Quimby, the people's ignorance had confounded Jesus with Christ, but it was only after Jesus had been baptized that he became "the Christ, the living God (or Science)." The term Christ was never intended to apply to the man Jesus but to a truth "superior to the natural man." Once Jesus was baptized, however, God took on the attributes of flesh and blood "to convince man of His power and save man from an endless eternity of misery." For Quimby, this meant that the "Christ or God in us is the same that is in Jesus, only in a greater degree in Him."[24]

According to Quimby, an "inward man" governed the "outward man," and when both were in tune, the body was healthy; when at variance, there was disease. This concept, similar to the Greek *crases*, implied a harmony of the body's humors or temperaments with the outer world. The concept would also have been very familiar to readers of Swedenborg; he wrote of the inner person as receiving good impulses from God and the outer person as being ruled by the senses.[25] As a healer, Quimby claimed the ability to place himself in communica-

tion with the inner (soul) and outer (body) person, acting as a mediator
between the two.

"Science of Life and Happiness"

In 1859, Quimby moved to Portland, Maine, where he met patients
Emma and Sarah Ware, Julius A. Dresser, Annetta G. Seabury (later
married to Dresser), Mary Baker Patterson (later Mrs. Eddy), and the
Methodist and later Swedenborgian clergyman Warren Felt Evans.
There Quimby developed a theory and practice that he variously called
spiritual healing, Christian Truth, or *Christian Science.* In this new
phase in his healing methods, Quimby emphasized spiritual rebirth
and the adoption of a life dedicated to "the Christ." His conversations
with patients were now intended to connect with their inner selves and
awaken them to the "science of life and happiness."[26] He believed that
his method of mental treatment was not dependent on any purported
revelation, book, or individual but, instead, operated on a verifiable set
of laws and principles that had the clarity of mathematics.[27]

Convinced that a person's happiness or misery depended upon his
or her beliefs, Quimby set out to separate that which was eternal in the
mind from beliefs that changed out of fear and ignorance. Believing
that God neither intentionally inflicted disease upon his creatures nor
intended that human beings should suffer from it, Quimby thought it
possible to discover the opinions, fears, and mental pictures that sowed
the seeds of error and to change them. Working with patients, he set out
to bring the individual to a state of self-understanding, meaning a state
of inner wisdom, peace, and goodness indicative of the Christ within.[28]

Quimby denied that Christ had performed any miracles when he
cured the sick. "I can produce a phenomenon that . . . is just like some
produced by Christ, and in the living, who speak for themselves," he
claimed. "I should like to know by what authority anyone dares to say
that it is not done in the same way that Christ did His works." The only
objection that could be made, he continued, is that such powers were
thought to be contrary to current opinion or belief, which "is not worth
anything." Instead, he insisted that all of humankind had the power
demonstrated by Jesus and his apostles.[29] Drawing from both his healing

experiences and from Bible reading, Quimby concluded that he had discovered Jesus's method of healing—instead of working miracles, Jesus had developed a highly scientific method of healing, the same technique that Quimby referred to as the "science of life and happiness." It was this that Jesus had come to reveal to humankind. The Bible contained a level of wisdom that Quimby called "the Christ," and this was Jesus's gift to the world—a mental healing method all could practice. In teaching this "Christ Science," Jesus showed humankind how to draw upon the divine wisdom within to overcome false beliefs.[30]

At this stage in his healing career, Quimby regarded his approach as that of "a lamp-bearer disclosing the way out of the dark places of the soul into the light of the divine wisdom." By this he meant that the patient had to see for himself in order for a cure to be permanent. Given the potential for human error, how was it possible to learn the truth? Was there a deeper science than that proposed by mesmerists, Spiritualists, and allopathic medicine? If we create what we believe, then what can we create that is truly worth believing? Having come to believe that each individual had the ability to access divine wisdom through intuition, Quimby concluded that in the discovery of that inner wisdom, patients found the guidance to deny what they had thought were their diseases or physical impairments. Once this wisdom was found, a spiritual transformation in the individuals essentially changed their view of life.[31]

Quimby first used the term Christian Science in an 1863 article titled "Aristocracy and Democracy." In it, he explained that healing was based on two distinct principles. The first was the idea that the divine wisdom Jesus taught could be found within the individual and serve as a guide to the true interpretation of the Bible. This explains his frequent use of the term "the Christ within." His second principle was that all causation was mental; every phenomenon was first conceived in the mind. Thus, Quimby intended the term "science" to mean wisdom, which was divine in origin and therefore superior to opinion. To the extent that Jesus taught science or eternal truth, he avoided opinion. Like mathematics, science could be reduced to "self-evident propositions" for the benefit of human understanding. Discoverable in the Bible, science could also be approached using "spiritual senses" or embraced as revelation that originated from God. "Science," explained Quimby, "is the name of that wisdom that accounts for all phenomena that the natural man or beast cannot understand."[32] Quimby spoke of Jesus as a man of opinions, and Christ as the scientific man. Between true science and true religion there was no conflict. Science, being true knowledge, was divine, relating to human beings through understanding. All true science encompassed genuine religion, which, if true, must also be scientific.[33]

According to Quimby, all people respected wisdom, which stood for "something superior to themselves that they cannot understand." Being naturally indolent, human beings were often deceived in their willingness to believe and therefore were easily drawn to false beliefs and opinions. In point of fact, the "natural man" (i.e., the man made of both truth and error)[34] was little more than a "brute" who followed the easiest path to understanding, a path that most often led him to follow public opinions or opinions of the masses and encouraged impetuous, reactive, and non-reflective decision making. In contrast, the "scientific man" schooled in the wisdom of God refused to believe what could not be proved. Never having compromised with the enemies of truth, the scientific man had a fuller understanding of life and happiness. Unfortunately, because the natural man was superstitious and easily distracted by the world's opinions, he found it difficult to interpret or understand the scientific man. "To be in the scientific world is to acknowledge a wisdom above the natural man," explained Quimby. "This is the condition of those who are thrown into the clairvoyant state."[35]

Quimby refused to have anything to do with organized religion, creeds, or priests. He considered them, along with the medical fraternity, the reason so many people were sick. His own religion was very simple. He acknowledged God or Wisdom, and nothing more.[36] He also believed in immortality and some form of progression after death. From his experiments, he concluded that there existed a "guiding principle" common to all humankind and that this principle affirmed a relationship between the soul and the divine mind. Knowing that one's spirit could act directly on another spirit convinced him that this action was evidence of the Divine in each soul.[37]

Healing involved recognition that the human mind was a far more complicated recipient of beliefs and ideas than previously understood. Like soil, the spiritual substance of the mind was a place where beliefs germinated and subsequently affected both the conscious and unconscious aspects of the body. Hidden in the mind, this substance was accessible to those spiritual healers who could discern its contents, bring those contents to the attention of the patient, and make them manifest. This was possible because there was a portion of every soul, regardless of illness, that was not sick. It was this portion that the healer summoned into action.[38]

Very much a homespun philosopher, Quimby found his way amid the orthodoxies of the day, relying on his own perception, creativity, and practicality. He enjoyed telling parables and repeated himself frequently in his notes. He insisted that a person's life was a progressive process and that health, wisdom, and happiness were realizable objectives. He furthermore taught that God was immanent in the world and that Christ was in everyone. "To believe in this God is to know ourselves," he wrote, "and that is the religion of Christ. It is Christ in us, not opinions we are in. Just as we know this truth, we are of and a part of God, . . . and will be guided by the Father of all truth."[39]

Given Quimby's limited education and the fact that he was charting new territory in healing, it is not surprising that he employed a vocabulary that was simple but sometimes contorted. Absent the language that would be used decades later to explain conditions or elements of the mind, he was nonetheless fully aware of the different mental states brought about by emotional disturbances. The term *subconscious,* for example, was not in his vocabulary, but this did not prevent him from identifying the elements of the inner mind that later experts identified with this term.[40] Having originated his healing technique within the mesmeric framework, his explanations of sickness and health were couched in terms that marked the period. Even though he broke ranks with the advocates of hypnotic trance, the limited vocabulary of the period followed him into his new beliefs. As explained by historian Catherine L. Albanese, "In writings that bear all the marks of their roughshod construction, Quimby hammered out a confused, but still commanding theology of healing, forming a charter document for American metaphysical religion."[41]

Despite Quimby's claims to the contrary, it is relatively easy to see the influence of Plato and Swedenborg, since so many of Quimby's metaphors were of light and shadow: the world of opinions versus the world of Science or Wisdom, the physical senses that were attached to opinion, the clairvoyant versus the natural state of human beings, truth being the wisdom of God and error being the god of opinions, and the sick being imprisoned because of their beliefs. Similar to Plato's analogy of the cave in *Phaedrus,* Quimby believed there were two worlds—one of opinion, belonging to the natural man, and one of wisdom or inner truth belonging to the scientific man. The former was a shadow of science, limited in its sphere, always changing, and seen by "natural eyes," while the latter had no limits and was always progressing. "To know Science," he wrote, "is to know Wisdom."[42] For Quimby, the natural man stood at the balance. "As his senses are in his wisdom and his wisdom is attached to his . . . body, his change of mind is under one of the two directions—either of this world of opinions or of God, or science; and his happiness or misery is the result of his wisdom."[43] It was people's duty to understand themselves and to overcome the kingdom of ignorance. Every person had the capacity for higher Wisdom and was encouraged to seek it. "What people call 'power' I call Wisdom," Quimby wrote. "Now if my wisdom is more than yours then I can help you, but this I must prove to you, and if I tell you about yourself that you cannot tell me, then you must acknowledge that my wisdom is superior to yours and become a pupil instead of a patient." Wisdom was potentially present in all individuals and represented the "Divine ideal of man in perfect health and freedom."[44]

Despite Quimby's references to human beings' "inner" and "outer" states, his use of the term *natural man,* his references to Swedenborg's self-induced trances, and his use of the term *Wisdom* to refer to divine influence, Quimby made no formal admission of Swedenborg's influence on his writings. The one exception is a reference to a brief conversation he once had with a minister of the New Church, the denomination founded by followers of Swedenborg after the Swede's death. One is tempted, however, to ask: If Quimby was knowledgeable enough to make reference to these various concepts, from whom did he derive the terms? Clearly, he was not alone among the nation's mental healers to have borrowed from (or, in other cases, even plagiarized) Swedenborg's works as he sought to understand the spiritual world. It would appear that this was a common occurrence among America's early spiritual healers and, in the absence of an international copyright law, done in conscious disregard of intellectual ownership. It also suggests the degree to which Quimby and other contemporary healers intended to put their distinctive stamp on a particular system of healing, believing theirs to be entirely different from all others.[45]

According to Horatio Dresser, since Quimby had not been a reader of philosophy and theology, it was unlikely that he had borrowed from Plato, or, for that matter, from either the Irish philosopher and idealist George Berkeley (1685–1753) or Swedenborg. "If . . . Quimby's spiritual exegesis might have been fulfilled in Swedenborg's science of correspondences," he observed, "we find nothing in his writings pertaining to the realms of evil spirits and angels, and nothing that tells us what for him was the content of the spiritual world. He is not at all interested in psychical experiences except so far as they imply belief in the spiritism of the day, and he opposes this because he finds it fundamentally misleading. . . . He is clairvoyant in high degree, but not as 'mediums' are, not through self-surrender, but through openness to Divine guidance and intuition."[46] In the end, Dresser concluded that Quimby might have discussed the teachings of Swedenborg with a local New Church minister, "but there is no indication of any influence coming from that quarter in Quimby's writings. The most we can say is that Quimby belonged to the new age whose coming Swedenborg foretold."[47]

Had not Horatio Dresser been responsible for leaving out numerous discourses on Spiritualism when he edited Quimby's manuscripts for publication, including references to séances that Quimby attended, one might be inclined to agree with his comment negating any connection with Swedenborg. The fact remains, however, that Quimby was an acquisitive thinker who, as historian Robert Peel notes, had attended both Unitarian and Universalist churches, which were hotbeds of Swedenborgianism. Moreover, since Warren Felt Evans, an author of a book on Swedenborg, was his patient and ardent disciple, it is difficult to accept Quimby's and Dresser's denials. This being the case, it is hardly reasonable that he would not have been acquainted with Swedenborgian ideas, a position made pointedly clear by Catherine L. Albanese in her book *A Republic of Mind and Spirit* (2007). For both Quimby and Andrew Jackson Davis, their denials were incompatible with their written words.[48]

The Diaspora

By the 1860s, Quimby was treating as many as five hundred patients a year and, over the course of his practice, sat with more than twelve thousand different patients.[49] Not much of a businessman, he took little interest in his accounts, treating both charity and regular patients equally and relying on each to pay what seemed appropriate. Nevertheless, he operated a booming business whose patients arrived daily by train or wagon and boarded in private homes or at the International Hotel in Portland. Most came from New England, with a scattering from the Middle West and West. As a strong Unionist and outspoken abolitionist, Quimby refused to accept patients from the South, scorning them for their use of the Bible to defend slavery as an institution of divine origin.[50]

Because of his patient load, Quimby often chose to treat through distant healing. "I feel as though I had explained to the spiritual or scientific man the cause of your trouble, which I may not have made plain in my letters to the natural man," he wrote to one patient in 1861. "So be of good cheer and keep up your courage, and you shall see me coming on the water of your belief and saying to the waters of pain, 'Be still,' soothing you till the storm is over." To another patient he wrote that while he had not been able until then to answer her letter, he had talked to her in spirit on several occasions. "I shall visit you as an angel," he explained, "till you are able to guide your own bark." To another he wrote: "I am with you now seeing you. I am in this letter and as often as you read this and listen to it you listen to me. . . . Take about one half hour to devote to reading and listening to my counsel and I assure you [that] you will be better."[51]

After moving to Portland, Quimby began writing out his ideas, employing Emma and Sarah Ware as well as his son, George, as assistants. The Ware sisters, the daughters of Judge Ashur Ware (1782–1873) of the US District Court in Portland, were entrusted with compiling, copying, and editing Quimby's writings under his close supervision. Despite Quimby's intention to set forth his teachings in a book, he failed to do so, due in no small part to the fact that he went through so many modifications in his thinking. Instead of a final product, he produced a series of short manuscripts, amounting to some eight hundred pages, some of which he loaned out to patients. One was a set of fifteen questions that had been put to him by a patient in 1862. In what became known as his *Questions and Answers,* he explained that it was not his intent to establish any religion or creed but simply to stand as an attorney on behalf of the sick. Copies of his *Questions and Answers* were circulated among patients as a way of providing supplementary instruction.[52]

Out of this practice emerged a group of highly successful disciples who carried his healing techniques into the broader marketplace of ideas and practices. Some, like Warren Felt Evans and the Dressers, chose to carry forward the work of their mentor without straying too far afield. Others, like Mary Baker Eddy, were anxious to export their own schemes for healing and personal gain. However familiar they may have been with Quimby's ideas, it would appear that his most prominent disciples were determined to formulate their own declaration of principles.

Julius A. Dresser (1838–1893), credited with being one of the founders of the New Thought movement, remained a strong acolyte of Quimby's methods. A native of Portland, he had become ill after taking up his studies at Waterville College in Maine, where he was preparing for a career in the Calvinist Baptist church. Fearing that his health was seriously deteriorating and that he might not live, he sought Quimby's help in June 1860. While undergoing treatment, he met Annetta Seabury (1843–1935) who, like himself, considered her time with Quimby a "turning point" in her life. Both, along with several other friends and pupils, became ardent disciples, meeting Quimby often in his office to discuss his methods and ideas, hanging on his every word, admiring his humanity, and inspired by his convictions and sincerity of purpose. Several chose to write articles about his theories, or what Quimby preferred to call "the Truth." "It was a rare privilege for those who were waiting their turn for treatment to listen to those discussions between the strangers and these disciples of his," recalled Seabury. On more than one occasion Quimby would enter into their conversations, expressing some idea "that would set us to thinking deeply or talking earnestly."[53]

Shut in a sickroom for six years, and having suffered through a variety of harsh regimens, Seabury had found Quimby to be a "kindly" man who met her with "sympathy and gentleness." Sometimes he simply sat silently at her side; on other occasions, he proceeded to explain her case. "Instead of telling me that I was not sick, he ... explained ... what my sickness was, how I got into the condition, and the way I could have been taken out of it through the right understanding." The "ease in his presence," she remembered, "put one in sympathy with that quiet strength or power by which he wrought his cures."[54] As a patient, she learned that every action of the mind set up vibrations affecting the body, and that if a spiritual healer could quicken those vibrations, he could heal the ills.[55] In recalling Quimby's healer-patient relationship, Seabury noted that he devoted much of his time trying to understand the disease as it appeared to the patient. Confident that it was a false idea, he proceeded to free the patient from the beliefs and opinions that held him or her in bondage. Once the patient saw through whatever had caused the problem, its power was lost and it did no further harm.[56]

Following her marriage to Julius Dresser, the couple moved to Webster, Massachusetts, where Julius published and edited the *Webster Times* and where their son Horatio was born. When they returned to Boston in 1882 they set up their own mental healing practice and began holding classes based on the "Quimby System of Mental Treatment," otherwise known as "Spiritual Science." Deeply religious in tone, the classes not only explained the restoration of health through spiritual means but also how to bring about changes in thought and lifestyle by reinforcing the preeminence of a person's inner world or "the Christ within." Their lectures, twelve in all, followed a detailed format:

1. A description and analysis of the life of the mind and the effect of erroneous beliefs.
2. Learning the power of thought and the part played by fear.
3. Discussion of divine immanence.
4. The nature of matter and the influence of the mind on the body.

5. The subconscious aftereffects of opinions and beliefs
6. The general mental theory of disease with constant reference to the New Testament in regard to the healing of disease.
7. The spiritual nature of human beings with the distinction between the historical Jesus and the universal ideal of Christ.
8. Dispelling the fear of death for an eternal spiritual life that was poised, calm, and free.
9. The real intent of human experience and "the wisdom of the situation."
10. The hidden effects of fear as "the backbone of disease."
11. The power of thought.
12. The fundamental principles of a comprehensive spiritual philosophy of life.[57]

During their years in Boston, the Dressers spent much of their professional lives expounding on Quimby's system and defending his reputation from Eddy's misrepresentations and the system she called Christian Science.[58]

In 1887, Julius Dresser published *The True History of Mental Science,* a compilation of lectures he delivered at the Church of the Divine Unity in Boston. In them, he explained his deep and abiding faith in the philosophy of Plato and his successors, the idealistic writings of Ralph Waldo Emerson, and the penetrating truths regarding Quimby's unselfish work in healing the sick. Like Quimby, Dresser taught that every individual was a potential healer for God. Julius's book was followed in 1895 by Annetta Dresser's *The Philosophy of P. P. Quimby,* which gave a historical sketch of Quimby's life, outlined his philosophy and healing methods, provided extracts of articles written in the press by supporters, and included selections from his unpublished manuscripts.[59]

* * *

Almost all the early pioneers of the mind-cure movement in America suffered as invalids at one time in their lives and, upon recovery, went forth as acolytes of a particular individual or set of principles. Such had been the experience of Quimby who, having restored himself to health, attracted a large number of patients, some of whom became well known and established healers in their own right. Quimby could justly be called the central figure in the mental healing movement of the mid-nineteenth century. Among his students, two stand out for their efforts to take Quimby's ideas and develop their own extensive systems of metaphysical healing: Warren Felt Evans and Mary Baker Eddy. While Evans gave full credit to Quimby as his mentor and originator of the mental-healing movement, Eddy would stun Quimby's students by claiming that he had based his healing system on her ideas rather than the other way around. Eddy's Christian Science arguably represents one of the offshoots of the New Thought movement, but it is an assertion that few of her contemporaries conceded due to the animosity that rankled both sides. As will be explained in the coming chapters, New Thought's largest religious denominations derived not as direct descendants from Quimby, but as defections from Eddy's Christian Science. Thus the true extent of Quimby's influence on the denominational side of New Thought is obscured by the widespread acceptance of Eddy's claims to have developed Christian Science herself. A comparison of Quimby's ideas with Eddy's, however, will show that without Quimby, Eddy would have had very little upon which to base her own system.

3

Competing Sciences

"What a man does, that he has.
What has he to do with hope or fear?
In himself is his might."

—Ralph Waldo Emerson, "Spiritual Laws"

Like many of the early pioneers of mind cure, Warren Felt Evans and
Mary Baker Eddy suffered as invalids during the course of their lives and
drew from their experiences to become pivotal figures in the mental-
healing movement. Grounded in the techniques and practices laid out
in Quimby's unpublished notes and manuscripts, they went beyond him
by placing disease and its cure within an intellectual framework steeped
in philosophical idealism and the ethical advancement of humanity.
They saw disease as essentially mental rather than physical, attributing
it to a loss of balance between the will and intellect. In developing their
theories of how to correct this discord, Evans and Eddy chose competing routes to the inner person and its relationship to the Divine. Both
denied the reality of matter and, therefore, of disease; emphasized the
mystical element of Christianity; and performed healings by placing
the individual in a state of increased suggestibility, by meditating, and
by communion with the Divine. Evans followed a spiritual but predom-
inately unchurched path while Eddy chose to create a more formalized
church structure. Eventually, Eddy's authoritarian and occultist behavior, as well as her many legal issues, served as a catalyst for defections
by her flock, some of whom formed churches and affiliated organizations that eventually associated under the broad umbrella of the New
Thought movement.

Warren Felt Evans

One of seven siblings born to a comfortable farming family in Rockingham, Vermont, Evans studied at Chester Academy and, in 1837, entered Middlebury College. A year later he transferred to Dartmouth, but he left before graduating to become a Methodist Episcopal minister. In 1840, he married M. Charlotte Tinker and continued with his ministerial duties at pastorates in Massachusetts and New Hampshire until 1856, when he began the study of Swedenborg. In 1863, he joined the Church of the New Jerusalem as a licentiate or lay teacher. His formal change in allegiance was due in no small measure to a book he wrote in 1862 titled *The Celestial Dawn; Or, Connection of Earth and Heaven,* which carried Swedenborgian overtones that troubled his Methodist friends and parishioners.

Having been in poor health since he was a young boy, and suffering nervous breakdowns in 1859 and again in 1862, Evans sought treatment from Quimby at his office in Portland. Impressed by Quimby's talents, he soon became a devoted follower and, after expressing an interest in healing, received encouragement to open his own practice in Claremont, New Hampshire. Sometime during this period, Evans reputedly received a medical degree from an eclectic medical school. Identifying the school is difficult. The only eclectic college in the New England region was Worcester Medical School (1846–59), which began as an Independent Thomsonian institution before turning to eclectic theory and then suspending classes. According to Eddy biographers Willa Cather and Georgine Milmine, Evans's degree was granted from "a chartered board of physicians of the Eclectic School," which suggests it may have been granted by a medical society formed during or after the Worcester school closed. There is, however, no indication that Evans received any formal medical training.[1]

In 1867, Evans and his wife opened an office in Boston and later, in 1869, at their home in East Salisbury, Massachusetts. There he operated a sanatorium known as the "Evans Home," devoting more than twenty years to spiritual healing. Following Quimby's example, Evans accepted all patients regardless of ability to pay and relied on voluntary offerings.[2] Evans also followed Quimby's lead by turning away from the deep hypnotic aspects of mesmerism, believing that patients treated in a conscious state were better able to conduct themselves through the mind-cure process. For those patients, suggestion became the key element in healing.[3]

Evans differed from Quimby's other students and followers because of his avowed membership in the New Church Society in Bowdoin Street, Boston, home to many Swedenborgian doctors and patients who, in addition to their spiritual quest, had left allopathy for the more vitalistic philosophies of homeopathy, eclecticism, mesmerism, and mental healing. Beginning in 1869, Evans incorporated Swedenborg's psychology and metaphysics with Quimby's system of healing in a manner that had significant implications for future healers. By the early 1880s, Swedenborg had become the therapeutic underpinning of his particular form of mental science and an attractive alternative to mainstream medicine.[4]

Evans's impact lies in his prolific writings, which influenced many of the mental healing components of the New Thought movement. Beginning with *The Mental Cure* (1869), published three years after Quimby's death, Evans authored a long list of books, several of which went through multiple editions. They included *Mental Medicine* (1872); *Soul and Body* (1875); *The Divine Law of Cure* (1881); *Healing by Faith* (1885); and *Esoteric Christianity and Mental Therapeutics* (1886). He also wrote several books that, while unrelated to New Thought, depicted his deep indebtedness to Swedenborg. These included *Divine Order in the Process of Full Salvation* (1860); *The Happy Islands; Or, Paradise Restored* (1860); *The Celestial Dawn; Or, Connection of Earth and Heaven* (1862); and *The New Age and Its Messenger* (1864). Aside from Mary Baker Eddy, whose publication *Science and Health* (1875) came several years after Evans's original work, Evans was one of a handful of followers who attempted to build upon Quimby's system of mental healing. By the time both Evans and Eddy had fulfilled their objectives, Quimby's mental healing system had been transformed into two similar but also distinctively different metaphysical healing movements—one highly authoritative and dogmatic, the other highly decentralized and including both religious and secular currents.

A year following his visits to Quimby, and before beginning his own healing practice, Evans published *The New Age and Its Messenger,* an intensive analysis of Swedenborg's theology, which he called "the herald of a new dispensation." In every epochal period, Evans explained, God had endowed certain individuals with the gift of extraordinary communication with their fellow human beings. Swedenborg had been such a revelator, chosen "to lift men's minds above the realm of sense, and to disclose the solid realities of an everywhere present spiritual world." Like Abraham in the Old Testament, Swedenborg had been God's instrument to usher in a new age of the Church, restoring to the world "the true idea of the unity of God." Just as importantly, he had shown that enlightened minds could once again commune with redeemed human spirits. The world of spirits was not only real and substantial, but close in spatial distance to earth. "It is an interior world," explained Evans, "and is within the material cosmos, as the soul is within and animates the body."[5]

Evans regarded Swedenborg's law of correspondences as essential to the new theology, giving a glimpse of what lay hidden from the human spirit. Having opened the spiritual keys to Scripture, the Swedish Seer had made available the treasures of divine truth by demonstrating a connection between the natural and spiritual worlds, namely, "that all things in the world of nature exist from and represent things in the higher spiritual realm." Between the two there was a relationship of cause and effect. The Word of God, written in the language of correspondence, gave spiritual meaning to all things natural. Swedenborg exalted Scripture as no one before him had ever achieved, bringing a spiritual sense of the Word to human understanding. By separating the apparent truth from real truth, he had given the "natural man" access to the spiritual mind and enlightened reason.[6]

With the publication of *The Mental Cure* in 1869, Evans began infusing Quimby's ideas with elements of Swedenborgian idealism. Well read, Evans honored his mentor by finding a correlation between Quimby's reasoning and the teachings of Swedenborg concerning the influx of divine life into the soul, the relationship of body and mind, the correspondence of all things natural with all things spiritual, the doctrine of spiritual spheres or auras, and the conception of causality as essentially spiritual. Evans admired Swedenborg as the "messenger of a new age" and Quimby's teachings as "an expression of . . . Swedenborg's doctrine on its practical side."[7]

Swedenborg's view that sickness represented the lusts and desires of the mind meant that illness corresponded not with heaven but with those souls living in various hells, for whom envy, hatred, adulteries, quarrels, fights, intemperance, and lasciviousness were everyday acts of conscious will. Every disease in the human race corresponded to an evil in the spiritualized world of hells. To the extent that one's spiritual life was committed to evil, the person's natural life became the victim of a related disease. The influx from the spiritual world varied according to its reception by each individual. When it flowed into good individuals, it bestowed intelligence and wisdom; when it flowed into the wicked, it turned into insanities of various kinds because of evils that either suffocated or perverted it. Provided that individuals lived a life of good, their smallest and most invisible vessels opened to heaven's influx, and when at length the body could no longer minister to its internal needs, it passed "without disease out of his earthly body into a body such as angels have, thus out of the world directly into heaven."[8]

Building on this bedrock of Swedenborgian physiology and metaphysics, Evans set out to establish the imminence of God in the spirit of the inward person. "The mind being the interior man," he explained, "is not confined to the brain, nor, as Descartes supposed, included in the Pineal gland. But it pervades and is interfused through the whole body. . . . The body is not merely an external robe, the outward shell of the living soul, but the mind interpenetrates every atom of it." The brain was the "connecting link" between the inner and outer person. Despite its plurality of functions, the brain proceeded from a fundamental unity first demonstrated by Franz Joseph Gall and best represented in the science of phrenology, a science that Evans considered still in its formative years.[9]

Every material body, Evans explained, was surrounded by a subtle emanation of corpuscles or atoms. This effluvia, expelled with a person's breath as a "celestial aura" or "hellish miasm," was noticeable to the senses. Like the odor given off by a rose, it had the potential to influence the thought of other individuals. Just as a body imparted radiant heat to surrounding objects, so every living being, including angels, gave off radiant circles or auras of force that were good, bad, happy, or depressing according to the inner mental state of the being. If the mental state was one of melancholy, its effluvia affected others with a like feeling. All mental states were contagious, which meant that people of a negative or passive nature were easily affected by these radiant influences. "[We] are like a vessel at sea," Evans observed, "impelled by sails, and at the mercy of every wind that blows." Many of the more troublesome thoughts and feelings were "excited in us by the sphere of those around us, and come to us from spirits in the flesh, rather than from those who have passed to the world beyond."[10]

Even the subtle forces given off by stones, metals, plants, and animal substances could be felt by certain highly sensitive persons. Evans referred specifically to the experiments of Joseph Rodes Buchanan in the 1850s on his students at the Eclectic Medical Institute of Cincinnati. Holding unidentified medicinal substances in paper wrappers in their hands, the students were supposedly able to sense the invisible effluvia given off by the drugs and react as if they had taken the substances internally. He likewise referred to the work of spiritual geologists William and Elizabeth Denton, whose two-volume *Soul of Things* (1863) recounted their psychogeologic examination of ancient rocks, which they claimed enabled them to write the history of geology based upon a "reading" of the rocks' auras.[11]

These subtle emanations were also embedded in written words. "A letter or a book may be charged with the divine magnetism of a spiritual life," Evans wrote. The words conveyed "mental treasures" that carried from one period of time to another. "Place a book in the hand, or on the forehead, of a person gifted with the psychometric sense, and enough of the spiritual life of the author will be still in it, to reveal his character."[12] Like a stone dropped in the ocean, sending the vibratory motion of its waves into the waters of the world, so a word, a mental picture, or associated sensations of light, heat, color, sound, and hardness became like so many vibrations that intersected in the ether and eventually entered the conscious mind. What made humans first among living creatures was their ability to absorb these impulses or vibrations, "read" them, and respond creatively and with purpose. Much existed in humanity's inner life beyond the world of consciousness.[13]

Evans made generous use of Swedenborg's psychology, noting that humankind was a recipient of divine life and therefore had an element of the divine spark that remained free of whatever vicissitudes befell the body. This included the abnormal state of disease, which represented a disturbance of the soul's inner harmony expressed in a corresponding abnormal condition of the body. Evans referred extensively to Swedenborg to explain the inner and outer aspects of human beings. He described an inner form that was the seat of all disease and the subsequent loosening of its correspondence with the external organs as the result of abnormal mental states. When the correspondence ceased, the outward body died.[14]

In explaining his own particular approach to healing, Evans started with the belief that human beings, in ignorance of their birthright, remained blind to the opportunities of this life, giving rise to mental and physical unhappiness. Any rectification of this unhappiness had to begin with the inner person (i.e., the spirit or soul), which received its form through influx from the Divine. Due to the law of correspondence and the intimate relationship between the body and soul, any change brought about in the spirit brought a corresponding change to the body. All causality operating in the physical world was, in the last analysis, spiritual in nature. The steps in the metaphysical healing process included the development of a mental picture; the mental picture producing nervous action; the nervous action registering through the tissues; and a corresponding bodily condition, which was more or less permanent. In time, every thought led to a corresponding action. Pure ideals perpetuated pure thoughts and inevitably right actions. Purity and health were coexistent.[15]

Implied in this reasoning was the assumption that when there was harmony between the will and the intellect there was both spiritual and bodily health. By contrast, disease represented a "loss of balance," the visible effect of an inner disturbance in the individual's mental state. Such conditions were contagious among those with similar inner states or feelings. Thus the impressibility of the mind on the body applied not only to the self but to others as well. The challenge was in finding a more desirable mental state in the individual so that the morbid state of mind would lead to a healthier inner life. "It is evident we can never attain to the highest well-being of either soul or body," wrote Evans, "until we come into the divine order of our existence, and employ the activity with which we are endowed, according to the laws of the celestial life."[16]

While philosophers had long sought the vital life principle in the universe, identifying it as nervous fluid, electricity, anima, etc., Swedenborg identified the principle as love. Love was the highest and most divine force and the only moving power whose derivatives were desire and affection. All truth proceeded from it just as light proceeded from a flame. Jesus and his apostles had transmitted this "sanative virtue" to the multitudes by way of their imposition of hands, by the silent prayer, and by the spiritual power of words. Their cures were not miracles but acts of love carried out in harmony with the laws of the universe. It was the vital force of the soul, the body's inmost life, explained Evans, that passed outward to become heat in the external organism.[17]

Material medicines could produce limited change in the body, but it was the intelligent application of mental force that made the most long-lasting effects. "We have thrown persons into a gentle perspiration in five minutes, without touching them," Evans reported, "and sometimes when they were miles away." Psychological influences could affect the physiological action of any organ of the body. In referring to the New Testament story of Jesus touching the eyes of two blind men and giving them sight (Matt. 20:34), Evans explained that Jesus had imparted some of his own vital force to these two blind individuals without any loss to his own self. The imposition of the hands never failed when directed by intelligence and love. It heralded a "new age" of the spirit world. "We believe, with the force of a prophetic conviction, that the time is coming, and draws near," Evans predicted, "when men will be educated into the normal use of their spiritual senses." At such a time, the spiritual world would no longer be compared to some unexplored land mass in the heart of Africa. With the help of God and angels, humanity would return to a harmonious state and the interior person would become independent of the outward body. In the new age to come, the soul would be set free of its fleshy bondage, the spiritual senses would be unveiled, and the inner powers of humanity unleashed.[18]

When Evans succeeded in removing the idea of disease from the mind of an invalid, he felt himself "standing on an established philosophical ground, an impregnable scientific position." At issue was not the affirmation or belief that this was possible, but the method or means of accomplishing it. In treating patients with the intent of removing morbid ideas from their minds, the healer had to form a true idea of the patients in his own mind and set it against the patients' own ideas of themselves. This, he reasoned, had been the way of Jesus. If the patients were in a receptive state and activated by a desire of recovery, the healer's impulses would affect the "inner ground" of their being. Jesus cured those who were receptive, explained Evans, "and left the unreceptive . . . as they were."[19]

Whether the phenomenon of imparting a mental state from healer to patient passed as mesmerism, psychology, animal magnetism, pathetism, hypnotism, or psychometry, it reduced to a single principle: the action of one mind upon another mind. By bringing the vibratory motions into harmony, one mind could "daguerreotype" itself upon another, a term that Evans adopted from Quimby's teachings. In this manner, explained Evans, Jesus had imparted the calm happiness of his own gentle heart upon the sick. "His habitual mental condition, when communicated to the afflicted, was the panacea for all their spiritual abnormality," he added. "His mind was a perfect harmony, everywhere exactly balanced, and thus contained in itself all that any one, however wretched, needed to restore his soul to soundness and health."[20]

According to this line of argument, thought transferences represented different planes or currents of consciousness, each with its own rate of vibration. The thoughts moved through a medium called the ether, a semi-spiritual essence that filled space and was sometimes identified as the "atmosphere of the inner world." Being universal, it was the means by which thought passed from one to another, including distances of a thousand miles or more. Ether was the soul of the world through which all objects were connected in sympathy. Through it, light flowed, electrical bodies operated, the senses were excited, and bodies were attracted to each other. It was the repository of spiritual images and human thoughts that filled space and connected all worlds. Human beings inhaled it, and through it received divine influx from above.

Drawing from Swedenborg, Evans explained that breathing connected the individual to this universal "Life-Principle." It was in this process that each particular life met and mingled with the Divine. This was how God made his presence known in nature and, as all human minds were connected through this Life-Principle, it was also how Christ entered into humanity and "deposited in it the germ of a new and higher life." Jesus conducted human beings to Christ, operating through individual minds according to their degree of receptivity.[21] Through the ether, individuals communicated with the spirit world, connecting the lower and higher spheres of life and intelligence. Some, like Swedenborg, had been able to hold conversations with spirits; others were able to summon the vision or spirit of a dead relative or friend; while still others were limited to evoking only rappings or voices from the spirit world. Notwithstanding these differences, this phenomenon enabled humans to escape time and space to see and hear what was transpiring in the remotest parts of the universe.[22]

Although assuredly not Baconian in his method of verification, Evans considered his system equivalent to the power displayed by Jesus, whose "inner selfhood was not in bondage to material limitations." To the degree that one attained the state exhibited by Jesus, one could cure diseases of the mind and body. Evans called this "prayer-cure," or *proseuchopathy*, a treatment capable of removing any pathological condition of the inner person. In the act of healing, the patient's inner self was renewed and spiritually healed. Those with the most passive natures were the easiest patients and those with the most magnetic power were the most successful healers. This was not supernatural or miraculous but simply a restatement of spiritual laws that governed the universe.[23] This apostolic mode of healing, reputedly practiced by the Swiss clergyman and exorcist Johann Joseph Gassner (1727–79), proved to Evans that the cures of Jesus were not miracles or deviations from "the established order of nature." They were simply the exhibition of mind over matter, a power consistent with the laws of nature and accessible to all.[24]

Evans did not insist that his system of healing would cure every disease. Instead, he believed that the world was living through a significant epoch demonstrating the fulfillment of numerous prophetic promises made in ages past. "This divine afflatus is coming out . . . upon the whole human family, quickening into life dormant faculties, and opening the organism to all invisible imponderable and spiritual influences and forces," he claimed. Just as the world was evidencing increased intercommunication by means of the telegraph, so people everywhere were becoming susceptible to magnetic and psychological impressions. The older systems of therapeutics, along with their antiquated *materia medica*, were being replaced by cosmic principles introduced by Mesmer, Reichenbach, and others, who had theorized that it was possible to capture and control the emanative spheres or auras that surrounded each individual. The connection with the ever-present spiritual world demonstrated by Swedenborg a century earlier had now become a successful psychopathic method in the cure of disease. The practitioner of this modern age, Evans said, was someone of high mental and moral character, whose predominant phrenological organs were similar to those of Jesus, and who had full faith and confidence in his psychic abilities. Those modern practitioners who ministered to the diseased had "breathe[d] the atmosphere of the divine and heavenly," and were in "open communion" with the spirit world.[25]

Like Quimby before him, Evans agreed that mesmeric sleep was no longer as important as placing the patient in a sympathetic, thought-reading, and clairvoyant state of wakefulness. The only thing necessary for a cure was for the patient to be in an "impressible conscious state."[26] When this was achieved, Evans instructed the patient to focus on a small silver cross. This assisted the patient in concentrating and thereby moving into a passive state. Simultaneously, Evans stared at the patient's forehead to aid in producing the impressible state. Once this was achieved, Evans placed one hand on the forehead and the other on the back of the head and neck. He said that this allowed for better control of the patient, rendering him or her insensible to pain by simple suggestion and infusing any weakened part of the body with a sanative level of spiritual force. A combination of spiritual psychology and the Swedish Movement Cure (massage) mutually reinforced each other in the treatment of chronic diseases. Applications of wet and warm cloths to the back of the neck produced the same effect.[27]

Evans's *Mental Medicine* was followed in 1884 by *The Divine Law of Cure,* marking the beginning of his transition from a strictly Swedenborgian point of view to one that, while still steeped in Swedenborgian terminology, would draw equally from the idealism of the Anglo-Irish philosopher George Berkeley and the German philosophers Georg Wilhelm Hegel (1770–1831) and Johann Gottlieb Fichte (1762–1814) to formulate a mind-cure system that he named *phrenopathy.* Representing the principle of applied idealism, it began with the proposition that "to think and exist are one and the same." Implied in this proposition was a change in emphasis about humans' spiritual nature from a strict focus on Swedenborg's concepts of will and love to a more intellectualized view of the mind. Rather than focusing on the spiritual world, Evans began to describe the mind as the "active power" in the universe. "The mind is the real man," Evans explained, "and its thoughts act on the body as a spiritual poison, or as a mental medicine, for health and disease." To the degree that a person thinks, feels, and believes himself to be sick or healthy, so he or she is. In this sense, thought became a creative force and, in the last analysis, reality (that is, the external world) was only a thought. Evans no longer spoke of healing as the action of one spirit on another or referred to drawing upon the spiritual world. Although he continued to emphasize the divine mind, he referred more often to thought in its intellectual rather than spiritual meaning. Just as his suggestion that "the spiritual physician . . . should speak and act from the Divine realm of his being, as did Jesus the Christ," became the touchstone for a generation of mental healers, so, too, his insistence that "thoughts are *things"* laid the foundation for the next generation of New Thought writers.[28]

In 1885, twenty-two years after the publication of his first book, Evans wrote *Healing by Faith: Or, Primitive Mind-Cure. Elementary Lessons in Christian Philosophy and Transcendental Medicine.* Intended as a textbook in self-healing, it contained features of the instruction that Evans believed had been given in the early decades of Christianity and that he now taught as an essential element in his practice. Sensing "an inward thirst, an unsatisfied craving for spiritual light" among his generation, he offered his book to assist people in finding the Christ within.

"When the reader shall have made the grandest discovery ever made in this earthly existence—the finding of his true *self*, and has identified it with the Christ, of whom it is but a personal limitation—we will gladly step down from the platform of the teacher," he wrote. At the book's core was an attempt to satisfy the craving for spiritual knowledge that Evans insisted was central to the healing process. Beyond the numerous systems of materialistic medicine that had uniformly failed humankind, there remained the "fountain of living water"—the universal Christ within—that offered the most complete method of healing. Drawing from Plato, the kabbalah, Swedenborg, and a succession of German philosophers, Evans explained that ideas were the "living and fixed forms assumed by thought." In the world of ideas, there is an ideal, immortal human. To find this ideal person, it was necessary to release the inward self from the bondage of matter. Doing so would make the ideal and immortal human become the actual and conscious human.[29]

In his *Esoteric Christianity and Mental Therapeutics* (1886), Evans responded to critics who categorized his works as too occult, explaining that his phrenopathic practice was no different from the healings recounted in the New Testament and practiced in early Christianity. The fundamental principle behind it remained the law of mental sympathy, including the intercommunion between minds and between the natural and spiritual worlds. Evans intended for the book to revive Christianity as a system of both salvation and mental cure, emphasizing Jesus as the saving principle in the universe. Jesus was the historical manifestation of the principle of health, the ultimate balance of soul and body, and the incarnate expression of the Christ. It was through Jesus that humankind came into communion with the wholeness of life. Without him, there was no conscious union with God, no health in the fullest sense of the word, and no completeness of human beings in God.[30]

The phrenopathic method of cure operated with a clear set of established rules relating to the influence of mind on mind and the doctrine of silent influence upon the mental sphere of others. This method was aimed at bringing the patient into the right mode of thinking and feeling through both a verbal and silent process. As with Quimby, Evans sat or stood beside his patients, surrounding them with the emanative sphere of his own life principle. This emanative sphere supposedly enveloped his patients and transferred his feelings of faith and hope. Although the distance between himself and his patients was sometimes only a few feet, in other situations they were miles apart. In either case, Evans held a positive attitude of mind, steadfastly thinking the truth and maintaining a correct idea of himself and of the patient. In accordance with the law of thought-transference, he influenced the patient in a manner proportional to the patient's susceptibility. "To modify a patient's thinking in regard to himself and his disease," explained Evans, "we employ the principle of suggestion or positive affirmation—not mental argument, as it is sometimes called, for argument creates doubt and reaction." The sick were not cured by one's mental reasoning or argumentation; rather, they were cured by knowing and affirming the truth.[31]

Evans's excoriation of contemporary medicine came at a time when its proto-orthodox proponents were beginning to pull away from the older therapeutic drugs of the *materia medica* and a priori principles to establish a combined rationalist-empiricist system built on a foundation of the sciences, information gathering, clinical exploration, hypothesis, and evidence-based outcomes. His criticism extended to mainline Christianity as well, believing that, having lost its bearings, it had departed from the healing message of Jesus and the early work of the apostles. For both medicine and religion, Evans offered a critique and a promise—a new age was coming that would merge these two contraries into a combined system of Christian healing. Like Quimby before him, he promised that a healthy body came by way of a healthy mind, uniting the human soul with the Divine.

Evans made every effort to demonstrate the compatibility of his phrenopathic system with Christianity's mystical traditions, Western idealism, and elements of Asian philosophy. An eclectic in the tradition of Victor Cousin, he held that elements of truth existed in all the great philosophies and religions. One needed to draw from each and all to formulate the broadest philosophical and religious truths. Nevertheless, at the heart of his mind-cure system was his affirmation of the practice of healing he believed had been carried out by Jesus and his apostles in the primitive Christian faith. Like Swedenborg, he accused the post-Nicean church of coloring Christianity with its own views on the worship of

Jesus, the power of prayer, belief in heaven and hell, and a vigorously materialistic view of disease. By rescuing Jesus from the priestly class, Evans hoped to return Christianity to a fuller recognition of humanity's true destiny, which was a union of the soul with God.

Those initially influenced by Evans included Egbert Morse Chesley, an active member of the Metaphysical Club of Boston; Charles M. Barrows, whose *Facts and Fictions of Mental Healing* (1887) drew from the philosophical idealisms of the past, including those of Asia; Mathilda J. Barnett, author of *Practical Metaphysics* (1880); and William J. Colville, author of *The Spiritual Science of Health and Healing* (1889). Their writings also reflected the influence of H. P. Blavatsky's Theosophy and the philosophies of Hinduism, Buddhism, and other Asian spiritual traditions, whose teachings were just beginning to penetrate the awareness of American popular culture.

In his attempts to understand the inner nature of his patients, Evans anticipated the Austrian neurologist Sigmund Freud (1856–1939) by more than a generation, though Evans traced nervous disorders not to a sexual instinct that could be understood through the interpretation of dreams but to errors in the individual's spiritual inner nature. The principal difference between the two lay in Evans's belief that there could be no purely mental cure, only one that was spiritual in nature, making divine wisdom its centerpiece. For Evans, faith became an essential element in the process of cure. "To believe that we can do a thing, especially if that faith is the result of an understanding of nature's laws," he wrote, "empowers us to do it. To believe that we are well, or that we are going to become so, excites a spiritual force within us that goes far towards making us so." By the same token, the lack of faith represented "the loss of one of the essential elements of a sound mental state, which underlies, as a foundation, a healthy bodily condition."[32]

Although not an original thinker, a characteristic that Evans held in common with almost all New Thought authors, he was able to bring together the esoteric beliefs of numerous philosophers to construct a practical system of idealism that resonated with the American psyche. Under his guidance, New Thought conceived of Christianity as the culminating religion of humankind, marshaling the best thinking from the world's great philosophers and mystics to assist in the healing process.

Mary Baker Eddy

Competing with Evans for the hearts and minds of the mental healing community was Mary Baker Eddy, who had also been a patient of Quimby. Married three times, she used several different names over the course of her life, including Mary Morse Baker, Mary Baker Glover, Mary P. Patterson, Mary Baker G. Eddy, and Mary Baker Eddy. This latter name, which she assumed in 1877 with her six-year marriage to Asa Gilbert Eddy, a sewing-machine salesman and active Christian Scientist, is the one by which she is most commonly known.

Eddy journeyed to Quimby's practice in Portland, Maine, in 1862, having departed from Dr. William Vail's Water Cure Sanatorium, a hydropathic treatment center in Hill, New Hampshire, where she had been seeking a cure for an unknown illness for nearly three months. Between 1862 and 1865, she paid high tribute to Quimby's reformed magnetic medicine in letters to the press and in her own private correspondence, soliciting his help on numerous occasions, defending him from charges of spiritism, and carefully explaining his "Spiritual Science" using the scriptural teachings of the New Testament. Eddy even composed poetry in his honor, including a poem prepared for the local newspaper upon Quimby's death. From a historical point of view, it is important to recognize these early efforts by Eddy to spread and defend Quimby's healing practices. Her early letters and poems are full of the gratitude of a pupil for a revered teacher, and they seem eminently more significant than her later efforts to discredit him.[33]

Beginning in 1872, however, Eddy changed course by presenting herself as the authentic discoverer of Christian Science and "accusing Quimby of having been a slave to animal magnetism."[34] What she once praised as Quimby's science of healing was now relegated to the dustbin; she claimed that his methods were stolen first from Mesmer and then from her own original ideas. To accomplish the objective of establishing herself as the founder of Christian Science, she constructed a story or narrative around its origins that accentuated its uniqueness, stressed its similarity with Jesus's healing, disavowed the materiality of disease and the efficacy of mainstream medicine, and laid claim to special communications from God.[35] Eddy made no claim of lineage to hypnotism, to mind-curists, or to faith-curists. "From my medical practice," she explained, "I had learned that the dynamics of medicine is Mind." Truth transcended the evidence of the senses; like Jesus's healing, there was no remedy administered apart from Mind.[36]

In a letter dated March 7, 1883, and published in the *Boston Post,* Eddy claimed to have laid out the foundations of her mental healing system as early as 1853 and, while Quimby's patient, to have encouraged him to write out his thoughts. She then claimed to have assisted him in correcting his methodology using a line of thought that she had already formulated.[37] Later, in a statement published in the *Christian Science Journal* in 1887, she went even further:

> I never heard him intimate that he healed diseases mentally; and
> many others will testify that, up to his last sickness, he treated us
> magnetically—manipulating our heads, and making passes in the
> air while he stood in front of us. During his treatments I felt like one
> having hold of an electric battery and standing on an insulating
> stool. His healing was never considered or called anything but
> Mesmerism. I tried to think better of it, and to procure him public
> favor, and it wounded me to have him despised. I believe he was
> doing good; and, even now, knowing as I do the harm in this
> practice, I would never revert to it but for this public challenge. I
> was ignorant of the basis of animal magnetism twenty years ago, but
> now know it would disgrace and invalidate any mode of medicine.[38]

In explaining her relationship to Quimby, whom she now referred to as a "distinguished mesmerist," Eddy claimed to have "rearranged" several of his essays and shared with him some of her own writings "which remained among his papers" and mistakenly attributed to him. Denying any claim of Quimby's influence on her own work, she instead insisted that Quimby's practice was tied to materialism, the antipode of Christian Science. While admitting that he had advanced mind cure on a material basis, she maintained that his views had in no way influenced her Science of Mind.[39]

In her 1891 book *Retrospection and Introspection,* Eddy again revised her claim, explaining that she discovered the science of divine metaphysical healing in 1866 (not 1853), a date that she changed to 1867 several pages later. Her science of divine metaphysical healing, she announced, was the first authentic metaphysical system of healing since the days of Jesus and his apostles. All other claims were simply plagiarisms of her *Science and Health.*[40]

The irony is that she made this claim after Evans had already written three books on the subject, all of which contained a full explanation of the principles and practices of metaphysical healing.[41] Moreover, the term "Christian Science" had been used as early as 1840 by Abram Cowles; by the Rev. William Adams in his 1850 work titled *Elements of Christian Science;* and by Quimby in 1863. In other words, Christian Science had been a term used simultaneously with metaphysical healing and mental science. This also suggests that the metaphysical world of Evans and Eddy was fundamentally the same.[42]

It was only after her recovery from a serious injury in 1866, Eddy explained, that she discovered the science of divine metaphysical healing that she eventually named Christian Science. Likening her experience to Jesus's withdrawal into the desert for forty days and nights, she claimed to have withdrawn from society for three years following her recovery, during which time she studied the Bible to learn *how* she had been healed. It was only then that she learned the true spiritual meaning of Jesus's teachings and that his so-called miraculous healings were not miraculous at all, but merely a demonstration of metaphysical healing, or Christian Science. It was during this time, Eddy said, that she put together the notes and ideas that she would eventually copyright in 1870 and publish as *Science and Health* in 1875.[43]

Long after Quimby's death, it was common knowledge among his former followers that copies of his unpublished manuscripts remained in circulation. One copy had been in the hands of the Dresser family until 1893, when it was returned to Quimby's son, George. Excerpts from two of Quimby's manuscripts had also been included in Annetta Dresser's *The Philosophy of P. P. Quimby.* As for Eddy, she once offered to publish the manuscripts provided that she was permitted to examine them first to determine which, if any, of the documents were those she had allegedly left with him. George Quimby and the Dresser family dismissed her offer, deeming it entirely consistent with what they thought of Eddy and her followers. Instead, Horatio Dresser remarked that "there is an assemblage of writings [in George Quimby's possession] that would have filled her mind with chagrin had she realized how fully Quimby's ideas were developed, long before she ever saw him." Besides, he added, the full canon of Quimby's writings made plain that the work was of "one mind, with continuity of thought from first to last." Not until 1920 did George Quimby give permission for Horatio Dresser to publish his father's manuscripts as a way to vindicate Quimby and his closest followers. To his discredit, Dresser imposed a somewhat skewed editorial hand on the particular aspects he chose to emphasize. Not until 1985 were the complete writings of Quimby assembled and published.[44]

Eddy's Writings

In a series of writings that began with the publication of *Science and Health*, Eddy laid out her metaphysical healing system in a manner that was intended to distinguish it from all other systems. She insisted, for example, that the Bible could only be understood when interpreted in the context of her book, which she described as "divine teachings" and "revealed truth."[45] In making this claim, she placed her *Science and Health* on equal footing with Scripture, reasoning that both had revolutionized the world by revealing the spiritual nature of the Word.[46] Even the clergyman and social reformer Henry Ward Beecher (1813–87) expressed his admiration for Eddy's book, remarking that it was "one of the most wonderful books ever written."[47]

Eddy reasoned that when the true Science of Mind was fully understood, Spiritualism, mesmerism, clairvoyance, and other semi-metaphysical systems would be judged as erroneous, having no scientific basis or origin, and no proof or power outside of human testimony. All had been the offspring of the physical senses, and those who adopted them were dependent upon human beliefs and hypotheses. Even if communication with the spirit world was possible, its connection with the mortal mind destroyed its presumed potential. In Christian Science, however, persons were free of all material investiture. Its understanding of God rested on divine principle, not on material personalities. By it alone the sick were healed. Only human beings in the likeness of God and as revealed in Science could be safe from sin and disease. The struggle, therefore, was between the competing claims of *mortal* minds and the *immortal* Mind. "Christian Science," Eddy claimed, "reveals incontrovertibly that Mind is All-in-all, that the only reality is the divine Mind."[48]

For Eddy, God was not a personality in the anthropomorphic sense of the word but a divine Principle for which she substituted "Life," "Truth," and "Love"—terms remarkably similar to Emerson's "Over-Soul." God was one, infinite, and triune. God was Life, Truth, and Love—all three in one essence, or Principle.[49] Only the power of Mind, or Principle, explained Jesus's instructions for healing the sick. It was the spiritualization of thought through the triumph of Christian Science that pointed to the elimination of sin and sickness. As demonstrated in the words and acts of Jesus, Christian Science revealed the divine Principle and denied the errors of the senses and of the so-called laws of matter.[50]

Eddy decried accusations that Christian Science was little more than pantheism, which advocated that the universe, conceived as a whole, was God. Those belief systems that embraced pantheism had made humanity "the servant of matter, living by reason of it, suffering because of it, and dying in consequence of it." Pantheism was nothing but belief in the intelligence of matter. Nor was Christian Science comparable to Theosophy, which she considered a corruption of Judaism blended with "Oriental magic" and the "false enchantments" of Brahmanism. The same applied to theism, which held the "personality and infinite mind of one supreme, holy, self-existent God, who reveals Himself supernaturally to His creation, and whose laws are not reckoned as science." In theism, Eddy wrote, the reason and will were human while God alone was divine. But if God is the creator of human beings, and theism also purports that human beings were creators, then there were two creators. She saw this as wrong. Christian Science had only one God; that was all that was real and eternal.[51]

Unlike Western healing practices, including mental healing, which relied on the action of the mortal mind, Eddy insisted that true healing would not occur until the "fleshy mind" yielded to the operation of the divine Principle as it had in Jesus's time. In her assessment of past healing practices, she observed that the primitive age of Christianity required neither hygiene nor drugs to heal the body. It demanded only right thinking and right acting. Since then, however, personal and material elements had stolen into Christianity's camp and removed its power to heal. Despite God's omnipotence, humanity had chosen to limit his power by means of phrenology, mediums, allopathy, homeopathy, and other material and quasi-metaphysical healing systems. While Eddy admitted that metaphysics was slowly turning weary souls toward a more spiritual understanding of disease and suffering, she feared that even homeopathy would "not recover from the heel of allopathy" even though it had "laid the foundation stone of mental healing."[52]

Christian Science practitioners claimed the capacity to heal functional, organic, chronic, and acute diseases without any assistance from mainstream medicine. "If the Scientist reaches his patient through divine Love, the healing work will be accomplished at one visit, and the disease will vanish into its native nothingness like dew before the morning sunshine," Eddy wrote. However, if vice found its way into the disease through an "unchristian practitioner," the cure would necessarily be delayed until the metaphysician cast out the "moral evils" within the patient. Unless the patient denied the existence of matter, the foundation of disease remained, with all its discordant symptoms. Under such conditions there could be no successful treatment of the disease. Only by removing the erroneous belief could the patient remove the effects.[53]

From her experience with allopathic, homeopathic, hydropathic, and electrical healers, Eddy concluded that the less material the medicine, the better the healing potential. One drop of a thirtieth attenuation of a homeopathic drug proved much more helpful than a heroic dose of the same medicine meted out by an allopath.[54] In one sermon delivered in Boston, she explained:

> The pharmacy of homeopathy is reducing the one hundredth part of a grain of medicine two thousand times, shaking the preparation thirty times at every attenuation. There is a moral to this medicine;

the higher natures are reached soonest by the higher attenuations, until the fact is found out they have taken no medicine, and then the so-called drug loses its power. We have attenuated a grain of aconite until it is no longer aconite, then dropped into a tumblerful of water a single drop of this harmless solution, and administering one teaspoonful of this water at intervals of half an hour have cured the incipient stage of fever. The highest attenuation we ever attained was to leave the drug out of the question, using only the sugar of milk; and with this original dose we cured an inveterate case of dropsy. After these experiments you cannot be surprised that we resigned the imaginary medicine altogether, and honestly employed Mind as the only curative Principle.[55]

"Metaphysics, as taught in Christian Science," wrote Eddy, "is the next stately step beyond homeopathy." In metaphysics, matter disappeared entirely from the medicine and mind took its rightful place. Christian Science rested on mind alone as the curative principle, acknowledging in the process that it was the divine Mind that contained all power. While homeopathy mentalized the drug with "thought attenuations" so that the drug resembled the intent of the mind, it still remained hostage to the mortal mind and materialism.[56] Eddy reasoned that the homeopath's cure came from the faith of the doctor and patient, which admittedly reduced the self-inflicted effects of the disease on the body. Faith, cooperating with belief, soothed fear and minimized the disease. But nothing in homeopathy was permanent unless the Science of Mind took charge.[57] All systems of medicine founded on the armamentarium of the *materia medica* were nothing but rank materialism whose "faith" was based on hygiene and drugs rather than on God. Such systems were a form of idolatry, and so long as individuals yielded to these material conceptions of medicine they would forever remain removed from knowing who God is and what he does. These were the same false conceptions of the spirit that had made historical Christianity shockingly material in its practices.[58]

In her Christian Science practice, Eddy began her treatment with techniques similar to Quimby's and Evans's by silently allaying the fear that often consumed her patients. To do this, she sought to fix in her patients' thoughts the image and likeness of God, where sin, disease, and death had no presence. After calming her patients, she then instructed their mortal mind with immortal Truth. Once patients understood that their sickness was but a "dream" from which they needed to be awakened and that their strength in overcoming their condition was in proportion to their courage, the patients took control over the body. "Speak the truth to every form of error," she advised her students. "Tumors, ulcers, tubercles, inflammation, pain, deformed joints, are waking dream-shadows, dark images of mortal thought, which flee before the light of Truth."[59]

In *Science and Health,* she gave a typical example of her healing experience:

> A woman, whom I cured of consumption, always breathed with great difficulty when the wind was from the east. I sat silently by her side a few moments. Her breath came gently. The inspirations were deep and natural. I then requested her to look at the weather-vane. She looked and saw that it pointed due east. The wind had not changed, but her thought of it had and so her difficulty in breathing had gone. The wind had not produced the difficulty. My metaphysical treatment changed the action of her belief on the lungs, and she never suffered again from east winds, but was restored to health.[60]

Until the world admitted to the efficacy and supremacy of Mind, Eddy cautioned, "it is better for Christian Scientists to leave surgery and the adjustment of broken bones and dislocations to the fingers of a surgeon." Nevertheless, she insisted there were "well-authenticated records" of cures attained by herself and her students using mental surgery alone to repair broken bones, dislocated joints, and even trauma to the spine.[61]

Christian Scientists were particularly adamant that their method of mental healing was in no way comparable to other systems. Eddy insisted that Christian Science did not heal by means of psychotherapy or autosuggestion; nor did it use hypnotism. In fact, it prohibited any form of suggestion on the "carnal mind of which sin and its resultant states, sickness and death, are effects." All cure came from the power of the divine Mind in human consciousness and was best achieved by emulating the example of Jesus, the Christ.[62]

Eddy was particularly emphatic in preaching against what she called *malicious animal magnetism,* a blanket term that included mesmerism and hypnotism. In a seven-page chapter titled "Animal Magnetism Unmasked" in her *Science and Health,* Eddy explains that animal magnetism was a force used to place one human being under the power or influence of another. While intended as a remedial agent, she insisted that it was a deceptive and dangerous practice based on the power of an erroneous mortal mind. In a similar vein, she taught that audible prayer, public prayer, long prayers, and creeds could never create true spiritual understanding. Only when understanding that life and intelligence were purely spiritual could the body separate the divine life from the "dream of material living." Only in the sanctuary of Spirit, she said, was one to know Truth, Life, and Love.[63]

Neither sin nor Jesus's sacrificial atonement were part of the Christian Science belief system. The sole purpose of Jesus's life was to show humanity the way "out of the flesh, out of the delusion of all human error." Jesus's death was "not to appease the wrath of God, but to show the Allness of Love and the nothingness of hate, sin, and death. . . . He atoned for the terrible unreality of a supposed existence apart from God."[64] As for death, it was but another phase of the dream that existence was material. Death was an illusion and controverted by the spiritual fact that "man *is,* not *shall be,* perfect and immortal." Having healed hopeless organic disease and "raised the dying to life and health," Eddy insisted that death could be mastered through Christian Science.[65] Because all things were part of the divine Mind, salvation was nothing more than being in harmony with all of its manifestations. This belief did away with historical Christianity's final judgment.[66]

Eddy's 1891 spiritual autobiography, *Retrospection and Introspection,* is a mixture of personal, historical, and religious reflections. It describes her alleged healing in 1866 and her subsequent founding of Christian Science. The first seven chapters recount her spiritual childhood and evoke images of Jesus as a youth doing his "Father's" business. Eddy spoke of the religiosity of her forbearers; the talent of her short-lived brother, Albert Baker, who was elected to the state legislature; the mysterious "voices" she began hearing at the age of eight; her early efforts at poetry; her admittance into the Congregational Church; and her initial questions and rejection of Calvin's decree of predestination.[67]

Chapters 8 through 10 recount the origins of Eddy's religious ideas and, once again, evoke images of Jesus's transition into public life. The chapters include her marriage in 1843 to George Washington Glover of Charleston, South Carolina, and his early death; the birth and handing off of her son to a family in northern New Hampshire; her second and unfortunate marriage, which included unsuccessful efforts to regain custody of her son; and an elaboration of her illnesses and subsequent discovery of the "magnetic" healer Quimby. Drawing comparisons to Jesus's withdrawal into the desert, where he came to know his purpose, Eddy claims to have used the time after Quimby's death to "ponder" her mission and search Scripture, where she found, at long last, the true Science of Mind. Guided by the mysteries revealed to her from reading Scripture, she, like Jesus, saw her role as introducing to the world the spiritual science of metaphysical healing, namely, Christian Science.[68]

The third stage of Eddy's retrospection (chapters 11–15) accounts for the preaching and eventual publication of her ideas—a task marked by self-sacrifice and love for her fellow human beings. Here, she found herself fighting the competing claims of allopathy, homeopathy, hydropathy, electricity, and various other healing "humbugs" that had "wandered through the dim mazes" of the *materia medica*. Recounting instances of her own notable cures, she reported that "a person healed by Christian Science is not only healed of his disease, but . . . is advanced morally and spiritually." Desiring to share the good news with others, she put her thoughts to pen, publishing *Science and Health*, which she claimed had been written under the supervision of God. She noted that while the first printing was of only a thousand copies, by 1891 it had reached sixty-two editions.[69]

Chapters 16 through 20 recount the early years of her public ministry, including examples of her extraordinary cures; the establishment of the Church of Christ, Scientist; and the steps taken to ensure her pastoral role. The chapters also recount her third marriage, to Asa Gilbert Eddy, and his devotion to the new religion; his organization of the Christian Science Sunday school; his remarkable talents in mind-healing; her organization of the first Christian Scientist Association in 1876; and her adoption of Ebenezer J. Foster-Eddy, a graduate of Hahnemann Medical College, and his embracing of Christian Science.

In her last ten chapters, Eddy reaches out with her teachings and ideas, revealing Mind as harmonious, immortal, and spiritual, and portraying herself as following Jesus's example in showing the way and the Truth. "Christian Science gives vitality to religion, which is no longer buried in materiality," she wrote. "It raises men from a material sense, into the spiritual understanding and Scientific demonstration of God."[70] Eddy takes note of the false claims made against her and her church, and her assumption of a role that combined both Jesus and the Virgin Mother in a messianic mission of the Christ. In this final phase, Eddy elevates herself to a position equal to Jesus as cofounder of the Science of Being.[71]

Organizational Structure

Eddy's significance lies less with her theories and whether they were original or borrowed than in her transformation of psychotherapeutic theory into an organized religion. In 1874, she and her followers formed into a society at Lynn, Massachusetts, where the first edition of *Science and Health* was published to explain her doctrines. In 1876, the society took the name of the Christian Science Association and, three years later, in 1879, the group voted to organize the Church of Christ, Scientist, to which she was ordained pastor and from whose pulpit she preached.

In 1881, after numerous schisms, excommunications, and defections, many by her closest followers, Eddy relocated to 571 Columbus Avenue in Boston, where she received a medical charter for training practitioners in Christian Science. During the next seven years, more than four thousand students matriculated at her Massachusetts Metaphysical College, paying $300 in tuition for a course of twelve lessons. Additional courses in metaphysical obstetrics ($100), theology ($100), and a summary of Christian Science principles ($100) were also available. Its graduates, most of whom were women, discovered a sense of physical and spiritual health as well as an opportunity for careers as practitioners.

Chartered for medical purposes but facing a litany of medical licensing issues, including manslaughter charges (the trial of Christian Science practitioner Abby H. Corner), Eddy's Metaphysical College closed October 29, 1889, only to open ten years later with a nonmedical charter as an auxiliary to the church.[72] Eddy's adopted son, Ebenezer Foster-Eddy, along with Edward Ancel Kimball (1845–1909), author of *Answers to Questions Concerning Christian Science* (1909), were among the school's faculty.[73]

Christian Science drew a disproportionate number of women into its ranks, with many choosing careers as readers, practitioners, teachers, and healers of both spiritual and physical ills. Women also constituted the majority of patients, finding the option of self-help more appealing than the helplessness of the prevailing limitations placed on their gender. With the exception of the church's executive positions, Eddy's church congregations averaged sixty-two women for every one hundred members. As with other sectarian movements of the day, including homeopathy and hydropathy, Christian Science had helped to enlarge the role of women in religious leadership and in health care.[74] Like Shaker Ann Lee and Theosophist Helena Blavatsky, Eddy deemphasized the masculine side of the Divine, offering instead a more impersonal, non-anthropomorphic Principle. Similarly, all three denied the Christian doctrine of the Fall, the need for an ordained clergy and, although having a somewhat ambiguous view of marriage, chose not to limit woman's sphere to mere motherhood.[75]

In 1883, the Christian Science Association began publication of the *Journal of Christian Science* with Eddy as its editor. Three years later, Eddy reconstituted the organization as the National Christian Scientist Association, which met in its first general convention in New York City on February 11, 1886.[76] By 1887, there were two Christian Science institutes and colleges advertised in New York, four in Chicago, one in Milwaukee, one in Brooklyn, and one in Colorado—each offering a course of twelve lessons and awarding the Bachelor of Christian Science (CSB). Those with several years of healing experience could seek the Doctor of Christian Science (CSD) and those with the lower degree who practiced for three years could seek the Doctor of Divine Science (DSD).[77]

By 1890, Eddy had consolidated all ecclesiastical power within the mother church. Demanding adherence of fellow believers to the church's rigid orthodoxies and accompanying them with a highly centralized authoritarianism, she was able to marginalize dissent and, at the same time, build a highly effective organizational response to competing religions. Whereas New Thought would celebrate the virtues of pluralism, voluntarism, and individualism with minimal doctrines and organizational structures, Christian Science chose a more cult-like response, preferring consolidation of authority and doctrine over loose association and eclectic religiosity. Unlike New Thought's easy tolerance, Eddy and her followers remained critical dissenters whose emphatic affirmation of health and spirituality brooked no linkage or affiliation with competing systems. By the end of the 1890s, Christian Science had expanded to 221 organizations spread widely across the American landscape, including such cities as San Francisco, Denver, and Cleveland. By then, too, there were 1,104 church buildings supported by nearly fifty thousand members.[78] At the time of Eddy's death in 1910, the Church of Christ, Scientist, had a "Mother Church" and a highly centralized governance system controlled by a self-perpetuating board of trustees.

Contending Parties

As the Christian Science movement took institutional form, it gathered speed, becoming a legitimate, albeit controversial, religion whose leader assumed Christ-like attributes. Seldom has a religion been viewed in such diametrical terms. Clearly, a goodly portion of the controversy surrounding the movement stemmed from Eddy's idealistic interpretation of metaphysics, her obsession with malicious animal magnetism, the matriarchal manner in which she controlled church doctrine and claimed theological and personal authority, and the implication of her ideas on issues of public health and healing. Nevertheless, given her physical and psychological impediments, from her disturbed childhood to a womanhood with sad and broken marriages, Eddy's accomplishments were extraordinary.

Although Christian Scientists insist their faith is derived from Scripture, mainline Protestants adamantly point to differences between themselves and Eddy's authoritarian teachings. For Christian Scientists, illness is an illusion, a form of evil derived from erroneous think-ing. Since God is good, God can in no way authorize or condone illness for any reason. Such an explanation detracts from God's glory and per-fection. When Christian Scientists spoke of healing, they did so in refer-ence to spiritual awakening, not blind faith. While both groups spoke of the importance of prayer, the term carried a different meaning for each. For mainline Protestants, prayer related to an appeal for God's interven-tion, while for Christian Scientists, prayer meant the use of the mind to control disease. The former saw spiritual healing as a miraculous accom-paniment to medicine; the latter viewed healing as a natural event, the outcome of correct thinking.

Other differences that separated Christian Science from mainline Protestantism include the degree of dependence on ritual practices and church attendance; the Christian Scientists' belief in spiritual healing as superior to conventional medicine; and Protestants' view of healing as a process resulting from materialistic reasoning rather than paranormal interventions. In other words, Christian Science was and is less likely to accept science and religion as distinctly separate epistemological routes to knowledge. Instead, Christian Science claims that its spiritual heal-ing occurs within a cognitive system distinct from those charismatic and metaphysical healing systems that insist on a dualistic approach to body and mind.[79]

Following the publication of *Science and Health*, the philosophies and practices of Eddy and Evans became the subject of a broad intel-lectual discussion across the metaphysical healing community. In the quarter century that followed, they and their supporters claimed own-ership of two competing mind-cure philosophies. Evans's phrenopathic system was distinctly philosophical, esoteric, impersonal, lacking in any dogmatic creed, free of any centralized leadership, and generally claimed Quimby as its originating source. Its proponents refused to accept Eddy's extreme form of idealism.

"In man's struggle through evolutionary processes of creation, to his present physical and mental stature," explained the popular New Thought writer Abel Leighton Allen, "it took millions of years to bring these five senses to their present degree of perfection, and they cannot be discredited by the bare declaration [by Eddy] that they are false."

Allen accused Christian Scientists of having erred by adhering to an exclusive set of teachings, all of which were issued under the rules of Eddy and her church. "Whenever an organization attempts to corral truth," he warned, "it is plainly evident that it has discovered only a small portion of truth."[80] Allen urged the proponents of New Thought to let the divine mind "find expression" in the thoughts and actions of their daily lives. The great achievement of modern psychology had been its discovery of the subconscious mind and the fact that through it, human beings had discovered the forces and powers of the soul within. It was this subconscious that united human beings with the Divine Soul, the kingdom of God within.[81]

Despite differences, there remained numerous points of similarity between the two competing movements. The businessman Henry Wood, one of the pioneer authors in the New Thought movement, predicted that, like other doctrinaire groups, Christian Science would probably soften over time, becoming more elastic and less authoritarian. Whatever Eddy's mistakes, he said, she deserved respect and would eventually be honored for her leadership and freshness of ideas. "This she will receive in future, whatever it may be lacking today," he surmised. There should be no rivalry between the two movements; each should rejoice in the success of the other. Instead of moving in opposite directions, he hoped that the two movements might converge sometime in the future.[82]

Notwithstanding Wood's hope for some form of merger, the two groups remained hostile to one another. New Thoughters accused Eddy of teaching a gross form of pantheism that absorbed God in nature and implied that the individual soul was only a modification of the divine substance. If the material universe existed only in the mind, they reasoned, it annihilated the human soul, which, in Christian belief, was destined for eternal life. This was not to say that Evans's followers denied all forms of idealistic philosophy; instead, they chose a pragmatic middle ground by explaining that matter existed and operated *in* God. The same was true of the human will. In other words, New Thought subordinated its idealism to the purposeful actions of the will. It saw itself as a progressive philosophy of growth, while Christian Science represented an extreme form of absolute idealism, stating that matter was but the illusion of human belief and asserting that the only realities were the divine mind and the divine idea. For Eddy and her followers, the five senses were not to be trusted; they were not to be believed. From New Thought's perspective, Eddy's system of belief failed to satisfy the more rational elements in the mental-healing movement.

* * *

The ideas of Evans and Eddy emerged from the same metaphysical womb and inherited similar genetic markers. Both advocated a spiritual view of healthy-mindedness derived from Quimby, who aligned the metaphysical imagination with unconventional healing practices. Each, too, articulated a philosophy that appealed to faith in the progressive tendencies of nature. Then again, both thrived among the urban and cosmopolitan middle and upper classes, serving as oracular spokespeople whose eloquence and persuasion rallied in defense of the body's inner harmony. But for all these likenesses, Evans chose a more secular and interdenominational understanding of the physical and metaphysical orders of healthy-mindedness, whereas Eddy preferred more structured pathways. Communicating to substantively different audiences, both tended over time to play to their base, which, for Eddy, bespoke of a more stylistic feminism, while Evans, more pluralistic in his discourse, became a voice for the changing spirit of American society, demythologizing the passing Victorian worldview. A sense of modernity entered more easily into his thought, justifying his conjectures, blurring the difference between the actual and the possible, and shrinking the boundaries marking divisions within the American society. Evans, more than the churches that would emerge as proponents of New Thought, served to influence a generation or more of secular writers who helped transform Protestantism and its moral code into an edification of mental harmony, positive thinking, and prosperity.

There seems to be little question that Evans's later writings had an affinity to Eddy's. Credited with being one of the first mind-curists to use the term "Christian Science," he nonetheless chose to stand clear from Eddy's extreme doctrines of idealism, divine revelation, authoritarianism, and pathological fear of malicious animal magnetism—elements that had made her a unique figure in the mind-cure movement, if not in the larger history of American religion. Unlike Eddy, he did not deny the reality of the material world; he believed it was only unreal when perceived as existing separate from the mind. God manifested himself to the world by way of the "Christ Principle," the universal or ideal human being, who was the source of love and intellect; the "Logos," which corresponded to the rational soul; and the "Universal Life Principle," which pervaded the material world without itself being classified as a material substance.[83]

More importantly, Evans refused to deny the usefulness of conventional medicine; instead, he saw it as a complement to the mental cure. Despite his sometimes rapturous idealism, he held firm to a more pragmatic system of mental healing whose approach was not so much mystical and esoteric as it was a form of positive thinking. Schooled in a combination of Methodism, Swedenborgianism, and the mind-cure techniques of Quimby, he acted as a bridge between the older pseudosciences (i.e., mesmerism, sarcognomy, and psychometry) of the nineteenth century and the emerging disciplines of psychology and psychoanalysis in the twentieth. In the last analysis, however, Evans held back from affirming the preponderantly secular tone of the new disciplines, preferring instead to retain a more religious and metaphysical approach to the concept of healthy-mindedness. It was an approach that emphasized the affirmation of prayer and the divine energy of perfect love over the more stressful implications of the subconscious and undetected depths of the mind.

In his analysis of the psychotherapeutic cults of the late nineteenth century, American psychologist James H. Leuba (1867–1946) explained that despite the often polarizing and distorted formulations of New Thought and Christian Science, their single common denominator was the power of mind over body. The discovery of this truth in the treatment of disease overshadowed the different markers used to distinguish the different modalities. Propagated from one end of the country to the other, the dualism long attributed to Descartes had ended and a restored body/mind or body/soul was announced to the world.[84]

4

Metropolitan Religions

*Whatever ... is in the mind is in the brain,
and from the brain in the body, according
to the order of its parts. Thus a man writes
his life in his physique, and thus the angels
discover his autobiography in his structure.*

—Emanuel Swedenborg, *Heaven and Hell*

While Warren Felt Evans chose a spiritual but unchurched approach to metaphysical healing, others with similar spiritual needs formed churches and affiliated organizations and associations. Many of these churches and groups were the result of schisms, defections, and excommunications arising from Mary Baker Eddy's doctrinaire methods and vendettas. Some of the prominent Christian Scientists who broke from the prophetess included George B. Charles and his wife Lizzie in 1884; A. J. Swarts and Katie L. Swarts in 1886; Ursula Gestefeld and Frank Mason in 1888; Joseph Adams in 1891; Ida A. Nichols in 1891; and Josephine Curtis Woodbury in 1899. Illustrative of the defectors was Luther M. Marston, MD, a graduate of both Harvard Medical School and of Eddy's class of 1883 who went on to establish the Mental Science and Christian Healing Association in 1886, followed by the Boston College of Metaphysical Science in 1888. As spokesperson for many disaffected Christian Scientists, he taught monthly classes on the science of spiritual and Christian healing, or what he called "Scientific Christianity," to distinguish his system from Christian Science. Referring to a power inherent in nature he variously called *vitality, anima, nervous influence, vital principle,* and *vis medicatrix naturae,* he viewed all things in terms of spirit and every person as a channel through which the influx of universal life force flowed. The spiritual person was the true and only reality; the person of the senses was only a shadow—one infinite, the other finite. The real person knew nothing of disease. It was only the finite person who suffered.[1]

"Teacher of Teachers"

Of Eddy's many defectors, the most significant was the theologian, writer, mystic, and feminist Emma Curtis Hopkins (1849–1925), a native of Killingly, Connecticut. The oldest of nine children in a farming family, Emma experienced the tragic deaths of several siblings as well as her father's loss of a leg in the Civil War, all of which left an imprint on the young girl. Following her primary education, Emma married George Irving Hopkins, a school teacher, in 1874. In the mid-1880s, the two were divorced, with indications that they had lived apart for some time prior to the official notice. Sometime in the early 1880s, Hopkins met Eddy, whereupon she became sincerely interested in Christian Science healing. She arranged to work on the editorial staff of the monthly *Christian Science Journal* in exchange for permission to pursue a practitioner's license at Eddy's Massachusetts Metaphysical College in the class of 1883. Thus began an association between student and teacher and the transfer of Hopkins's membership in the Congregational Church in Killingly to Eddy's First Church of Christ, Scientist, in Boston.[2]

In 1885, shortly after being appointed editor of the *Christian Science Journal,* Hopkins had a falling out with Eddy and was summarily dismissed from her post. Choosing to leave Boston, she moved to the Midwest. There she charted a new course in metaphysical healing, relying on a network of sympathetic female healers, many of whom were also defectors from Christian Science. From 1895 until her death in 1925, she carried on an extensive practice in metaphysical healing and became a spiritual mentor to many in the literary and artistic world. Her *Scientific Christian Mental Practice* (1888), *Class Lessons 1888, Bible Interpretations* (1892), and *High Mysticism* (1888) were hallmarks of her syncretic metaphysics. There were also books prepared by students that represented compilations of her teachings.

Hopkins accepted many of Eddy's principles and, for a brief time, even appropriated the term "Christian Science" for her own Christian Science Theological Seminary (1886), which she later renamed the Emma Hopkins College of Metaphysical Science (1889). By 1893, her college had ordained 111 ministers.[3] New Thought, as represented by Hopkins and her competing brand of theology, charted a course from the Midwest to urban churches on the West Coast, focusing on the central elements of healthy-mindedness, spirit, purity, and selfhood. She sent forth a group of disciples who spawned churches and organizations such as the Unity School of Christianity and affiliated associations in the Midwest; Divine Science churches and schools in Denver and San Francisco; and Home of Truth associations along the Pacific Coast, including Canada.[4]

Known lovingly by her disciples as the "teacher of teachers," Hopkins mentored the poetess Ella Wheeler Wilcox; Charles and Myrtle Fillmore, cofounders of the Unity School of Christianity, who she ordained in 1891; Charles and Josephine Barton, publishers of *The Life* magazine in Kansas City, Missouri; D. L. Sullivan, who taught classes in St. Louis and Kansas City; Helen Wilmans, author of *Conquest of Poverty* (1899) and editor of *Wilman's Express;* New Thought publisher Elizabeth Towne; Helen Van-Anderson, founder of the Boston New Thought Church of the Higher Life; Malinda Cramer, cofounder of Divine Science and first president of the International Divine Science Ministry; and Kate Bingham, who instructed Nona L. Brooks and Fannie Brooks, cofounders of Divine Science in the West. Others included physician Harriet Emilie Cady, MD, author of the Unity textbook *Lessons in Truth: A Course of Twelve Lessons in Practical Christianity* (1896); Annie Rix Militz, founder of the Home of Truth associations; the prolific New Thought author William Walker Atkinson; and Ernest S. Holmes, who went to Hopkins for private instruction and founded the church Religious Science.[5]

In *Spiritual Law in the Natural World* (1894), a collection of Hopkins's lectures published by her students under the pseudonym of "Eleve," Hopkins expressed her intent to save humanity from natural laws that had led to a procession of "undesirable phenomena" such as disease, starvation, hatred, pain, and death. Her teachings were about the spiritual law (i.e., the teachings of Jesus) that "is sure to heal you if you read it—heal you of pain, of physical disease, of feebleness, of indeterminate will, of faltering by the wayside of your human walk." Her writings were intended to teach the laws and conditions of "right thinking" by breaking down the shell of materialism and cleansing the mind of its prejudices. Once aware of the impediments of wrong judgments, individuals were supposedly able to cure disease in themselves and in others by thoughts alone. In terminology similar to Plato's analogy of the cave in *Phaedrus*, Hopkins spoke of the "shadow system" through which most saw the world, and which hid its true meaning. It was only in seeing the light through these shadows that "we would know the divine idea of creation and the design of our own life."[6] Drawing from Plato, Berkeley's idealism, and Emerson's transcendentalism, she reiterated her belief in spiritual knowledge and the unreality of material things. "Plato was quite right, the world of sight, or sense, is a cave, in which we are blinded to the real and true," she wrote. "Out of this we must come and leave the shadows on the wall, which are the beliefs in mortal things as being real or as having any pleasure in them."[7]

So potent was truth, Hopkins explained, that merely repeating the appropriate word brought the power represented by that word to the mind. Similarly, if an individual believed that there was something in the universe that was "good" for his or her use and contained no mixture of evil, it was obtainable simply by wanting it. With an understanding of truth, she insisted, "we cannot be sick or poor or unhappy or in doubt or fear."[8]

> Whatever we declare we are sure to have, for God has created all things good, and for us, and it is our office to speak the word that will make them show forth. All round about us is an invisible power (invisible to the senses) that our word acts upon, bringing it into action. Whatever we desire can be invoked into sight. We have just what we invoke. If we continually speak of hateful things they will surround us. We can speak into visibility exactly what we wish.[9]

Reflective of Eddy's Christian Science doctrine, Hopkins viewed sin, sickness, and death as dreams, not realities. Matter did not exist in

Truth, Life, and Love. God was all and good. God was the only sub-stance. God was humanity's *terra firma,* and could be discovered through repeated affirmations such as "God is Life, God is Truth, God is Love; God is Substance; God is Intelligence." Through these affirma-tions, the individual discovered an "inner seeing that is keener, clearer than physical sight."[10]

Hopkins's gift was in the clarity of her language. Unlike Eddy, whose words were often difficult to parse and who insisted on the authority of the Mother Church to control interpretation, Hopkins's words were transparent in their meaning. More educated in historical and contem-porary philosophies, she expressed herself in a manner that appealed to a broad band of followers eager to carry her ideas to the far corners of the continent. She shared the belief of many in her generation that a new wave of thinking was fast approaching that would be wholly spiritual. As all of history had come and gone in "cycles" or "mental waves," she pre-dicted the coming of a new spiritual wave that would rescue humanity from its delusions by showing "that God is everywhere and at all times as near to us as we are to ourselves."[11]

As with other metaphysical healers in her day, Hopkins refused to accept the germ theory of disease, arguing that thought, not bacte-ria, was the cause of bodily sickness.[12] In her instructions to students regarding healing, she explained that "there is in reality no heal-ing done at all." Instead, it was bringing forth the health that already existed in the mind but was hidden by "clouds of error."[13] Believing that words must be repeated until felt, she gave examples of affirmations used in treating the sick.

For Weakness without Pain

You believe in God and know He is with you always. He is health, strength and rest. Nothing else can be where He is. There is only God. God is all. (several times) You have health, vigor, strength and courage, for God fills you full of them. Spirit is all there is, and is with you and in you. You are whole, now.

For Catarrh

You know that God is everywhere. God is Spirit and is with you; is all around you. The sweet healing Spirit that is health itself is all about you. You breathe it with every breath. It is all through you, over you, and you are one with it. Nothing can come near you to hurt you for it protects you. You must be perfectly well in this presence and you are well and whole—clean and wholesome, now.

Epilepsy

You are not afraid of anything, for you are safe. God folds you round with loving care and protection. You know that God is everywhere. You have heard that if you go down into the sea, or even under the earth, that God is there. You cannot get away from God . . .You cannot be sick for you breathe only health. You are well for God enfolds you. His everlasting arms uphold you. You are whole.

Blindness

"Let there be light." You are bathed in a sea of light for God is light and He is all around you. You are in the glorious presence of God always. God is sight itself. You see with His sight. He sees through you and for you. You have perfect sight now. "All is light."[14]

Hopkins even had affirmative thought prayers intended to ward off poverty.

Great and bountiful Spirit, I rejoice in the full supply that Thou hast given me. I thank Thee that I am supplied with all that I can ask for. Thou art all good. The symbol of good is gold, thus a plentiful supply of gold is mine, for Thou art the fullness of supply. It is thy delight to give; Thou art more willing to give than we are to receive. I am supplied with all I want, for I am one with Thee. All that is Thine is mine. . . . The Almighty is my defense and I have plenty of silver.[15]

Hopkins served as midwife to a host of sects gathered loosely under the umbrella of New Thought and representing the denominational side of the movement. She is also credited with introducing some of the earliest lectures on what she called "The Good" (as reflected in the phrase "There is Good for me and I ought to have it"), which eventually evolved into the prosperity gospel.[16] Having repudiated the authoritarianism of the Christian Science movement, Hopkins and her disciples organized fledgling societies, associations, colleges, institutes, and sanitariums that swirled in and around the more generic New Thought movement. Many of them remain to this day independent and autonomous, while others are affiliated in some manner to the four New Thought groups known as Unity, Divine Science, Religious Science, and Home of Truth.[17]

Hopkins eventually relocated to New York City, where she lived out the rest of her life exploring mysticism and practicing healing among a notable group of acolytes, including homeopath Harriet Emilie Cady and the writer and social activist Mabel Dodge Luhan.[18]

Unity School of Christianity

The Unity Church of Kansas City, Missouri, better known as the Unity School of Christianity or simply Unity, was founded in 1889 by Charles Fillmore (1854–1948) and Myrtle Fillmore (1845–1931). The Fillmores (including sons Lowell Page and Waldo Rickert and grandson Charles) developed Unity as a form of what they termed *Practical Christianity*, meaning the promotion of a positive approach to life without the embellishments of a creed, dogma, or ritual. They supported spiritual healing, taught the creative power of thought and the importance of taking personal responsibility for one's actions, stressed the combined merits of prayer and silence, affirmed the divinity of Christ in each person, and accepted reincarnation as God's gift to human beings of a second chance at perfection.

Mary Caroline "Myrtle" Page Fillmore decided early in her youth to reject the dogmatic teachings of her Methodist parents. She attended Oberlin College, followed by a brief stint teaching in the public school system in Clinton, Missouri. Diagnosed with tuberculosis, she followed the advice of family and friends to move to the dry climate of Denison, Texas. There she met Charles Fillmore who, although lacking much formal education, was a great admirer of Emerson, Spiritualism, and the occult. Like Myrtle, Charles complained of suffering from long illnesses. Following their marriage in 1881, the two lived briefly in Gunnison, Colorado, before moving to Pueblo, where sons Lowell and Waldo were born. The family then moved to Omaha, Nebraska, and finally to Kansas City, Missouri. In 1886, while living in Kansas City, the Fillmores attended the New Thought classes of Dr. E. B. Weeks, a former follower of Eddy and later a student of Emma Hopkins, from whom they learned how to recover from their chronic health problems.

Drawn to the calling, the Fillmores began publication of the magazine *Modern Thought* in 1889 and, a year later, organized the Society for Silent Unity. In 1891, they went on to publish the popular monthly magazine *Unity*, which they advertised as a "Hand-book of Practical Christianity and Christian Healing," explaining the practical application of Jesus's beliefs; the actions of the mind; the mind as the connecting link between God and human beings; and how understanding divine law produced harmony, health, and peace.[19] In addition to poems and Bible lessons for achieving spiritual growth, the magazine offered information concerning upcoming meetings, correspondence and testimonials from subscribers, directories of teachers and healers, quotes from famous celebrities, and notices of metaphysical articles and books for sale. It also kept subscribers up to date on legislation restricting the practices of various healing groups, including the Christian Scientists, whom they admired for their political acumen.[20] Of the magazine's many subscribers, over seven thousand were members of the Fillmore's Society of Silent Unity. Even though separated by hundreds of miles, the members joined every evening at nine o'clock for five minutes of silence to make a "unity connection." At the end of the silence, each asked for something: "Ask what ye will in my name, and it shall be done unto you." Through this process, they reputedly received answers to their requests.[21] Fillmore's books include *Christian Healing: The Science of Being* (1917), *Jesus Christ Heals* (1936), *Mysteries of Genesis* (1936), and *Teach Us to Pray* (1941). There are also a number of posthumously compiled collections of his writings, including *Atom-Smashing Power of Mind* (1949), *The Revealing Word* (1959), *Dynamics for Living* (1967), and *The Twelve Powers of Man* (1999).

For Unity, it is the creative power of thoughts, words, and actions that gives each person the ability and responsibility to realize spiritual health and prosperity, learning always from the master teacher Jesus, who set the example for all. The term "Christ," used to convey Jesus's divinity, is also intended to express the potential divinity of every individual to the extent that he or she seeks universal Truth. Each individual has the responsibility for awakening the divine nature within and living with a conscious understanding of the journey into spirituality. Unity believers use prayer and meditation as their roadmap into spiritual awakening. Regarded as the highest forms of creative thought, prayer and meditation provide the means through which individuals experience God in their souls. By aligning their creative powers with the power of God, they awaken their lives to their divine nature.[22] The principal beliefs of Unity include:

1. God is the source and creator of all. There is no other enduring power. God is good and present everywhere.

2. We are spiritual beings, created in God's image. The spirit of God lives within each person; therefore, all people are inherently good.

3. We create our life experiences through our way of thinking.

4. There is power in affirmative prayer, which we believe increases our connections to God.

5. Knowledge of these spiritual principles is not enough. We must live them.[23]

Many of Unity's core beliefs are found in the writings of Harriet Emilie Cady (1848–1941), who began her career as a schoolteacher before enrolling at the Homeopathic College of New York City, from which she graduated in 1871. Inspired by the Bible and the writings of Emerson, she pursued spiritual and metaphysical studies, eventually becoming a student of Hopkins and associating over the years with the Fillmores; the spiritual teacher Ernest S. Holmes (1887–1960); and Albert Benjamin Simpson (1843–1919), founder of the Christian and Missionary Alliance (1897). Cady authored *Finding the Christ in Ourselves* (1891), *Lessons in Truth: A Course of Twelve Lessons in Practical Christianity* (1896), *God, a Present Help* (1910), and *How I Used Truth* (1916). Her *Lessons in Truth*, which has sold more than 1.6 million copies, addressed the importance of denials and affirmations as well as going into the silence to find the indwelling God. "When you withdraw from the world for meditation," she explained, "get all your thoughts centered on God, and upon your relations to the Creator and Upholder of the universe. . . . Think of some truth, be it ever so simple." The ultimate aim of each soul was to come into the consciousness of the indwelling God, which Cady called "Father-Mother."[24]

Once the principles covered in *Lessons in Truth* were understood, Cady directed her followers to Fillmore's *Christian Healing: The Science of Being* to gradually introduce them to the healing aspects of Practical Christianity. His book, intended as a series of lessons to be applied with the precision of mathematics, entailed affirming or denying, both audibly and mentally, a thought or suggestion. This technique, when carried out to the letter, "set up new thought-currents" in the mind and body that, applied daily, made way for spiritual illumination. The object of the lessons was to quicken consciousness, which in turn increased understanding. For those who sought self-healing, Fillmore explained, it was important to talk mentally to your body as you would to a patient. For those who wished to heal another, "hold him in mind and mentally repeat the denials and affirmations, which will raise the consciousness to Spiritual Reality, where all the healing power originates."[25]

The first stage of any true healing was the recognition by both healer and patient that God was present as an "All-Powerful Mind" and capable of healing any and all types of organic and functional diseases. For this reason, Fillmore and other metaphysical healers chose to begin their treatments with the Lord's Prayer, as it raised the mind to "Christ Consciousness." Once this was done, the outer senses were quieted and thoughts became "obedient to the Word."[26]

Fillmore provided sample affirmations to treat nervousness, influenza, indigestion, liver and kidney disorders, and throat infections. The treatments carried the patient through six steps or degrees:

1. Having the mind perceive and affirm Truth to be a universal principle

2. Believing that faith is the working power of Truth

3. Accepting that Truth takes form in the mind

4. Using the Will to carry Truth into action

5. Discerning the difference between Truth and error

6. Utilizing thought and word to express harmony with Truth.

With affirmations and denials carried out each day over a six-day course of treatment, he promised that the seventh day would result in "a peaceful confidence and rest in the fulfillment of the Divine Law."[27]

Fillmore argued that hypnosis and mediumship were not legitimate forms of mind cure. "Any system is radically wrong that suppresses the will," he warned. "It is the work of the true healer to instruct the patient, to show cause and remedy from the viewpoint of spiritual understanding. All other methods are temporary."[28] Similarly, he doubted the relevance of biomedicine's germ theory. "To apply a remedy to the poor little microbe is like trying to stop the manufacture of counterfeit money by destroying all that is found in circulation," he mused. It was the intellect that produced the microbes of anger, jealousy, malice, avarice, lust, ambition, and selfishness. "If we had microscopes strong enough we would find our bodies . . . composed of living microbes, doing to the best of their ability the tasks which intellect has set before them."[29]

In 1914, Unity merged with several other ministries to become the Unity School of Christianity. By 1918, there were Unity churches in Denver; Seattle; Los Angeles; Boston; St. Louis; New York City; Oakland, California; Portland, Oregon; and Spokane, Washington. In 1929, the church's central offices relocated to Lee's Summit, Missouri, and it opened its school for ministerial training at Unity Village, Missouri.

Borrowing heavily from Theosophy, theism, Spiritualism, Hinduism, and other non-Western sources, particularly in its teachings of reincarnation, Unity remains predominantly a Christ-centered movement emphasizing the power of positive thinking as a means for realizing physical health and happiness. Although its publications are intended for its own churches, an impressive number find their way into the Protestant mainstream. Included among Unity's many authors are Frank B.

Whitney, Annie Rix Militz, Frances W. Foulks, Dana Gatlin, Ernest C. Wilson, Richard Lynch, Evelyn Whitell, Clara Beranger, Gardner Hunting, Imelda Octavia Shanklin, and Zelia M. Walters.

Divine Science

The Church of Divine Science was founded in San Francisco by Malinda Elliott Cramer (1844–1906). Inspired by Hopkins, Cramer and her husband also founded the Home College of Divine Science (1888) and the magazine *Harmony* (1888), which carried tidings of the emerging New Thought movement. She also served as first president of the International Divine Science Association (founded in 1892). In Colorado, a parallel effort was undertaken by Nona L. Brooks (1861–1945) and her sisters Alethea Brooks Small (1848–1906) and Fannie Brooks James (1854–1914) who, like Cramer, had been students of either Hopkins or one of her many disciples. Ordained by Cramer as a minister in the Church of Divine Science, Nona founded the Divine Science College in Denver in 1899 to instruct teachers, practitioners, and ministers.

Malinda Elliott Cramer was born in Greensboro, Indiana. Plagued in her early life with health issues, in 1870 she moved to San Francisco, where she met and married Charles Lake Cramer. In 1885, she became interested in Christian Science and claimed that a divine revelation led to her improved health. Soon thereafter, she took classes from Emma Hopkins and began a career as teacher and practitioner of metaphysical healing.[30]

Chartered for educational, ethical, therapeutic, and religious purposes, Cramer's Home College of Divine Science, located at 3360 Seventeenth Street in San Francisco, provided instruction in four departments: primary, for teaching fundamental principles; training, for mental discipline in right thinking, teaching, and application; theological, for the spiritual and scientific study of the Bible; and normal, for the special training of teachers. Those who successfully completed her course work, offered in the form of classroom instruction and through correspondence courses, were eligible to become teachers and ministers of Divine Science.[31] As president of the college and its principal instructor, Cramer taught the "law of expression," meaning that through mental discipline, concentration, and change of habits one could obtain peace, health, prosperity, and happiness. During silent meditation and affirmation of "the Good" (following Emma Curtis Hopkins's use of the same term), a mental change occurred that removed all erroneous belief and negativity.[32]

Divine Science represented the Christ method of healing. Using language loaded with the words *God, Spirit, Divine, Good, Mind, Truth, Principle, Absolute, Infinite, Being, Indivisible, One, Omniscience,* and *Omnipresence,* Cramer replicated many of Eddy's beliefs, including her business model. As a metaphysician of Divine Science, she perceived the individual as a pure spirit in both visible and invisible garb. As a healer, she taught that false beliefs were the cause of disease and the remedy was Truth, which bore away all suffering. Cramer taught that it was necessary only to focus on correct thinking. "If you earnestly think that you are perfect in Being you will realize that perfection," she wrote, "and it will be manifest in the body. If you think that you are imperfect, sick, or sinful, the same will seem real to you."[33] As with Unity, Cramer's method of healing was through silent treatment, removing her patient's false judgments by drawing attention to the consciousness of Being. It was only then, she taught, that true healing occurred.[34]

Cramer's instructions to patients included "going into the silence" twice a day for at least twenty minutes. This required the patient to recline in a chair or sofa and concentrate solely on the repetition of Divine Science's "Statement of Being" ("God is Spirit; Mind; Principle; Infinite Being. God is Immutable; Indivisible; One. God is Life; Love; Truth; Omnipresent.").[35] Those who held themselves in Truth, concentrating their thoughts on being the Christ in God, reduced all discordant feelings and diseased conditions. "Begin to think and speak Truth for yourselves without even pausing to take a glance at what has seemed to be obstacles," urged Cramer. "Affirm there are no obstacles; I do not fear, there is nothing to fear."[36] When truthful thought took the place of error, all disease, sorrow, and trouble were dispelled. For Cramer, affirmation brought realization, a process that represented the very heart of Divine Science and the New Thought movement.

Like disease, poverty implied a negativity or lack of harmony. To do away with this deficiency, which was another name for ignorance, was to know the Truth. Knowledge was always and at all times the remedy for ignorance. Since it was intended by the Creator that all humans should be happy, healthy, and successful, Cramer reasoned that overcoming false and erroneous beliefs would bring all the riches that rightfully belonged to humanity.[37] "Spiritually speaking," she wrote, "if you are one with God, money is yours just as much before it comes into your hand as it is after."[38] She expounded her philosophy in books that included *Unity of Life and the Methods of Arriving at Truth* (1888); *Lessons in the Science of Infinite Spirit* (1890); *Basic Statements and Health Treatment of Truth* (1895); and *Divine Science and Healing* (1902). Cramer died as a result of injuries suffered during the San Francisco earthquake of 1906.[39]

The cofounder of Divine Science, Nona Lovell Brooks, was born into a large, upper-middle-class family in Louisville, Kentucky. Following a decline in her mother's health, the collapse of the family business, and her father's sudden death, the family found itself living in more constrained circumstances in Pueblo, Colorado. There, in 1890, Nona attended normal school with the intention of becoming a teacher. It was during this period of the family's misfortune that Nona and her sisters, all of whom complained of health problems, learned of Emma Hopkins's classes on healing and felt called to her faith. Although Nona never met Hopkins, she studied with Mrs. Frank Bingham, a former Hopkins student; it was through Bingham that she and her sisters discovered New Thought. After meeting Cramer and becoming close friends, Nona and her sister Fannie organized themselves under the name of Divine Science, creating the Divine Science College in 1889 and the First Divine Science Church of Denver in 1899. In 1922, Nona aligned the Church of Divine Science with the International New Thought Alliance.[40] Nona took leave of her duties to work for a brief time in Australia before returning to the States to continue her lecturing. From 1938 to 1943, she served as president of the Divine Science College in Denver.[41]

The first convention of Divine Science organized in San Francisco in 1894 under the auspices of the International Divine Science Association. Its second convention opened in Chicago, followed by Kansas

City, St. Louis, then back to San Francisco in 1899. By 1925, Divine Science churches had spread from Colorado and California into Oregon, Massachusetts, Washington, Missouri, Ohio, Illinois, Kansas, and the District of Columbia.[42]

Religious Science

Religious Science or Science of Mind was founded by writer and spiritual teacher Ernest Shurtleff Holmes (1887–1960). He is credited with establishing the Institute of Religious Science and Philosophy in 1927; in 1953 it became the Church of Religious Science, and it is known today as the United Church of Religious Science.[43]

Leaving his native Maine at an early age to find work in Boston, Holmes attended the Leland Powers School of Expression and, soon afterwards, joined Eddy's Church of Christ, Scientist. In 1912, he moved to Venice, California, where he began a career in city government. In his pursuit of a life of independent thinking, he discovered the writings of Emerson, Quimby, Horatio Dresser, Hopkins, Ralph Waldo Trine, and William Walker Atkinson. He was especially drawn to the optimistic creed of Christian D. Larson (1874–1962) and Thomas Troward's (1847–1916) law of attraction. These and other writings eventually caused him to abandon Christian Science for a ministry in the Divine Science church.[44]

After debuting as a lecturer at the Metaphysical Library in Los Angeles, Holmes received invitations for repeat engagements, leading to a nationwide tour and the publication of his first book, *The Creative Mind and Success* (1919), followed by *Science of Mind* (1926) and a magazine with the same name. His other writings include *Creative Mind: A Series of Talks on Mental and Spiritual Law Delivered at the Metaphysical Institute* (1919), *The Bible in the Light of Religious Science* (1929), *New Thought Terms and Their Meanings* (1953), *Mind Remakes Your World* (1941), and *Discover a Richer Life* (1961).[45] His spiritual philosophy went on to influence the positive-thinking teachings of Protestant preacher Norman Vincent Peale (1898–1993).[46]

Holmes's religious views were syncretic, drawing together a number of ideas common among the churches and affiliated organizations within the New Thought movement. The following statement of beliefs was written by Holmes and reflects a clear statement of his core principles:

> We believe in God, the Living Spirit Almighty; one indestructible, absolute, and self-existent Cause. This One manifests Itself in and through all creation but is not absorbed by Its creation. The manifest universe is the body of God; it is the logical and necessary outcome of the infinite self-knowingness of God.

> We believe in the incarnation of the Spirit in everyone and that all people are incarnations of the One Spirit.

> We believe in the eternality, the immortality, and the continuity of the individual soul, forever and ever expanding.

> We believe that heaven is within us and that we experience it to the degree that we become conscious of it.

> We believe the ultimate goal of life to be a complete emancipation from all discord of every nature, and that this goal is sure to be attained by all.

> We believe in the unity of all life, and that the highest God and the innermost God is one God.

> We believe that God is personal to all who feel this indwelling Presence.

> We believe in the direct revelation of Truth through the intuitive and spiritual nature of the individual, and that any person may become a revealer of Truth who lives in close contact with the indwelling God.

> We believe that the Universal Spirit, which is God, operates through a Universal Mind, which is the Law of God; and that we are surrounded by the Creative Mind which receives the direct impress of our thought and acts upon it.

> We believe in the healing of the sick through the Power of this Mind.

We believe in the control of conditions through the Power of this Mind.

We believe in the eternal Goodness, the eternal Loving-kindness, and the eternal Givingness of Life to all.

We believe in our own soul, our own spirit, and our own destiny; for we understand that the life of all is God.[47]

Fenwicke Lindsay Holmes (1883–1973) assisted his brother in many of the church's activities. Ordained a minister in the Congregational Church where he served for six years, he turned to New Thought after reading the works of Thomas Troward and Christian D. Larson. In 1917, Fenwicke opened a metaphysical sanitarium in Long Beach, California, and joined his brother in lecturing in the Los Angeles area. Along with his brother, Fenwicke published *Uplift Magazine,* serving as its editor. His first book, *The Law of Mind in Action* (1919) became an instant success, and soon after he became a lecturer for the League for the Larger Life in New York City. In 1927, he assisted his brother in establishing the Institute of Religious Science and School of Philosophy. After serving as minister at the Divine Science Church of the Healing Christ in New York City, he became president of the International College of Mental Science in Santa Monica, California. His books include *Healing at a Distance* (1917) with his brother Ernest; *How to Develop Faith that Heals* (1919); *The Unfailing Formula* (1919); *Being and Becoming* (1920); *Practical Healing* (1921); *Text Book of Practical Healing* (1943); and *Healing Treatments in Verse* (1943), many of which are still in print.[48]

Home of Truth

A schoolteacher in San Francisco when she first attended one of Hopkins's classes, Annie Rix Militz (1856–1924) became an early advocate of the New Thought movement. As with so many of its leaders, she claimed numerous health issues and disabilities before finding a cure. In 1890, she was ordained at Hopkins's Christian Science Theological Seminary in Chicago and went on to found the Christian Science Home in San Francisco, later renamed Home of Truth. At the World's Columbian Exposition in Chicago in 1893, she met Hindu teacher Swami Vivekananda, causing her to turn away from an exclusively Christian view of New Thought to a more pluralistic interfaith. Reflective of this change, Annie, along with her sister, Harriet Hale Rix (b. 1863), founded the West Coast Metaphysical Bureau, which was dedicated to the study of world religions and philosophies.

Along with the Fillmores, Militz became a pivotal figure in the early years of the Unity movement, teaching monthly courses at their center in Kansas City. In lessons serialized in *Unity* magazine and eventually published as *Primary Lessons in Christian Living and Healing* (1904), she demonstrated her ability to provide a spiritual interpretation of Scripture, an element that had all the earmarks of Swedenborg's influence.[49] Her writings included descriptions of God as Love; heaven as a state of consciousness rather than a place; the correspondence between the natural and spiritual worlds; the root of health being spiritual rather than material; the Last Judgment as something that happened in the spiritual present, not something that was put off to a future end of days; and an understanding that those who pass from the physical plane continue to learn of the Truth as they retire into the spiritual regions of the universe—all themes that are also found in Swedenborg's writings.[50] However, she was clearly influenced by a number of sources; for example, like the Fillmores (but unlike Swedenborg), she was enamored with the possibility of physical immortality and viewed abstention from sex as a regenerator of life force.[51]

Beginning in the summer of 1907 at the Home of Truth in Los Angeles, and later before audiences in cities around the country and abroad, Militz delivered public lectures on the subject of concentration. Many of these lectures were published in *The Master Mind,* a magazine that she edited from 1911 to 1919, before being collected and published as a book in 1918. Calling attention to the importance of developing the mind, she reaffirmed Joseph Rodes Buchanan's "science" of psychometry.[52] She also gave numerous examples of how concentration could become the key to worldly success. Her method, which she called *Christian Yoga,* was a combination of the Hindu practice of spiritual concentration known as yoga and "taking on Christ." In recommending this approach, she discounted the "worldly methods of thought-control" as imperfect and misleading. Instead, she emphasized the power of repose (i.e., "letting the thought rest in your mind") and reflecting on the "Christ-self," by which she meant the shadow of the real self that is one with God. Achieving this made for clear thinking and the removal of the three Hindu impediments: *tamas* (inertia), *rajas* (negative passions), and *sattvas* (self-righteousness). Militz devoted many of her lectures to the art of "decomposing" (relaxing the muscles) and the power of silence.[53] It was through concentration that one entered through the "Christ-Door" to enjoy the benefits of "cosmic consciousness" and the ability to overcome disease and life's other discomforts. Achieving this came by way of the bhakti yoga, the heart way; raja yoga, soul way; gnana yoga, mind way; and karma yoga, self way.[54] If this was done, whatever one desired would be fulfilled. In *All Things Are Possible to Them That Believe* (1905), she reasoned that God was "as willing to give us good gifts as is any earthly father." By saying the words "it is," the individual brought to reality whatever was wished.[55]

Militz codified the elements of her Home of Truth in the following principles:

> God is All and All are One.
> Respect all paths, all people and ourselves.
> Forgiveness is the key to happiness and inner peace.
> God is Love and Love is who we are.
> Love extends itself. Love prevails.
> Peace is our single goal, the aim of our living here.
> We choose Peace.
> We are responsible for the world we see and our experiences here.
> What we sow, we reap.
> Giving and receiving are one.
> Gratitude is our way to Love.[56]

Everyone had the ability to enjoy healing power, Militz explained. It was a gift given to Jesus "to awaken man out of his false dream about himself, his neighbor and his God, and restore him to the consciousness of his powers and how to use them." Provided the application was repeated daily, healing became instantaneous, lifting the healer and patient into "Christ-consciousness." This applied to old chronic diseases as well as those diseases pronounced incurable. Healing required the consent of the patient and a week's course of treatments either in the presence of the patient or through absent treatment. Once during the day and again later at night, healers were directed to silently call the patient's name three times and then reason with the patient using the following statements:

First day: Deny inheritance of the flesh and its evil. Deny lust and sensual desire. Affirm man's inheritance from God, and his true state to be pure and his desires spiritual.

Second day: Deny the deceptive influences of evil and the delusions of matter. Affirm Good as the only influence, Spirit as the only substance, and the law of the Spirit, the only law.

Third day: Deny the power of sin. Deny the power of selfishness, pride, avarice, envy, jealousy and malice. Affirm divine Love and Forgiveness, omnipresent and omnipotent.

Fourth day: Deny fear, guilt and shame. Affirm faith and peace.

Fifth day: Deny weakness, ignorance and foolishness. Affirm strength, knowledge and good judgment.

Sixth day: The Spiritual Baptism, affirming and confirming the healing with words of unity and satisfaction.[57]

By 1911, Militz had broken with the Unity Church, taking her Home of Truth on a more independent course but remaining a member of the International New Thought Alliance. Home of Truth spread through numerous cities in California, including Alameda, Los Angeles, San Diego, Oakland, San Jose, Sacramento, Berkeley, and Sierra Madre. Militz's other writings include *Primary Lessons in Christian Living and Healing* (1904), *Spiritual Housekeeping* (1910), *Prosperity Through the Knowledge and Power of Mind* (1913), *The Renewal of the Body* (1914), and *Concentration* (1918), some of which helped to fuse Christian virtues to the prosperity gospel.[58] Her books and articles, along with her founding of the University of Christ in Los Angeles, provide ample evidence of her influence on the New Thought movement. Later, as an officer of the National New Thought Alliance and as president of the New Thought Exposition Committee that helped organize events for the Panama-Pacific International Exposition in

San Francisco in 1915, she added her own perspective to further crystalize New Thought's beliefs in healthy-mindedness, happiness, and prosperity.[59]

When Militz died in 1924, her followers delayed burial for several days, hovering over her casket in the firm belief that her corpse would return to life, a promise she made to her "chosen ones" before she died. Disappointed that she did not return, they reasoned that "she has simply found the land to which she went too interesting and beautiful to leave."[60]

Affiliated Churches and Independent Associations

As the mind-cure movement spread across the country, its churches, clubs, and associations created any number of perplexities for their respective members. For one thing, their shared opposition to dogma and formalized structure left few, if any, instructions on the proper conduct for their services and activities, some of which were essentially spontaneous while others drifted in and out of structure. Similarly, the negative feelings harbored against the dogmatic extremes of Eddy's metaphysical idealism often led to crises of conviction, solemnity, and self-scrutiny. Hints of fissures worried ministers and parishioners alike as they promoted the benevolent dispositions of their organizations and awakened excitement among those wishing to mobilize ever-larger interdenominational societies and associations. Companions in the cause of Christ, they worried that, as instruments of New Thought's ecumenical designs, they might bring harm to their own local organizations. Ameliorating these concerns was the realization that the New Thought movement included many whose motivations were broad-based and spirited. Having repudiated wire-drawn metaphysics and become convinced that the sciences had been vulgarized by materialism, they forged ministries that were strong on personal development, affections, sympathies, and hopes—a union of intelligence, public spirit, and moral principle.

In 1894, Sarah Jane Farmer (1847–1916), assisted by Frederick Reed, who would later become secretary of the Metaphysical Club, organized the Green Acre Conferences at Eliot, Maine. Like other leaders in this newly minted movement, Farmer considered Jesus to be one among many great prophets who had shown the path to the good life. She was as fond of quoting Emerson and the Scottish historian Thomas Carlyle (1795–1881) as she was referencing Jesus and the Vedas. The conferences, held under the pines at Green Acre, were rich in spiritual suggestion, revelation, and lessons of the soul. They were the outcome of the World's Parliament of Religions held in Chicago during the Columbian Exposition of 1893, which witnessed scholars from Hindu, Buddhist, Confucian, Parsi (Zoroastrian), Muslim, Christian, and Jewish faiths come together to discuss their common interests in an atmosphere of openness. From this event, a new consciousness filtered among America's alternative religious movements, bringing waves of counterculture ideas into the conversation of those seeking new religious truths. The result was a flowering of scholarship, much of which was absorbed into the budding New Thought movement.[61] Green Acre became home to both Christian-oriented gatherings and those that expounded the Vedanta philosophy of Hinduism as well as, later, the Bahá'í faith of Persia. Messengers from multiple religions came there to whisper their revelations on life and happiness while their hearers realized a communal union from the conference's varied lessons. "The summer at Green Acre," explained Mary Hanford Ford, a frequent lecturer at the conference, "leaves one with the joyous certainty that the day of God has come, and that more and more, both within us and without, divine power and love are altering the conditions of the world."[62]

Green Acre helped in the founding of the Procopeia Society, which organized in Boston in 1894–95, and the Metaphysical Club, which formed in 1895 "to promote interest in and the practice of a true spiritual philosophy of life and happiness; to show that through right thinking one's loftiest ideas may be brought into perfect realization; to advance the intelligent and systematic treatment of disease by mental methods." The club, whose originators included L. B. Macdonald, J. W. Lindy, and Frederick Reed, not only aroused public interest in mental healing, but displayed an ongoing openness to the world's great religions. It even constructed a "silence room" where members could sit and contemplate spiritual truths.[63]

Among the Metaphysical Club's earliest lecturers were abolitionist and feminist poet Julia Ward Howe (1819–1910); writer and preacher Minot Judson Savage (1841–1918); professor and physicist Amos E. Dolbear (1837–1910), author of the influential *Matter, Ether and Motion* (1903) and *Science and Theism* (1897); and essayist and critic Hamilton Wright Mabie (1846–1916). The club set the standard for societies elsewhere and was a clear indication that the mental healing movement was seeking a more inclusive audience. In 1898, the club's magazine, *The Journal of Practical Metaphysics*, with Paul Tyner as editor and Horatio W. Dresser as associate editor, merged with *The Arena*, which was published in Boston. A year later, *The Arena* moved to New York, where it ceased to be connected with New Thought. In its place, the periodical *Practical Ideals* was established under the editorship of Jonathan W. Winkley to represent the club's thinking. Through all these changes, mental healing remained the focal point of the club.

Out of the Metaphysical Club emerged the International Metaphysical League, which first met at the Tremont Temple in Boston in 1899, then a year later at Madison Square Garden Concert Hall, and at annual meetings in Chicago, St. Louis, and other cities. It was at the Tremont Temple convention that its delegates began using the term "New Thought." Reorganized in 1906, the League transformed itself into a federation of New Thought centers. In 1908, the League changed its constitution and name to become the National New Thought Alliance. Between 1908 and 1914, its conventions offered classes on such subjects as "God in Man," "Practical Metaphysics," "Psychical Secrets," "The Way Unto the Perfect," "The Evolution of Christ in Consciousness," "Masters of Yourself and Your World," "Symbol Psychology," and "Unfolding Individuality."[64]

In 1914, the Alliance changed its name to the International New Thought Alliance (INTA). That year, the INTA held its annual convention in England under the auspices of the Higher Thought Centre and, a year later, opened in San Francisco in connection with the Panama-Pacific International Exposition. In 1916, the INTA defined its purpose: "To teach the infinitude of the Supreme One; the Divinity of Man and his Infinite possibilities through the creative power of constructive thinking and obedience to the voice of the Indwelling Presence, which is our source of Inspiration, Power, Health, and Prosperity." Over and over again, INTA representatives reiterated the fact that their movement made no claim to being a new religion but rather a highly porous system of metaphysics that found both church and unchurched expressions of mental powers. The INTA made no effort to ask people to leave their churches, only to become better members of their own churches and associations in order to carry forth the message of Christ to all people.[65]

Even with centers located in Boston, New York, Chicago, Kansas City, and San Francisco, the New Thought movement lacked the organizational regimentation of the major religious dominations, leaving it vulnerable to the whims of localized interests, some of which were compelling and others less so. Like so many national movements, New Thought had less influence in the rural South and Southwest, whose citizens seemed content adhering to the anti-materialist and anti-evolutionary dicta of fundamentalist Christianity. Nevertheless, in addition to the churches and organizations listed above, numerous smaller groups have affiliated under the umbrella of the New Thought. The ones that remain active today will be discussed further in chapter 9; some examples of groups that did not survive include:

> **The Church of the Higher Life.** Founded in Boston in 1894 by the Rev. Helen Van-Anderson (b. 1859), the church claimed no formal creed. Stressing a combination of God's immanence and a principle of love similar to Swedenborg's, the church revolved around friendly fellowship; healing services, which included sending out cheerful notes to invalids confined in hospitals and reformatories; an Emerson Study Club whose meetings included discussions of life's problems; meetings for the benefit of mothers; and training classes to promote greater spirituality.[66]

> **The Church and School of the New Civilization.** Founded by Dr. Julia Seton (1862–1950) in 1905, the church operated centers in Boston, Manhattan, Brooklyn, Cleveland, Buffalo, Chicago, and Denver.[67] Each of the ministries represented a philosophy grounded in individual freedom. Its mantra was that sin and evil had no place in the world, and it emphasized that each individual

must seek his or her fullest potential within divine will. Church members were profoundly religious in a very open and nonsectarian manner. By the outbreak of the First World War, the church represented a set of tenets that included God as omnipotent and omnipresent, Spirit as the ultimate reality, human selfhood as divine, divinely attuned thought as a positive force for good, disease as mental in origin, and right thinking as having a healing effect.[68]

Altrurian Society. Founded in 1911 by Lawrence Augustus Fealy in Birmingham, Alabama, the society had as its goal "To Heal, Teach Abundance and Happiness, and otherwise perform the ordinances of God." The society disappeared in the 1930s, but not before it had published numerous pamphlets.[69]

League for the Larger Life. Founded in New York City in 1916, the League provided Sunday services as well as weekday classes and lectures on such topics as mental health, prosperity, and biblical study. Its first president was writer, businessman, and physician Orison Swett Marden, MD (1850–1924). Early supporters of the organization and its annual conferences included the Vedanta Society, Higher Thought Centre, First Church of Divine Science, and the Freedom Fraternity.

Psychiana. Formed in 1929 in Moscow, Idaho, by Englishman Frank Bruce Robinson (1886–1948) as a mail-order enterprise, it recruited followers through direct mail solicitations and magazine advertisements. Promising health, wealth, and happiness through positive thinking, Robinson presented himself as a prophet who offered books and biweekly correspondence lessons to subscribers. Following legal problems concerning his citizenship, Robinson was ordered to leave the country. Eventually, with the aid of Senator William Borah, he returned to become a naturalized citizen. Following his death in 1948, the organization collapsed.[70]

* * *

As a predominantly metropolitan movement celebrating the American philosophy of optimism, New Thought grew at a prodigious rate, impelled by the use of spiritual and metaphysical language to espouse a belief in healthy-mindedness, prosperity, and personal magnetism. As the various churches and groups that formed under the New Thought banner struggled to define a coherent, unified vision, what emerged was an idealistic, syncretic, and hybrid set of beliefs, built from a combination of ancient and modern religious and metaphysical systems as well from ideas drawn loosely from science and pseudoscience. Drawing from this potpourri of principles, its proponents proclaimed that the mental or spiritual world was the only true reality and that thought-as-power (i.e., the cultivation of the divine within each person) was the basis for inner truth about the self and otherness. Recoiling from the biblical God who had reputedly sent life's sorrows as tests of human beings' faith, New Thought practiced visualization, affirmation, and prayer as a means for realizing health, harmony, peace, and prosperity. Thought-as-power became the basis of this "Christ Science" or "mind-cure" system begun by Quimby and matured through a generation of writers, lecturers, and publishers intent on accentuating life's positive attributes.

Teaching the divinity of each individual and the infinite possibilities available through the power of creative thinking, New Thought's churches and affiliated associations organized for the purpose of finding and exploiting the routes to personal happiness. Built on the notion that success was a sign of virtue, they looked to the best ways of holding to a positive attitude and thinking one's way to wealth and happiness. They concluded that since thoughts can materialize, success lay in the ability to attract, persuade, and influence one's fellow human beings. Success was the outcome of the quality of mind, its character, and its temperament. Provided that the individual exercised perseverance, determination, energy, and patience, anything was possible and likely probable.

5

The Psychologies of Healthy-Mindedness

*Psychotherapy . . . is a most terrifying word,
but we are forced to use it because there is no
other which serves to distinguish us from
Christian Scientists, the New Thought
people, the faith healers, and the thousand
and one other schools which have in common
the disregard for medical science and the
accumulated knowledge of the past.*

—Richard C. Cabot, MD,
"The American Type of Psychotherapy"

At the dawn of the twentieth century, psychology in the United States contained a rich overlay of religious content that was both fundamental and far-reaching in its influence. Although the labors of French neurologists Jean-Martin Charcot (1825–93), Pierre Janet (1859–1947), and other European leaders in abnormal psychology paved the way for a largely academic and secular interpretation of psychology, Americans were notable for imposing a more religious motif on the discipline. Whether referring to works such as Daniel Garrison Brinton's *The Religious Sentiment: Its Source and Aim* (1876), Henry Rutgers Marshall's *Instinct and Reason* (1898), Morris Jastrow's *The Study of Religion* (1901), William James's *The Varieties of Religious Experience* (1902), James Henry Leuba's *The Belief in God and Immortality* (1916), or James

Bissett Pratt's *The Religious Consciousness* (1920), American psychologists used religious beliefs to explain key elements in human nature, i.e., feelings, sentiments, moral values, repressed tendencies, or simply instincts. Religious belief, with its hypotheses of God and immortality, was an essential factor in the examination of self-consciousness and the issues of abnormal psychology. Religious-based psychologies were used to interpret the complexities of consciousness despite limitations with respect to objectivity, applicability, and reliability. God was the object of meditation and cognition and the symbol of social values, while non-belief became the explanation for deviance. Mind was not an instrument of genetics or adaptation, but a principle of awareness aspiring toward some universal, perfect Mind or Selfhood. Even the discovery of subliminal consciousness took shape within the confines of a worldview that included an indwelling Spirit and the inner self's aspiration to merge with the cosmic or universal Mind. In the world of psychoanalytic scholarship, divinity had become the object of humanity's aspiration, and its antithesis was considered the reason for its less admirable traits and failings. In spite of the uniqueness of this narrow view, America's early psychologists used this religious aspiration, or the lack of it, to define personal character, repressed desires, moral reform, social justice, democracy, and humanism in general.

William James

The psychologist and philosopher William James (1842–1910) made an enormous impact on philosophy, psychology, and religion. Son of the Swedenborgian theologian Henry James Sr. (1811–82) and brother of the prominent novelist Henry James (1843–1916), he found himself constrained through much of his life with physical and psychological ailments, including depression. After taking up scientific studies at the Lawrence Scientific School at Harvard, he moved on to medical school, earning his MD in 1869. Instead of embarking on a medical practice, he chose to teach anatomy and physiology at Harvard beginning in 1873, rising to professorships in psychology in 1889 and philosophy in 1897. Drawn to the study of the human mind and what he called "soul-sickness," he studied the work of Hermann Helmholtz (1821–94) and

Pierre Janet, who were developing psychology into a science. He also joined in lively philosophical discussions with Charles Sanders Peirce (1839–1914), Oliver Wendell Holmes Sr. (1809–94), and Chauncey Wright (1830–75); participated in the early activities of the Metaphysical Club; and influenced numerous later luminaries such as Boris Sidis (1867–1923), George Santayana (1863–1952), G. Stanley Hall (1844–1924), Ralph Barton Perry (1876–1957), Morris Raphael Cohen (1880–1947), and Clarence Irving Lewis (1883–1964). James's writings include *Principles of Psychology* (1890), *The Will to Believe, and Other Essays in Popular Philosophy* (1897), *The Varieties of Religious Experience* (1902), *Pragmatism, A Pluralistic Universe* (1909), *The Meaning of Truth* (1909), and *Some Problems in Philosophy* (1911). His eloquent writings, in which he juxtaposed the so-called "sick soul" with healthy-mindedness, provided compelling evidence that those individuals possessed of optimism, courage, hope, and trust were better able to throw off the effects of depression and melancholy. Aware of both the sunny and dark sides of life, James struggled to find common ground.

Despite, or perhaps because of, his Harvard medical degree, James openly opposed medical licensing laws, viewing them as a not-too-subtle mechanism designed to defend the status quo in science and therapeutics. Instead, he advocated a much broader definition of healing, namely, one that was inclusive of so-called irregular methods such those found in homeopathy, Christian Science, Spiritualism, osteopathy, magnetic healing, naturopathy, and other unconventional therapies. His opposition to the Massachusetts Medical Registration Acts of 1894 and 1898 represented a clarion call for a more open-ended approach to healing, recognizing that the state of medical science was far from complete. Unlike his colleagues, who were appalled by the level of chicanery occurring outside mainstream medicine, James defended unlicensed healers, persuaded that there was value in allowing people to choose their own therapies. Indeed, he viewed conventional medicine's history as one of "ignorance clad in authority, and riding over men's bodies and souls."[1]

A champion of radical empiricism, James nonetheless took a strong interest in Spiritualism and the paranormal, willing to set aside his scientific groundings to explore more esoteric belief systems. He showed particular interest in hypnosis, suggestion, and other related mind-cure therapeutics. Here, he believed, was the Achilles's heel of conventional medicine. Ruling out such therapies had forced allopathic medicine into a too-narrowly defined reductionism that precluded a wealth of new knowledge. To be clear, however, he was not effusive in his support of these unconventional theories. As he remarked to Boston neurologist James J. Putnam, "I am not fond and cannot understand a word of their jargon except their precept of assuming yourself well and claiming health rather than sickness which I am sure is magnificent."[2] He was also not oblivious to the self-deceptions that often mixed in with these unconventional therapies. Some of it was "so moon-struck with optimism and so vaguely expressed," he once observed, that "an academically trained intellect finds it almost impossible to read it at all." Nevertheless, New Thought and Christian Science said much about the practical character of the American people and had an important influence on both religion and medicine. James's particular interest in the teachings of these two groups stemmed from the fact that, pragmatically speaking, they oftentimes "worked." As a physician and psychologist, he was quick to appreciate the importance of the role the mind played in relation to health and disease. He considered the writings of Horatio Dresser, Ralph Waldo Trine, and Henry Wood among the more coherent representations of this literature.[3]

In his 1900–1902 Gillford lectures given at the University of Edinburgh on the "Religion of Healthy-Mindedness," and afterwards published as *The Varieties of Religious Experience,* James spoke of the growing affinity between religion and happiness that had become popular within Christian culture. He detected among its advocates a "cosmic emotion" that took the form of freedom from the "sinister theologies" of the past and an enthusiasm for what they perceived as a "union with the divine." "We all have some friend, perhaps more often feminine than masculine, and young than old whose soul is of this sky-blue tint, whose affinities are rather with flowers and birds and all enchanting innocencies [sic] than with dark human passions, who can think no ill of man or God, and in whom religious gladness, being in possession from the outset, needs no deliverance from any antecedent burden," he wrote.[4] He found examples of this temperament on the fringes of the Roman church and among the antinomian and latitudinarian elements of Protestantism, particularly the Unitarians. It was a temperament characterized by a passionate and almost mystical emotion, something that the poet Walt Whitman considered even pagan in its defiant celebration of life.[5]

James gave the name "mind-cure" to the New Thought movement, describing it as "an optimistic scheme of life, with both a speculative and a practical side [and which] . . . must now be reckoned with as a genuine religious power." He traced its ideas to six distinct sources: Scripture, Emersonian transcendentalism, Berkeleyan idealism, spiritism, optimistic evolutionism, and Hinduism. Common to all these sources was "an intuitive belief in the all-saving power of healthy-minded attitudes . . . and a correlative contempt for doubt, fear, worry, and all nervously precautionary states of mind." They shared the rejection of evil and of all invasive elements of negativity, including disease. Nevertheless, James refused to subscribe to New Thought's belief that sin and evil were only "conditions" that existed in the mind; he never lost sight of the reality of human existence. Healthy-mindedness did not mean isolation from reality any more than the healthy soul could exist without bodily nourishment. The power of healthy-mindedness was not without limits.[6]

With the popularity that followed the publication of *The Varieties of Religious Experience,* James turned his attention to the germinal elements of psychology embedded in New Thought writings, which had tapped into powers that conventional medicine had barely considered but that had already proven their utility. By accessing the subconscious, whether through suggestion, silence, breathing exercises, visualization, relaxation, or repetition, healers of various stripes had succeeded in adding value to the existing armamentarium of therapeutic practices.[7] In fact, the powers inherent in suggestion and belief had trumped much of Western medicine's reductionist claims. The power of an idea was a force unto itself that, properly utilized, set the individual on a course of bodily and mental health. Mind cure was a force to be claimed rather than rejected out of hand as a tool of the impostor or quack. In James's open universe, healthy-mindedness demanded receptivity to all of life's healing energies—a readiness to accept both material and mental forces that can interact with the body as well as with the mind's subconscious levels. By itself, reductionist medicine was incomplete; only when partnered with healthy-mindedness did it overcome the fear and pain expressive in the "sick soul."[8]

James addressed the movement of healthy-mindedness from a psychological point of view, but also with a perspective that included the existence of a personal God or impersonal Force. He explained that the cultivation of healthy-mindedness as a religious attribute was the distinguishing reason for its optimism, its rejection of evil, its acceptance of the theory of evolution, and its concept of universal progress. While New Thought contained within its fold a number of competing and sometimes truculent sects (James considered Christian Science an element within the New Thought movement), their agreements were much more profound than their differences in that they all showed a practical side that was intimately connected with healthy-mindedness. Choosing to ignore the disagreeable ailments of life that varied from some level of existence to nonexistence, they attacked the beast of fear by replacing it with a subliminal consciousness focused on the Divine. It was misalignment of the subliminal consciousness that explained negative behavior. For the followers of New Thought, the union of the self with the More, a goal common to numerous religions and religious experiences, came by way of a process that included relaxation; going into the silence; and trusting in the care of higher powers to take care of one's destiny. The importance placed on the oneness of the individual with God and "relaxing by letting go" were traits surprisingly similar in character to those he found in elements of Lutheranism (justification by faith), Puritanism (concept of piety), and Wesleyanism (acceptance of free grace).[9]

As explained by James, there was a force beyond consciousness that brought help to the sick soul. While secular psychologists interpreted this force as a certain something within the subconscious self, New Thought attributed the force to an external source. Both, however, chose to use relaxation, concentration, and meditation as tools to acquire it.[10] James could not decide if this force that helped the sick soul existed in the senses and intellect or transcended the individual self. Regardless of its source, he admired this abandonment of self to the More and its embodiment in healthy-mindedness. He made no claim to the authoritative nature of this More; he simply accepted the practical value of the belief and its effect.

In the tradition of Alfred Binet (1857–1911), Josef Breuer (1842–1925), Pierre Janet, and Sigmund Freud, James explored the inner eruptions that surfaced through hallucinations, pain, and other symptoms of the body and conscious mind. Like them, he rejected the heavy-handed therapeutics of biomedicine with its myriad of drugs and appliances. Similarly, he judged the leading figures among the world religions of Christianity, Islam, Buddhism, and Hinduism as "morbid-minded," having posited evil as an essential prop around which humanity was to find its compass. Instead, he found himself attracted to a wider meaning of life, one that was humanistic, transcendent, and boldly passionate about life's possibilities. In this schema of things, immortality played only an ancillary role to the quality of existence. His was a pluralistic universe whose possibilities exceeded its dissonance. He repudiated monistic religion and imperious rationalism in favor of a more accidental universe where the material and spiritual elements of the self intermingled in bliss. This explains his admiration for the varied forms of mind-cure therapies prevalent in his day, because they tended to link health and happiness with an ambitious optimism rather than with any sense of evil, denial, or bodily mortification. It was the therapeutic function of belief—however tinged by religious, agnostic, or even atheistic origination—that healed the troubled soul more convincingly than biomedical reductionism. While Freud and his disciples had chosen to isolate the psychological problems with certain periods and residual feelings within the life cycle, James was content to place his bet on the creative energy, luminosity, and moral helpfulness of the religious experience.[11]

In James's universe, nothing was absolute or absolutely simple; even the most insignificant experience was related to something else. In such a universe, the goal of healthy-mindedness afforded an opportunity to exercise creative thought (including intuition) and experience by putting ideas to work and evaluating their results in a manner that the British physician and psychologist Havelock Ellis (1859–1939) epitomized in *The Dance of Life* (1923).[12] Those individuals who went through life in a spiritually joyful manner and with minimum awareness of evil were those who lived a more meaningful life. This explains James's preference for the New Thought movement and its deliberate choice of good as the very essence of existence. For those who were healthy minded, or potentially so, the message was one of courage, hope, and trust. It was a realization that humanity, at one with the Divine, was immune to the prospect of fear, disease, and other negative habits. For those who found the message of mind cure agreeable, the power of suggestion affected both the conscious and unconscious, turning the individual into an engine of personal strength and comfort.[13]

The strength of the mind-cure movement was not found in its theology but in its practical results, a characteristic that James found especially attractive. Regardless of the origination of its power—whether from inside or outside the person—mind cure "worked," and its successes were strikingly similar to those attributed to Jesus and the early Christian church. This mental energy, which took the form of emotional excitement, volitional effort, and abstract ideas, became the subject of his talk "The Energies of Men," delivered in his presidential address to the American Philosophical Association in 1906. In it, he recounted various political, scientific, philosophic, and religious conversions and the manner in which these conversions loosed energies that challenged the will. He took special note of the converts to New Thought, Christian Science, metaphysical healing, and other forms of spiritual philosophy whose ideas were focused on healthy-mindedness and optimism. Their common feature, he explained, was their tendency to suppress what he called "fearthought." He wondered openly to his listeners how far the mind-cure movement was destined to prevail and what ultimate powers it might energize through the exercise of affirmation, suggestion, and repetition.[14]

Horatio W. Dresser

Among James's more admiring students was Horatio Willis Dresser (1866–1954), a philosopher and religious thinker who spent much of his life defending the healing theories and techniques of the New Thought movement. Born in 1866 in Yarmouth, Maine, the year of Quimby's death, he moved with his parents and siblings around the country as his father took up various forms of employment. At age thirteen he left school to learn telegraphy, and at sixteen assumed charge of a railroad station on the Central Pacific line in Pinole, California. In 1882, he moved with his parents, Julius and Annetta Dresser, to Boston, where they opened a mental-healing practice. There, Dresser became a reporter, learned the business of the publishing world working for the *New England Farmer,* and he also began a lifelong study of Emerson. Two years later, he joined his parents in their mental-healing practice at 14 West Chester Park in Boston, where he helped with lectures and catered to the burgeoning market of aging Spiritualists, troubled transcendentalists, curious Unitarians and Universalists, and former Eddyites. There, too, Dresser prepared himself to enter Harvard in 1891. The initial funds to support his education came from a local patroness through the auspices of Richard Hodgson (1855–1905), a psychical researcher and secretary of the newly formed American Society for Psychical Research, in anticipation of Dresser being trained as a "scientific medium." When Dresser learned the purpose behind the support, he declined the money and secured his own resources to complete his degree. Dresser believed in clairvoyance and telepathy but viewed the possibility of his own mediumship abilities as secondary to the study of philosophy.[15]

While working on his baccalaureate, Dresser wrote and delivered public lectures under the general title of "Talks on Life in Relation to Health," one of which was subsequently published as *The Immanent God: An Essay* (1895). In it, he spoke of God as love, the only reality in which all activity originated (Emerson had given its best expression in the term "Over-Soul") and where evolution, not creation, was the law of life.[16] That same year, he published his first full-length book, *The Power of Silence,* which by 1903 had gone through fifteen editions. He also found time to help organize the Metaphysical Club of Boston and the International Metaphysical League. In addition, he founded the monthly *Journal of Practical Metaphysics* (1896–98) to advocate for a "more harmonious, rational, and ethical life, and to derive this help from all the resources of human thought." In 1898, the journal merged with *The Arena,* a literary and political magazine devoted to social and economic reform founded by Benjamin O. Flower in 1889. Dresser served for a short time as *The Arena's* associate editor, using its pages to introduce readers to New Thought ideas and concepts, but left to found *The Higher Law* (1898–1902), a magazine that was dedicated to advanced ideals. During this time, he also conducted correspondence courses in spiritual philosophy through the auspices of the Philosophical Publishing Company. In 1898, he married Alice Mae Reed (1870–1961), a graduate of Wellesley, whose brother Frederick Reed managed the Green Acre New Thought summer program in Maine.[17]

In 1904, Dresser earned his master's degree in philosophy from Harvard, followed by his PhD in 1907, studying under William James and working as an assistant to the idealist Josiah Royce (1855–1916), whose metaphysical views were strikingly similar to those of Hegel. Dresser's doctoral dissertation, *The Element of Irrationality in the Hegelian Dialectic,* was signed by James, Hugo Münsterberg, and G. H. Palmer on May 1, 1906. It formed a major part of his *The Philosophy of the Spirit,* published in 1908. During this time, Dresser was a frequent contributor to the Fillmores' *Unity* magazine, writing on Plato and Emerson, emphasizing the former's belief in the essential goodness of human beings and stressing the latter's penetrating insight into the times; demonstrating the importance of the laws of compensation, correspondences, and degrees; and writing on the progressive nature of the Spirit.[18] From 1903 to 1911, he taught philosophy at both Harvard and Radcliffe, served a short time as professor of applied psychology at the Massachusetts College of Osteopathy and, in 1911, was appointed professor of philosophy and education at Ursinus College in Collegeville, Pennsylvania, which had been established by the German Reformed Church. He taught there until 1913, when he resigned to resume his literary work.[19]

In the months before Europe plunged into the First World War, G. P. Putnam's Sons of New York and London published Dresser's *The Religion of the Spirit in Modern Life* (1914). The book is important in that it signifies a restatement of New Thought's religious spirit from one that was predominantly Christian in expression to one that was much more representative of the world's philosophies. As with many of New Thought's representative spokespeople, Dresser had been greatly influenced by the World's Parliament of Religions in 1893, and he presided over a series of subsequent conferences held between 1909 and 1912. These experiences gave him a much deeper understanding of the currents of spirituality common across the world's religions. He found among their discussions an inner center or heart that was more constructive than any partisan creed. As a consequence, his book was intended to discern that which was essential and practical among the great religions as they spoke of the divine presence in the soul. The object was not to find a theological or philosophical basis on which all could agree, but to understand how each, despite their doctrinal and ritualistic differences, sought out the Indwelling Spirit.

An admirer of Victor Cousin's philosophy of eclecticism, Dresser held that all the great philosophies and religions contained elements of truth. When assembling meaning out of their distinctive traditions, spiritual thought grew at the expense of sectarian beliefs and practices. What Dresser desired most was recognition of a spiritual household where all of God's children, of whatever race or tongue, could come together as one family in mutual love and common worship. By this he did not mean their absorption into a single denomination but a community of spirit, of mutual respect, devotion to knowledge and righteousness, sympathy, and helpfulness to every soul.[20]

Dresser found three tendencies in modern life that represented departures from prior belief systems. First was the tendency to reinterpret life in social terms, a sharp departure from the individualism of the nineteenth century; second was the growth of idealistic philosophy; and the third was the realization of the presence of God in each individual. For Dresser, the more significant of the three tendencies was the latter, which had come to him by way of Emerson and then was reinforced by Plato, Hegel, and Royce. But it was William James who had influenced him the most by emphasizing the practical value of the relationship between the soul, God, and society. In 1917, Dresser published a collection of essays titled *The Spirit of the New Thought* (1917), followed by *Handbook of the New Thought* (1917), considered two of the more important representations of the New Thought movement.[21]

In 1918, Dresser enlisted for service in the Fourth French Army as director of a *Foyer du Soldat,* a program arranged between the War Work Council of the American YMCA and the French Army to improve soldier morale by providing books, stationery, entertainment, and canteen service to the troops at the front.[22] Upon his return after the war, he became a minister of the General Convention of the Church of the New Jerusalem, followed by a brief stint as pastor of a Swedenborgian church in Portland, Maine. He continued to write throughout his life. His *A History of the New Thought Movement* (1919) laid out the movement's complete history to date; he edited the first formally published collection of Quimby's writings, *The Quimby Manuscripts* (1921); and he also wrote *Psychology in Theory and Application* (1924), *History of Ancient and Medieval Philosophy* (1927), and *A History of Modern Philosophy* (1928).

Entering the Silence

In *The Power of Silence; a Study of the Values and Ideals of the Inner Life* (1906), Dresser offered a practical method for bringing the principles of philosophic study to all. The book consisted of a series of lectures delivered before various metaphysical societies in and around the Boston area explaining a form of meditation he called the "power of silence" or "entering the silence." Much like Quimby and Evans before him, silence was not intended to infer quietude, or making the mind a blank, or the loss of consciousness. Nor, for that matter, did it imply pantheism based on Eastern religions or yogic exercises. Rather, he intended it to describe a method of concentrating the mind on a single uplifting idea such as found in an inspiring book, poem, artistic performance, or scriptural passage. His book also signaled a revised view of mental healing from that held by Quimby and his parents' generation. Believing that suffering was not just a state of mind but a condition of the entire person, he emphasized activity that was both mental and physical. One's whole conduct or mode of life, not merely one's thought, enabled one to live reposefully and purposely through the "tide of life."[23] Philosophi-

cal thinking, he explained, required the power of silence in order to realize the meaning and spirit of belief. Access to divine wisdom lay not in
reasoning, since "no attempted logic is more absurd than the endeavor
to prove the existence of God."[24] Rather, it was the experience of God's
immediacy and immanence in the world and revealed through silence.
Although God was not identical with the world, the world was made
real by his immanent presence.[25]

Dresser intended for his writings to bring evolutionary philosophy
and life into a closer and more practical relationship by conjoining the
two seemingly contradictory terms "pragmatic" and "wisdom." It was
this objective that distinguished his theistic philosophy from other
mysticisms. "Our existence in the universe is made known through
experience," he wrote. "By studying experience, testing our theories by
further experience, and keeping close to the assured results, we may
not only solve our practical problems but gain knowledge of life as a
whole."[26]

The mental life that best revealed the divine presence required individuals to consider what nature is and how it is made known. Nature was
spread before humanity as a vast banquet made tangible through what
the conscious mind understood from the senses. It was the conscious
mind that became the medium through which the world was known.
But as individual thinkers penetrated deeper into their consciousness
they began to blend with the All. The deepest self was not physical or
intellectual, but spiritual.[27] Humanity's objective was to realize this
relationship to the All through inward repose. With God as immanent
and evolution as the true statement of life's process of becoming, it was
important for the individual to establish a "centre of repose" that was
receptive to the spirit.[28] Being restfully silent was to cultivate life, not as
an intellectual, but as an artist or poet who is able to penetrate beyond
self-consciousness to breathe in silence before the divine presence. "Not
until we live reposefully," Dresser wrote, "do we begin to experience the
benefit of our powers."[29]

Although the century had begun as an initial triumph for materialism, Dresser concluded that none of the evidence that bore upon
the origins and tendencies of the human species had been as dramatic

as the new science of psychology and the light it threw upon the inner world of human experience as a reasoning being. To understand the benefits of this inner world, he focused on three value-laden questions: What sort of world ought one to build from within? What is real? And what is worthwhile?[30] As noted above, he found that the value derived from silence had enabled individuals to realize life's true meaning. As social beings, humans achieved their highest level of the subconscious mind when they turned away from the "hurrying" world and, in calmness, reason, and intuitiveness, found harmony with other minds. Studying the mind as a manifestation of the Divine served to guide the soul unharmed through its many encounters. "He who thus knows himself, whose motive is right," he wrote, "may go forth into the world unconcernedly; for the conditions we attract depend upon the attitude within."[31]

Awake to a world of consciousness, Dresser viewed each individual as played upon by impulses, forces, emotions, and all manner of phenomena that concealed the inner world of the soul. In attempting to explain these workings—and drawing heavily from Swedenborg's descriptions of the interaction between soul and body—he referred to three states of the mind: *acute consciousness,* which included sensations, moods, ideas, and emotions; the *subconscious,* governed by suggestions offered by the conscious self; and finally, the *higher or reflective self,* which implied the use of insight, reason, and guidance. It was this latter state that served as a unifier; with it, one learned fully to know oneself. Unfortunately, too many individuals remained prisoners of the sense world and never experienced the soul's aspirations. Only a few felt the soul's awakening, and when it occurred, it became a turning point in life. Nevertheless, this inner self could be discovered early as well as late in life. Whenever this happened, it gave unity to life, sustaining and guiding it through times of weakness, supported by a divine presence that soothed the troubled mind and reassured it against the silence of the universe. Dresser described this experience as a "vibration," "force," "substance in motion," or "vortex motion in the ether" through which God spoke. "It is not all of God," he admitted, "but is that measure of the perfect which the imperfect can apprehend."[32]

Unlike the exponents of Eastern thought whose perception of the Absolute was that of an infinite ocean where the individual was little more than a ripple in the water, Dresser, like Emerson, insisted on keeping the principle of individuation an essential factor in the cosmos. Individual thought could never be set aside for another's wisdom, no matter how important. "I must ever have the courage of my convictions," he insisted, "and not only think, but express them." This was not a personal self-assertion masquerading as individuality, but an individuality that maintained itself with balance, repose, sociability, and practicality. As a devoted acolyte of Emerson, the prophet of self-reliance, Dresser viewed individuality as an escape into greater freedom. It was a positive quality that, when augmented by self-reliance, humility, love, and the desire to attain a higher self, led to the Christ ideal.[33]

At the heart of Dresser's self-reliant individual was the Christ-centered soul. "It would be the Christ ideal made real," he explained, a "harmony of action between the Father's will and the son's will, inseparably one, yet individually distinct in each of us." Each individual soul operated in a spiritual environment that allowed it to expand and grow, combining the best active thinking with calm, self-possessed direction, leading to a quickening of the Christ ideal. Each person had the potential for self-consciousness, self-adjustment, self-direction, and self-realization. That is what constituted individuality. It was each person's task to find his or her special place in the world, to learn the wisdom of his or her circumstances, to become a center of force or consciousness, and to do justice to the whole and its parts, to the individual and to God, and ultimately, to self and society.[34]

In addressing the seeming dichotomy between his belief in individuality, which was so much a characteristic of American thought, and the tendency in Eastern philosophy toward the impersonal, Dresser explained that the principle of individuation was an essential factor in any relationship to the Absolute—an explanation in which he seemed to be seeking common ground between the conflicting beliefs of James and Royce.

> True individuality is obviously the escape into freedom; and the probability is that the freer we are, the more individual. Absolute Being itself would seem to be served better by free individual

spirits; and freedom in this sense suggests a possible relationship to Absolute Being, which preserves our relative independence, and at the same time justifies our existence as parts of that Being. The center of Absolute Being, then, may be said to be successively in each and every individual. Each soul is as real as the Over-soul, for there is in reality no separateness; and from each soul-centre the whole is differently perceived and differently served. Absolute Being is thus absolute because and only because of individuals, without whom life would be an utterly cold and barren monotony.[35]

The soul's most fulfilling moment was as part of the eternal wisdom of God. For that reason, Dresser doubted that it was simply another product of evolution, having begun in time and subject to change and even extinction. If so, its temporary existence gave no hope for immortality. Alternatively, if the soul was "a pure and perfect essence" in no way bound by the conditions of life, then it had no need for this life. In resolving this conundrum, Dresser suggested that the Christ ideal brought the individual and Absolute together in unity. New Thought began, therefore, as a plea for individualism, free will, and self-activity, but the objective was not an egoistically individualistic world; instead, its objective was a world of social harmony and love born of the Christ ideal.[36]

Recognizing that the challenge before him was in finding the proper relation of the individual to society, Dresser set out to throw new light on this problem by expressing it as a contest between the spiritual ego, which was a free moral agent, and the environment, which he saw as mechanically determined. Noting that every individual was a "fresh revelation of God," and that the purpose in life was self-knowledge, self-mastery, and self-expression, he turned to James, whose philosophy of the practical described how the human soul could be opened to the fullness of human freedom. Humans may not have been born equal and free, but each must have the opportunity to realize these objectives in his or her own individual way. Doing so depended on the degree to which each soul moved consciously and deliberately toward self-analysis, judgment, and interaction with other minds. It also meant avoiding those creeds, dogmas, customs, habits, and authorities that kept the individual in servitude to other masters. Only by strengthening individuality could one realize real freedom. Such was the riddle of unity amid variety.[37]

Dresser saw freedom as bound by degrees, the elements of which contained labyrinths of ignorance, settled convictions, and false prophets. "If your insight bids you follow the doctrine or advice of another," he cautioned, "let it not be because of the greater strength of the other's mind, but because you have reflected upon the subject long enough so that your wisdom discovers the rationality of his." Otherwise, such allegiances led back to dependence. This required the application of "nonattachment," meaning that at the moment of belief, one should become its owner rather than its disciple; one should possess it and not become its property. Only then was an individual spiritually free to begin an ascent into liberty and an ever-broadening life that came through personal effort and self-understanding.[38]

Dresser praised his parents' generation for having labored to emancipate society from the physical aspects of cure, including those superficial mental theories based on animal magnetism. To their credit, they had replaced hypnosis with gentle reasoning and discovered the keys to self-control, equanimity, and poise. The conditions required for true spiritual healing, Dresser said, involved openness to suggestion as well as openness to the higher faculties of the human soul. While the physician defined disease as material and physical in nature, thus relegating the mind to a "secondary accompaniment," Quimby and his parents' generation of healers had focused their healing efforts on the patient's state of mind.[39]

As with Evans, receptivity played a critical factor in Dresser's view of spiritual healing. This did not mean receptivity to another's influence, but rather a readiness to be healed by the power of the Spirit. The sufferer's receptivity varied with habits and lifestyle. A person who was generally unreceptive in the outer world of experience behaved much the same in the interior world. This applied to the sufferer's openness to auto-suggestion and the desire to actively participate in the healing process. The same applied to the healer who sought to bring about a new and wiser attitude on the part of the patient. Obviously, if the healer had once been a sufferer, it made the process easier because of shared experiences. Having once suffered, the healer was more able to discern a patient's inner feelings. As an instrument of a higher power, the intuitive healer was able to sense the "atmosphere" of the patient and therefore be better able to read and guide him or her in thought.[40] The essential elements to a successful healing experience included the calmness of the healer, together with the patient's willingness to cooperate in the process. Dresser invoked Swedenborg's concept of prevailing or ruling love—that is, the thing that one loves more than anything else—to convey the idea that loving the right things results in an openness to divine influx. Quiet, poised, and master of the moment, the healer enveloped the patient in a harmonious atmosphere where the mind became free of its inner discord. The healing power was a vibration that moved through the ether and, after communicating with the patient, created a oneness with God and a realization of the divine ideal.[41]

Dresser's method applied to both disease and sin since, in each instance, the individual was brought in contact with the "omnipresent Wisdom." To the extent that an individual was capable of drawing upon Wisdom to conquer sin, he or she was also able to conquer disease. Putting faith to practice was to live as Jesus intended, recognizing divine guidance and purpose, and adjusting one's innermost thoughts and external actions to the fullness of God's love. Similarly, health represented the seizing and redirection of the mind toward a more spiritual life by freeing the inner self using uplifting and hopeful mental pictures.[42]

Swedenborg's Psychology

Dresser's most revealing work was an unpublished manuscript written over a period of several decades in which he sought to construct an integrative psychology using Swedenborg's law of correspondences and concept of divine influx. Like Evans before him, Dresser was infatuated with the breadth and depth of Swedenborg's genius and his efforts to undertake a comprehensive view of human personality. Swedenborg had provided an explanation of human beings' mental life, or inner world, replete with meanings, moral principles, and scientific truths.

In doing so, he had sought to restore to their proper place the role and meaning of the natural and spiritual worlds.

Though Swedenborg himself did not use psychological terminology when describing his visionary experiences, Dresser found precursors to modern psychology in *Arcana Coelesia* (1749–56, also known as *Secrets of Heaven*), followed by further elaborations in Swedenborg's *Divine Love and Wisdom* (1763) and *Divine Providence* (1764). In these works Swedenborg disclosed the reality and nature of the soul and the relationship between the workings of the mind, ethics, and religion. In *True Christianity* (1771), he laid out the psychology of regeneration. Central to his understanding of the workings of the mind, Swedenborg taught that humans lived in two worlds—one natural and the other spiritual—covering the full sphere of human experience.

Dresser found hidden within Swedenborg's elaborate system of thought a "remarkable psychology, unique in quality and meaning." However, because so many of his investigations into the "inner life" were classified as mystical or visionary, he had been either ignored or misjudged. Just as it was easy for Emerson to classify Swedenborg among the mystics in his *Representative Men,* so it was easy as well for the psychological world to relegate Swedenborg's insights into an archaic type of seership unbecoming of the modern world.[43] Yet Swedenborg's psychology of the inner life and of the intimate correspondence between internal and external states of mind and body, encased within a system of Christian theology, "carried forward the idea of science into a religion . . . long before there was either a psychology or a philosophy of religion."[44] If there was to be a science of the soul (in contrast to theories of mental life without a soul) addressing the relationships of the natural and spiritual world, Dresser felt that Swedenborg's inquiry was truer to the mark than the theories of Theosophy and spiritism popular in Dresser's day.[45]

In contrast to the English philosopher and sociologist Herbert Spencer's (1820–1903) view of evolution (i.e., evolution is change from an incoherent homogeneity to a coherent heterogeneity), Swedenborg had proceeded from the highly organized to the simple, believing that real knowledge did not begin with observed or tested material facts but with Divine Truth. Thus, he approached the study of the soul from the vantage point of the universe as a whole and, from there, to deduce knowledge of the natural world. His was a spiritual psychology, dealing with the innermost region in human nature where the individual was in "untrammeled relation with God." Hence, the soul was to be understood with respect to its most interior quality.[46]

In *Economy of the Animal Kingdom* (also known as *Dynamics of the Soul's Domain*) Swedenborg explained that psychology—which he defined as "the science which treats of the essence and nature of the soul, and of the mode in which she flows into the actions of her body"— was the most important of the sciences.[47] As explained by Dresser, Swedenborg did not depend on experiences that fed into the self-authored *tabula rasa* of Lockean psychology to explain the essence of the soul; nor was he influenced by the contemplative methods of Eastern philosophy. Instead, he studied the formation of affections and ruling loves. Human life in all its phases, from innocence and childhood to wisdom and maturity, was the consequence of loves and desires that flowed from the spiritual to the natural world. Nothing in the natural world was explainable by itself, since nothing existed without connection with the spiritual world.[48]

Swedenborg's quest for the soul through anatomical studies ended when he devoted himself to more direct means of spiritual perception through revelatory interpretation of Scripture. He believed that everything in the natural world corresponded to a spiritual reality, and that behind the literal stories in Scripture were clues to humanity's spiritual history. In this larger view, Swedenborg developed the idea of God as Love and Wisdom, the creative first principles of the universe. The spiritual life of the individual was as "a child of God, wrapped around with the Divine presence, with no barriers between."[49] As explained by Dresser,

> In spirit man moves and wills, thinks and understands from Divine
> life which in itself is open and free. In and through the body man
> loves by means of sensibilities, thinks and wills through the brain,
> moves or acts by aid of the body's structure as an organic whole.
> Where he is in perfect possession of his spiritual faculties, he would

possess the open vision of spiritual perception. In actuality most of us are greatly hampered by bodily conditions, in the closed world of existence in the flesh, where we value things above spiritual truths, pursuing wealth and personal pleasures. Hence the need for a profound teaching to enlighten us concerning the falsities and other obscurities which limit both our vision and our affections.[50]

The human brain, according to Dresser's interpretation of Swedenborg, not only held the basis of a person's will and understanding, it was so organized that the person's ideas were "fixed" in the light of the spiritual influx flowing into it. The brain was the body's natural organ or instrument and corresponded to the "series" and "orders" adapted from the heavenly influx. Thought could not inhere in the mind without its complement of organic forms in the brain; but just as importantly, thought could not inhere without the flow of divine influx.[51] This was Swedenborg's explanation for spiritual psychology: a brain formed for sensation and action, but adhering to a connection with the divine influx that flowed into it.[52]

Dresser lamented the failure of European psychology to concern itself with the harmony of body and soul. Indeed, there was even the question of whether the soul existed at all. From physiology and biology had emerged the view that, regardless of religious faith, mental life ceased with the death of the body. Despite this perception, Dresser viewed the individual first and foremost as a spirit that no force could destroy.[53] "Man ostensibly lives in the body, on whose functions he seems solely to depend," he wrote. "Yet he is the more truly in the spiritual world as a spirit, however remote from what . . . his interior relationship may appear to be. In spirit man is already in the light of heaven, while his body is in the light of the natural world."[54] The internal or inward was that which made humanity unique. From inner spirit to the outward body, human nature was by "series" and "degrees" transformed into a "garment" and "instrument" of the Spirit.[55]

The idea of the Universal Human was central to what Dresser identified as Swedenborg's social psychology. All the souls of people who had died and gone on to live in heavenly societies formed its limbs and organs. Since all heavenly societies were arranged according to this particular form, all social groups on earth corresponded to it as well. Similarly, whatever was meant by personality was apt to suggest discrete degrees of difference between spiritual and natural qualities and loves. It was the vitalized organism whose wisdom and love actuated what it conceived as most enduring, real, and significant.[56]

Dresser seemed initially surprised that Swedenborg had such a fully developed theory of psychology. "It does not seem credible," he remarked, "that the same person who has passed through a period of experiences of a visionary type may also have precise convictions concerning the best known facts in mental life in relation to the brain." Nevertheless, his psychology ("science of the soul") represented an elaborate spiritual excursion into the inner life with an emphasis on the affections and will as well as preparation for the life to come. Human personality had come in a combination of body, mind, and spirit. Spiritual psychology was a method for studying both the natural and spiritual worlds and humanity's preparation for future life.[57]

Unlike Emerson, who had described Swedenborg as a mystic, Dresser preferred to see him as someone who was "calmly intellectual" and no more a mystic "than an artist or inventor who works by intuition." While union with God had been Swedenborg's psychology, the "self" retained its individuality along with the blessedness of heavenly life. Each "self" was incomplete without its own individuality, which at the same time participated in the life of similar souls in a heavenly society.[58] Even the most elemental sense-experience was spiritually generated from above. Born in the age when the forces of the Reformation were strong, Swedenborg appreciated the nearness of the spiritual world and the presence of its ministering angels, with whom he conversed. The soul was a subtle, living fluid, imbued by the Creator and linked to the body by way of the cortex. The body was the soul's instrument, not just its dwelling place. Thus, Swedenborg viewed the inner soul as discoverable only as the individual became a more rational being. To the extent that the soul flowed into the body, it gave form to the divine influx; and after death, the soul relinquished its connection with the corporeal life and continued as a pure spiritual essence. In this manner did Swedenborg's psychology play into the hands of New Thought proponents, forging a conception of the body and its relationship to the soul and to a spiritual world that continued the soul's quest after bodily death. "Souls will be in communication with one another, as indeed we now communicate more or less directly," explained Dresser, "but the communication will be more immediate, by auras and atmospheres which reach to any distance. Heaven will be the society of happy souls."[59]

Swedenborg's psychology became New Thought's entree into the spiritual quest of humanity. The brain, as the body's principal organ, existed as the instrument through which the senses were seen, heard, touched, smelled, and tasted. Without these organs, the body failed to receive information with which to fulfill its basic needs. Added to these sense-organs was an "interior sight" that opened into the spiritual world and enabled the individual to perceive the spiritual meaning of things. Formed in accordance with the law of correspondences, this interior sight discerned that which pertained to the spiritual world. The brain was not an independent entity, but served the mind; it was a bodily organ whose functions corresponded to the purposes and ends of the heavenly influx.[60]

In representing the qualities of the spirit, the body acted responsively to its purposes and ends. It became the soul's outward expression. Love was not only the life of the soul but the body as well. The body did nothing but what was actuated by the soul, and whatever was true for one was true for the other. This larger view of humanity began with the idea of God as universal Love and Wisdom. To the extent that love was an individual's central motive, its spirit partook of activities fitted to the purpose. "Man's being from moment to moment is sustained by this indwelling Love," explained Dresser, "infilling his own love-nature, renewing him so that each pulsation of life, each rhythm of activity within him is from the same Divine source." Thus psychology became an expression of God's dynamic love, which was the life of the body as well as the life of the mind. It was also the power of truth. To the extent that humans lived in response to love and truth, their interiors opened to heavenly influx and their bodies acted in perfect correspondence with the divine order. In such a state, health became their natural condition and disease not even a remote possibility.[61] When manifold, love turned toward the world with an affirmative attitude of hope and aspiration. This constituted a kind of "fourth dimension." Just as certain odors surrounded a plant and helped to define its genus and species, so spheres of love manifested themselves and became a person's signature image that extended outward into the world. In this manner, one could trace an individual's sphere to a particular heavenly society to which he belonged. No sphere was completely hidden; everyone's sphere was an open book.[62]

Disease formed no part of the divine plan; nevertheless, it came under the law of correspondences by correlating what was interior to what became exterior. Behind every excess was the manifestation of a specific disease. "As man's life is from the spiritual world, anything which interferes with the spiritual influx is not merely a defect or obstruction, but a disease," Dresser wrote. The seriousness of a particular disease was a reflection of the individual's departure from goodness and truth. While Dresser distinguished between functional and organic diseases (i.e., those diseases to which an individual might be subject through no direct fault), there remained the tendency to emphasize the relationship of all disease to the spiritual world, suggesting that at some time in the distant past, even organic disease had resulted from some particular spiritual infirmity.[63]

After taking time to study briefly with Swiss psychiatrist Carl Gustav Jung (1875–1961) and Austrian psychotherapist Alfred Adler (1870–1937), Dresser joined the Associate Clinic of Religion and Medicine, also known as the Associated Counseling Service, a consortium of churches and clinics in Brooklyn. There, from 1931 through 1953, he provided part-time service in applied psychology. Along with minister and social activist John Howland Lathrop (1880–1967), who headed the First Unitarian Church in Brooklyn, the two men pioneered in providing a combination of religion, psychology, and medicine for parishioners. Lathrop even suggested Dresser as a possible director of the Emmanuel Movement in Boston. Into his late sixties and seventies, Dresser continued to give lectures on the general topic of health and inner control. He died in Boston in 1954 at the age of eighty-eight, survived by his wife, son Malcolm, and daughter Dorothea.[64]

Emmanuel Movement

Within the New Thought movement, various associations, clubs, and churches brought much-needed help to the urban poor. In cities from the Northeast to the Far West, New Thought organizations staffed nurseries, offered meals and clothing, involved themselves in settlement house activities, created homeless shelters, looked to the needs of prisoners, and introduced mind-cure methods to the victims of tuberculosis, alcoholism, deviancy, and recidivism. In order to realize this latter objective, New Thought leaders recognized the need to form partnerships outside their own organizations. For some, this translated into an advocacy of quasi-socialist objectives and building some type of alliance with parties or groups fostering a social and economic agenda. Notwithstanding the fact that such examples did materialize, particularly in the Midwest, the greater part of the New Thought movement sought to define its social and economic objectives in a manner that was more theological than political.

The term *psychotherapy,* employed in the United States and Europe to designate the scientific practice of mental healing, owed its development to a legion of practitioners whose work in the treatment of hysteria revealed physical and mental problems that could be addressed through hypnosis. Suggestion also played a significant role in treating functional maladies and even specific types of organic diseases. With or without the aid of hypnotism, investigators in Paris and Berlin found that, when deftly applied, both methods offered effective access to subconscious mental states that often hid the real cause of certain maladies.[65] Doctors in France, Germany, Holland, and Sweden won acceptance of these therapeutic methods independently of religious considerations, but this was not the case in the United States, where physicians, even those with considerable international stature, hesitated in using them for diagnostic and therapeutic purposes. While American doctors recognized the work of Ambroise-Auguste Liébeault at Nancy and Jean-Martin Charcot at the asylum of Salpêtriére in Paris, they were reluctant to give psychotherapeutics their full support. This was due in part to the extravagant claims made initially by the proponents of hypnosis, but even more important was their concern for the patient's potential loss of control during hypnosis, a factor that reflected the nation's high regard for individualism and self-reliance.[66]

Because of these concerns, the American pioneers in psychotherapy—William James, Mark Baldwin, Morton Prince, Lewellys F. Barker, W. J. Hudson, Isador H. Coriat, James J. Putnam, Frederick Peterson, Boris Sidis, Henry Wood, and Horatio Dresser—deliberately chose to share elements of their psychotherapeutic responsibilities with church ministries. This was particularly evident in the Emmanuel Movement, which epitomized the church-based nature of American psychotherapeutics.[67]

Initiated in 1905 by Elwood Worcester (1862–1940), pastor of the Emmanuel Episcopal Church in Boston; his associate Samuel McComb; and Joseph H. Pratt, MD, of the Massachusetts General Hospital in Boston, the Emmanuel Movement represented a collaborative effort of the church and the medical profession to address the needs of the city's poor. Its healing regimen, which was confined to functional nervous disorders, resulted in a distinctive blend of Christian healing and pre-Freudian psychiatry aimed at bringing fulfillment to both the spiritual needs of wealthy parishioners seeking an outlet for their charity and the often-dire needs of the poor, who suffered from a broad range of untreated physical and mental complications. The method eventually spread through many Episcopal, Baptist, Congregational, Unitarian, and Universalist churches in the United States before migrating to Great Britain.[68]

Herein lay much of the difference between European scientific psychotherapy and American mental healing practices. While the former was grounded in a naturalistic set of psychological principles, the latter represented a heterogeneous combination of religious and secular ideas that claimed neither an authoritative spokesman nor a unitary theory of healing. At best, it shared a common belief that the individual, using individual efforts and those of some external force, had the power to overcome adversity. However, in its conjoining of secular and Christian principles of faith, American psychotherapy often failed to distinguish between functional and organic disease. This lack of distinction had far-reaching implications and eventually brought unwelcome criticism to many New Thought healers and their techniques.[69]

Worcester's Emmanuel Movement represented the closest approach to European psychotherapy that American physicians were willing to undertake at the time. As an ordained Episcopal clergyman trained as a physiological psychologist by Wilhelm Wundt (1832–1920) and Gustav T. Fechner (1801–87) in Germany, Worcester held that mental states were dependent upon the brain's state or condition. He rejected the strictly religio-metaphysical doctrines of New Thought and Christian Science on the basis that a person's religious or metaphysical beliefs should be kept separate from psychological and physiological facts. He considered it wrong, therefore, to confuse or misrepresent speculative or religious doctrines as science. The word science belonged to physics, chemistry, biology and psychology; beyond the sciences were the fields of metaphysics, religion, and theology. In the interest of mental healing, the two should be viewed separately.[70]

Notwithstanding these distinctions, Worcester predicted a religious awakening that would see the application of psychological principles to religion. In doing so, he and his colleagues drew their ideas from two specific lines of thought. From French philosopher Ernest Renan (1823–92), German theologian and historian Adolf von Harnack (1851–1930), and theologian Karl Theodor Keim (1825–78), they learned to study the life of Jesus and the tasks to which he had consecrated his life. And from Gustav Fechner, William Wundt, and William James, they absorbed the idea of the essential unity of human nature, meaning that the body and soul together constituted a full human being. From psychology they also came to recognize the subconscious and the importance of suggestion if skillfully placed before a receptive mind.[71]

In their initial undertaking, Worcester and his colleagues set out to treat twenty-five consumptives living in the city's tenements using a combination of medicine and Christian principles. Backed by a board of medical advisors that included doctors Joel E. Goldthwait, Richard C. Cabot, and James G. Mumford, the church clinic used the functions of the physician, psychologist, clergyman, and social worker to address the conditions of their patients. Treatment consisted of confronting the disease with the most modern medical therapies along with a combination of moral elements identified as discipline, friendship, encouragement, and hope. The results reputedly compared with the best private sanatoria, a factor that led Worcester to conclude that a partnership of the physician and clergyman had an important mission to discharge and that they could do so effectively and for the community's ultimate benefit.[72]

Over time, the sphere of these combined efforts expanded to include alcoholism, drug addiction, sexual perversion, and phobias considered nervous or functional. Here again, nothing was done without the cooperation and advice from medical advisors. "We have confined our practice to that large group of maladies which are known today as functional nervous disorders," Worcester explained. "It is in the field of functional neuroses that all its real victories have been won." For that reason, the movement focused its energies on neurasthenia, hysteria, psychasthenia, hypochondria, alcoholism, and other affections of the personality. All were thought to spring from moral causes, where the use of drugs and similar regimens had limited effect. The intent was to improve the mental disposition of patients and, by means of psychotherapy, facilitate their cure. This meant that trained clergy were to confine themselves to the religious and ethical side of the patient's problem, leaving the physician and the trained social worker to handle the physical and neurological aspects of the patient's needs. Each provided their own special knowledge and experience to the task without confusing their respective roles.[73]

Believing that humanity was living in the midst of a new era of spirituality, the movement's organizers were all the more convinced that the churches could no longer address persons simply as "disembodied spirits." Those who participated in the movement dispensed with dogma and returned to the Christ of the Gospels in a renewed belief in prayer and with the expectation that one's religious and spiritual state could affect health. "If the nineteenth century was materialistic and critical, the first half of the twentieth century promises to be mystical and spiritual," Worcester and his associates explained. "Already we are conscious of a general revolt in the name of the soul."[74]

In *The Christian Religion as a Healing Power,* Worcester and McComb wrote that Christ's role as a physician and healer had been more or less ignored since the fourth century, explained away as having only allegorical meaning. Nevertheless, the fact that Jesus had attached great significance to his healing had been clearly reflected in the New Testament. "The psychic energy of His personality was so great," they explained, "that He was able to move powerfully the forces of the inner life, which, in turn, reacted upon the physical state." Pleading for a return of this spirit, they did not mean for it to replace the discoveries of medical science, but to work in tandem with it to serve humanity. The tools used by Christ against physical and moral disorders had already been noticeable among numerous early Christians, whose success was proof of the continued presence of Christ's powers in the world.[75]

According to Worcester and McComb, the work of Wundt, Fechner, Freud, James, and others had proven the significance of the subconscious in the physical, mental, and moral lives of individuals—a fact that could no longer be disputed. The weapon of choice in addressing these problems lay in the "re-education" of the conscious powers. "Just as an athlete can train particular groups of muscles to do his bidding, so we can exercise particular groups of thoughts until they dominate the mind, and this domination leads of necessity to the elimination of other groups of thoughts which we regard as undesirable," they explained. Their aim was to establish a harmonious relationship among the individual's physical, mental, moral, and religious attributes based on the proposition that there was a unity of mind and body, and central to that unity was the knowledge that the universe "lives in and is sustained by the eternal life of God, and that this life is the source of all healing agency." Accordingly, the Emmanuel Movement stressed the integration of suggestion, psychic analysis, reeducation, work, and rest in their therapeutic procedures. Together, they stood for a new attitude toward life and "a return to the attitude of Christ."[76]

Worcester and his colleagues began by asserting the power of suggestion, but eventually substituted the New Thought principle of divine wisdom as the motive force, believing that the presence of God was more important in the healing encounter than any physical force. While the secular psychologist saw little difference between spiritual consciousness and therapeutic suggestion or auto-suggestion, the religious therapist insisted that the presence of God was central to healing.[77]

"When our minds are in a state of peace, and our hearts open and receptive to all good influence, I believe that the Spirit of God enters into us
and a power not our own takes possession of us," Worcester wrote. Later,
in his *The Living Word* (1908), he even made room for the role of angels
in the healing process.[78]

The Emmanuel Movement saw itself as the rightful successor to
New Thought's earlier mental-healing practices and a legitimate alternative to Christian Science. Nevertheless, the Christian Scientists accused
Worcester and his colleagues of having compromised too many of their
spiritual principles to material medicine, including the dangerous use
of hypnosis. In their defense, Worcester and McComb characterized
their particular form of moral, educational, and suggestive treatment
as a "hypnoidal state" in which the mind of the patient was passive but
where there was no loss of consciousness. Unlike Christian Science, the
Emmanuel Movement had not broken its ties with academic medicine.
In point of fact, its supporters made every effort to cooperate and support the work of the medical profession by bringing spiritual medicine
into partnership with material medicine. While Christian Science drew
its principles principally from Eddy's *Science and Health,* the Emmanuel Movement made no such dogmatic claims. Equally important, while
Christian Science made no distinction in its willingness to treat both
organic and functional disorders, the Emmanuel Movement chose only
functional cases, leaving the former to the medical profession alone.
Finally, while Christian Science professed to be a healing religion, the
Emmanuel Movement insisted that such a claim represented the height
of "folly and ignorance."[79]

Despite their differences, Worcester encouraged reconciliation with
the Christian Scientists, whose numbers continued to increase:

> Unless we are prepared to confess ourselves utterly at a loss to
> explain this infatuation, we must be able to pass beneath the
> vulgar and repulsive exterior of Christian Science and to find a
> truth in it, a gift for men, a spiritual power answering to men's
> needs which the churches at present do not possess. With all its
> obscurity we find in the Sacred Book of Christian Science great
> truths—freedom from the fetters of sense and passion, the power

of the soul over the body, victory of the mind over its tyrants fear and anger, the presence of God manifested with power; above all, the promise of an immense immediate good as the result of faith. Here lies the source of the power of Christian Science. It does unquestionably bestow certain great benefits on believers: it makes men happy, it improves tempers, it frequently weans men from evil habits, it can reduce or remove pain, it cures certain types of disease and it gives courage to endure these which it cannot heal. It concerns itself with the present and its effects are direct, practical, immediate. Therein lies its great superiority to preaching that is vague and impractical and which deals largely with a distant future.[80]

By 1908, the church-based clinics of the Emmanuel Movement had found supportive outlets in popular women's magazines, including *Good Housekeeping,* which had contracted with Dresser to write on the subject. This prompted numerous imitators of the movement in Brooklyn, Chicago, San Francisco, and other major cities. One example was Bishop Samuel Fallows (1835–1922) of the Reformed Episcopal Church, who drew upon the counsel of Dr. Harold N. Moyer, Dr. Sidney Kuh, and other neurologists and physicians to extend the work of the Emmanuel Movement to St. Paul's Church in Chicago. Believing in the power of faith and in the role of prayer as an intercessor to a personal God, Fallows encouraged the expansion of the principles learned in the Emmanuel Movement to awaken the church to a sense of responsibility and check what he considered had been a "drift" among certain groups to "theological quackery." For convenience's sake, he characterized the effort as "religious therapeutics," meaning the application of faith as a cure for functional disorders of the nervous system. He believed that this treatment, shared between physicians and the clergy, represented a return to the healing practices performed by the early Christians.[81]

In spite of these initial efforts, clear differences remained among the American advocates of psychotherapy. In 1909, Oliver Huckel (1864–1940), pastor of the Associate Congregational Church in Baltimore, Maryland, published a set of lectures under the auspices of the Young Men's Christian Association for students at the Johns Hopkins

School of Medicine. The lectures sought to untangle the relationship between physicians and the clergy in their respective treatments of the "sick mind." Noting that there had been numerous attempts to bring the two professions into closer cooperation in matters of health and healing, Huckel nevertheless warned that serious dangers lurked amid the "extravagances" of psychotherapeutic theories put forward by the churches, including "grave ethical dangers" in the use of hypnotism by ministers practicing the Emmanuel style of healing. Looking to find a wiser and safer method of cooperation, he offered a perspective on how a minister might supplement the work of the medical doctor.[82]

The potential for cooperation had been growing for some time at Johns Hopkins, pushed along by generous endowments from patrons and encouragement from the school's leading professors—Drs. William H. Welch, Lewellys F. Barker, W. S. Thayer, and Henry M. Hurd. The intent was not to turn the clergy into physicians but to make them more effective in the care of the sick in their respective ministries. Their effort was intended to reassert the dominant role and responsibility of the physician and the supportive role of the clergyman. Recognizing that the Emmanuel Movement had claimed numerous successes, Huckel intended to borrow what was best but leave behind its clinics and hypnotic treatments. "In a word," he explained, "we aim at something of permanent value, independent of all passing movements."[83]

Even Dresser found himself responding to the growing popularity of the Emmanuel Movement's imitators, criticizing the tendency of medical doctors to focus their attention on germ theory rather than on the conditions that rendered people immune. The result of this type of thinking was to regard disease as "something that seizes a man from the outside, almost without regard to the state of mind and body." The failure to realize the importance of divine immanence with respect to health, Dresser explained, was one of the great tragedies of the modern age. Neglected for too long by the Christian church, it was only lately that the psychological principles of this great truth in Christian teaching had returned in the form of the Emmanuel Movement.[84]

However, it was not only Christian clergy and Christian thinking that influenced this aspect of New Thought. According to historian

Andrew R. Heinze, Jewish psychologists played a "disproportionate role" in the development and marketing of the psycho-religious, humanistic, and positive psychologies of the twentieth century. This claim, if true, goes counter to the prevailing belief in the resounding influence of Protestant pastoral theology. Clearly, Donald Meyer's *The Positive Thinkers,* Richard Weiss's *The American Myth of Success,* E. Brook Holifield's *A History of Pastoral Care in America,* John Burnham's *How Superstition Won and Science Lost,* and Robert Fuller's *Americans and the Unconscious* place the locus of twentieth century popular thought in the post-Puritan narrative of perfectability. Nevertheless, as Heinze has suggested, a corpus of works written by Jewish authors were subsumed into the Protestant mindset. Specifically, writers such as Hugo Münsterberg, Boris Sidis, Abraham Arden Brill, Abraham Myerson, Alfred Adler, Walter Béran Wolfe, and Isador Coriat helped shape the salient characteristics of America's culture of popular psychology. Although the bulk of popular literature on self-improvement, visualization, and healthy-mindedness embraced a Christian motif (i.e., Jesus as a psychological healer), the sources for much of the psychological data derived from Jewish writers, many of whom were agnostics and atheists. Where Jewish thinking veered from popular thought was in its rejection of mystical interpretations of the unconscious as found in Spiritualism and Christian Science, both of which were deemed dangerous. This explains in part, perhaps, why the self-help and human perfectability genre of the early twentieth century diverged from the divining aspects of nineteenth-century Spiritualism with its séances and mediums as well as from the heavy draughts of Christian dogma and ritual.[85]

Positive Psychology

In 1998, ninety-four years after the radical empiricist William James delivered his address on "The Energies of Man" before the American Psychological Association, University of Pennsylvania psychologist Martin E. P. Seligman (b. 1942) delivered his own presidential address before the association on the subject of "positive psychology" and its role in the pathology of healing.[86] Unlike James, who analyzed healthy-mindedness from the vantage point of personal and anecdotal testimonies, Seligman emphasized quantitative assessments, meaning a meta analysis of those persons undergoing interventions in various control groups.[87] Psychology was not just for the curing of disease and illness; it also could be used to make the lives of people and their communities qualitatively better. Seligman's aim, and those of his colleagues, was to create a "science of positive subjective experience, positive individual traits, and positive institutions."[88]

For much of the history of academic psychology, explained Seligman, its proponents had devoted their efforts to healing or repairing some aspect of human functioning. As a consequence, psychology came to see itself as a mere subfield of the health professions and one whose empirical focus centered on assessing and curing individual suffering. But psychology was not just the study of disease, weakness, and mental damage; it was also the study of strength and virtue. "Treatment is not just fixing what is wrong," he cautioned, "it also is building what is right. Psychology is not just about illness or health; it also is about work, education, insight, love, growth, and play. And in this quest for what is best, positive psychology does not rely on wishful thinking, self-deception, or hand waving; instead, it tries to adapt what is best in the scientific method to the unique problems that human behavior presents in all its complexity."[89]

Believing that the disease model did not move the profession any closer to the prevention of these problems, Seligman looked for those human strengths that could serve as buffers against mental illness. At the heart of this approach was the idea of "learned optimism," meaning the ability to understand, learn, teach, and reinforce those virtues best capable of protecting the individual from the negative traits of depression and anxiety that led to various forms of mental illness. This practice was just as applicable to families, education, communities, corporations, economics, and even government policy.[90]

Seligman's work in positive psychology has been the centerpiece of numerous books and articles appearing in the scholarly and popular press. It has been furthered as well by the creation of a Character Strengths and Virtues (CSV) scale for measuring its six virtues and twenty-four strengths of character; the establishment of Positive Psychology Centers at the University of Pennsylvania, the University of Michigan, the University of Illinois, and Claremont Graduate School; and the widespread dissemination of findings through the Positive Psychology Network and its numerous websites.[91]

One of the eager spokespeople for positive mental health is the University of Illinois psychologist Edward Diener (b. 1946), better known as "Dr. Happiness," who has focused his research on understanding what makes people feel satisfied with life. He, along with Seligman, Ray Fowler of the American Psychological Association, and Hungarian-born Mihaly Csikszentmihalyi, have identified the three key components for a satisfied life as pleasure, engagement, and meaning, with pleasure being the least consequential.[92]

Seligman's efforts and those of psychologist Sheldon Cohen at Carnegie Mellon to make people happy through positive reinforcement of the human psyche transformed psychology—both scholarly and popular—into more nuanced strategies correlating happiness with wealth, marriage, health, and longevity. Some of these strategies, such as the study of longevity among nuns in a 2001 University of Kentucky study, were rigorously researched. Not surprisingly, however, positive psychology has spilled over into popular culture. While it remains an academically rigorous discipline, it has also opened its doors to any number of lay professionals seeking to claim a piece of the market. As Chris Peterson of the University of Michigan astutely remarked, "There's a temptation to bullshit in positive psychology."[93] Although researchers suggest that the level of individual satisfaction is determined largely by character and attitudes and less by money or disability, this clarification seems not to have been noticed by many of the movement's more popular advocates. The parade of happy-ologists spouting positive psychology have given vent to a litany of positive-thinking modalities that define a less scholarly underpinning.

* * *

New Thought went through numerous stages in its development before transitioning to the subconscious mind and the importance of suggestion. In this latter phase, emphasis was placed on the idea of affirmation. God became more impersonal and was referred to as "Principle" or "All Being," terms that easily substituted for a more pantheistic or even mystical view in place of Christianity and the teachings of Jesus. Also evident in this latter stage of the New Thought movement was a greater emphasis on individualism as distinct from authority; elements of optimism and affirmation in the goodness of life; freedom from old forms of bondage, including the emphasis heretofore given to the role of heredity and environment; and greater reliance upon experiences and intuitions. In a sense, this was an affirmation of the term "realization," meaning that the future was in the hands of each individual and what he or she decided to make of him- or herself. "To realize the value of an affirmation is to grasp the implied truth or law, to think it out, enter into its spirit, assimilate its life," explained Dresser. Obtained through silence and meditation, realization became a favorite expression across the multitude of churches and organizations under the umbrella of New Thought.[94]

6

 Evolution's Divine Plan

The old physics showed us a universe which
was more like a prison than a dwelling place.
The new physics shows us a universe which
looks as though it might conceivably form a
dwelling place for free men, and not a shelter
for brutes—a home in which it may at least be
possible for us to mould events to our desire
and live lives of endeavor and achievement.

—Sir James Jeans, "Address," 1934

In a nation built on the shoulders of its denominations and creeds, New Thought purports anything but a fixed system of beliefs. Nevertheless, among its representative spokespeople—both past and present—a repetitive stream of terminology such as "Law of the Good," "Law of Attraction," "Law of Degrees," "Law of Supply," "Law of Success," and "Law of Correspondences" suggests a set of unwavering principles that are both certain and progressive. Believing that the remedies for all human defects are in the realm of metaphysical causes that are mental and spiritual in nature, these spokespeople focus on the lives of individuals who are at home in the mental world of the inner self as distinct from those swept along by their senses. In using the term *inner self,* the proponents of New Thought emphasize the mental experience of the individual insofar as it involves practical beliefs and attitudes within the subconscious. New Thought speaks of a directive power and presence operating in the universe where God, the unifier whose love serves as its centerpiece, is the sole healer and sustainer.[1]

More than any other law or theory, the literature of New Thought can best be judged by the extent to which it succeeded in transforming Darwin's *The Origin of Species* (1859) into a positive force for spiritual growth and accomplishment. To do so, however, it had to drown out the scientific materialism of Baron d'Holbach's *Système de la nature* (System of nature, 1770) and Julien Offray de La Mettrie's *L'homme machine* (The man-machine, 1748), which served as distant echoes of eighteenth-century pronouncements concerning the physical universe. It also had to confront the triumph of Jean-Baptiste Lamarck's *Philosophie zoologique* (Zoological philosophy, 1809), Auguste Comte's *Cours de philosophie positive* (Course in positive philosophy, 1830), and Ernst Haeckel's *The History of Creation* (1876), which had bequeathed to the Victorian imagination a whirl of blind matter in a universe governed by physical laws. Natural or "unconscious" selection left little room to harmonize the human soul with its Creator, much less argue that natural selection itself must have been designed. Yet, despite the ominous influence of realism, pessimism, agnosticism, and atheism that worried religious thinkers, *fin de siècle* literature was ripe with descriptions of a world that remained under the guidance of divine providence.

Beginning in the 1880s, the mind-cure movement was modified by the popular effects of evolutionary theory on American culture, suggesting that mind cure could have a spiritual significance beyond the healing techniques developed by Quimby and his contemporaries. New Thought repudiated a materialistic view of evolution and, with equal vigor, repudiated any theology that conceived of God as outside nature. The energies found in nature were the currents of the Divine Spirit expressing itself in progressively more creative acts. Science had brought to life the presence of an all-inclusive Wisdom whose upward sweep compelled belief in a glorious future for humanity.

In what historian Stow Persons described as "an age of restatements" of faith and belief, New Thought's scientific theism was well positioned to explain and defend both religion and science.[2] Avoiding outworn Christian idiom, its apologists transformed the universe into a living organism whose God was both immanent and transcendent, and where the unknown was becoming known as humanity moved in step with nature's plan. The Christian deity was effectively transformed into a Divine Mind to which individuals were encouraged to harness their own mind power. Grounded in theistic evolutionism, the proponents of New Thought saw themselves working as co-creators with God to realize wellness, harmony, and prosperity. Theirs was a friendly universe whose Immanent Spirit encompassed all and where human beings, emulating the Christ, used intuition to recapture the healing powers of Jesus and his apostles.

Risorgimento

Rich in analogy and imagery, late nineteenth-century evolutionary literature colored all aspects of the culture—from physics, chemistry, geology, and natural history to religion, moral philosophy, and mysticism—with an outlook that was remarkably anti-materialistic. Whether through the writings of John Fiske's *Outlines of Cosmic Philosophy* (1875), *The Destiny of Man* (1884), and *The Idea of God as Affected by Modern Knowledge* (1885); Henry Ward Beecher's *Evolution and Religion* (1885); Edward Payson Powell's *Our Heredity from God* (1887); Joseph Le Conte's *Evolution: Its Nature, Its Evidences, and Its Relation to Religious Thought* (1897); Myron Adams's *The Continuous Creation* (1889); Henry Drummond's *Natural Law in the Spiritual World* (1884) and *The Ascent of Man* (1894); Lyman Abbott's *The Theology of an Evolutionist* (1897); or George Holmes Howison's *The Limits of Evolution* (1905), the implications were clear. Evolution became the preferred method for explaining growth and change in the universe, but the process that was once called creation, and now natural selection, was interpreted as the immanent God making himself known. After the "opening whoops and war cries" that filled the years immediately following the publication of *The Origin of Species,* explained D. H. Meyer, "the clash between faith and reason stirred not jingo sentiments but a range of emotions, extending from the hopeful confidence that a new philosophical synthesis would create a truly scientific religion to deep anxiety and longing, what [William] James called a mood of 'speculative melancholy.'" Purpose and order were refabricated, resulting in a personal religion of the mind that, while holding the scientific method as its standard, rejected agnosticism and atheism for a cosmic consciousness where the Divine was both within and without.[3]

With evolution came the inference that humankind was not only of one blood but also of one origin and one destiny. The solidarity of the species was the century's great lesson. Each and all were sensitive to the tides and currents of mental forces traveling the universe. The telegraph and the laws of electromagnetism provided a much-needed analogy between the practical embodiments of the applied sciences and the world of spirits. Americans had come to appreciate the importance of the practical applications of science and their extension, by analogy, to the metaphysical currents toiling in and about the earth and its inhabitants—both past and present. All parts of the universe were governed by law, from the smallest atom to the largest planetary system. Modern science had proclaimed not only the universal reign of law, but the unity of all substances. The divine intelligence had awakened in human beings the realization of their kinship with the rest of creation and the conviction that they stood at the summit of all beings, the product of the evolutionary process. As Abel Leighton Allen, the author of *The Message of New Thought* (1914) explained, quoting an ancient Sufi proverb: "God sleeps in the rock, dreams in the plant, stirs in the animal, and awakens in man."[4]

Against the ominous implications of Darwin's dysteleology, with its existential sense of meaninglessness for otherworldly aspirations, the proponents of New Thought offered the English-speaking world a plausible alternative, namely, the primacy of spirit over matter. Rather than confront the religious and metaphysical consequences of a biological world formed by random variations in a struggle for existence, they combined Darwin's scientific vocabulary with Swedenborg's concept of divine influx to create a language that encompassed both the physical universe and human consciousness. In this universe, unconscious matter took a back seat to the metaphysics of consciousness. Plato, Swedenborg, and Kant became its revelatory spirits by offering meaning beyond earthly existence. For the proponents of New Thought, the threat of spiritual nothingness gave way to optimism and intimations of reincarnation and immortality.

Along with these celebratory feelings was a more sobering realization that the organized churches were, by slow degrees, losing their preeminent role in society. Both the Bible and the pulpit had become less authoritative and therefore less weighty in their ability to direct individual and collective thought and activity. No longer did the dogmatic accounts of endless punishment, election, and material resurrection carry the day. The Bible, once the centerpiece of Christian faith and practice, became more of a guide, inspirer, and illuminator—none of which dishonored its purpose, but it most assuredly lessened its former authority. Humanity's view of the world was moving away from the supernatural to a more orderly and natural sense of change; nature, in its widest sense, was unfolding the outlines of a divine plan. The rules of faith were yielding to the voice of God heard in the human soul.[5]

In reflecting on the overall character of the late nineteenth and early twentieth centuries, Horatio Dresser predicted that while many chose to view the period as predominantly one of invention, discovery, and sociological inquiry, it would be far better known as a time when no organism, society, institution, philosophy, religion, or nation stood apart from the biological selection method of individual variation and competition. Notwithstanding this prediction, he denied that the process in any way implied an absent God. It was absurd to think that God "impressed His energy upon the primeval nebulous mass" and then retired "we know not where." Evolution may be the law of life, but God's continued ontological presence was essential to sustaining the endless workings of force against force. "Either God is revealed through the cohesive force which holds matter together, and holds the planets in their positions in space, through the love which draws man to man, and the fortunes and misfortunes which characterize his progress," observed Dresser, "or there is no divine Father."[6]

For himself, Dresser preferred a strictly theistic approach to God rather than one that was anthropomorphic, pantheistic, or mystical. God was immanent *in*, rather than identical *with*, the world. Best expressed in Christian theism, life was the result of a "continuous divine communication" and not just the product of a momentary force or event. To the extent that creation was continuous, it was important for humanity's "wise adjustment to and intelligent cooperation with" the world. Acceptance of divine immanence required that individuals adjust their inner lives to the thought of God. "I advocate that interpretation of life which places the responsibility largely upon ourselves," Dresser explained, one that "encourages us to look within to find the ever-present resource." The ultimate test of belief in an immanent God was to be found in individual conduct and the values each associated with his or her actions.[7]

Those like Dresser who sought to reconcile design with natural selection explained that God had available a treasury of potential variations that were introduced over the course of time. Evolution represented the continual unfolding of revelation and became the means whereby humans, as moral beings, participated in the creative process. This restated argument from design included the gradual adaptation of species by means of chance or random variations for which there was an intervening providence. Through the sometimes messy process of evolution, revelation mingled with natural selection as the divine mind revealed itself to the world of intelligent creatures. Evolution was essentially creation through time by conscious intelligence—both human and divine. Conscious intelligence was an independent force in nature, the very embodiment of the divine being, with the moral individual as both a participant in the process and its final product.

Dresser thought it an "unwarranted generalization" to claim that evolution was simply another name for "steady advancement," since there was ample evidence that evolution also allowed for "downward growth." He nonetheless accepted as a general principle humanity's natural "tendency to aspire" and that "with the appearance of new forms and superior standards," the old gave way to a better world. "We may confidently declare that we are spiritual beings in the rough," he concluded. In this manner, he and other New Thought writers took ownership of a progressive conception of humanity's mental powers and of human history. The dynamics of human evolution were different from the lower orders, whose lives were natural, impersonal, unreflective, and unconscious. Theirs was a veritable struggle for existence, where nature progressed through the survival of the strong and the destruction of the weak. By contrast, humans had supplanted strict biological evolution with mental evolution in which, after achieving a critical level of brain power, advancement came through actions aimed at blunting the brutish aspects of life's struggle. The mind was an organ whose activities were aimed at controlling the environment rather than reacting to it, and where group activities, idealized pursuits, and foresight trumped immediate personal wants.[8]

In a strange sort of way, therefore, Dresser seemed undisturbed by the potential dysteleology in Darwin's theory of evolution. Unlike many in his generation, he admitted that evolution through natural selection and survival of the fittest was no guarantee of "progress," "victory," "permanent advance," or "goodness." It could just as easily stand for "atrophy," "reversion," and even "failure." In fact, he reasoned, without failure and the freedom to do wrong, without novelty and the consequences of chance, there could be no moral order, no lessons learned, no free will, and no personal responsibility.[9] Physical evolution was real, but it came *after* spiritual involution, which both controlled and modified it. This pointed to the supposition that there was a single law of the universe that, as the foundation of all things, reaffirmed the oneness of life. Conversely, ignorance of this law and its universality led humans to sin and suffering.[10]

As appealing as natural selection was for American and European intellectuals, the idea of random variations left its apologists ill-equipped to accept the full range of its consequences. Out of this dilemma emerged a host of ameliorating theories, each with a different set of explanations embedded in an almost uniform protest against the harshness of an unguided and unconscious process. Since the theory of natural selection sported many elements of irregularity, indeterminacy, and chance, it proved to be far less compelling to the New Thought movement than the more purposive Lamarckianism, whose mechanism of will or desire (i.e., needs determine use) seemed to explain how God's love could work on a cosmic scale. The Lamarckian alternative to natural selection guaranteed progress not only in the context of the prevailing environment but against the broader context of life's struggles. Nevertheless, there would be no softening the harshness of the struggle.[11]

Given increasing doubts in an anthropometric God, New Thought writers found solace in postulating a transcendent energy that, while perhaps unknowable, exercised its love and providence through evolution. The alternative, which they uniformly rejected, was to continually adjust their beliefs to each new theory of creation. Thus, while the idea of biological evolution stood as a symbol of a revitalized science and an important challenge to the long-held assumptions of Christian believers, New Thought writers' faith in science became a welcome answer to old doubts that had been lingering since the days of the early Church fathers. The soul's habitation was safe, secured not by cosmic indifference, accident, or randomness, but by an emergent process acting out a cosmic purpose. It remained only for believers to show confidence in the purposefulness of that process through their commitment to some form of practical or applied idealism.

For New Thought's proponents, evolution was God's method of creation, a power and a process that he shared with his creatures once they had progressed sufficiently in intelligence and reasoning. The corollary to this view was that God and humanity constituted a single, complete system—one Intelligence—reconciling the evidence of evolution with the concept of universal design. To the extent that humans sought to emulate the life of Christ and express the will of the Divine Intelligence, they could contribute to the emergent universe. The growth of consciousness became one of the culminating aspects of the evolutionary process, offering humanity a creative role in the unfolding of the divine plan. Thus, during the storm that broke over Darwin's *The Descent of Man* (1872), it was not so much the immediate biological issues that excited New Thoughters as it was the new perspective on the origin of the human mind and the gradations between reason and instinct, on the development of and differences between consciousness and self-consciousness, and on the power of memory, attention, and abstraction.[12]

New Thought's concept of evolution was one of development and growth, manifesting itself in more perfect forms. This assumed that the forces within evolution were guided by an intelligence that pervaded every atom, controlling its functions and activities. When New Thought practitioners found what they believed was the power of individuals "to tap the universal mind" to create health, ability, character, or any other desirable quality, they felt they had at last discovered their potential. In following the universal mind, humanity was progressing to a fuller understanding of the soul. Through modern psychology, explained Abel Leighton Allen in *The Message of New Thought,* humans were discovering themselves. Through it, they were gaining "faint glimpses of the powers of the great soul within, of that reservoir of intelligence and wisdom" to which they were finding access. When ultimately awakened to the forces within, humans would "look upon man as he is today as a pygmy and a dwarf." As Henry Harrison Brown (1840–1918), publisher of the New Thought magazine *Now,* explained:

> Man as thinker shapes the universal energy into forms of use and beauty, through his thought in mechanics and art. The absolute creates within itself by bodying itself forth in a universe cognizant to the senses of man, first as cosmic energy, then as matter. Man is thus the absolute, becoming cognizant of himself. Man is God thinking; elsewhere all creation is God working. . . . Man is God individualized. The kingdom of God is within you. Kingdom: power, thought is this kingdom. . . . Man controls that subconscious divinity which he is. The conscious man controls the God in man.[13]

Regenerated Humanity

The major tenets of middle-class American Protestantism mellowed over the course of the nineteenth century. In the emerging theology, human beings were only temporarily sinful, and becoming less so under the guidance of the Christ. Changes in the visible universe remained under the direct supervision of providence, but now occurred through strictly natural processes. Middle-class Protestantism struggled to believe in the harmony of science and religion—that true science and true religion were one, the former being truth, and the latter being faith in the truth. The belief was that God governed the world but was not the world itself. God was in the process of uniting humanity to itself, but this did not necessarily mean that human beings received direct communication from God. Such "enthusiasm" went beyond God's intent and the workings of the natural world. New Thoughters envisioned a regenerated humanity and a visible outpouring of God's love into the creative process where human beings and Jesus expressed themselves in the ever-emergent values of unity, justice, love, and community.

New Thought openly confessed to a teleology that joined the intelligible universe with the birth of human thought and its role, albeit limited, in the cosmic process. Its writers clothed natural history in spiritual garments that suggested a more meaningful pattern of cause and effect. No longer considered corrupt, human nature became the means through which God unfolded his plan, molded by natural forces and the revelations of science. The encounter of God, nature, and mind was openly announced as the commencement of a great and glorious new age made fruitful by the labors of each participating soul. In this encounter, God reunited humanity with himself by revealing a spiritual philosophy that connected faith in the cosmic order with New Thought.

The stirring sermons of New Thought preachers and their secular counterparts were resonant with confidence. No longer was faith built on the basic propositions of the fall of humanity and its badge of lost innocence. Rather than take refuge in the conventional landscape of orthodoxy, they spoke of a world where humans decided their own ends and could participate in the divine plan under their own power. As New Thought religious and secular writers learned to appreciate the wonders of the new sciences, they invariably turned to contemplation of the divine perfection revealed in the evidence of order and coherence in the universe. They looked upon God without terror. Such was the spirit that the theory of evolution had bequeathed. These were preachers of scientific sobriety moving cautiously away from the mechanism of natural selection to become worshippers of cosmic order.

As explained by writer and publisher Elizabeth Towne, God was the First Cause whose thoughts were "ever changing within Him." God, she said, had not been content with Nirvana. Had he been, there would have been no human race. "The evolution of man is the involution of God; evolution is the concentration of God's life, nature, character, into countless millions of images and likenesses of himself." In other words, the human race was a copy of God and, as such, its purpose was to carry forward his blueprint for the world. Humanity "took up the work of evolution" in the dominion given it over the earth with its multitude of creatures. It took humanity to put the "finishing touches" to God's work, Towne added. "God made man . . . to help him think still farther and better . . . to make a paradise out of this earth and then conquer the stars."[14] Humanity's role was as a co-worker in the evolutionary process, assisting nature; together they inched toward perfection. Thus the adherents of New Thought worshiped the indwelling God, not a God distant from the human race. God was a universal spirit diffused over all of nature, finding its highest expression in a race that was molding itself into the divine likeness. "The Father and I are one," reported Abel Leighton Allen. This, he loudly proclaimed, was the true meaning of New Thought.[15]

In *The New World and the New Thought* by James Thompson Bixby (1843–1921) and *Evolution and Man, Here and Hereafter* by John Wesley Conley (b. 1852), both published in 1902, the authors repudiated any materialistic interpretation of evolution, and similarly any concept of God outside nature. Renouncing the implications of a purposeless universe, both counted themselves among those who interpreted evolution as a theistic and progressive revelation. While Conley applied the language of Christianity to explain evolution, Bixby preferred to substitute an all-inclusive Wisdom or Infinite Power. For both, however, the Darwinian elements of random variations and wanton struggle were softened with the purposefulness of a cosmic plan. For these two authors, each individual was a free being whose ability to succeed came from within the limits of his or her ability and fulfilled a specific role in the cosmic plan. This variation on the theme of progress found instant acceptance in the American psyche—a hopeful philosophy nurtured and sustained by an equally hopeful nation.[16]

Bixby, pastor of the Unitarian Congregational Church in Yonkers, New York, wrote of the immense expanse of the universe as revealed by recent discoveries in astronomy, but insisted that humans remained "the chief subject of divine care and [the] earth as the moral and spiritual centre of the universe." Science did not diminish the world to simply the outcome of matter and force, but actually multiplied the proofs of the intelligibility and rationality of the universe, making it far more majestic than previously conceived. The human race remained the "climax of the ascending evolution, . . . its end and goal." The reason for existence lay outside the material things of the world, all of which served the spiritual universe.[17]

A believer in immortality, Bixby insisted that humanity had not one savior but many. "If man's soul is immortal," he wrote, "its salvation must be under universal laws, not a thing due to the accident of birth in a Christian nation or the visit of some missionary with a Bible or the presence of a priest with drops of holy water." The doors to immortality were as open in China and Japan as they were in New York and London. Similarly, they were as open in the millions of planets in the universe as they were on the planet earth. "Not alone to our earth and in the flesh of its humanity has the love of God been manifested and incarnated," he insisted, but "to every part of the cosmos where souls have come to need it, in every abode of planetary and stellar society."[18]

Bixby viewed death as merely an "incident" in the soul's onward progress. Similarly, he rejected any concept of the soul relegated for eternity to some infernal hell; this was simply the relic of the older geocentric view of the universe. Instead, he conceived of the disembodied soul as "possessed of the freedom of the universe, and carrying its own heaven and hell within its happy or remorseful consciousness." The soul was in continual ascent, both before and after death, with its earthly existence being but "a mere tick of the pendulum of eternity." The whole of the universe was God's home, with the divine life pulsating through all souls as they proceeded onward and upward from their separate worlds.[19]

Modern science in no way infringed on Bixby's view of religion, which he believed had moved away from the theology of Thomas Aquinas (1225–74) and the poetry of Dante (1265–1321). In fact, science had discovered wondrous new gifts, transforming the universe into a spiritual home for humankind. What Darwin, Spencer, Huxley, Alfred Russel Wallace (1823–1913), and evolutionary biologist and physiologist George Romanes (1848–94) had confirmed with their research went only so far in establishing science's elementary bearings. These "modern Jeremiads" had come up with an evolutionary process that on the surface seemed selfish and cruel, without elements of righteousness and helpfulness. In fact, however, the outcome was entirely the opposite. The theory of evolution, explained Bixby, should not be judged by its elementary roots but as the sweep of a divine process that unfolded itself in a grand moral and spiritual end. "The term nature, properly used, means the whole of creation, not its lower half," he reasoned, "and the great victory of modern science has been precisely to show that man is as much a part of nature and under nature's laws as the vegetable or the animal kingdom." By the same token, human evolution culminated in "the unfolding and perfection of the spiritual nature." Even in the lower stages of life, there was an altruism that acted contemporaneously with the egoism of evolution. The deeper one studied evolution, the more irresistible the conclusion that altruism, self-restraint, self-sacrifice, devotion, social impulses, and the care for others were its most overpowering attributes. Morality did not come about through the invention of priests or statesmen, but from an "irresistible growth" in the human heart. It was the product of the Divine operating in the universe and moving it out of chaos and into a more spiritual plane. The universe was "God's unfenced and all-inclusive communion table" to which all souls were invited. It was a universe permeated with forces and laws that were unitary—a universe forever climbing forward, growing and unfolding, proceeding according to intelligible plans and purposes.[20]

For Bixby, evolution had broken once and for all the unwholesome grasp of Christian conservatism and the destructiveness of its creeds. Evolution was here to stay. "It is too late to turn it out of the mansions of modern thought," he wrote. The real question at hand was whether belief in God and in the soul could exist under the same evolutionary roof as the "chilling frosts of materialism and skepticism." While he admitted to aspects of evolutionary theory that remained narrowly materialistic, he denied that this represented an irreconcilable conflict. Evolution was a method, not a cause in itself. It demanded a divine creative force as its starter. Instead of removing God from humanity and the universe, evolution had brought God closer, setting human beings "face to face" with the universe that was God's soul. The universe was simply the secular name for the indwelling God "incessantly moulding and forwarding His work."[21]

Another favorite scientist and philosopher admired by the New Thought movement was geologist Joseph Le Conte (1823–1901), a student of both Louis Agassiz (1807–73) and Asa Gray (1810–88) at Harvard, who spent his professional career at the University of California, where he taught from 1874 until his death in 1901. Along with Bixby and Conley, he came to view God-centered consciousness as the "directive force" of evolution.[22] "In a word," he wrote, "there is no real efficient force but Spirit, and no real independent existence but God, in whom, in the most literal sense, not only we but all things have their being; in whom all things consist, through whom all things exist, and without whom there would be and could be nothing."[23]

> But the upward tendency which runs through all nature does not stop with man. It is again taken up by man and carried forward in a higher sphere. As spirit in the womb of nature gradually grew to higher and higher conditions until it broke away and came to birth and freedom in man, so the spirit of man immediately enters into a new and higher embryonic condition, to reach by evolution a new spiritual birth and a higher moral freedom as *regenerated man*. As nature through all geological times struggled slowly upward to reach its final term, its goal, its *ideal*—in a word, to *finish its work* in man; so man immediately enters upon a new race to reach *his* goal and ideal—the *divine man*.[24]

Le Conte explained that organic evolution reached its completion in the ideal human, meaning Christ. The goal for humans was the completion of their animal evolution and elevation to a higher spiritual plane of life. The divine spirit was in embryo in humans and came to birth in Jesus, the Christ. It was through Christ that the human race reached union with God. "As man, the ideal animal, is a union of the animal with the spiritual; so the Christ, the ideal of human evolution, is a union of the human and the Divine," he wrote.[25]

As a champion of evolution, Le Conte tired of the contentious argumentation in his day and settled on a view that, according to philosopher Herbert W. Schneider, interpreted evolution "as a process of continuous creation by an immanent will in nature."[26] In this sense, Le Conte was not unlike Henri Bergson (1859–1941), professor of philosophy in the Collège de France, Paris, who viewed the world and humanity as being in a process of creation, becoming and passing through an evolutionary growth and development. For both men, there was a psychic element in life that molded matter to its own purposes. Where there was life, creation was going on.[27]

Another of New Thought's evolutionary enthusiasts was John Hamlin Dewey, MD (1828–1918), honorary vice president of the New Thought Federation (1904), who explained evolution as God's method of creation and the means by which humans would reach divine kinship. Evolution was the manifestation of the immanent God bringing forth the kingdom of God in the race-life of humans; it was through evolution that the race ascended the scale of existence to a new and higher embodiment. Since Spirit is God, the operations of life in nature were the manifestations of an immanent God and a superintending Providence. Evolution was the method of creation, the unfolding of life from within, lifting life through wave after wave of evolutionary activity to the eventual realization of the Christ ideal.[28]

A new age was approaching when an illuminating spirit in the soul of humanity would awaken. This, Dewey explained, would be symbolized by the second coming of Christ—not Christ in an outward form but rather an inward presence in the souls of his followers. This described the new conception of the spiritualized human and the kingdom of God in the world. While latent in humanity, this divinity was awakened and brought to organic expression by means of evolution. Evolution did for all humans what God had done for Jesus, namely, lift them to the level of the Christ life. The transformation of humanity into the Christ ideal represented the embodiment of spiritual principles and the attributes of divinity through the prophecy of evolution. While the processes of evolution below the human race were largely spontaneous, the processes after humanity's creation included "self-will, or a self-directing and self-determining power." Admittedly, in the early savage stages of the race, the inventive faculties were governed by physical necessities. As intellectual powers developed, however, and humanity moved forward utilizing science, philosophy, and invention, it formed a standard of ethics. Having come to a level of intellectual and moral consciousness, humanity at last became "a co-worker with God."[29]

Not content to leave the explanation of evolution to others, businessman Henry Wood explained that as humans had grown more materialistic over the centuries, they had lost awareness of their own divinity.

Every person possessed the spiritual capacity to know the Divine, a capacity hidden beneath the shadows of a more sensuous material nature. "It has been said that God is nearer to us than we are to ourselves," he explained, "but if we are unconscious of the Presence, it has no meaning." The scriptural texts that taught the indwelling of the Spirit had been ignored for too long. As a result, the Spirit was perceived only on rare occasions. Nevertheless, those who believed that "Divine revealment is in any manner limited to the Bible" or through some other exclusive channel available only to a few had missed seeing the Divine overflowing in the soul of the individual.[30]

For Wood, who William James had once singled out for special praise as one of the more articulate mind-cure authors of the time, the concept of progress was everywhere engrained in evolution, whose theory, until recently, had been regarded as allied to materialism and contrary to religion and revelation. This had certainly been the position held by the more fundamentalist elements within Protestantism, who accused it of undermining church authority and the scriptural narrative. But those who had denied the findings of science failed to recognize that not only was evolution true, but it was "absolutely confirmatory of whatever is vital and inherent in true religion." For Wood, evolution was best defined as "the act of unrolling or unfolding." It was "a process of growth and development" applied to every living organism as well as to all human institutions including religions, theologies, civilizations, ethics, and spirituality. In effect, evolution was a universal trend that encompassed the entire cosmos. Borrowing language from Spencer and Le Conte, he described evolution as an eternal law that "involves progress from the lower to the higher; from the simpler to the more complex; from the less perfect to the more perfect; from the indeterminate to the determinate." It was a philosophy that, like other natural laws, proved indispensable in conceptualizing the grand harmony, economy, and unity of the cosmos.[31]

If the law of gravitation did not disturb humanity's belief in God as the sustainer of the universe, there was no good reason to believe that the law of evolution would disturb it either. "In the great everlasting cycle of creation," explained Wood, "the primal energy which God first evolved into the lowest, most general, and indeterminate conditions is, at length, through a series of grand steps, gathered, organized, individuated, and evolved into sons of God, in which form the return is made to the Father's House." Each individual was made in the image of God, but it was Jesus, the Christ, in whom God's divine and spiritual identity was perfectly manifested. Jesus served as a powerful ideal presented to the human mind; he was God's agent in the evolution of human character, drawing the human race upward like a great magnet.[32]

For the New Thought philosopher and mystic Ralph Waldo Trine (1866–1958), the Immanent Spirit was present everywhere in the universe. In an effort to harmonize science with the idea of immanence, he overlaid the hypothesis of evolution, which he interpreted theistically. Within this context, he said that individuals who opened themselves to the influx of the Spirit, placing themselves in harmony with the Infinite, would find themselves not lost in some Absolute but at the center of power, linking themselves with purpose to the life forces around them. By participating in the Divine Life, they would find harmony in the fullness of life. Trine expressed this message best in his *In Tune with the Infinite* (1897).

> The great central fact in human life is the coming into a conscious,
> vital realization of our oneness with this Infinite Life, and the
> opening of ourselves fully to this divine inflow. In just the degree
> that we do this, do we actualize in ourselves the qualities and
> powers of the Divine Life. You will exchange disease for ease,
> unharmony for harmony, suffering and pain for abounding health
> and strength.[33]

Charles Fillmore, cofounder of Unity, taught a similar lesson. Since Spirit and mind were the same, God dwelled in the mind that he used to move creation forward. In this sense, each individual became a vehicle of evolution, a visible expression of Spirit. This was not the natural selection of Darwin and Huxley, nor was it the notion of a humanized God sitting at the center of the universe and ruling things; rather, it was a theistic form of evolution where the infinite and finite met in the mind to carry out the mysteries of creation. Through each human being, who became a willing worker with the Divine Mind, God formed and manifested the universe to his liking.[34]

Thomas Troward's popular *The Edinburgh Lectures on Mental Science,* first published in 1904, continued to receive adulations through its eighth printing in 1922. Intending to explain the natural principles governing the relationship between mental action and the quality of a person's material condition, or what he called the "livingness of Life," he took note of the marked distinction between the "cosmic intelligence" and individual intelligence. With this distinction manifested by the presence of *individual* volition, Troward set out to find ways to move ideas about human evolutionary ascent from chance variation to a more purposeful process. His objective was a "unity of the spirit," by which he meant aligning the innermost nature of being with the cosmic intelligence of God. As with others of his generation, Troward stressed the critical role of intuition—which was the tool of the subjective mind—and the law of attraction in prompting the objective mind in the right direction.[35]

With "trained thought" there was no limit to what mental science could enable humanity to make of life. Given the law of correspondences, the externalization of that thought would always be in accord with the internal principles that gave rise to it. "Belief in limitation is the one and only thing that causes limitation," Troward warned, "because we thus impress limitation upon the creative principle." But as humanity lays its imperfect beliefs aside, its boundaries will expand, bringing abundant blessings to all.[36] This was the ultimate goal of evolution and should be the "great end of our studies," he concluded. "There is a correspondence of the constitution of the body to the faculties of the soul, and there is a similar correspondence of the faculties of the soul to the power of the All-originating Spirit."[37]

Divergent Roads

There were at least two social consequences of New Thought's acceptance of evolutionary theory. The first was an uncompromising individualism that drew sustenance from its conviction that the soul was in direct communication with God's divine plan. The second was a practical or scientific humanitarianism that substituted a combination of individual perseverance, self-reliance, personal accountability, and a scrupulous regard for nature's laws for the charitable side of Christianity. The day had long passed when those blessed with nature's bounty were obligated to share a portion of their wealth with the society's poorest or to dissipate their energies through the enactment of institutional protections aimed at softening the rawness of life's struggles. Getting the weak and poor of society on their feet did not entail soup kitchens or doles; nor did it require legislation to enforce safety rules, minimum wages, or maximum hours for work.

In his book *The Christ Ideal,* published in 1901, Dresser explained that Jesus had been a radical of the inner life, counseling people to seek the Kingdom of God within. Jesus was not, however, a social reformer in the typical sense of the word. His social gospel began with each person's own mental development, knowing that "new ideas gradually work[ed] their way from the individual to the social mind." Instead of going forth to coerce and accelerate social change, the individual must cultivate repose and trust. Responding to comments that Jesus was a socialist, Dresser explained that Jesus's advocacy of spiritual equality did not imply equal distribution of material wealth. "There is a diversity of gifts," he pointed out, "and men should be free to choose that kind of external life which is most in keeping with the inner ideal." If Jesus were to visit earth again, he would hardly ally himself with any of the schemes of social reform. He would come as a man of peace "quickening spiritual presence" among the living. That said, spiritual growth and moral reform were not truly Christian if they applied only to the individual. "The mere individualist, one who seeks his own good, to be free from the ills and annoyances of life," he warned, "will find small comfort in the Christ world."[38]

In similar fashion, Henry Wood urged readers to avoid extremes of all types. By keeping a "level head," the individual could remain indifferent to social or class conflict and approach change in a gradual and orderly process. Accordingly, he condemned socialism to the extent that it implied the forcible expropriation of material wealth by law and the assumption of the productive agencies of society by the state. Any interference with the natural laws of distribution only led to idleness and anarchy. "If through any ostensible legalized process men can get what they do not earn," Wood reasoned, "production will be diminished and decay ensue." This had been the outcome of many well-meaning philanthropies. If, on the other hand, socialism meant the cultivation of an unselfish character in humanity through the awakening of a spirit of love and altruism, then he had no objections to the use of the term. This form of benign socialism taught individuals through character reinforcement that the best way to help themselves was not through the pursuit of material wealth but through unselfishness. "Only as human consciousness is lifted into the spiritual zone and the image of God uncovered," he reasoned, "will that harmony and wholeness be realized which is able to transform the earth into a paradise."[39]

As for moral and social reforms, Wood considered New Thought to occupy a "deeper realm" and therefore a role above politics. It was about the evolution of spiritual character in the individual, knowing full well that social, political, and ethical reforms would follow. As a movement, it should remain unencumbered by so-called "surface work." The real work of New Thought was in forming the correct principles. Unfortunately, cautioned Wood, many would-be reformers engaged in activities that were manifestly dishonest because of flaws in the fundamental principles that made up their character. Individuals could not be made honest by legislation or by any other form of government intervention and the whole of history was witness to that fact. So long as reformers occupied themselves with the external aspects of reform, plastering goodness on people "instead of awakening the forces . . . latent within," their efforts would fail. "The most important mistakes of the world have been its attempts . . . to override or disregard the Established Order," Wood preached. "Men think that they can formulate some plan more expeditious than inner and evolutionary processes." Such shortcuts were only temporary acts that changed nothing. Outward reform was powerless without the inner spirit standing firm behind it. In this sense, New Thought served as an important philosophical plank in the intellectual construct of Progressivism, an American reform movement between 1890 and the 1920s that centered around the transformative influence of the individual rather than the government on social, political, and economic issues.[40]

In the exercise of Christian charity to ameliorate the needs of the nation's underclass, New Thought conditioned its concept of social justice by teaching that it was impossible to improve the conditions of society except by the very forces that gave rise to them. In the end, competition and the advantages of a market-driven economy were the stern props on which all parties found justice. Beyond access to opportunity, there was only indiscriminate charity that, when left to its own devices, undermined any hope for a worthy life. Holding up examples such as Andrew Carnegie and Henry Ward Beecher, poverty was associated with vice and sin. As Beecher explained, "looking comprehensively through city and town and village and country, the general truth will stand, that no man in this land suffers from poverty unless it be more than his fault—unless it be his *sin*."[41] Hasty philanthropy, given for whatever reason, made virtue of vice, leaving its receivers to live in the dullness of the sins that forged them. Only when churches and benevolent associations were hardened with foresight and realism could they truly benefit the poor and the needy.

New Thought's religious and secular leadership was ideologically prepared to meet the high standards set by scientific philanthropy. This temperament, widely prevalent in the waning years of the nineteenth century, carried forward into the twentieth century as the righteous use of wealth by those who created it. Here the harmonization of science with religion left the middle class with an equanimity of soul that glided comfortably over life's gritty paradoxes. Utilizing the objectivity of the new social sciences, they expounded an arbitrary and impersonal philanthropy that defined and explained away the detritus of *laissez faire* capitalism. Until the Depression years, when questions arose over the future of capitalism and the preconditions for social justice, this remained the most desirable and legitimate form of philanthropy. Reflective of Andrew Carnegie's famous article "Wealth,"[42] New Thought writers viewed Christian charity in the context of realism, espousing the view that philanthropy should be scientifically administered to avoid hasty and foolish handouts that undermined personal responsibility and middle-class virtues.[43]

Poet and inspirational author James Allen (1864–1912) is credited with pioneering in motivational thinking. His books were inspiring, including *From Poverty to Power* (1906), *All These Things Added* (1903), *Through the Gates of Good* (1903), *Eight Pillars of Prosperity* (1911), *Foundation Stones to Happiness and Success* (1913), and *The Divine Companion* (1919). His *As a Man Thinketh* (1903) became a template for hundreds of books and pamphlets on self-help and motivational thinking. For Allen, the discovery of the law of evolution in the material world enabled individuals to better understand the mental world of thought, where the good survived because it was "fittest" and where evil ultimately perished. The law of "survival of the fittest" was not founded on cruelty but on justice. "It is one aspect of that divine equity which everywhere prevails."[44]

Allen pushed these beliefs even further by arguing that breaking the chain of poverty required the individual to cease complaining and, above all, cease all self-pity. "By so ennobling your present surroundings," he advised, "you will rise above them and above the need of them, and at the right time you will pass into the better house and surroundings that have all along been waiting for you, and that you have now fitted yourself to occupy." Individuals were to utilize their poverty to cultivate hope and courage. Similarly, they were to treat a tyrannical employer with patience and self-control. There was no way to rise above poverty or any other undesirable condition except by eliminating the selfish conditions within. The path to wealth and power lay in self-control, self-government, and self-purification.[45] "A man does not come to the almshouse or the jail by the tyranny of fate or circumstance," reasoned Allen, "but by the pathway of groveling thoughts and base desires." Poverty, disease, and health were all rooted in thought. Until thought was linked with purpose, there was drift and aimlessness that led inevitably to failure, unhappiness, and disease. Those who were unprepared for the apprehension of a great purpose were bound to fail. Thought allied to purpose, on the other hand, became a creative force with which the individual could do anything.[46]

Until 1898, explained Richard Ingalese in *The History and Power of Mind* (1902), the Adamic curse ("In the sweat of thy face shalt thou eat bread.") was upon humanity. As evolution of the race advanced, some people had been able to use the laws of nature for their own individual benefit. In this manner arose the relationship of employer and employee. Employers, he went on to argue, had become civilization's mental workers as distinct from physical workers and physic-mental workers, both of whom were tied to some level of physical labor. The mental workers learned to use their minds and mental forces so fully as to "receive whatever they desire without manual labor of any kind." These had become the conscious users of the Law of Opulence. The successful mental worker is the individual who can make a positive picture of what he desires, create it mentally, and demand it be so. "Your experiences with prosperous business men and all successful persons in the world," he observed, "show that unconsciously they work along these lines."[47]

Apart from the disdain New Thought writers showed for patching society's unsightly blemishes, they did not dismiss outright the need for service nor the importance of maintaining decent human relations. Change without direction was not an end to be sought or endorsed. The "success vibration" in the New Thought movement had been overworked. Material prosperity was a desirable objective and tended to invigorate individual initiative, but it carried no magic charm and should be subordinated to other goals. "It is legitimate to make money in an honorable way," Wood explained, "but it is a degradation to make the new philosophy a money-making scheme." The great accomplishments of humankind were planned and shared in a covenant between human beings and God. Change needed to be purposeful, marked by conscious decisions and willful choices. This implied the use of human faculties to discover the natural forces and tame them to be extensions of a person's soul and contrivances for his or her greater happiness. This did not mean transforming the state through feats of civil engineering into a refuge of strident unselfishness; the object lesson was to ensure a climate conducive to supporting a self-contained matrix of a God-infused, self-reliant individualism.[48]

A similar argument came from Theodore F. Seward (1835–1902), author of *The Don't Worry Philosophy* (1894) and *Spiritual Knowing* (1901), who explained that just as materialism had as its watchwords "the strenuous life" and "survival of the fittest," so the thought-world had as its mantra "spiritual knowing," a process of moral and spiritual development that rediscovered and applied the spiritual gospel of Jesus. Seward's scientific conception of the spiritual life did not belong to the older pietism but rather to the strenuous life of right thinking that included both trust in a divine guidance and in the ideal of freedom for all.[49]

Yet another New Thought writer was businessman Charles Benjamin Newcomb (1845–1922), author of *All's Right with the World,* published in 1897. According to his analysis of the closing decades of the nineteenth century, the world had wearied of complaints suggestive of social discontent, economic depression, and hard times. For too long, Americans had been looking for remedies to address their personal condition, not recognizing that the "banquet of life" was always spread and that "none is really shut out of the feast except the self-exiled." The cause for suffering, including financial deprivation, was to be found in the individual, since life was a combination of "opulence and equity." The horizon of nature's laws was always changing. Yesterday gravitation was discovered; today, magnetism; and tomorrow, levitation. The mysteries of hypnotism, once learned, passed quickly into Spiritualism. The seekers of truth were travelers who carried little baggage and lived off the land through which they journeyed.[50]

In keeping with this ratiocination, Newcomb warned readers to avoid becoming slaves to the past, including its rules, opinions, and laws. Referring to Emerson, he urged his devotees to revise yesterday's "standard works," as they were valueless in unlocking the secrets of the future. Nature was "fluidic" and its fixed opinions were dangerous, taking little or no account of the laws of growth. Principles, he advised, were the only absolute laws. "The real science of life," he explained, "is ever fresh adjustment." It was important to live in the now rather than in the past or the hereafter. Being a true son of God meant having control over one's destiny.[51]

Newcomb compared New Thought to the discovery of the X-ray in that it replaced the scattered ideas of thought-forces in previous philosophies with an abundance of new opportunities and applications. The X-ray had revealed the existence of a radiant energy that enfolded humankind. It was a "light within the light" whose vibrations were so rapid as to be invisible except under special conditions. "Let us study the correspondence of this truth in philosophy," he urged, as it changed many of the old bearings of life. New Thought taught that all heredity, environment, and interior conditions were controlled by the soul, not by any outside circumstances. The world was humanity's "plastic clay," ready to be molded by the intelligent use of subjective consciousness.[52]

Newcomb took notice of those egalitarian views that had surfaced with the publication of Henry George's *Progress and Poverty* (1879), Henry Demarest Lloyd's *Wealth Against Commonwealth* (1894), and Edward Bellamy's *Looking Backward* (1888) and *Equality* (1897). Each had explained that the nation's addiction to happiness and prosperity had produced a plutocracy instead of a commonwealth. Admittedly, reforms such as social purity, Bellamyite Nationalism, and Christian socialism appealed to women in the movement, but such radical designs for rectifying social inequality failed to elicit approval from the majority of New Thought writers. As explained by Newcomb, sympathy was a vice that, if spread, created only discord. "Let us take the black borders from our stationery, and gild our thoughts and words with love, and confidence," he urged. "We will not, then, mistake the vice of so-called sympathy for the virtue of encouragement, which brings always health and gladness as a welcome guest."[53]

The combination of evolutionary theories, biblical criticism, and the steady rise of secular philosophies turned many of Protestantism's more liberal leaders (such as Washington Gladden and Walter Rauschenbusch) toward some form of adjustment with science, pluralism, and the darker side of unregulated capitalism. As Martin Marty explained in his *Righteous Empire* (1970), "mainline Protestants saw much of their intellectual leadership adopt various versions of the new theology and much of their reformist passion shaped into a new social gospel."[54] For them, the kingdom of God became an idealized restatement of society girded by fidelity to a social gospel designed by religious liberals and progressives who shared their new alignment with an increasingly secular culture. By contrast, however, most of the proponents of New Thought—both religious and secular—proceeded unabated on a course of positive thinking, healthy-mindedness, and happiness. Sidestepping the theological concerns of evangelical Protestantism and the liberal agenda of Protestant modernism, New Thought struck a path that placed full responsibility for an individual's plight in the social, political, and economic world on the individual and the rightness of his or her thinking. Untouched by irony, New Thoughters remained conscious of society's evils but considered them unimportant in the greater scheme of things. The challenges encountered in the upheavals that from time to time shook the social and economic structure were peripheral to acknowledging the indwelling spirit of God, a generous regard for the good of others, seeing poverty as the result of vice and sin allied with ignorance and indolence, and knowing that godliness was in league with good habits that included industry, frugality, and foresight.

New Thought's writers placed the soul on a transcendental plane where mental rather than physical attributes prevailed and where spiritual advancement carried with it a full social heritage that matured into rich minds, material prosperity, and healthy bodies. Accompanying this phenomenon was a neo-Malthusian belief that quality over quantity in human population (i.e., birth control) would gradually disarm society of its evil aspects and the life cycle of humankind would enter an age where acts of will and mind would check humanity's lower instincts. While procreation was a constructive life purpose, only voluntary parenthood of the most perfected human beings offered the promise of spiritual, physical, and economic abundance.[55]

Accompanying this reasoning was the introduction of "scientific charity" and the pressing concern among social scientists that unless there was a sound approach to addressing poverty and its effects, benevolence could turn into state-sponsored pauperism. Regardless of good intent, careless charity (i.e., direct handouts) could have a corrupting effect on the moral fiber of the body politic. In an era of emerging foundations like Carnegie and Rockefeller and larger-than-life reformers such as Henry George, Edward Bellamy, Henry Demarest Lloyd, and Susan B. Anthony, observers within the New Thought movement saw the need to develop a therapeutic agenda for use by the nation's political and philanthropic leadership. As Newcomb explained, those who considered themselves agents for God's work often erred in thinking that such service entailed sacrifice or denying of self. "If we believe that God governs our own lives," he reasoned, "why cannot we believe that he governs equally those of our friends and children, however they may appear to us for the moment?" God was neither blind, powerless, or failing in love. His estates, forever plentiful, could not be wasted. Yet the world suffered from the "despotism of mistaken kindness" and "foolish anxieties concerning the welfare of others." This, he explained, was Christian atheism in that it represented a denial of God's sovereignty. "No life can become a 'victim' to another," he reasoned, "else God does not govern absolutely." If God truly governed all worlds at all times, then it was foolish to doubt his purposes, Newcomb continued. Doing so makes people atheists masquerading as Christians. Doubting God is to lack confidence in the inner voice of one's own self. Believing that all was good and that God was in each individual, Newcomb offered as an antidote what New Thought called the "vibratory law":

> I am well.
> I am opulent.
> I have everything.
> I do right.
> I know.[56]

The breadth of New Thought literature was cosmic in its proportions, capturing within its orb all that had transpired from earth to the heavenly planets and beyond. If questions could not be settled by the authority of the Bible, then its writers were just as willing to draw from Eastern philosophies as well as from lay and professional authorities. New Thought writers never lost the chance to wax eloquent on some unexplained perplexity, the importance of human reasoning, the promise of human perfectibility, or to scorn literalness and orthodoxy. They preferred focusing on cosmic piety rather than conversion, faith rather than grace, science rather than mystery, and discourse rather than argument. With equal measure, they avoided zealotry, abstruse issues, authoritarianism, and human depravity. They seem not to have doubted their own beliefs, making it abundantly clear that their guidance came from a multitude of sources.

This so-called cosmic consciousness, an attitude of mind that some arrived at naturally and others achieved through practice, was likened to the religious experience of conversion. While many sought it, few were actually able to attain it. Like conversion, it meant turning to God, the "Cosmic One," and imitating Jesus. The Canadian psychiatrist Richard Maurice Bucke, MD, (1837–1902) explained that the individual who came to the new consciousness viewed the cosmos as a "living presence" where all things worked together for the good of each and all, and where the founding principle was love. These were the attributes of the cosmic mind. Although Bucke was licensed to practice medicine, he chose to throw his energies into the study of consciousness and spiritual evolution. A profound optimist, he wrote that "the universe is so built and ordered that without any peradventure all things work together for the good of each and all, that the foundation principle of the world is what we call love and that the happiness of every one is in the long run absolutely certain."[57]

* * *

When William James spoke of a pluralistic universe, he touched on a spiritual crisis of faith that affected many writers and intellectuals at the *fin de'siècle*. This crisis of faith, which had thrown vast amounts of Christian theology into doubt, did not have the same effect on Christian metaphysics, where the literal sense of Scripture was now interpreted in terms of an intelligently and purposefully designed cosmology. Rather than devolve into militant agnosticism, the choice between belief and disbelief was deferred as New Thought's writers, lecturers, and philosophers reconciled final causes with a theistic theory of evolution. Darwin's dysteleology was blunted by an elusive "inward" spirit that found friends in both religious and secular form. In their quest for certainty, they chose an assortment of metaphysical propositions with which they made sense out of existence. Longing to feel at home in the universe, they shrank from the implications of natural selection by restoring a sense of intimacy between the individual and the universe. In the process, they found in their inward turning a cosmic reassurance that was moral, aesthetic, and emotional. Thus armed, they found within the mind a higher purpose to existence, namely, a divine presence. Humanity was not a rival of God but a manifestation of Divine Intelligence and, as such, a co-creator. In a world that was benignly indifferent to the individual, this inner awareness of divine presence brought cosmic comfort and reassurance to many a troubled soul.[58]

In addressing these troubling questions, New Thought reached out to Adam Smith, Herbert Spencer, and Charles Darwin to understand the complexity of morality as it intersected with sympathy, generosity, self-interest, organic and intellectual development, and the conduct of an ethical life. If, through complacency, the preconditions for benevolence were replaced by habitual handouts, the purposes and ends became unwanted and unsocial perversions, destroying the character of the giver and turning the receiver into a perpetual outcast.

The plethora of New Thought books published in the wake of evolutionary theory called attention to the sense of personal self that Emerson celebrated as an unfinished but purposeful goal of humanity. It was not a self of habit or of accommodation, but the self of rich social relationships, conscious of a larger bond of union with fellow human beings and with nature itself. It was that larger sense, specifically the self prompted by love of fellow human beings, that created the ethical dilemma. Haunted by the evidence of poverty, hunger, and disease among society's underclass, New Thoughters sought to work through the burden of their awareness in a manner consistent with their belief that the evils in society were the byproducts of wrong thinking. But what was the proper approach? Could a person exercise benevolence, altruism, and sympathy without undermining individual responsibility? And if one refused to interfere with life's unpleasantness, would this be interpreted as a cloak of selfishness? How can one settle for inequality without affecting moral sentiment? How can the perception of indifference be made not only to seem right but to be right? What are the rules that define the purposes and limitations of sympathy and benevolence toward society's weaker elements? And how does this line of conduct affect character in both the giver and the receiver?

Perceived as beneficiaries of the century's materialism, New Thought writers were loathe to replace their beliefs with an oversimplification of Christian virtues. They did not flinch from confronting the vicissitudes of life's struggles, provided of course that the experience proved illuminating. They avoided zealotry of all types and shapes—from labor unions and religious frenzies to all shades of egalitarianism—judging it to be dangerous and destructive of the body politic. Determined to run no such risks, they satisfied their spiritual needs without being submissive to emotional or metaphysical outbursts. Rather than show concern for the issues of equity and justice that so broadly resonated within the mainstream churches of the social gospel movement, New Thought took a different course, namely, one that substituted the mental and spiritual elevation of the individual for the troubled waters of social and economic reconstruction. New Thought offered a new, syncretistic alternative to the social gospel's solution of redrawing the social and economic landscape: relying on intuition, self-assertion, and positive thinking.

It would have been more courageous had the New Thought movement stated at the outset that its evolutionary theory was grounded in the old design argument, but it refused to do so. Having agreed to a muddled peace with both science and teleology, it found itself occupying the uncomfortable position of arguing for a God who maintained a treasury of variations that he introduced into nature as part of the normal course of events—a combination of special providence and accidental variations. Change would come by degrees and stages from the Divine Mind so as to correspond with the levels of complexity exhibited in humanity's unfolding consciousness. Those in the New Thought movement who supported the hand of providence in natural selection were also inclined to adhere to progressive salvation, the natural growth of intelligence, and more modified versions of personal growth.

Like others of their generation, New Thoughters were enamored by evolutionary theory, convinced that it represented a divine plan of life and of society. Biological evolution became a congenial framework for reinforcing the fading of doctrinal divergence in religion, the need for society to adapt to the environment, and faith in an orderly process of creation working itself out through divine immanence. Even though they were transitory, elements of the material world fit together in a harmonious whole that corresponded with the sum total of eternal truths that existed in the mind of God. God acted of his own free choice but did so in accordance with a divine pattern imprinted in his creatures and expressed through the laws of evolution. God remained sovereign but was neither capricious nor ruthless. Endowed with a divine nature, human beings lived with an understanding that as chief among the world's creatures and imparted with both imagination and insight, they could perceive his part in the essential unity of life.[59]

In general, the devotees of New Thought taught a reverence for science that represented the truth as discovered by human beings acting in conscious communion with God. Personal happiness and prosperity were reformulated and given social, altruistic, and religious connotations. In the process, the Yankee traits of prudence, soberness, industriousness, and self-reliance were dressed in social Darwinistic clothes and called forth to justify their cumulative achievements. New Thought's idealism tended to shift attention away from real problems to the fervent belief that all would be set right in the end. Evolution sufficed to furnish confidence in both a supernaturalism and in the participation of human powers furthering the cosmic moral order.

Material bounty was no longer an obstacle to grace, but evidence of it. The new moral individual had the evidence of his or her regeneration in the professed holiness of external gifts. For a time, numerous New Thought churches were transformed into social welfare agencies devoting their energies to a social-gospel style of good works. The God within and the God without were drawn together and made incarnate in the world. But this effort was not long lasting, as too many feared that an active program of social reform would endanger the very individuals who participated in the process by furnishing the materials for a very unpredictable course of events. Eventually, the social-reform culture within the churches chose undertakings that carried more limited liability.

7

The Marketplace
of Healing

I do not know what I may appear to the world,
but to myself I seem to have been only like a boy
playing on the sea-shore, and diverting myself in
now and then finding a smoother pebble or a
prettier shell than ordinary, whilst the great
ocean of truth lay all undiscovered before me.

—Sir Isaac Newton , *Memoirs*

Concepts of health and disease are intimately entwined with the world-view of specific groups and cultures, and, depending on their scientific and religious traditions, the implications can vary significantly. In non-Western societies, for example, healing includes a much closer alignment of spirituality with disease, which is commonly understood to have both natural and unnatural or paranormal causation. On the other hand, in Western societies the relationship between religion and science has been much more bifurcated. To be sure, early Christianity contained a strong element of faith healing, but those practices were generally abandoned sometime during the first three centuries. Nevertheless, in both the Roman church and among the various Protestant denominations and sects, individuals were known to be associated with healing. These included English Dissenter and founder of the Religious Society of Friends George Fox (1624–91); cleric, theologian, and cofounder of the Methodist movement John Wesley (1703–91); Shaker leader Mother

Ann Lee (1736–84); the prophet, teacher, and leader of the Latter Day Saints movement Joseph Smith (1805–44); the Scottish evangelist and faith healer John Alexander Dowie (1847–1907); and the Alsatian cobbler turned faith healer Francis Schlatter (1856–96). Their supposed "healings" provided marvelously creative theories regarding the extent of their powers.[1]

Notwithstanding these exceptions, Western views on the relationship between body and mind since the time of Descartes resulted in a division of spoils between science and religion. On one side, Western religions generally focused their energies on saving the immaterial soul, which they saw as separate from the material body, while Western medicine chose to view the body/mind as a construct of material forces to which it applied only biological and other natural principles. Rather than ascribe religio-medical explanations to cures that involved the mind, the medical profession chose the more benign terms "suggestion" and "placebo," both of which lacked divine manufacture. Within Western medicine's communities of healers, only its unconventional elements chose to regard health and wellness as an expression of the individual's harmony with some form of "otherness." Thus, Cartesian dualism put science and religion on separate tracks, leaving the reductionist sciences as the only recognized tenants of the medical arts. Into the late nineteenth century, evidence of this separation continued unabated, except for the advocates of metaphysical healing (including Christian Science) and select evangelical groups, some of whose leaders claimed to be particularly possessed of special healing powers. These groups insisted that Spirit was the exclusive channel for healing and proceeded on a course independent of materialistic medicine.[2]

New Thought's nonmedical approach to healing offered two distinct explanations for the source of the cure. The first, that of *transcendence,* drew from occult traditions to recapture powers once exercised by Jesus. The other, that of *immanence,* drew from preponderantly non-Western traditions to explain the capacity present in every individual for well-being and self-healing, but also postulated a separate life force derived from a cosmic source. For New Thought's religious and quasi-religious followers, both transcendence and imminence offered a concept of the mind, body, and spirit that complemented rather than competed with reductionist medicine. Even so, New Thought found itself in competition with numerous systems of healing, each offering a "return" in exchange for belief.

Allopathy

Despite what appeared at times to be a strong condemnation by New Thought of allopathic medicine, the relationship between the two was far more accommodating than either had with Christian Science. Generally speaking, New Thoughters chose not to reject biomedicine. In fact, several of its leading spokespeople trained as physicians, including Orison Swett Marden and Luther M. Marston, both graduates of Harvard Medical School.[3] This helps to explain why New Thought organizations such as the Emmanuel Movement not only consulted with doctors but worked hand in hand with their hospitals and dispensaries. It was not that they considered reductionist medicine to be wrong; they simply felt that in its limited view of the whole person, it failed to provide a full explanation of disease causation. Without taking into consideration the emotions, attitudes, beliefs, spiritual choices, and discords ruminating within the individual, the physician could only approximate but never fully understand disease causality.

Viewed as imperfect, medical orthodoxy was nevertheless judged to reflect humanity's present state of development. "The vast majority of medical practitioners are conscientious and self-sacrificing," observed Henry Wood in his *New Thought Simplified*, "and deservedly stand high in public estimation." They were exponents of a system under constant change, and eventually humanity would outgrow its reliance upon drug treatment and other materialistic regimens. "But so long as men regard themselves primarily as material beings they will rely mainly upon material means for the healing of disease," Wood explained. New Thought was not so much an alternative healing system as a new consciousness whose remedial powers were a reflection of changes in the spiritual interior of humans. Until spirituality was fully realized, Wood said, patients should continue to utilize those materialistic regimens they could see and feel, even if imperfect. Nevertheless, change was underway as doctors replaced the aging system of *materia medica* with newer agents such as electricity, massage, X-rays, colored light, fresh air, hygiene, diet, music, gymnastics, and a host of other noninvasive applications. In the meantime, he warned against the use of vaccines as detrimental to the purity of the body. Since time immemorial, drug medication had been "mingled with uncertainty and empiricism." Soon, Wood predicted, humanity would rely upon the body's inner recuperative powers alone to heal the body of its physical imperfections.[4]

More than anything else, the *materia medica* served as point of contention between allopathic medicine and the mind-cure movement. Since the body represented the outward expression of the inner person, the application of material drugs, with their ability to excite or depress the nervous system, was thought to have a demonstrably negative effect on the body's ability to heal. The *materia medica* might be a respectable system for allopathic medicine, but for mental healers it could be only temporary. In her popular *Healing Power of Mind,* published in 1884, Julia Anderson Root explained that since disease was mental in origin, drugs in whatever form were "delusions and snares." To the extent that humans were able to increase their spirituality, it was in their power to reduce their dependence on material medicine. All they needed was to understand God's laws and know how to apply them.[5]

For pioneer mental healer Leander Edmund Whipple (1848–1916), editor of *New Thought Magazine,* the *materia medica* assumed a "resident energy in material objects which have no life or force in themselves." Because all poisons injured the body, some part of the body's nervous mechanism was inevitably affected. When this occurred, the mind, the only intelligent element of vitality in the human body, was prevented from working at its highest level of effectiveness. Patients expected that drugs would act with a curative effect upon disease, but every drug that entered the circulation did so in a manner that impeded the system. "The atomic construction and molecular form of drugs is unlike that of any part of the human system," Whipple claimed. "There is no health either in a poison or in any of its attendant effects." In such conditions, corrective mental action was prevented from expressing itself, and while drugs sometimes provided temporary relief they did so at a cost to the life of the organism.[6]

Ursula Gestefeld (1845–1921) was a once-trusted devotee of Eddy who broke away to found her own group known as Science of Being. She attributed disease not to the power of the germ but to the body's mental passivity to negative thoughts. The physical body was not the seat of the disease but only the "plane of its visibility." Avoiding disease entailed "mental breathing," which amounted to bringing Christ into the soul, thereby inoculating it with eternal life. In this way individuals made themselves safe against the "mortal sense germs."

> The soul-atmosphere is filled with the emanations of souls, the thoughts which humanity has been thinking for generations. It is full of these germs, loaded with them. All the mortal beliefs of Adam-souls are in this storehouse and we breathe in that atmo-sphere constantly, inhaling, drawing into the soul-organism the germs of all kinds of sickness, suffering, and death; for these thoughts are the germs with which the soul is inoculated and which breed their consequences so long as the soul is susceptible to them. And the soul is susceptible so long as it is passive to sense-impres-sions, so long as it remains the Adam-soul. While this passivity continues the human race is bound to be disease-ridden, for the causes of disease are constantly at work and effects must follow. Not till resistance to thought-germs instead of passivity becomes the order will disease disappear, for the soul leaves it behind through growth, and in no other way.[7]

With the advent of cosmic consciousness, there was reason to believe that disease, along with crime and poverty, would eventually become relics of the past. "It may well be that the next hundred years of human progress will show man as victor over disease and pain, show him master of his own physical organism," ventured New Thought pub-lisher and author Charles Brodie Patterson (1854–1936).[8] "The mind can make the body whole and strong, or the mind can make it weak or dis-eased," he reasoned, "the result is purely a question of mental poise or lack of it." For Patterson, intuition came before reason, life before doc-trine, and the true gospel of healing before medical science.[9]

As allopathic medicine tied itself to the coattails of reductionist sci-ence, gaining notable advances in the last quarter of the nineteenth century due to advances in germ theory, pharmaco-therapeutics, hygiene, diet, immunizations, aseptics, and surgery, many of mental healing's proponents moved perceptively away from mind cure (although never really leaving it) as a closed system of therapeutics. Truth to tell, reductionist medicine outperformed society's expectations to the point of relegating much of metaphysical healing to the backwaters of New Thought thinking and opening the way for a more public discussion of positive thinking and its impact on happiness and prosperity.

Homeopathy

In contrast to allopathic medicine, which New Thought writers judged to be tainted by excessive materialism, homeopathy was praised for its bold advance into the mysteries of healing. Its infinitesimal doses supposedly aroused the organism's vital principle and drove out the intruding disease without inflicting harmful substances on the body. This was a "spiritual advance of no small magnitude," inasmuch as it acknowledged the presence of a divine life principle (i.e., vitalism) in the organism, explained author Helen Bigelow Merriman (1844–1933) in 1888. Nevertheless, to the extent that homeopathy relied on material means, however small, it remained estranged from the full benefit of this life principle.[10] Homeopathy's remedies were judged effective in proportion to their attenuation, meaning the degree to which they "approached more nearly to spirit." New Thought healers valued homeopathy as a spiritual advance in therapeutics whose ultra-molecular dilutions more than demonstrated its ability to work through the mind. Indeed, "the greatest effects were produced by those high attenuations in which there was no appreciable quantity of the drug left," explained Mathilda J. Barnett in her popular *Practical Metaphysics* (1880). Asserting that the most powerful remedies were those where the only thing left remaining in the medium was the dynamic or spirit power of the drug, Barnett praised the homeopathic effort to substitute "pure spirit" as the agent of healing. She predicted that in coming years homeopaths would prescribe only ultra-high potencies for treating the ills of humankind, a prediction that proved remarkably prescient. Today, homeopathic drugs are attenuated into the millions, leaving no molecular trace or imprint of the original drug in the solute.[11]

Mesmerism and Friends

By the second half of the nineteenth century, mesmerism, including hypnosis, was regarded as a form of "mental bondage" or mind control unrepresentative of American values. Though opponents of the practice admitted that it was more ethereal than any material drug and potentially an effective agent of cure, they argued that it relied on the power of mind control radiating from the healer's body. So destructive was this supposed force on healer and patient alike that Quimby reportedly took frequent vacations of total rest to recover from its effects. Years later, osteopaths were warned that their spinal manipulation of patients could result in the outflow of vital magnetism through their hands. "It is not conducive to the good health of the Osteopath, or magnetic healer, to use both hands while treating the sick," advised Richard Ingalese in his book *The History and Power of Mind* (1902). Immediately after treatment, he urged osteopaths to bathe in hot water, rubbing their arms and hands from the elbow downward to the tips of the fingers to remove any low-vibrating atoms from their bodies.[12]

Henry Wood proposed "Ideal Suggestion" as a worthwhile substitute for mesmerism, believing that it carried no alien element or personality into the individual psyche. Its mental impression was pure, spiritual, and impersonal. Wood gave the following instructions on how to prepare for its application:

1. Retire each day to a quiet apartment, and be alone IN THE SILENCE.

2. Assume the most restful position possible, in an easy-chair, or otherwise; breathe deeply and rather rapidly for a few moments, and thoroughly relax the physical body, for by suggestive correspondence this renders it easier for the mind to be passive and receptive.

3. Bar the door of thought against the external world, and also shut out all physical sensation and imperfection.

4. Rivet the mind upon the "meditation," and by careful and repeated reading absorb its truth. Then place the "suggestion" at a suitable distance from the eyes, and fasten them upon it

for from ten to twenty minutes. Do not merely look upon it, but wholly GIVE YOURSELF UP TO IT, until it fills and overflows the entire consciousness.

5. Close the eyes for twenty to thirty minutes more; behold it with the mind's eye, and let it permeate the whole organism.

6. Call it into the field of mental vision during every wakeful hour of the night.

7. If disordered conditions are chronic and tenacious, there need be no discouragement if progress is not rapid, nor if "ups and downs" occur. Absorb the ideals REPEATEDLY, until no longer needed. The cure is NOT magical, but a NATURAL GROWTH. Ideals will be actualized in due season.[13]

New Thoughters took a similarly dim view of channeling. First made prominent in mid-nineteenth century with the popularity of the Fox sisters and the phenomenon known as Spiritualism, channeling (i.e., where a medium goes into a trance to receive a spirit or entity that speaks in some form) gathered momentum through the second half of the century, clinging to the coattails of notable public mediums whose séances reportedly included a mixture of paranormal experiences, including rappings, voices, levitation, tablet-writing, and flying objects. As with mesmerism, channeling was viewed as a corrupting influence dependent upon some level of spirit control that could potentially injure the medium and/or the patient. "To yield our will . . . to the control . . . of others, and become a mere automaton for their intelligence and opinions," remarked John Hamlin Dewey, "is destructive of our individuality and personal character." The true source of illumination with the Divine came not from "disorderly spirits" who still roamed the earth but through divine inspiration.[14]

Channeling was practiced in the late nineteenth and early twentieth century by Edgar Cayce (1877–1945), Emma Hardinge Britten (1823–99), Allan Kardec (1804–69), and the Davenport Brothers (Erastus [1839–1911] and William [1841–77]), and in more recent times by mystic Judy Zebra Knight (b. 1946), English-born Spiritualist C. Doreen Phillips (1927–2003), poet and psychic Jane Roberts (1929–84), clairvoyant Margaret McElroy (b. 1946), and spirit channeler Esther Hicks (b. 1948). They see themselves as vessels through which noncorporeal entities in the spirit world (i.e., Ramtha, ascended Masters, Brahma Kumaris, Abraham, and Kryon) communicate with humans in the natural world. According to Michael A. Brown in *The Channeling Zone: American Spirituality in an Anxious Age* (1997), much of what passes as metaphysical channeling has become a materialized commodification of spirituality, with money as the most sought form of energy.[15]

Ironically, while New Thought writers were singularly hostile to channeling, they were generally supportive of Joseph Rodes Buchanan's science of psychometry, which held that highly sensitive individuals could "read" the history or character of an object or individual simply by pressing the artifact (i.e., rock, signature, or article of clothing) to the forehead. As a form of "superior vision," it supposedly allowed the psychometrist to "feel" the aura emanating from an object and thereby intuit the full identity and character of its owner.[16] Along with Buchanan, William and Elizabeth Denton were credited with having discovered psychometry and the resulting mental telegraphy between the soul-world and living beings. "Though ignored by the scientific authorities and schoolmen of his day," Dewey was convinced that Buchanan's work would eventually be recognized.[17]

While both channeling and psychometry were different in that the former involved bringing the thoughts or vibratory forces of an *outside* entity into the consciousness of a living person while, in the latter situation, the person absorbed the vibratory forces emanating from *within* an inanimate object, both relied upon paranormal explanations inimical to the epistemological foundations of reductionist science. That channeling would be deemed inappropriate while psychometry was welcomed into New Thought seems strange, particularly since the former was more broadly accepted in the popular culture.

Prayer Cure

Religious groups that employed prayer as a form of petition for worldly needs were challenged by the proponents of New Thought who considered it little different from begging, pleading, or otherwise beseeching God for intervention. Such prayers were never answered, insisted Jane W. Yarnall, author of *Practical Healing for Mind and Body* (1891), because they were made without a "righteous conception of God." To be effective, prayers must be "of acknowledgment, of thanksgiving, of affirmation or recognition of what is already provided." One should never expect to change the plans or purposes of God by pleading. "We must be reconciled to God as He is," she advised, "not God reconciled to us."[18]

In more recent years, Unity minister Catherine Ponder (b. 1927), author of *Pray and Grow Rich* (1968), explained that the reason so many prayers went unanswered was due to the fact that prayer was really a matter of going within. As spiritual beings made in the image of God, humans were intended to use prayer as the "connecting line between God and man."[19] True prayer always began with the purification or cleansing of one's thought. This required using the word "no" to erase all unhappy thoughts, followed by the release of all willful attitudes and relationships. When this occurred, a channel opened to receive God. In other words, prayer was not a petition but a genuine illumination into the Spirit.[20]

Jewish Science

British inspirational speaker and author William Wilberforce Juvenal Colville (1859–1917) was one of many New Thought healers who decried the use of terms that gave Christianity special status in metaphysical healing. He found Christian Science particularly objectionable, since it led unsuspecting people to suppose that the power to heal was a closely held secret confided to Eddy alone and obtainable only by paying hard currency for her proprietary courses. In reality, he explained, Eddy simply shared a belief held by many that the body could be made subservient to the mind. That she would lay claim to a secret healing method revealed only to those who paid her a fee represented the most "pernicious form of superstition."[21] Equally importantly, Colville objected to Christian Science because it slighted Jews and other non-Christian believers who were doing fully as much good as anybody who had ascribed to Christian Science. There was no reason to make metaphysical cures the sole property of Eddy, Jesus, or anyone for that matter. Christian Science was nothing more than a mental culture whose underlying principles applied to materialists as well as those who viewed health as a matter of religious blessedness. The culture of good habits and humane thoughts were within the capacity of all—believers and nonbelievers alike. Recognizing that the words "Christ," "Christian," and "Christianity" were unpleasant terms for Jews, theists, Spiritualists, and Free Religionists, all of whom might practice various forms of mental healing, Colville recommended the more neutral term "Spiritual Science."[22]

To be sure, America's Jewish population was not immune to the issue of divine healing or the growing influence of Christian Science and New Thought. In fact, many Jews had gravitated to Eddy's metaphysical healing system in the late nineteenth and early twentieth century.[23] Historian Michael A. Meyer estimated that as many as fifty thousand Jews were affiliated with Christian Science in New York City alone during the 1920s.[24]

In response to the appeal of Christian Science and New Thought to the members of the American Jewish community, Rabbi Alfred Geiger Moses (1878–1956), who served his rabbinate in Mobile, Alabama, from 1901 to 1940, sought to win back errant Jews by saying that the Jewish faith had its own healing traditions. Rejecting Eddy's absolute idealism, he explained that both matter and spirit were real and that the true fabric of one's health involved the integration of both.[25] In his book *Jewish Science: Divine Healing in Judaism* (1916), Moses referred to a similar Hebrew tradition that he called *chochmoh,* meaning *divine wisdom* or *science,* meant to address the subject of divine healing as it unfolded in the history of the Jewish people. Faith cure was Jewish in origin, he insisted, having been an integral part of Jewish scriptures thousands of years prior to the claims of Eddy and her disciples. In more recent history, it was explicitly expressed in the prayer book *Tefillah of Israel,* which contained prayers for divine healing.[26]

Moses intended to win back to Judaism those who had been assimilated into the non-Jewish world. "Christian Science and similar faiths are not needed by the true Jew who knows and loves his Religion," he

explained, since Jewish Science contained "every important principle in the art of Divine Healing."[27] He recognized that many Jews who
had either suffered from illness or had seen another suffer had sought
out homeopathy, osteopathy, New Thought, vibration cure, or animal
magnetism before trying Christian Science. "A drowning man clutches
at a straw," Moses opined, "and the distracted Jew begins his course in
the school of Mrs. Eddy . . . and the bible of Christian Science becomes
his Bible."[28] Thus, when Jews were told that Eddy's *Science and Health*
was the first declaration of the principle of divine healing, they turned
to it without reflecting on their own religious traditions "No Jew needs
to become a Christian Scientist in order to find the Law of Healing by
Prayer," he insisted. "Christian Science offers absolutely nothing new to
the Jewish Mind. It is simply Judaism, veneered with Christology or the
belief in the divinity of Jesus."[29]

For Moses, the psychological factor, or agent, in faith cure was the
power of auto-suggestion inasmuch as all strong suggestions help in the
healing process, something that was known to both the medical doctor
and the rabbi. In other words, faith and science were in harmony in the
treatment of disease. And, as with all suggestions to the subconscious
mind, none seemed more appropriate to Moses than "the pure idea
of faith in an All-Good God."[30] Moses's *Universalism and Nationalism
in the Prophets* (1901) and *Jewish Science, Psychology of Health, Joy and
Success: or, the Applied Psychology of Judaism* (1920) became important
sources for the emerging movement of Jewish Science.

Moses also disclosed that the healing practices popular within the
eighteenth century Chasidic movement in Russia, Poland, and Gali-
cia represented a protest against the rigid legalism that had crept into
Judaism. In this movement, the Podolian Rabbi Eliezer Baal Shem Tov
(1698–1760), also known as Besht, became for the Chasidim what Eddy
had become for the Christian Scientists. Unlike Christian Science, however, Chasidism employed a combination of prayer and material medicine. Besht's principal ideas, characterized in the Chasidic creed, are
religious pantheism and the idea of communion between God and
human beings.[31] Chasidism had its greatest growth in the early decades
of the nineteenth century when, after being legalized by the Russian

government, it spread through Eastern Europe and played an important role in shaping subsequent Jewish thought. [32]

Another leader in Jewish Science was Morris Lichtenstein (1889–1938), who grew up in Cincinnati, Ohio, where he was ordained at Hebrew Union College in 1916 before continuing his education at Columbia University and subsequently serving as a rabbi in Amsterdam and Troy, both in New York state, and also in New York City. Together with his wife, Tehilla Hirshenson, he founded the Society of Jewish Science in 1922, institutionalizing what Moses had started and providing a Jewish identity to the healing effects of right thinking. [33] Both physical and spiritual health were derived from affirmative prayer and, although Jewish Science chose to distance itself from Christian Science by not discarding medical intervention, it did hold with a view that God or some energy force was responsive to prayers offered in silence. Lichtenstein's radio broadcasts and magazine *Jewish Science Interpreter* effectively served as a counterweight to Christian Science and the New Thought movement. His books include *Conquest of Fear* (1922), *Jewish Science and Health* (1925), *Peace of Mind* (1927), *Cures for Minds in Distress* (1936), *How to Live* (1938), and *Joy of Life* (1938). [34]

In his *Cures for Minds in Distress*, Lichtenstein provided one of the more articulate explanations for the treatment of the nervous ailments (i.e., neurasthenia, melancholia, mania, hysteria, epilepsy, paranoia, dementia praecox, complexes, abnormal impulses, and insomnia) proving so injurious to the modern world. Although not all of these nervous conditions were life-threatening, their spread across civilized life had intensified humanity's struggle for existence to the point of exhausting energies so necessary for endurance in "the common race for success." [35] While some of the nervous instability in modern society was the result of individuals' neurotic dispositions, it was wrong to presume that heredity accounted for the notable increase of nervous diseases, especially the milder varieties such as neurasthenia. It was clear to Lichtenstein that there was a marked difference in the pace of modern society from previous times. The busy schedules, the new curricula in schools, the additional mental demands of advanced civilization, the competition that was part of every profession and business, and the life of haste had caused many to "overstrain themselves in order to keep up satisfactorily with the required standards." All of these factors had come at a time when religious beliefs and practices had deteriorated under the harsh glare of science.[36]

Lichtenstein chose not to deny the roles that medicine, psychoanalysis, and religion all had in the treatment of mental distress. No system of therapeutics had a monopoly on healing. In fact, most curative methods had proven their worth by facilitating recuperative powers already ingrained in humanity. Thus, any particular remedy or system of therapeutics that enhanced this quality was a valued factor in the physical, mental, and spiritual health of the individual. Medicine, with its foundations in physiology and anatomy, had done much that was praiseworthy, especially in the fields of surgery, immunization, instrumentation, and diagnosis, but it had achieved little success dealing with mental maladies. Allopathic medicine had been successful in treating the corporeal aspects of the body much like a good mechanic treated a machine, but its solution to abnormal mental conditions had been much less effective, notwithstanding the fact that mental states had definite influences on the body.[37]

Lichtenstein was also interested in psychoanalysis, which chose to look at the origin of various psychoses not as a physical problem but as an experience locked away in the vast storehouse of the unconscious. Citing the examples of dream theory and suppressed sexual longings, he outlined Freud's proposition that every neurosis was some form of disguised but frustrated sexual demand, meaning that neurotic symptoms were simply substitutes when normal gratification of the sexual instinct was suppressed or denied. For Freud, Breuer, and Jung, the remedy came by way of *abreaction,* meaning the purging from the mind of these hidden complexes. By bringing the complexes to the light of consciousness through dream analysis as well as free association, they ceased to be troubling.[38]

For Lichtenstein, however, psychoanalysis was built on a "chain of assumptions, none of which has actually been demonstrated as an immovable truth." He saw no reason to believe there was a relationship between the suppressed wish and the method of abreaction. Moreover, he doubted the entire theory of suppression, viewing it as unfounded. "Do we not observe in nature in general and in man in particular that the tendency on the part of nature is not to conserve its wounds but rather to *outgrow* them?" he asked. "Why should the fate of the sex misconceptions and maladjustments of childhood be any different from all the other misconceptions and maladjustments of that age?"[39] Lichtenstein concluded that psychoanalysis was not only erroneous in its theory but detrimental in practice to both the patient and the general population.[40]

The spiritual method of treatment remained Lichtenstein's preferred choice, recognizing that it also served as an important adjunct to regular medicine as well. In order to make clear his concept of spiritual healing, he insisted that the power that heals is "a universal Mind whose presence is in everything that exists."[41] Since the universal Mind or Power dwells in every phenomenon, including each individual, no human power can be credited with healing; rather, it is the product of the wise, creative, and benevolent God. Whether offered with the lips or in silence, affirmative prayer created a mental image of the state in which the individual desired to be. As the mind concentrated on this image, individuals placed themselves in tune with the Infinite Mind, making them susceptible to its influx.

> Divine healing may be conceived as coming from within or from without. The Divine Mind fills the Universe and dwells both within and without man; Divine help may therefore be visualized as welling from the depths of the consciousness of man or as coming from infinite sources outside of man. . . . In picturing the process . . . one should, in the first part of his prayer, visualize healing as coming from an infinite fountain of health; and in the second part of his prayer he should see himself as healthy and thoroughly restored.[42]

Jewish Science formulated ten fundamentals. Unlike Christian Science, these were not creeds that every adherent was required to accept; rather, they were beliefs that Jewish Scientists hoped to attain through conviction and experience. Not imposed on believers, they were simply representative of a search for spiritual truth.

1. The Jewish Faith is the only faith we acknowledge. Jewish Science is the application of the Jewish Faith to the practices of life.

2. We believe wholeheartedly in the efficacy of prayer. We believe that no prayer, when properly offered, goes unanswered.

3. We shall endeavor every day of our lives to keep serene; to check all tendencies to violence and anger; to keep calm even in the face of unpleasant and discouraging circumstances.

4. We shall strive to be cheerful every day of our lives. The Talmud says that the Divine Presence departs from one who is in gloom.

5. We shall seek to cultivate an attitude of love and good-will towards everyone. We shall make no room in our heart for hatred or bitterness. The world was created on a plan of divine love, and to admit thoughts of hatred or malice is to violate the plan of God.

6. We shall cultivate a disposition to contentment, envying no one, and praising God for the good He has already bestowed upon us. Contentment is the greatest friend of happiness; envy, its greatest enemy.

7. We shall make conscious effort to banish worry and fear from our lives. We regard these two as the greatest enemies of mankind and give them no place in our consciousness.

8. We shall trust in God's goodness in every circumstance of our life.

9. We believe that death is an elevation to eternal life, and not a cessation of existence.

10. We believe that God is the Source of Health and the Restorer of Health.[43]

Jewish Science served as a direct counterforce to Christian Science by proposing a more rational and progressive approach to disease and healthy-mindedness than the metaphysics of Mary Baker Eddy.

Theosophy

Theosophy ("god-wisdom") is a syncretic system of Eastern and Western religious and philosophic thought with trace elements from Plato (429–347 BC), Plotinus (204–270), and Jacob Boehme (1575–1624). Considered a white, middle-class, and essentially feminine movement, Theosophy was one of several esoteric groups to explore the religions of the East. Organized in New York City in 1875 by Russian immigrant Helena Petrovna Blavatsky (1831–91) and lawyer and writer Henry Steel Olcott (1832–1907), it purports to be the esoteric wisdom of the world's greatest religious prophets (i.e., Moses, Krishna, Lao-tzu, Confucius, Buddha, and Christ) handed down by gifted seers known as "adepts" or "masters" in the form of "materialized letters" interpreted and published by Blavatsky in *Isis Unveiled: A Master Key to the Mysteries of Ancient and Modern Science and Theology* (1877) and *The Secret Doctrine: The Synthesis of Science, Religion and Philosophy* (1893). As seekers of certain truth, Blavatsky and Olcott claimed to have discovered a cosmos characterized by absolutes and a nondemocratic hierarchy of masters teaching spiritual and racial evolution.

Theosophy viewed the prevailing orthodoxies in medicine, psychology, and religion as having done little to minimize the ravaging afflictions of the body. It opposed the use of drugs and physical practices such as osteopathy as well as hypnotism, mesmerism, Christian Science, and mind cure as having purported healing when the only outcome was to make the patient more dependent on the healer. These cures, from the Theosophical perspective, were due simply to the application of occult powers on the lower planes *(prana)* of nature and misunderstood metaphysics. By contrast, the laws of health as taught by Theosophy had been formulated into doctrines by the "wise men and true physicians" of antiquity who had developed and perfected the physical, mental, psychic, and spiritual components of humanity to near perfection. The seat of true health was the astral body, whose electrical and magnetic essence operated independently of the physical body, guiding it through the fields of experience lying within the animal, vegetable, and mineral world.[44]

For the devotees of Theosophy, the seeds of disease were located primarily in the mind and they created havoc among the inner currents of vibrations that passed through the physical body. Unlike mind-cure healers who saw the spiritual body as free from disease, the Irish-born mystic and occultist William Quan Judge (1851–96), who helped form the Theosophical Society, considered it like a container of seeds that, if left unattended, "sprouted again and again as physical diseases as well as those purely mental." Rather than treat the physical body with palliatives, he looked to the mind and its effects on the "inner body."

> The ethereal body has its own current-nerves, for want of a better word, changes and methods of growth and action, just as the gross body has. It is, in fact, the real body, for it seldom alters throughout life. . . . The inner currents emanate from their own centers and are constantly in motion. They are affected by thoughts and the reflection of the body in its physiological changes. They each act upon the other incessantly. (Every center of the inner body has its appropriate correspondent in the physical one, which it affects and through which it is in turn acted upon.) It is by means of these subtle currents called "vital airs" when translated from the Sanskrit that impressions are conveyed to the mind above, and through them also are the extraordinary feats of the séance room and the Indian Yogi accomplished.[45]

Based on a belief that the universe developed through seven stages of evolution and that the whole of humanity moved through an ascending arc of reincarnation to arrive at pure consciousness ("I am"), Theosophy's philosophy and practices include a belief in planes of psychic intuition, occult racial theories, bursts of energy or chakras, pulsating prana (breath of life), and spiritual enlightenment. Despite vigorous denials, evidence of fraud surfaced in the mid-1880s and continued to attach themselves to the alleged marvels at the Theosophical center in the Indian city of Adyar, where Blavatsky had established herself. For the remainder of her life, Blavatsky's claims were viewed under the dark cloud of skepticism. Even her coadjutor Olcott had a somewhat jaundiced view of her. "If there ever existed a person in history," he wrote, "who was a greater conglomeration of good and bad, light and shadow, wisdom and indiscretion, spiritual insight and lack of common sense, I cannot recall the name, the circumstances, or the epoch."[46]

After Blavatsky's death in 1891, the movement split into several groups, with Annie Besant (1847–1933) as leader of the society based in Adyar, beckoning believers in a more Asian direction. Another group, led by Katherine Tingley (1847–1929), was headquartered in New York City until resettling in Loma Linda, California, where she founded the Raja-Yoga School and Theosophical University.[47] Yet another branch was founded by Austrian philosopher and esotericist Rudolf Steiner (1861–1925) who, insisting that Christianity remain as the core element of its philosophy, broke with Besant and her allegiance to Jiddu Krishnamurti, the incarnated "Christ," to establish his own Anthroposophical Society.[48]

Theosophy created considerable debate within the New Thought movement, with many warning that reincarnation was merely a hypothesis, and not a very credible one at that. Elizabeth Towne was even less gracious, accusing Blavatsky of doling out the wisdom of the Mahatmas when it best suited her purposes. "Why have all these anthropomorphic Lords and Mahatmas between you and a sublimated God who cannot talk to you direct?" Towne asked. It seemed to her that Theosophy was little more than a "trituration of polytheism." The more Lords, Masters, and Mahatmas that believers found in creation, the more distant they were from God. Better to do without them. "Wipe them off the map!" Towne urged.

> Nobody is any closer to God than you are. Nobody has any more
> of a monopoly of God than you have. See that nobody has any
> greater faith in the God within him than you have. See that nobody
> depends more absolutely upon the God within him than you
> depend upon the God within you. Do the will of God within you,
> and you shall know what to believe on all manner of subjects. . . .
> Call no man Master, call no teacher Master, call no Mahatma
> Master, call no Lord Master. Only One is your Master, the One
> within you.[49]

Notwithstanding New Thought's reluctance to accept the full measure of Theosophy, selective groups within the New Thought movement, including Unity, laid claim to reincarnation as the final stage of humanity's spiritual development, arguing that it proved helpful in understanding the importance of affirmation, optimism, and awakened spiritual consciousness.[50] Like the St. Louis Hegelians and the many contributors to Paul Carus's (1852–1919) Open Court Publishing Company and *The Monist* (1890–present) journal, Theosophy sought to identify some common ground between the polarities of religion and science. Encouraged by the founding of Ramakrishna-Vivekananda centers and the popularity of the World Parliament of Religions in 1893, Theosophy became an integral part of America's journey into selflessness and transcendence.[51]

Christian Theosophy

Despite a pronounced skepticism of Blavatsky's Theosophy, an element within the New Thought movement attempted to find a bridge between the two systems. Eventually dubbed Christian Theosophy, these writings contained both Western and occult elements, including reincarnation, but were predominantly Christian in focus. A prominent example was Rudolf Steiner's Anthroposophy and, more recently, prophetess and clairvoyant Ann Ree Colton (1898–1984) and her system of Niscience, meaning beyond academic knowledge.

Charles Brodie Patterson explained the principles of the system in his *The Measure of a Man* (1904): "there is no separation between your soul and the soul of the universe." Humans were just an individualized expression of the one Spirit. Humanity was God incarnate.[52] This inclusion of humanity in God created a particular set of dynamics when addressing the topics of sin, sickness, suffering, and death. But how could humans so destined be subject to moral evils?

In resolving the puzzle, various New Thoughters, including Henry C. Sheldon, attempted to bridge the gap between Theosophy and New Thought by explaining the individual as a work in progress, a soul transitioning to a higher attainment. So-called moral evils were only indications of a lack of development. All disease originated in the emotional life of the individual and proceeded from mental aberrations of fear and other negative activities. While the *materia medica* reflected the current state of human development, the next hundred years or more would witness humanity's victory over disease and pain. Similarly, crime and poverty would become things of the past.[53]

New Thought writer and physician John Hamlin Dewey practiced medicine for nearly twenty-five years before turning to the purely mental and spiritual side of healing. As proprietor and teacher at a school of applied psychology in New York City, he described three planes of consciousness through which individuals exercised their faculties. First was the plane of the physical senses, where personality became visible through use of the mental, moral, and social faculties. The second plane, that of the occult functions (the sixth sense), opened consciousness and awakened the interior faculties. The third plane was the purely spiritual and divine, the highest and most interior sphere of consciousness. It was this latter sphere that acted in "perfect unity and oneness with the Father." The human species alone was capable of achieving this inward divinity and thus stood between two worlds, a blending of the animal below and the Divine above.[54]

Dewey's version of Christian Theosophy was heavily laced with Swedenborgian concepts, although there is no reference in his various works of his having read any of Swedenborg's writings. In his *The Way, the Truth and the Life: A Handbook of Christian Theosophy, Healing, and Psychic Culture, A New Education, Based on the Ideal and Method of the Christ* (1888), Dewey's division of creation into the three planes noted above were comparable to Swedenborg's three levels of the mind and existence (natural, spiritual, celestial). His works also contained concepts similar to Swedenborg's law of correspondences; his rejection of ecclesiasticism and theological dogmatism; his emphasis on the inner and outer person; and his concept of matter as a condition of spiritual substance made visible for divine purposes. Where Dewey differed from Swedenborg was in his belief that individuals could attain occult knowledge and power. Among Swedenborgians, that ability was believed to have been given to Swedenborg alone and not shared with other humans. For Dewey, however, Christian Theosophy was the only philosophy that adequately embraced the existence of an overruling intelligence and divine government. Neither materialism nor pantheism could make this claim, nor could those theologians whose claims rested upon the Bible as the only direct and authoritative revelation of God. Christian Theosophy was attained not by revelation but by direct insight or illumination into the divine mind. This belief of Dewey's differed from Blavatsky's Theosophy, which taught that illumination came by way of the secret Brotherhood of Mahatmas.[55]

Behind the veil of the physical universe in Christian Theosophy lay a spiritual universe of incomprehensible magnitude with infinite gradations of beings whose environment corresponded with their interior states of wisdom and holiness—a concept also found in Swedenborg's writings. While clairvoyants were able to use their inner vision to behold scenes of this inner world and even converse with its souls, a few select individuals were transported into the more interior regions of the heavens to witness scenes "so vastly above and beyond anything corresponding therewith in the natural world, as to baffle every attempt at description."[56] Dewey's reliance on Swedenborg was never as clear and obvious as his description of the planes of life in the world of spirits.

> [T]he personal life of every one, whether conscious of the fact or not, is in conjunction with the corresponding plane of life in the world of spirits, in which we all exist even now by virtue of our interior organism, though held to the outward world by the physical body. Hence the unfolding of our spiritual nature and life here will lift us into conjunction with corresponding planes of heavenly life and influence, and with the opening of the divine life within comes the opening also of the door of conscious communion and fellowship with heavenly societies, who are one with the ascended Christ in the ministry of heaven to earth.[57]

Like many representatives of New Thought, Dewey believed that the mission of Jesus was not to teach but to establish a method by which all might come to the immediate and intuitive knowledge of truth through inward illumination. Explaining this direct and immediate knowledge of God, which was accompanied by the attainment of both physical and spiritual perfection, was the task of Christian Theosophy. This was to be achieved not by turning to Indian Theosophy, Buddhism, or even Spiritualism, but by bringing Christianity back to its esoteric origin, meaning, and purity. The Theosophy of the Christ was not a secretive Brotherhood of Mahatmas serving as channels of communication. The covenant that God had made with human beings began with Jesus as the God-anointed mediator, leading by example— the "Great Exemplar."[58]

Dewey attributed the origins of modern metaphysical healing to Quimby, who had discovered that what people called disease was a delusion of the mind. It was "a disturbed or deranged condition of vital action, to which all physical organisms . . . are liable under abnormal conditions."[59] Removing the disturbance and restoring harmony to the vital processes resulted in removing the disease and restoring health. Since the body's condition in both health and disease is a reflection of the mental state and therefore the mind, it is the mind, not the body, that is the proper subject for treatment. By bringing forth the spiritual nature of a person, the mind is enabled to assert and achieve supremacy over the body.[60] Although light, heat, magnetism, electricity, and chemical affinity are active in the world, they remain subservient to powers of consciousness, thought, and volition. The power of mental supremacy cannot be overstated or underestimated. Faith was the key that unlocked the soul's resources, bringing forth an inward fountain of possibilities. Denying the power of disease in the body, he wrote, one destroys its force. Recognizing God as the source of life is to empower one to overcome every evil.[61]

It was the function of the inner sixth or psychometric sense to acquire knowledge of the corresponding qualities and conditions of things. The development of this psychic power awakened the mind. Drawing upon the works of W. F. Evans, Dewey directed his readers to the power of inner concentration, namely, forming a mental picture and holding the attention upon it. The perfection of this "inner sight" forced the bodily sensations and conditions to come under its control, thereby unfolding the higher gifts of the Spirit to the outward person. "Remember," advised Dewey, "that desire is the only true prayer, and that all desire for good, focalized in faith or expectation of receiving it, is the prayer of faith which secures the blessing."[62]

Whether designated as "nature" by the materialists, "od" by Baron Reichenbach, "vril" by Edward Bulwer-Lytton, "divine influx" by Emanuel Swedenborg, "akasa" by the Adept Brotherhood of India, or other terms such as "The Divine Thought," "The Celestial Ocean," "ether," or "Holy Ghost," all life was sustained by one or more life principles. For Christian Theosophists, "divine influx" permeated every crevice and every tissue. It did so from above and below, surrounding and pressing upon every side. Eager to be admitted into the soul, it was filled with the divine intention to bless and to heal, if only humanity would allow it to do so.[63]

* * *

To this day, unconventional medicine stands against the empirically-tested system of reductionist medicine, offering a thinly veiled vitalistic doctrine that defines the life principle as something distinct from processes explicable by the laws of physics and chemistry. Vitalism refers to a "spark," "energy," or "principle" that explains the causation of life and is also responsible for the health of a living organism. By the middle of the twentieth century, this curative principle not only included the metaphysical systems of New Thought and Christian Science, but also homeopathy, osteopathy, naturopathy, acupuncture, chiropractic, and other unconventional therapies. All expressed their healing modalities in the context of a nonspecific paranormal causation outside the known sciences.

8

The Prophet Margin

*Opulence is the law of the Universe, an
abundant supply of everything if nothing
is put in the way of its coming.*

—Ralph Waldo Trine, *In Tune with the Infinite*

In matters of faith, the religious mind of nineteenth-century America was formed by Puritan dissidents whose depictions of God and humanity laid the groundwork for the nation's rigorous morality. Central to their beliefs was the conviction that humans were lost in sin, saved only by the grace of God and not by any merit or effort on their own part. Nevertheless, the elect and the damned were each accountable for their condition. Over time, strands of this conviction enabled the founding of innumerable churches, all sustained by belief in the omnipotence of a sovereign and inscrutable God. Even though the doctrine of salvation decreed that God's grace rather than human efforts opened the gates of heaven, and that nothing an individual did could in any way "earn" that access, the doctrine had the effect of unleashing an intense activism among believers who concluded that grace, once bestowed, must result in a thoroughgoing change—both internal and external—in the sinner's now-sanctified life. Salvation was the centerpiece of life's drama, whose proof lay in the visible evidence of the regenerate's saintliness. Not surprisingly, the test of regenerating grace was brought face to face with the judgment of the community that demanded to see the evidence in external signs of conduct, including changes in the former sinner's material worth. The fusion of spiritual and materialistic signs of favor lent a social dimension to the religious experience, suggesting that mere moral conduct was itself no final proof of regeneration. Instead, the judgment of the community was brought to bear on the whole individual for signs of God's choice. Unless faith was conditioned by visible signs, there was no way of knowing who God had arbitrarily chosen, or, for that matter, to whom society should look for guidance and leadership. This became known as doctrine of the covenant, the theological concept that God had contracted with the human race to allow for a reasoned understanding of the relationship between grace and good works.

The circumstances that had led to the broad acceptance of covenant theology blurred over time as positions were either forgotten or abandoned, replaced by a public creed that became more and more inclusive. Religious diversity remained an important expression of American Protestantism, but its success in large part was due to the easy crossover among church members who chose their churches for socioeconomic reasons rather than as a reflection of any doctrinal beliefs. Over the course of time, the steady drift toward a more democratic theology and an optimistic worldview served to moderate the religiosity of church organizations, the emphasis on human sinfulness and the need for redemption, and the focus on the overpowering nature of God's love. Religion became less of a bedrock for separating saints from sinners and more of an episode in the personal quest for meaning.

The practical side of this new spirit expressed itself in an even more liberal covenant, suggesting that if the individual earnestly sought grace, he or she would not be denied. Not only did God condescend to treat humans as equals, he allowed that they should have the power to be the best that they could be. This resonated well with the popular disposition for simple virtues, a preference for happiness over contemplation of a wrathful God, a recognition that business and profits not only absorbed more of the time previously allocated to religion and salvation but created a complementary set of worthwhile virtues, and an assurance that all could secure the glory of Christ's visible kingdom when infused with God's grace. Empowered by a culture of positive thinking and a radicalized belief in self-reliance, the markers of dour Calvinism gave way to belief in the innate goodness of humanity and the eventual elimination of disease, poverty, and evil. Along with these changes, the motivational representatives of the age presented society with an ubiquitous vision that included the contact of mind with mind; the tactile and tele-pathic delivery of emotional states of mind; verbally based suggestions and affirmations; the relevance of trust, confidence, power, and oneness with God; and the extension of healthy-mindedness to include a new gospel of success for business and life generally.

This transformation was helped along in the last quarter of the nine-teenth century by the emergence of national brand advertising and the dramatic shift in publishing from regional to mass circulation of maga-zines and books. It was at this time that much of the pre-canonical litera-ture of early New Thought writers gained broad acceptance, exploding into the wider cultural arena—both denominational and secular—and muting the divide between the socioeconomic classes. Issues such as socialism, class conflict, labor unrest, and poverty took a back seat to a plethora of literature touting the self-made nature of poverty, the importance of individual hard work and achievement, and the promise of material comfort that was only a wish away. New Thought's readers learned that the only barriers to personal health, happiness, and pros-perity were self made, meaning that failure was due to personal fault. In essence, the literature of New Thought transformed the deepening social and economic contradictions of the age into issues of personal success or failure. New Thought's self-appointed instructors, counselors, and prophets offered a combination of guidance and wisdom intended to explain how individuals could heal themselves, thereby restoring health and autonomy. Arguably, the ideas put forth by these writers, lec-turers, and publishers confirmed the dominant ideology of American capitalism by blaming any weaknesses on personal failure. The key doc-trine in this pernicious thinking is the so-called "prosperity gospel" or "prosperity theology," which teaches that God blesses those he favors with material wealth—the visible sign of God's redeeming grace.

The Potency of Character

As explained by cultural historian Richard Huber, the Ameri-can idea of success, sanctioned by religious injunction and embed-ded in Calvinist values, expressed a "character ethic" best epitomized in McGuffey's Readers, whose moral virtues included self-discipline, hard work, honesty, and deferred gratification. True success was not defined by the acquisition of material wealth alone but by adherence to a concept of stewardship that tempered wealth's material benefits with more sober social obligations tied to service. Success, however defined, entailed public responsibility. Reinforced in the works of Cotton Mather, Benjamin Franklin, Henry Ward Beecher, Horatio Alger, and Freeman Hunt's monthly *Merchants' Magazine and Commercial Review* (1839–48), this character ethic began eroding with the writings of New Thought authors, whose amalgam of science, pseudoscience, transcendentalism, idealism, psychology, and self-affirmation promised health, prosperity, and happiness to all who accepted the proposition that being one with God would conquer life's challenges. As Huber explained, "Since you are divine and one with God, by thinking you are one with God, you cannot be poor, because God cannot be poor. Poverty being in its root a wrong belief, change the belief and it will cure the poverty. By faith we are thus made prosperous."[1]

Once weakened, the nation's character ethic was eventually replaced by a "personality ethic" that was evident in the works of Charles F. Haanel, Frank Channing Haddock, Dorothea Brande, William Makepeace Thayer, Elbert Hubbard, Orison Swett Marden, B. C. Forbes, Claude Bristol, Bruce Barton, and Émile Coué before exploding in the hugely popular works of Napoleon Hill and Dale Carnegie. For this latter group of writers, success could be attained not through virtues stemming from hard work but through mind power and positive thinking. Wisps of ideals were kept alive by frequent references to Emerson, McGuffey, and Alger, whose lessons of life were told over and over again, but these newer writers and philosophers appeared all too content to judge the future in more material terms. For them, materialism became a virtue unto itself, with little or no concern for the inherent dangers earlier writers had warned their readers about. With the emergence of the personality ethic, the cult of service succumbed to an economy of consumption and an identity shaped by manipulation, hypocrisy, and ultimately self-deception.

As this intention played out, terms such as *capitalism, profit,* and *rugged individualism* replaced the popular and well-used concepts of *public virtue* and *self-reliance.* The same was true of the words *psychic, magnetism, energy, force, thought waves, mental control, suggestion, immi-nence, vibrations, attraction,* and *influence,* which had carried authorita-tive meaning through most of the nineteenth century. They gave way to terms such as *determination, perseverance, prosperity, personal well-being, thought power, mental power, financial betterment, ambition, suc-cess, happiness,* and *potential.* This suggests that the newer spokespeople for New Thought found that traditional Christian virtues no longer fit their needs. Meekness and contentment were now considered little more than stolen robes that concealed morbid sentimentalism and even cowardice.

In their decision to use visualization, word repetition, and affir-mation to realize material gains, New Thought's prosperity gospelers turned money into an end in itself, a "calling" whose spirit and ethos substituted expectation for self-discipline. To be sure, there was a mea-sure of moral obligation (i.e., good works) that stood in the way of free indulgence. For many, however, this was short-lived, secure in the assur-ance of God's glorifying reward. Work was the prophylactic against sloth but valued only when seen in the context of its fruits. This explains how riches were no longer seen as a danger to the soul but had become the object of one's calling. Seldom did New Thought's prosperity writers question the world of money-making; nor did they foresee the dangers that such a utilitarian objective might bequeath. No longer a means, material wealth became its own just reward, a rationalization removed from otherworldly motives. The Calvinist outlook that once defined an individual's responsibilities and his or her calling was not so much replaced as it was redefined by rationalizing life and salvation in terms of material wealth.[2]

Good Tidings

Along with Emma Curtis Hopkins, whose gospel of "the Good" represented an early materialization of the prosperity gospel, the writ-ings of Anna W. Mills became one of the first contextual examples of combined health, hope, happiness, and prosperity in the New Thought movement. In her *Practical Metaphysics for Healing and Self Culture; Or, the Way to Save Both Soul and Body Now* (1896), Mills looked to the teachings of Jesus as the font of a new philosophy of practical metaphysics. The course of lectures set forth in her book laid out a method of self-culture and a belief that those loyal to God and to Christ would be fulfilled spiritually, physically, and materially.[3] Similarly, Home of Truth founder Annie Rix Militz adopted the Hindu practice of yoga to teach spiritual exercises in the power of concentration and acquiring the power of silence, which led to what she called "cosmic consciousness," meaning the opportunity to know the bliss of heaven while still walking the earth.[4] By thinking, speaking, and doing, the power of belief bore fruit. Provided that one's words and deeds were consistent with one's thoughts, whatever was desired in prayer was ultimately received. It made no difference what one asked. "Have no doubt in your mind of God's willingness to give you any good thing that you would give yourself," she assured readers. Early groups influenced by this rationale included the Christian Assembly, founded in 1900 by William Farwell and operated in association with Militz's Home of Truth; and the Altrurian Society, founded in 1911 by Lawrence Augustus Fealy in Birmingham, Alabama.[5]

As with his peer writers on prosperity, Unity cofounder Charles Fillmore explained that the Creator had provided for the needs of his creatures and would not have allowed their minds to desire what was not possible. Instead, he "provided a universal seed substance that responds with magical power to the active mind. . . . What we need to realize above all else is that God has provided for the most minute needs of our daily life and that if we lack anything it is because we have not used our mind in making the right contact with the supermind and the cosmic ray that automatically flows from it."[6] Given that prosperity did not mean the same for all, there was no limit to what the mind of each individual might desire. Prosperity was a condition brought about by certain ideas that were allowed to rule in each individual. "The sin of riches is not in the possession but in the love of money, a material selfishness," he explained. It was not a crime to be rich or a virtue to be poor; the sin lay in what was done with it. "Those who put wealth into useful work that contributes to the welfare of the masses are the salvation of the country," he explained. "Tell me what kind of thoughts you are holding about yourself and your neighbors, and I can tell you just what you may expect in the way of health, finances, and harmony in your home."[7]

The philosopher and mystic Ralph Waldo Trine (1866–1958) was admired by William James for his contributions to mind cure. An Illinoisan by birth, Trine received his baccalaureate degree in 1891 from Knox College and, a year later, attended the Emerson School of Oratory in Boston. There he participated in many of the proto-New Thought discussions led by school's founder, Charles Wesley Emerson. He later studied history and political science at the University of Wisconsin and at Johns Hopkins University. His widely sold books became life-transforming experiences for many, including American automaker Henry Ford, who shared their contents with a number of his industrial colleagues. In *What All the World's A-Seeking; Or, the Vital Law of True Life, True Greatness, Power, and Happiness,* published in 1896, Trine focused on the following questions: "How can I make life yield its fullest and best? How can I know the true secret of power? How can I attain a true and lasting greatness? How can I fill the whole of life with a happiness, a peace, a joy, a satisfaction that is ever rich and abiding?" The answers to these questions formed the *summum bonum* of life and involved placing one's self in harmony with the universe by living the Christ-life. One awakened the God within not by trumpeting his or her accomplishments before others but by choosing silence for short periods every day to contemplate God, by regarding wealth as a private trust to be used for the good of humankind, and by recognizing that character ("living the life that tells") was the greatest power in the world. "Let this great principle of service, helpfulness, love, and self-devotion to the interests of one's fellow-men be made the fundamental principle of all lives, and see how simplified these great and all-important questions will become," Trine wrote. This was living the life of a true Christian; it was living the Christ-life.[8]

Another proponent of the good life was the minister, lawyer, and writer Russell Conwell (1843–1925), best known as the creator of the inspirational story "Acres of Diamonds," which was published in book form in 1890 and delivered thousands of times as a lecture over the course of his career. The book recounted the story of an ancient Persian who owned a farm by the sea but who, after a visit from an old priest, concluded that he "was poor because he was discontented, and . . . discontented because he thought he was poor." In search of diamonds, which the priest explained would make him richer, the man sold his farm and traveled the earth in vain, only to drown in a great tidal wave. The story did not end there, but continued with the man who purchased the Persian's home and property, only to discover the diamond mines of Golconda in his backyard. Conwell went on to recount several similar stories, concluding that people who think they are poor are actually possessed of great wealth that they need only to discover. All true success, including business success, was based on taking an interest in one's fellow human beings and working for their welfare. "He that can do the most to elevate, enrich, and inspire others," Conwell explained, "shall reap the greatest reward himself. Not only so says the Holy Book, but so says business common sense."[9]

Over the decades, material happiness became an ever-increasing theme among New Thought's writers, who were fond of explaining that the greatest discovery of the human race was the realization that humans possessed all the powers that formerly had been ascribed to God. This meant that each had the ability to accomplish any purpose formed in the mind. "We have emancipated ourselves and find good reason to believe that we are quite at home in the planet earth and have nothing to gain by leaving it," exclaimed Charles B. Newcomb in *All's Right with the World* (1899). "We do not sigh for liberty, since we have learned that we possess it." This meant that humans no longer needed to talk of poverty, since they were already the "preferred stockholders" in the universe. Discoveries through the phenomenon of Spiritualism had provided humanity with firsthand knowledge of the world beyond. This knowledge made it clear that humans lived in a universe governed by the law of evolution and that death left them unchanged. Above all, this meant that excuses such as being "prisoners of poverty," "victims of injustice," or "creatures of circumstances" had little meaning in the broad span of time. "All prisons are mental," Newcomb explained. "Truth gives us the passkey to all doors, the control of all the environment, deliverance from all injustice and disease."[10]

Newcomb was also fond of arguing that the principal human fallacy had been ascribing disease and poverty to the mysteries of Providence. These conditions proceeded not from fate, destiny, or accident, but from a condition of mind; they were crimes of ignorance for which the sufferer alone was responsible. Being one with God meant one was never forgotten or overlooked. "We are never denied anything we crave," he insisted. "The power to wish and the power to execute are one and the same. All things are ours as soon as we recognize and appropriate from the universal life. This is done without cost or deprivation to our neighbor." In remedying disease and poverty, humans had only to realize that they were in control of their surroundings and responsible for the results of whatever progress they achieved. They succeeded because they expected themselves to succeed. Individuals created their own destinies and must not rely upon outside forces to meet life's challenges. The kingdom of God was within each.[11]

Newcomb's *All's Right with the World* became a watershed moment for the New Thought movement, turning the purpose in life from "self-sacrifice," "humility," "meekness," "prudence," and other so-called Christian virtues into a joyful celebration of life's banquet. For too long, vices had been distorted into virtues. It was time for stock-taking and finding a new classification of virtues and vices. "Let us examine anew some of the things we have thought vicious," urged Newcomb, "and revise our definitions where we find it necessary."[12]

Newcomb's literary contemporaries showed little hesitancy in selling the secrets to material success. Helen Wilmans's *The Conquest of Poverty* (1900) and Elizabeth Towne's *How to Grow Success* (1904) represent two early examples of the prosperity gospel. Wilmans made frequent use of her own life experiences to teach that any individual could rise above life's impediments by virtue of knowing and valuing his or her own powers. "I have known poverty most thoroughly," she reminded her readers. "I was held in a belief of its power all through the earlier part of my life; not during my childhood, however, but beginning when I was a very young woman and continuing until I found there was a Law that could command opulence, which by slow degrees I put in operation and became free." It was in the wisdom gained from knowing herself that Wilmans learned she could accomplish anything. Knowledge of the self was a "lifting power" that brought the individual to the conscious plane of growth. As with her peers, she emphasized the potency of desire and, with it, the correlation of thought to the objects of desire.[13]

New Thought's most noted publisher, Elizabeth Towne (1865–1960), started her company in 1900 at the young age of thirty-five. Over the decades, her stable of New Thought authors grew to include such personages as Charles Fillmore, William Walker Atkinson, Annie Rix Militz, H. Emilie Cady, Frank B. Whitney, Wallace Wattles, Kate Atkinson Boehme, Paul Ellsworth, Frances W. Foulks, Elinor S. Moody, Clara Beranger, Imelda Octavia Shanklin, Zelia M. Walters, and Clara Palmer. Towne also published the hugely popular New Thought magazine *Nautilus* (1898–1953), with a circulation of approximately 150,000, which explained that success was the "liberty to command, coupled with a clear conscience and loving heart." Although she cautioned that the successful individual was not necessarily rich in a monetary sense, it did not exclude the power to command money as a way to gratify one's aspirations, provided that the intent was good.[14] As with others, she insisted that "as you think of yourself, so the world thinks." Every person got out of the world what he or she put into it, meaning that individuals had to think their world into existence. "The money you attract," she explained, "is the exact measure of value of the Ideas you have succeeded in externalizing." The art of making money was a form of self-expression that gave one the opportunity to do good for the world.[15]

Author, physician, and hotel owner Orison Swett Marden, MD, (1850–1924) was yet another believer in the power of the "great within." As editor of *Success Magazine* (1897) and author of *He Can Who Thinks He Can* (1908) and *The Miracle of Right Thought* (1910), he reasoned that the Creator would never have mocked humanity by instilling yearnings for things that it had no ability to attain. No matter what hurdles existed in life, "we were intended to be and do what we were made to do," he insisted. The great curses of the human race were fear and worry, as they destroyed harmony, poisoned thoughts, and ruined the mental potential in the individual. His writings centered on the proposition that everyone ought to be happier than they are and that each person's life is intended to be richer and more abundant. "What we try persistently to express we tend to achieve even though it may not seem likely or even possible." That expression applied to both health and material success. The daily habit of picturing oneself in a condition of success, health, power, and prosperity replaced the imperfect individual with a better "God-self." The injunction by God to be perfect was not given to mock humans but to offer the possibility of realizing his likeness.[16]

As Marden explained, too many people settled for less, believing that the luxuries and comforts of the world, including fine houses and good clothes, were beyond their capacity to either want or achieve. But the limitation was in ourselves. God wanted all of his creatures to have the good things of the universe. There was no poverty and no want in the Creator's plan. The earth was full of resources that humans had barely touched. "We have been poor in the very midst of abundance, simply because of our own blighting limiting thought," he wrote. Humans lived their own thought-habits and surrounded themselves with their own creations. While they were not forced to grovel, many chose poverty due to their own fear and worry. "Whatever your condition may be in your home, or business, or social life," he advised, "it is the legitimate offspring of your own thought, your own ideals, and that you have nobody to blame but yourself."[17]

Marden cited Theodore Roosevelt, Andrew Carnegie, J. P. Morgan, and John D. Rockefeller as examples of individuals who mentally created the conditions that had made them prosperous. They were great achievers who built with their thoughts; they were practical dreamers whose minds reached out to create and produce what their ideals and ambitions had sought. Their environment corresponded with the nature of their thoughts, their mental attitudes, and their positive creative condition. Unfortunately, Christianity taught humanity's debasement with original sin. This was an error of significant magnitude since, in truth, humans had always been advancing. "The man God made never fell," he insisted. "It is only the sin-made man that has fallen. It is only his inferior way of looking at himself, his criminal self-deprecation, that has crippled and deteriorated him."[18]

Paul Ellsworth, author of *Direct Healing* (1914) and *Mind Magnet: How to Unify and Intensify Your Natural Faculties for Efficiency, Health,* and *Success* (1924), explained that New Thought was not just a method of thinking, but a way of living. When the spirit in individuals "quickened" and became one with the Universal Spirit, their regenerated life changed to one of creativity and power. For such people, life became free of encumbrances and limitations. The individual became master, "not a beggar," and his or her kingdom became one "of peace, of plenty, [and] of good will." The key to self-regeneration was love of the spirit, a love that "giveth freely of all its treasures."[19] Not until individuals became channels through which flowed the Christ-spirit would they take control of their bodies and minds. "Remember that the All-Father did not put us here to be servants or laborers," he often remarked. Instead, God surrounded humanity "with physical conditions which should quicken within us the desire to rule, and so bring us to the realization of our own true being." Ellsworth urged his readers to repeat the statement: "I am wealth; the spirit of Infinite Wisdom and Power and Love flows into me and through me, and at all times I bring forth those physical things which I need to fulfill my highest desires." In time, he assured them, this silent prayer would harmonize with the vibrations of the unseen and enable the full realization of these requests.[20]

Ellsworth cautioned that infinite wealth, health, and love did not by themselves cure spiritual maladies. Spiritual harmony was founded upon the principle of universal and impersonal love, or, as the Puritan Jonathan Edwards expressed it, a benevolence toward Being.[21] When material things became ends in themselves, a spirit of decadence took control of its owner. This was especially evident among second and third generations of the rich, whose inherited property came without the desire to use it for the good of humankind. Not having earned that which they inherited, they lacked the spirit to master it. In effect, they lacked impersonal love and the light from that love that allowed one to possess wealth without being possessed by it. Nevertheless, everyone had the power to draw from the "universal storehouse" that included love, wisdom, power, and substance. The spiritual person lived serenely by drawing that which he or she desired, "whether it be a brush and a palette or a touring car." Only when it was acquired under the guidance of wisdom was it of real value; otherwise it was simply an encumbrance that had the power to injure. The best description of perfect harmony between the individual and the material world was the Christ statement: "All mine is thine, and thine is mine."[22]

The Law of Attraction

William Walker Atkinson (1862–1932), one of the more influential spokespeople of the prosperity gospel, pursued careers in business and law before suffering a physical and mental breakdown in the early 1880s. In his search for health and inner peace, he turned to the healing practices in the emerging New Thought movement and soon began writing about his newly discovered religion of healthy-mindedness. Within a short spate of time, he was hired as associate editor of the journal *Suggestion* (1900–1) and followed shortly afterwards with editorships of *New Thought* (1901–5) and *Advanced Thought* (1906–16). He founded the Psychic Club (1901), opened the Atkinson School of Mental Science (1905), and teamed with several publishers, including Sydney Flower's New Thought Publishing Company and the Elizabeth Towne Company, to produce a virtual library of New Thought literature. Writing under his own name as well as various pseudonyms (i.e., Yogi Ramacharaka, Theodore Sheldon, Theron Q. Dumont, Swami Panchadasi, The Three Initiates, Magus Incognitus), Atkinson reached into the homes of millions of readers with more than a hundred book titles.[23]

In his *The Law of the New Thought: A Study of Fundamental Principles and Their Application* (1902), Atkinson provided a thorough overview of the New Thought movement, tracing its historical origins and explaining the most recent research in the conscious and unconscious. He placed New Thought among the oldest philosophies in existence, containing teachings that stretched back in time to the schools of ancient Greece, the temples and shrines of Asia, the songs of the earliest poets, and the writings of the mystics. He explained that the movement carried the "sacred fire" of truth from each of the great religions and illuminated as well the insight of writers from Shakespeare, Bacon, and Pope to Browning, Emerson, and Whitman. New Thought reaffirmed Victor Cousin's intent, through his philosophy of eclecticism, to sweep up the best ideas of antiquated wisdom without the artifacts of dogma, creed, superstition, intolerance, selfishness, and prejudice. Finally, New Thought brought together for humanity's betterment the principles of freedom, independence, success, health, and happiness to form a simple teaching: "I Can and I Will."[24]

Like his contemporaries, Atkinson acquainted readers with the latent powers within themselves, specifically their own personal magnetism or "mind-power." Most writers had their own pet theory to account for this. Some attributed mind power to a vegetarian diet, others to celibacy.[25] Atkinson recommended that individuals learn to absorb the magnetic forces of the universe using a combination of the law of attraction and deep breathing, charging the body with mind-power in a manner reminiscent of a storage battery. Mind-power was one of the greatest manifestations of energy in the universe. It was the living, throbbing, pulsating power from which everything emanated. Those who understood its use could make for themselves whatever they desired. The positive thought expressed in the words "I can," "I do," "I will," and "I am" manifested a power of mind that was "as steady as the arrow from the bow of the skilled archer." Believing that the real self was a spirit that used the mind and body as tools, Atkinson announced that humanity was growing into a "new plane of consciousness" that included oneness with the Absolute.[26]

Adopting the principle of *similia similibus curantur* (like cures like) from homeopathy, Atkinson reasoned that thoughts were attracted to similar thoughts—good thoughts to other good thoughts and thoughts of strength, happiness, and so on with other like-minded thoughts. "When we think, we send out vibrations of a fine ethereal substance which is as real as the finer vapors or gasses," he explained. While one cannot see, smell, or taste thought, its vibrations passed through bodies and exerted a force equivalent to a powerful magnet. Every thought projected vibrations into space and affected the minds of others in varying degrees. Some thoughts could be directed in a straight line from one mind to another while others branched out in the form of undirected waves. He used the term *volation* to describe the conscious effort of the will to direct thought vibrations to a specific person. At short range, it was exerted through a personal conversation; at long range, it was accomplished by *telementation,* or thought-transference. Atkinson offered exercises designed to acquire a working knowledge of these powers.[27] The mastery of this form of personal magnetism applied to qualities such as success and happiness and even to material things such as money. "Money, regarded as mere money," he pointed out, "is not a high ideal, but regarded as the means of surrounding ourselves with the best things of life, it becomes no unworthy goal for human endeavor."[28]

The ether was constantly filled with these meditative currents streaming out from individuals in ever-widening circles and drawing into their center minds of similar mental attraction, personality, and influence. Known simply as personal magnetism or mental suggestion, it explained how crowds or mobs acted; how various towns exhibited certain common traits; how great generals like Caesar, Alexander the Great, and Napoleon affected their armies in battle; how religious revivals excited people; and how seduction worked. Mental magnetism could provoke otherwise sober minds into joining a raucous camp meeting revival or reacting emotionally to William J. Bryan's "Cross of Gold" speech at the Democratic National Convention in 1896.[29] This power drew, coaxed, induced, allured, and attracted people to their views, creating mental images that were both convincing and seductive. To protect against unwanted magnetism, Atkinson directed individuals to form the thought "I am," accompanied by a mental conception of the self that imparted a psychical barrier impervious to outside vibrations. "By a full appreciation and recognition of the higher self, you will surround yourself with a thought aura, which will protect you, without any voluntary effort of the mind from outside mental influences," he wrote.[30]

Although the phrase "thoughts are things" was common language among the proponents of New Thought, Atkinson taught that a more correct phrase was "thoughts are forces," since forces were always active, never inert. Force was the pulse sent into every living fiber, vitalizing body and soul. These powers, once considered to be exclusive, were available for all to exercise. "Anything is yours, if you only want it hard enough," Atkinson promised. "Just think of it. ANYTHING. Try it.

Try it in earnest and you will succeed. It is the operation of a mighty Law."[31] The channels through which these words expressed themselves included the ear, eye, and touch. The ear could discern an expressive tone or feeling; the eyes could reveal excitement, steadiness, or intensity; and the "conductivity" of the hands in a handshake could express signs of strength or weakness.[32] Atkinson encouraged his readers to cultivate these channels, as they served as windows into the soul. With proper exercise, he said, anyone could use them to produce emotional responses or feelings in others.[33]

The focal point of Atkinson's teaching was the "I"—the thinker, knower, feeler, and actor. It was the central authority of the mind and constituted the essence of the so-called Master Mind whose will was its garment. While the slave obeyed orders derived from desires, feelings, and emotions, the Master Mind concentrated on those attributes that best enabled the mind to understand the thought forces and store them away for use at a later time. This Atkinson called "memory training," which consisted of fixing the mind on a particular subject, holding the mind firmly upon it, and shutting out extraneous elements. This level of attention constituted the best of intellectual power—the true work of character building. To the extent that one's Master Mind built up a character to suit his or her tastes and ambitions, it acted with purpose to solve life's problems.[34] "Inspect and pick out your own mental material," he advised, "so that nothing but the best quality of thought and action may be produced!"[35] This became the basis of character building, of engraving substance upon character. It was a "plastic thing" that could be modified by one's thoughts and mental attitude and improved, changed, or altered at will.[36]

"Remember," advised Atkinson, "the only thing to fear is Fear," a sentiment that Franklin Delano Roosevelt borrowed for his famous remark, "The only thing we have to fear is fear itself."[37] Similarly, Atkinson wrote in 1908 that "laughter is the only thing that keeps the race from madness. . . . Try it the next time you get stewed up with 'high statements,' 'basic truths,' and 'axiomatic principles.' . . . Apply the chemical of laughter, and ascertain whether the stuff bleaches."[38] One suspects that Norman Cousins might have borrowed this idea as the basis of his best-selling *Anatomy of an Illness as Perceived by the Patient: Reflections on Healing and Regeneration,* published in 1979.

Another prophet of the prosperity gospel was the psychic healer Richard Ingalese (b. 1863), who wrote and taught the techniques of visualization. When an individual wanted something, the intensity of the thought determined the promptness of the response. "And if there should be a delay . . . the fault will be in yourself; because you do not think clearly enough or hold your thought picture sufficiently long."[39] The more concrete the picture, the more tenacious the hold, and the sooner the material reality was realized. "The constant or frequent vibration which your thought causes," Ingalese taught, "sets the Universal Consciousness surrounding you and your picture into action."

> If you desire success, social position, any spiritual, mental or physical thing, it can be gained by simply creating and holding the picture in your mind. It makes no difference whether the thing you create is good for you to have, or whether you use or misuse it after you get it, you will get whatever you clearly picture. If you want a thousand dollars for the purpose of helping a poor family or to hire a man to murder another, it makes no difference with the operation of the law. Your demand will be met if you make your picture of the thousand dollars.[40]

> Do you want money? Then make a concrete picture of the amount you want—say a one-hundred-dollar bill; or if you do not want your money all of one denomination picture a sufficient number of bills, of the denomination you want, to make the amount you desire. But in any event make a picture of a definite amount and after making it, hold to it till it stands out as distinct as though it had materialized and you could see it before you.[41]

World War I

The years leading up to the First World War revealed dissonance between the celebration of Emerson's cult of individualism and the cadence of a world increasingly indifferent to the hopes and aspirations of the individual. For a growing number of writers and thinkers, the power of the individual as a free agent in the world seemed illusory. This contradiction in the culture, made poignant in Frank Norris's *The Octopus, A Story of California* (1901) and also evident in the fashionable disease of neurasthenia, or "American nervousness," gave striking evidence of the fissures that marred the optimism of New Thought and the principle that each could become the master of his or her circumstances.[42] Emerson remained the father of optimism and the literary sage of New Thought in this new consumer culture, but those who referenced his writings did so less as a celebration of self-reliance than as an effort to authenticate abstruse aesthetic values. As H. L. Mencken reflected in 1919, "What remains of [Emerson is] . . . a debased Transcendentalism rolled into pills for fat women with vague pains and inattentive husbands—in brief, the New Thought—in brief, imbecility."[43]

America's entry into the war served as a watershed event for the New Thought movement, interpreted by its revelators as the moment when the nation had moved out of its isolationist shell and joined in brotherhood with the world. More than any other event, the war gave New Thought's proponents the opportunity to draw a contrast between the discovery of the inner life in the century that had recently passed and the discovery of the great social, economic, and geopolitical issues that propelled the world into war. Pleading for a moral and spiritual basis for cooperation, they looked to the war's end as a hopeful sign that humanity would again find God immanent and, in the process, understand the importance of humans as social beings. "Democracy frees the soul from man-made shackles," explained one of the bulletins of the International New Thought Alliance in 1918, "and New Thought teaches it to depend upon the Divine."[44] In many ways, this statement represented the unofficial view of New Thought—echoing President Woodrow Wilson's address on April 2, 1917, before a joint session of Congress seeking a declaration of war against Germany—identifying the war as the beginning of a New Age. It was a war to make the world "safe for democracy."[45]

With the dawning of peace after the hostilities ended, Horatio W. Dresser and other New Thought spokespeople viewed their work in terms of erecting democratic governments and announcing a spiritual awakening of which New Thought was a vital part. Optimistic that a new age had arrived, the outcome of which was evident in temperance, the rights of women, the League of Nations, and greater spirituality, Dresser saw the world entering a golden age, rich with opportunity and evidence of the presence of God in the affairs of humankind.[46]

Despite the aspirations emanating from Dresser and a few other stalwarts of New Thought idealism, the post-war years constituted a spiritual crisis for America and the world of nations. With Europe left in shambles, the New Thought movement faltered as the rosy optimism of the pre-war decades all but vanished amid the chaos that so profoundly marked the outcome of the world conflict. Those who at one time had embraced the ideals of liberal religionists and secular progressives soured into a profound pessimism. Disillusioned by the realities of war, many of Dresser's colleagues shifted from idealism to enlightened self-interest. In the wake of this change, a new generation of New Thought motivational speakers and writers argued convincingly for a culture of prosperity. This new era, which cultural historians have described as the "Roaring Twenties," reflected a nation that had tired of idealism and now yearned to return to normalcy—meaning a return to the business of making money.[47]

This shift in thinking took time to occur, but occur it did as Americans turned increasingly insular and isolationist, showing little interest in reform and human betterment. The once-popular Progressive movement found itself in full retreat, attacked by turbulent criticism from both the right and the left. Reflective of this change, William F. Ogburn explained in his presidential address before the American Sociological Society in 1929 that "sociology as a science is not interested in making the world a better place to live [but only in] discovering new knowledge."[48] This was expressed even more forthrightly by Read Bain in an editorial in his *American Sociological Review*, remarking that "a scientific society should never approve or condemn a war, a Fuehrer, a labor union, a New Deal or Old Deal, an epidemic, nor a hurricane. These are natural phenomena to be studied by natural science. The *Review*, as an organ of a scientific society, should reflect this strict, 'pure,' non-moral position."[49] Notwithstanding the theology of Karl Barth (1886–1968) and Reinhold Niebuhr (1892–1971) whose neo-orthodoxy cast a long shadow over modernism's Gatsby-like indifference to the human condition, the sermons that marked New Thought's popularity in post-war America seemed gloriously immune to the soft underbelly of the nation's fragile social order. It was during the 1920s and 1930s that New Thought chose to wrap itself in a heavy dose of materialism at the expense of the spiritual self. New Thought writers—both secular and religious—used their literature to justify the accumulation of wealth and prosperity as a self-directed right. Millions gravitated to these celebrity writers selling personal success as a way of coping with the world around them.

A broad change in thinking spread across society in the mid-1920s, signaling the beginnings of functionalism among the nation's religious and spiritual elite. By functionalism is meant the intent to emphasize what religion and/or spirituality can *do* rather than argue how its ideas came about and what particular creeds were true. The new emphasis was on its usefulness in physical health and spiritual well-being. As explained by William James in his *The Varieties of Religious Experience*, it represented "the feelings, acts, and experiences of individual men in their solitude, so far as they apprehend themselves to stand in relation to whatever they consider the divine."[50]

From the 1920s onward, New Thought turned its metaphysics of healthy-mindedness into a set of physical laws giving individuals the power to attract, persuade, influence, and control others. In other words, in an age of increasing indifference to the individual as a free agent, New Thoughters now saw Emerson's self-reliant individual as being helped along by physical laws set in nature. For a nation whose people wanted to grow rich and powerful, New Thought's appeal was in its "get-rich" philosophy, offering success and prosperity to those with the "calling." The newest generation of writers and teachers were business oriented, selling their secrets of personal charm, energy, ambition, and determination for profit. These included Charles F. Haanel, author of *The Master Key System* (1917) and *The New Psychology* (1924); Frank Channing Haddock, author of the "Power-Book Library" series (1907–16); Bruce Barton, author of *The Man Nobody Knows* (1925); Robert Collier, author of *The Secret of the Ages* (1926); Kate Atkinson Boehme, author of *Real-*

ization Made Easy: For Health, Wealth, Supply, Self-Direction (1918); and Napoleon Hill, whose magazine *Hill's Golden Rules* (1919–20) and books *The Law of Success* (1925), *Think and Grow Rich* (1937), and *How to Sell Your Way Through Life* (1939) provided inspiration for millions.

The Personality Ethic

A native of St. Louis, businessman and author Charles F. Haanel (1866–1949), often called the "Father of Personal Development," was always curious as to why some individuals realized their ambitions while others failed. He attributed the difference to the creative force of the mind, which he believed constituted the sole difference between individuals. As he explained in *The Master Key System,* abundance, however defined, depended on the mind, and only those who put themselves in harmony with its creative force could reap its benefits.[51] Like Atkinson, he believed that the "key" to this knowledge lay in the cultivation of mental power. Using the law of attraction, thought became a creative energy that brought desired objects into manifestation. Wealth was but the conscious offspring of this power, a conscious intention brought into existence by the creative energies of the mind.[52]

The minister, attorney, and self-help author Frank Channing Haddock (1853–1915) took up training for the Methodist ministry before turning to law and trying his hand as a New Thought writer and lecturer. His "Power-Book Library" series, which included *Power of Will* (1907), *Power for Success Through Culture of Vibrant Magnetism* (1919), *The Personal Atmosphere* (1916), *Business Power* (1919), *The Culture of Courage* (1910), *Practical Psychology* (1915), and *Creative Personality* (1916), enjoyed a huge posthumous popularity during the 1920s and 1930s. His *Power of Will* alone sold over six hundred thousand copies by 1923.[53] Through a series of exercises, he encouraged his readers to assert themselves using willpower, personal magnetism, courage, confidence, and auto-suggestion. Quoting heavily from Andrew Carnegie, William James, and Orison Swett Marden, he taught that commercial and financial success depended on personality and the skill to use the power within. For this to happen, there must be a "winning personality" that was expressive of the inner person—"I am power! I am equal to anything that may come up in my life. I will unfold personal power. I make real within dynamic business power!" His books laid much of the foundation for the self-help books that followed. In each of his volumes there was a sufficient body of information to provide later generations of writers with instructions, examples, resolutions, affirmations, and remedies. After him, there is very little written among New Thought writers that was new or different—only variations on his numerous themes.[54]

Businessman, advertising executive, and US Congressman Bruce Barton (1886–1967) became for cultural historians a transitional figure in the prosperity gospel and stereotypical of the nation's view of modern business. After attending Amherst, where he graduated as valedictorian, Barton wrote for the religious monthly *Home-Herald* in Chicago and managed the women's magazine *Housekeeper* before moving on to the publishing company P. F. Collier and Sons in New York in 1912. Early in his career, he immersed himself in many of the progressive issues of the day, including prostitution, race relations, worker wages, class conflict, and national apathy. In his *A Young Man's Jesus,* published in 1914, Barton used his pen to ask what Jesus's response might be to the evils weighing down on society. Choosing a route away from the muckraking journalism of the time, he called for business to be the force for righteousness. Instead of appealing to the usual run of social gospelers to ring the changes on greed and inequality, he looked to the business and corporate world for the convictions that he thought Jesus would hold. The son of a Congregationalist minister, Barton drew heavily from his father's family, whose male members had raised themselves out of poverty as self-made men. In particular, he was drawn to the admonitions of his father, who held strong views drawn from Scripture urging a combination of patience and vigorous persistence in overcoming life's impediments.[55]

In his best-selling *The Man Nobody Knows,* Barton drew from his father's ministerial background to contextualize the triumph of Christianity in the pagan world as a feat of outstanding proportions. Using metaphorical tools drawn from the world of business, commerce, and advertising, he explained how Jesus had taken twelve men from the lower rungs of society and trained them to forge an "an organization that conquered the world."[56] Jesus's role in Christian theology as the son of God was downplayed to his abilities as a CEO capable of identifying a vision and a spirit that promoted individual interest and, at the same time, supported the collective good. Barton's Jesus was no longer the man who cleansed the temple at Jerusalem of its money-changers, but the person who stressed individual (and corporate) responsibility and used his "regenerate" disciples as mechanisms to reform society.[57]

Nurtured in an environment of liberal Protestantism, Barton identified Christian doctrine with the economy of abundance. However, his ideas seldom strayed from the expectation that each of society's producers should carry an ethic of hard work, self-denial, savings, and a service or "producer ethic" to accompany any personal or corporate success. No supporter of hedonistic consumption, he insisted that material success was a commodity tempered by a "business ethos" that included societal responsibilities. Unfortunately, while Barton placed his business ethos above profits, it was the latter that surged into prominence among his readers, making profits the most compelling, if not the only, *raison d'etre* for God and country.[58]

Indeed, from the first decade of the twentieth century to the Great Depression, the nation's religious leaders had used their pulpits to celebrate with rhetorical flourish the salesmanship authenticated through the life and character of Jesus.[59] As explained by William T. Doherty in a 1954 retrospective in *The Business History Review*, business became "an equal partner of God in setting right the world."[60] For two years, Barton's book remained at the top of the best-seller list, selling 250,000 copies in eighteen months.[61]

For Robert Collier (1885–1950), another of America's inspirational and success authors, the greatest discovery of modern times—what he called "the secret of the ages"—was nothing more than the "life principle" that each individual could call upon at will to achieve health, happiness, riches, or success.[62] Desire was the first law of gain; it was that special "something" that drove Columbus to cross the ocean, Napoleon to win battles, and Thomas Edison to become an inventive wizard. This "genie of the mind," or inner self, had enabled persons to rightfully claim their inheritance jointly shared with God. Only by controlling the mind and making it a storehouse of knowledge and power was this possible. The power of the mind was unlimited. "Whatever of good you may desire," Collier promised, "it can bring to you." The secret was in concentrating on one thing at a time and making it the thing most desired— of seeing oneself having or possessing it. It had to become the center of the individual's creative power and a mental image clear and vivid in every detail.[63]

Collier combined his secret with what he called "the law of supply," meaning that nature was lavish in all that she did. "There is plenty for everyone," he insisted. "[Nature] is your estate. It owes you not merely a living but everything of good you may desire." The true kingdom of God was to be found in health, happiness, and prosperity.[64]

> Don't worry. Don't doubt. Don't dig up the seeds of prosperity and success to see whether they have sprouted. Have faith! Nourish your seeds with renewed desire. Keep before your mind's eye the picture of the thing you want. BELIEVE IN IT! No matter if you seem to be in the clutch of misfortune, no matter if the future looks black and dreary—FORGET YOUR FEARS! Realize that the future is of your own making. There is no power that can keep you down but yourself. Set your goal. Forget the obstacles between. Forget the difficulties in the way. Keep only the goal before your mind's eye—*and you'll win it!*[65]

Collier's books include *The Book of Life* (1925), *The Secret of Gold: How to Get What You Want* (1927), *Be Rich! The Science of Getting What You Want* (1947), and *The Law of the Higher Potential* (1947). Packaged as a series under the title *The Secret of the Ages,* he sold more than three hundred thousand complete sets.[66]

Among the more notable representatives whose popularity derived from selling "secrets" was the journalist, attorney, and lecturer Napoleon Hill (1883–1970). Like Collier, he became an undisputed master of self-help, motivation, and positive mental thinking. He is best known for transforming visualizations into a formula for personal achievement and financial success best expressed in his *The Law of Success* (1925) and a series of home-study courses detailing his "Philosophy of Achievement."

His other books include *The Magic Ladder to Success* (1930), *How to Sell Your Way Through Life* (1939), and *Success Through a Positive Mental Attitude* (1960) with W. Clement Stone.[67] Among his many public services, Hill became known as an unofficial advisor to President Franklin D. Roosevelt during the Great Depression.

It was Hill's *Think and Grow Rich* (1937) that transformed him into a national celebrity. At the time of his death in 1970, the book had sold twenty million copies.[68] Every chapter revealed how various individuals had made their fortunes through knowledge of a particular secret. Awareness of this secret was originally brought to Hill's attention by the Scottish captain of industry Andrew Carnegie (1835–1919), who, Hill recalled, "watched carefully to see if I had brains enough to understand the full significance of what he had said to me." When he obliged Carnegie by telling him that he understood the idea, the Scotsman then asked Hill if he was willing to spend a lifetime teaching the secret to the world. With help from Carnegie, he did just that, explaining how various individuals including Henry Ford, John Wanamaker, William Wrigley Jr., John D. Rockefeller, Theodore Roosevelt, Dr. David Starr Jordan, Woodrow Wilson, William Howard Taft, and Clarence Darrow had utilized the secret and, with it, accumulated success and fortune. With chapters bristling with examples of inspiration, auto-suggestion, self-discipline, imagination, persistence, and decision making, Hill conveyed Carnegie's secret, namely the power of "organized and intelligently directed knowledge" as the key to success. Notwithstanding this "natural" power, Carnegie also referenced the power of the paranormal, namely telepathy, clairvoyance, and the application of a sixth sense through which the subconscious brain could access the "Infinite Intelligence." It was from the sixth sense of intuition that one received flashes of insight, hunches, or inspirations.[69]

While writers like Atkinson, Wattles, Collier, and Hill included both normal and paranormal techniques to realize mind-power, it was the writer and lecturer Dale Breckenridge Carnegie (1888–1955)—no relation to Andrew—who focused on using the five senses, leaving all other spiritual planes, auras, visualizations, and vibrations to polite indifference. The power of visualization was transformed from a product of the occult to a manifestation of a positive mind, thus discarding past theories for a more straightforward, secular interpretation.

Carnegie's teachings rose to cult-like status in the 1940s and 1950s, providing a canon of machismo-like messages—both conscious and subliminal—intended to win over the most hardened of skeptics. His popular *How to Win Friends and Influence People* (1936) taught that the power of communication was to be found in the method or technique of delivery. For the millions who read his book or attended his courses and lectures, success lay in mastering the rituals of communication. Once learned and practiced, they became the magical tools for success—comfort food for those anxious to find their identity in personality rather than character. As historian Gail Thain Parker observed, Carnegie's books and workshops were "a mirror of the popular mind [and] a pulse point in cultural history."[70]

Unlike his New Thought peers, Carnegie chose a singularly secular rhetoric to convey his vision of a richer, happier life. Unable or unwilling to delve into life's deeper meanings, he used his talent for communication to express the outward signs of success. It was the outer-directed individual to whom Carnegie's books were meant to appeal, not the inner-directed soul with questions, concerns, and issues. This change can be explained in part by the fact that Carnegie was himself never particularly articulate in discussing deep philosophical issues. In place of thoughtful conversation, he found it easier to communicate with pieced-together phrases plus a combination of stylized gestures and smiles. Throughout his life, he was more interested in *how* something was said than *what* was said. Words were used to convey slogans, nothing more. It was not the importance or logic but the rhythmic sound of pleasing slogans that, along with appearance, smiles, expressions of interest, and looking people in the eye, served to enable and motivate people. Teaching his followers to be outwardly sincere was Carnegie's passion. It was of no purpose that individuals should reveal their most private feelings or vulnerabilities. His character was the essence of solipsism, preaching a conscious hypocrisy that demanded nothing more out of life than surviving each day without having to consider, much less contemplate, a deeper meaning to the human condition. More than eight million individuals enrolled in his training program, which consisted of five steps: build greater self-confidence, strengthen people skills, enhance communication skills, develop leadership skills, and improve attitude and reduce stress. At the time of his death, his bestseller had sold five million copies in thirty-one different languages.[71]

With Carnegie's book, the full coup d'état had been carried out, replacing McGuffey's character ethic with a personality ethic that turned the power of healthy-mindedness into a gospel of consumption. In this new personality ethic, the opinion and control of others trumped personal virtue and self-identity. As Huber explained:

> The personality ethic dilemma of hypocrisy versus sincerity was shaped by the necessity in a consumption economy to manipulate people for personal or corporate gain. What happens to moral honesty when people become objects, when relationships are stained by the need to sell, when the self is soiled by the demand to sell the self? In personal affairs the insincerity and deceit of Dale Carnegieism becomes a smiling conception of human relations. In administrative affairs hypocrisy and deception sink into the moral relativism of a public relations mentality in which truth is no longer in principles but in public opinion polls.[72]

For those who found the secular nature of Carnegie's teachings bereft of spiritual value, Dr. Norman Vincent Peale (1898–1993) offered an antidote. Born in Bowersville, Ohio, Peale earned degrees from Ohio Wesleyan University and the Boston University School of Theology. Ordained a Methodist minister in 1922, he joined the Reformed Church in 1932 and ministered to the Marble Collegiate Church in Manhattan for fifty-two years, where he enjoyed celebrity status. Peale's radio program "The Art of Living," sponsored by the National Council of Churches, became an instant success in 1935 and eventually migrated to the television set. In 1940, he joined forces with Smiley Blanton to write *Faith is the Answer: A Psychiatrist and a Pastor Discuss Your Problems* (1940). Five years later, Peale, along with his wife and several businessmen, founded *Guidepost* magazine, which used inspirational stories to launch its nondenominational teachings. In 1947, he co-founded with

Kenneth Beebe the Horatio Alger Association to honor the nation's leaders. But it was his hugely popular *The Power of Positive Thinking,* published in 1952, that projected him onto the national scene. The book remained on the best-seller list for many weeks, selling over five million copies in fifteen different languages.[73]

Using anecdotes impossible to substantiate because of unnamed and unknown sources, Peale presented a strategy intended for enhanced self-analysis, self-confidence, and self-help. His repetitive techniques, common among New Thought writers, represented a form of auto-suggestion hidden under a plethora of "formulas," "methods," and "prescriptions." Similar to the hypnotist Émile Coué, whose writings jumped to national prominence in the 1920s, Peale taught a mental habit that was deceptively simple, namely, a panacea of repetitive prayers.[74]

Peale is also remembered for his Republican politics, which included attacks on presidential candidate Adlai Stevenson, anti-Catholicism and, in particular, his outspoken opposition to the candidacy of John F. Kennedy for president. Stevenson reportedly responded to Peale's attacks with the quip: "Speaking as a Christian, I find the Apostle Paul appealing and the Apostle Peale appalling."[75] In 1968, Peale officiated at the wedding of Julie Nixon and David Eisenhower and was awarded the Presidential Medal of Freedom by President Reagan in 1984. He died in 1993 at the age of ninety-five.

* * *

The idea of the self-made individual has become part of the very fabric of the American dream of an open society where persons with character and talent can rise to unprecedented heights. This idea became the mechanism for making the middle class, and it unfolded as the rightful outcome of such disciplinary values of the Protestant ethic as sobriety, thrift, self-restraint, and industriousness. From Horatio Alger onward, the churches and secular institutions of the nation perpetuated the imagery of this hero. Instead of the frontier, the business world became the stage upon which individuals played out the spirit of independence, self-reliance, and the other icons of the Protestant ethic. Here individuals transformed their environment and themselves through hard work, initiative, and mastering obstacles, which now took the form of business and government bureaucracies and regulations. Here, too, is where expressions of self-confidence, personal charm, magnetism, and sheer willpower made the difference between and among individuals. In other words, the myth was nuanced by separating conception from execution, meaning that material success was valued more than self-improvement, cunning more than character-building, and aggressive competitiveness more than social responsibility. For the minor expense of a book or workshop, the faceless individual could seize the moment and surface from the crowd wearing a mask of success and self-fulfillment.

9

Dream Weavers and Money Changers

When you pray you quiet your mind, body, emo-
tions, vibrations. Prayer gives you a sense of peace
and tranquility that are attracting powers. In one
way or another, prayer first makes you more
attractive, and then gets busy attracting your good to
you. Prayer makes you irresistible to your good!
And, most certainly, to all the risks of confident
living, including adequate financial supply.

—Catherine Ponder, *Pray and Grow Rich*

In the decades following the Second World War, the celebrity spokes-people of New Thought churches and secular organizations turned to the mass media to explain (and sell) their multistep formulas for health, prosperity, and self-discovery. As weavers of stories, dreams, and visions operating loosely under New Thought's global tent, they signaled a challenge to mainstream religion's hegemony by using media attuned to the emerging pluralism—media that advanced highly personal and nondogmatic approaches to spirituality, including experimentation with both Christian and non-Western methods of healing and self-discovery. In this setting, denominational exclusivity fell before a consumer culture whose marketers promised healthier, wiser, happier, and more prosperous lives. Rather than seeing modernity as a threat, these religious and secular celebrities saw power in advancing the principles embedded in science, the social sciences, and metaphysics. Combined, they became the theoretical underpinning for New Thought's explanatory content, offering up ever-evolving forms of self-discovery as replacements for the older institutions and their dogmas.[1]

With the advent of postmodernism, the medium for New Thought's messages multiplied as celebrities touted their "secrets," "keys," "laws," and "steps" for health and happiness through books, magazines, CDs, videos, talk shows, infomercials, meetings, courses, workshops, conferences, and the Internet. The books and videos of Stephen R. Covey, James Redfield, Deepak Chopra, Jon Mundy, Caroline Myss, Byron Katie, Rhonda Byrne, and Eckhart Tolle became representative examples of how New Thought's genre of self-discovery took root in mainstream thinking. The importance of the personal human experience (including visions and dreams) as distinct from modernity's materialistic and reductionist personhood resonated far beyond Western culture's more esoteric currents and traditions. Western esotericism, which once was contained in the gnostic currents of Christianity, was now secularized with the addition of quantum physics and its kindred sciences.[2]

The metaphysical world of postmodern American society is not too unlike the metaphysical world of the early nineteenth century, which accommodated a myriad of scientific, pseudoscientific, spiritual, and occult journeys into self-discovery. Despite greater acceptance of non-Western philosophies, and changes in the technical language to incorporate quantum physics, bioenergetics, cosmology, and other esoteric combinations of philosophy, medicine, and psychology, the purposes have remained fundamentally the same. This is not to deny the presence of occult phenomena such as auras, sheaths, chakras, vibrations, subtle bodies, and energy vortices in the present literature, but merely to point out that there has been a reworking of its component parts with the use of language, symbols, and meanings drawn from the gray area between modern physics and philosophy. Such terms continue to invite a personal and community discourse intended to make people happy about themselves and their prospects.

For the representatives of the contemporary New Thought movement, Spirit remains the ultimate reality, with the resulting conclusion that the self is divine and therefore attuned to the forces of good. Having trust and confidence in Spirit means that impediments such as worry and envy fail to find traction. With trust in Spirit, a positive mood of optimism and healthy-mindedness has taken the high ground, preventing either mental or physical disease from taking hold. Oneness with Spirit opens individuals to a cosmic power that transforms their lives, bringing to them the fullness of health, vigor, and plenitude. Here church and unchurched metaphysical groups and associations have made curious bedfellows, coming together (albeit rhetorically, not organizationally) to share in their healing roles. With their combination of channeling and other mental healing techniques with quantum physics and the newer sciences, both have staked claims to the present age.

New Thought Today

Many of the New Thought groups that got their start around the turn of the twentieth century continue to thrive into the twenty-first, in many cases spinning off new organizations or ordaining ministers who went on to establish their own independent churches and associations. Besides their common spiritual interests, they cooperate in job and wedding referrals; provide information on incorporation issues for independent churches, including instructions on obtaining IRS 501(c)(3) tax exempt status; share information on church record-keeping; partner in the delivery of workshops and seminars; hold tax-deductible annual conferences; and offer bookstore discounts to members across the movement. They also maintain websites that explain New Thought history; encourage dialog among interested viewers through blogs and other forms of social networking; announce forthcoming events; and sell DVDs, books, and related items.[3]

Unity is arguably the most widespread New Thought group in the United States today, with its single largest representative being the Association of Unity Churches. One of the association's most popular publications, boasting several hundred thousand readers, is the *Daily Word,* a series of daily inspirational quotes and prayers that the church makes available in both print and digital formats.[4] The organization also reaches out to its followers via online radio, blogs, and its bimonthly

Unity magazine. The physical center of the association is Unity Village, a 1,400-acre campus near Kansas City, Missouri, that includes a hotel and conference center, library, bookstore, swimming pools, a nine-hole golf course, and several chapels. Unity Village is also home to the Unity Institute, which offers ordination for Unity ministers and classes for interested laypeople. Estimates for the size of the organization range between four hundred and six hundred churches worldwide, in addition to one hundred to three hundred study groups.[5]

Unity has also given rise to a number of independent associations, such as the Unity-Progressive Council in Clearwater, Florida, and the Universal Foundation for Better Living (UFBL) in Chicago, Illinois. The UFBL was founded by the Reverend Johnnie Colemon, who, as with many leaders in the New Thought movement, was first introduced to New Thought when she was diagnosed with a terminal illness in her mid-thirties. Ordained as a Unity minister in 1956, she founded a church in Chicago the same year. In 1974, she broke with the Unity church organization over accusations of latent racism, renaming her church the Christ Universal Temple and establishing the UFBL.[6] The UFBL retains many of the teachings of Unity, with a heavy emphasis on the Bible as a source of inspiration. The group was also the inspiration for actress Delloreese Patricia Early, known professionally as Della Reese (b. 1931), who used Colemon's teachings when founding her Understanding Principles for Better Living Church in Inglewood, California.[7] The UFBL currently has more than a dozen churches in the United States, the Caribbean, and Africa as well as numerous study groups.[8]

Another offshoot of Unity is One Spirit Ministries, otherwise known as God's Church. Its founder, the Rev. Dr. Holly A. Heinz, established the association in 1988 and formally incorporated it in 1992 as God's Church. In 1998, the name was changed to One Spirit Ministries. Unlike the UFBL, One Spirit emphasizes the esoteric and metaphysical side of New Thought, including the unity of all religions. The organization offers ordination through the Affiliated New Thought Network's Emerson Theological Institute (see below).[9]

The second-largest New Thought denomination in the United States is the United Church of Religious Science, which now identifies itself as the United Centers for Spiritual Living, with more than four hundred centers in the United States and a presence on almost every continent.[10] Like Unity, they promote their ideas through books, audio and video recordings, and magazines such as *Science of Mind* and *Creative Thought*. They offer spiritual training and ordination through the Holmes Institute, and, like Unity, they have given rise to a number of independent organizations and teachers.

One such is the Rev. Michael Bernard Beckwith, who founded the Agape International Spiritual Center in 1986. This trans-denominational spiritual community, located in Culver City, California, is built on a set of teachings that Beckwith calls "New Thought-Ancient Wisdom." Beckwith, whose promotion by talk-show host Oprah Winfrey launched him into the national spotlight, began his inward journey in the 1970s when he looked for universally true principles in the spiritual teachings of both West and East. Ordained a minister of Religious Science, Beckwith teaches meditation, including the technique known as the "Life Visioning Process™," utilizing guided meditation, music, yoga, and relaxation. He is author of *Life Visioning: A Transformative Process for Activating Your Unique Gifts and Highest Potential* (1998), *Inspirations of the Heart* (2004), *40 Day Mind Fast Soul Feast* (2000), *Spiritual Liberation: Fulfilling Your Soul's Potential* (2008), *Your Soul's Evolution* (2009), *Living From the Overflow: A Practical Guide to a Life of Plentitude* (2010), and the popular *Science of Getting Rich* videos.[11]

Another outgrowth of Religious Science is the Affiliated New Thought Network (ANTN), which was founded in 1992 by a group of independent Religious Science ministers. Originally intended to support Religious Science practitioners, the organization has grown to include all types of associations and fellowships that adhere to the ideals and beliefs of New Thought. The ANTN currently has approximately thirty member centers and supports a number of independent ministers.[12] The operational arm of the ANTN is the Emerson Theological Institute in Oakhurst, California. Its curriculum was developed by the futurist and writer Barbara Marx Hubbard (b. 1929), currently the president of the Foundation for Conscious Evolution, formed in 1990. The institute offers on-site and online programs that range from bachelor degrees through a doctorate degree in humane religious studies, as well as practitioner and ministerial credentials for interfaith, religious science, and animal chaplaincy.[13] Open to all New Thought practitioners, ANTN's core values include caring, consciousness, integrity, service, spiritual growth, and freedom of expression.[14]

Two other denominations founded by students of Emma Curtis Hopkins continue to survive today: The Divine Science Federation International, keepers of the teachings of Malinda Cramer and Nona L. Brooks, currently has approximately a dozen churches in the United States and supportive groups in Australia, England, and South Africa.[15] The Home of Truth, founded by Annie Rix Militz and Harriet Hale Rix, maintains a center in Alameda, California.

Another independent church that dates from the early days of New Thought is the Church of Truth. Founded in 1913 by Dr. Albert C. Grier (1864–1941) in Spokane, Washington, it was the first of twenty-two churches he organized in the early decades of the twentieth century. After graduating with a degree in science from the University of Michigan in 1886, Grier became a minister in the Universalist Church in Spokane and was recognized as a prominent leader in the New Thought movement. Today, the Churches of Truth in Santa Clarita Valley and Pasadena, California, are among the most prominent in the New Thought movement.[16] Grier's Center for Awakening Consciousness, formed in 1922 in Pasadena, California, was a spiritual community and an affiliate of the Church of Truth that taught that through meditation, contemplation, and virtuous living, one could access the power of "Christ consciousness" to heal the twin problems of poverty and disease.[17]

The Metropolitan Spiritual Churches of Christ, an African-American denomination that is part of the Spiritual Church movement, was founded in 1925 in Kansas City, Missouri, by Bishop William F. Taylor (1886–1942) and Leviticus L. Boswell (b. 1871). It grew especially strong in the 1940s and 1950s during the long tenure of the Rev. Clarence H. Cobbs (1908–1979), better known as "Preacher." An urban phenomenon, its popularity followed in the wake of the soil depletion in the South, the invasion of the boll weevil, and the migration of rural blacks into the industrial North. In adjusting to the economic and social strains placed on their livelihood and personhood, these rural migrants created or joined numerous associations—both secular and religious—as a means of protection and comfort.[18] The Metropolitan became the largest African-American spiritual association in the country. Syncretic in scope, it drew elements from Catholicism, Voodoo, Islam, Judaism, Pentacostalism, Methodism, Christian Science, New Thought, and even astrology. Its churches include both male and female pastors and trustees and, as of 1968, claimed 125 congregations and over ten thousand members. Asserting the possibility of communication with those who had passed into the spirit world, the Metropolitan nonetheless eschews séances and, like the Mormon Church, explains that paranormal communications are restricted to only a few of the congregation's members. Over time, as members have risen in economic and social status, the congregations have tended to emulate mainstream denominations in ritual content, organization, and outreach. Overall, they share common values concerning prosperity and healthy-mindedness. The Metropolitan is particularly active in cities such as Chicago, Detroit, Kansas City, New Orleans, and New York, competing with Holiness, Pentecostal, and other sects, including the National Baptist Convention and the African Episcopal Church.[19]

Another active group is Seicho-No-Ie, a hybrid of Japanese spirituality and New Thought whose name has been variously translated as "House of Growth" and "The Home of Infinite Life, Wisdom, and Abundance." The sect was founded by the Rev. Masaharu Taniguchi (1893–1985) in 1930 after reading Fenwicke Holmes's *The Law of Mind in Action*. As with contemporary New Thoughters, Taniguchi denied the reality of evil and taught that human beings, as souls, were perfect. Through lectures and extensive literature, Seicho-No-Ie encourages a form of meditation called *shinsokan* or "meditation to visualize God."[20] Its goal is the realization of a world of Grand Harmony for all living things. Taniguchi encouraged the cross-cultural study of religions and philosophies along with deep meditation. This training, he taught, resulted in divine inspirations that could lead to miraculous healings, personal happiness, and prosperity. Through the power of mind, one has the capacity to awaken the kingdom of God within and transform one's environment, replacing negativism with positive beliefs.[21] Headquartered in Japan, Seicho-No-Ie has over a dozen centers in the United States, mostly in California and Hawaii, and internationally in Canada, Brazil, England, Germany, Portugal, France, Switzerland, China, and Korea.[22]

In addition to these more focused denominational groups, there are two major organizations that serve as umbrellas for the movement: the INTA, whose origins were discussed in chapter 4, and the Association for Global New Thought (AGNT). Formed in 1996 in Santa Barbara, California, following a leadership struggle within the INTA, the AGNT consists of ministers, laypersons, and directors of New Thought churches, organizations, and centers numbering over seven hundred. The association, with Michael Beckwith as cofounder and president, sponsors such programs as the Season for Nonviolence, a campaign dedicated to the goal of healing, transforming, and empowering lives and communities. The association also sponsors gatherings such as the Synthesis Dialogues with the Dalai Lama and the Awakened World Annual Conference.[23]

Over more than a century of existence, two constants in the New Thought movement have been the diversity of beliefs and practices that fall under its broad banner and a respect for the right of each individual to choose his or her own path, even when respect between the individuals themselves is lacking. As a result, attempts to articulate a single vision for New Thought have always ended with sweeping, general statements, making it difficult to quantify any changes or developments in overall philosophy. It can be illustrative, however, to compare a single document as it has been adapted to the changing needs of the community.

In 1917, at the third annual congress of the INTA meeting in St. Louis, delegates adopted a "Declaration of Principles" that included the following:

> We affirm the freedom of each soul as to choice and as to belief, and would not, by the adoption of any declaration of principles, limit such freedom. The essence of the New Thought is Truth, and each individual must be loyal to the Truth he sees. The windows of his

soul must be kept open at each moment for the higher light, and his mind must be always hospitable to each new inspiration. . . .

We affirm health, which is man's divine inheritance. Man's body is his holy temple. Every function of it, every cell of it, is intelligent, and is shaped, ruled, repaired, and controlled by mind. He whose body is full of light is full of health. Spiritual healing has existed among all races in all times. It has now become a part of the higher science and art of living the life more abundant.[24]

We affirm the teaching of Christ that the Kingdom of Heaven is within us, that we are one with the Father, that we should judge not, that we should love one another, that we should heal the sick, that we should return good for evil, that we should minister to others, and that we should be perfect even as our Father in Heaven is perfect. These are not only ideals, but practical, everyday working principles.[25]

In 1957, certain specific references to Christianity were removed from the "Declaration of Principles," which now celebrated the inseparable oneness of God and humanity and the unique combination of spirituality and the creative power of thought:

We affirm the inseparable oneness of God and man, the realization of which comes through spiritual intuition, the implications of which are that man can reproduce the Divine perfection in his body, emotions, and in all his external affairs.

We affirm the freedom of each person in matters of belief.

We affirm the Good to be supreme, universal, and eternal.

We affirm that the Kingdom of Heaven is within us, that we are one with the Father, that we should love one another, and return good for evil.

We affirm that we should heal the sick through prayer and that we should endeavor to manifest perfection "even as our Father in Heaven is perfect."[26]

In 2002, the INTA amended the "Declaration of Principles" once again, intending them to articulate the needs of the second millennium:

We affirm God as Mind, Infinite Being, Spirit, and Ultimate Reality.

We affirm that God, the Good, is supreme, universal, and everlasting.

We affirm the unity of God and humanity, in that the divine nature dwells within and expresses through each of us, by means of our acceptance of it, as health, supply, wisdom, love, life, truth, power, beauty, and peace.

We affirm the power of prayer and the capacity of each person to have mystical experience with God, and to enjoy the grace of God.

We affirm the freedom of all persons as to beliefs, and we honor the diversity of humanity by being open and affirming of all persons, affirming the dignity of human beings as founded on the presence of God within them, and, therefore, the principle of democracy.

We affirm that we are all spiritual beings, dwelling in a spiritual universe that is governed by spiritual law, and that in alignment with spiritual law, we can heal, prosper, and harmonize.

We affirm that our mental states are carried forward into manifestation and become our experience in daily living.

We affirm the manifestation of the kingdom of heaven here and now.

We affirm expression of the highest spiritual principle in loving one another unconditionally, promoting the highest good for all, teaching and healing one another, ministering to one another, and living together in peace, in accordance with the teachings of Jesus and other enlightened teachers.

We affirm our evolving awareness of the nature of reality and our willingness to refine our beliefs accordingly.[27]

These principles retain an emphasis on freedom; on the oneness of God—who is now specifically defined in terms of a more abstract universal Spirit—and humanity; and on the presence of heaven in the here and now, although it is no longer seen as being specifically "within us." The newer principles, however, include the idea that we are spiritual beings and that our attributes are a natural outgrowth of existing in a spiritual universe—whereas in earlier versions of the declaration, spiritual attributes are the result of being one with God. There is also a specific statement that our mental states are carried into manifestation as a result of the laws of the spiritual universe. Tellingly, in the newest version of the declaration there is an absence of any principle listing healing as a duty to others; healing is now relegated to being a benefit that we can enjoy for ourselves. While all of these concepts existed in New Thought from the beginning, the change in emphasis away from a God-centered view of the universe and toward a more mechanical, self-centered view suggests that the movement has not been immune to the shift toward the secular in the broader popular culture.

Prosperity continues to be an important element in the literature of both the churched and unchurched side of the New Thought movement today. This can been seen, for example, in the programs of conferences such as those sponsored by the ANTN that are attuned to the "secrets" of one's spiritual journey; sharing the sacred sounds of Native American flute music; discussing effective energy healing techniques; and drawing out the potential greatness in individuals and in their communities. The magazine *New Thought*, published by the INTA, features articles such as "Prosperity for the New Age," "World Healing," "Self Management and Soul Unfoldment," "Love Your Way to Success," "Staying Centered," and "Building Your Own Spiritual Website." As with the "Declaration of Principles" cited above, this suggests that the beliefs and practices of New Thought have not changed dramatically from those expressed by its spokespeople in the late nineteenth and early twentieth century. This is confirmed by the continued republication of earlier authors and the virtual pirating of their ideas time and again by contemporary ministers and motivational speakers. New Thought continues to emphasize God's presence for practical purposes such as success and healing and to reaffirm both the law of attraction and self-treatment.

The voluminous writings and website articles of Alan Anderson and Deborah Whitehouse, both of whom are members of the executive board of the INTA, represent the most current expression of New Thought. Their book, *New Thought: A Practical American Spirituality* (1995; revised ed. 2002), recounts the movement and its relationship to science, the expansion of New Thought into wealth and happiness, and its overall affirmation of self-discipline, mastery, and freedom. They consider New Thought to be very similar to New Age practitioners and their organizations in their relationship with the Ultimate, their common lack of hierarchical organizations, their strong optimism for society and the planet, their ideas of immanence and transcendence, their emphasis on the importance of meditation, and their desire to harness the power of mind as a complementary source of healing. The major difference, the authors explain, is the tendency of New Age proponents to drift into the occult, something that New Thought practitioners once explored but now generally leave alone. Overall, however, the view of Whitehouse and Anderson is not much different than that of Henry Wood's comparison of New Thought with Christian Science. For Wood, both were destined to have more in common than their advocates were willing to admit. Nevertheless, he predicted that New Thought would remain opposed to the hierarchical structure of Christian Science. Similarly, for Anderson and Whitehouse, New Thought and New Age will probably continue on their separate journeys, with New Age remaining aloof from any form of organized spirituality or religion.[28]

As a spiritual movement, New Thought today is undoubtedly as diverse and as vocal as its early proponents were. However, both churched and unchurched spokespeople for the movement are dwarfed, both in number and in influence, by charismatic media personalities who admit no connection to New Thought even as their teachings repeat and rehash the principles of early New Thought authors. Whether pushing the power of the mind to cure disease, the secrets of untold wealth and power, or the key to spiritual enlightenment, these celebrities arguably represent the "newER" face of modern New Thought.

Oprah Winfrey's Friends

Exemplary of how New Thought ideas and materials have entered the American psyche without the overt application of religious rituals or creeds has been the media host, actor, producer, and philanthropist Oprah Gail Winfrey (b. 1954), whose various media portals include *The Oprah Winfrey Show;* her own radio channel, most recently branded as Oprah Radio; a book club; and *O, The Oprah Magazine.* Together, they represent an eclectic religiosity using idealistic and even mystical versions of empowerment through thought. Winfrey's roots lie in the Baptist church, but her media conglomerate markets a hybrid philosophy in keeping with the New Thought worldview that the mind can overcome any of life's problems—whether poverty, sickness, or despondency. In disseminating the message of thought-as-power, her various media portals draw upon an American tradition steeped in a transcendent view of personhood that defies life's many impediments.[29]

Arguably one of Winfrey's most popular guests, the Australian-born celebrity Rhonda Byrne (b. 1951) was listed in 2008 by *Time* magazine and by *Forbes* among the top one hundred people who have helped shape the world. Her film *The Secret,* released in 2006 and later accompanied by the book *The Power* (2010), is an eighty-seven-minute series of interviews with various individuals representing medicine, religion, philosophy, finance, coaching, and physics explaining how, by repeated affirmation, the law of attraction results in achieving anything wanted or desired. Byrne explains the law of attraction thus: "Everything that's coming into your life you are attracting into your life. And it's attracted to you by virtue of the images you're holding in your mind. It's what you're thinking. Whatever is going on in your mind you are attracting to you." This law, the most powerful in the universe, is *The Secret* to life, wealth, relationships, health, and happiness. It not only explains that what you are at any given time is the result of past thoughts and feelings, but that everything you will become in the future depends on what your mind is shaping in real time. By consciously attracting what you want through thoughts and feelings, you take control of your future. Once you visualize a need, the universe responds. Those interviewed by Byrne for her film included Rusty G. Parrish, John Assaraf, Michael Beckwith, John Demartini, Bob Proctor, Jack Canfield, James Arthur Ray, Esther and Jerry Hicks, Morris E. Goodman, Denis Waitley, and David Schirmer. As with many of New Thought's successful spokespeople, Byrne drew from the personal failures of her early life to convey her journey of discovery.[30]

When discussing the significance of *The Oprah Winfrey Show* and of Byrne's *The Secret*, it is impossible not to include the spirit channeler Esther Hicks (b. 1948) who, together with her husband Jerry Hicks (d. 2011), a former musician and successful Amway distributor, published numerous books including *Ask and It is Given: Learning to Manifest Your Desires* (2004), *The Amazing Power of Deliberate Intent: Living the Art of Allowing* (2005), *The Law of Attraction: The Basics of the Teachings of Abraham* (2006), and *The Vortex: Where the Law of Attraction Assembles All Cooperative Relationships* (2009). In *The Secret*, Esther recounted her channeling experiences with a group consciousness known as "Abraham" or "Abraham-Hicks," who teaches how individuals create their own reality through thoughts of love, joy, and sex. Until disagreements arose between Byrne and Esther over the distribution of profits from the film, the two women were strong allies in the law of attraction. However, once *The Secret* became an international success, Esther insisted on renegotiating her share of the profits. Failing to reach a settlement, the second version of *The Secret* had both Esther and Jerry edited out of the film.[31]

Notwithstanding what Byrne allegedly discovered in *The Secret*, there is little in her "documentary" that is not found earlier in works of New Thought celebrities Wallace Wattles, William Walker Atkinson, Elizabeth Towne, Prentice Mulford, and Robert Collier. Nevertheless, the popularity of the film and book, enhanced with endorsements and interviews by other television celebrities, including Montel Williams, Matt Lauer, Cynthia McFadden, Ellen DeGeneres, and Larry King, resulted in millions of copies sold internationally. Both the book and the film continue to be marketed through various New Thought churches, centers, and associations. Currently living in Los Angeles, Byrne's production company, known as Prime Time Productions, creates films and books designed around the law of attraction and, for a price, offers to share *The Secret* to healthy-mindedness. In recent years, Byrne has been plagued with a plethora of legal suits and depositions involving former colleagues, disputes over money, and claims of fraud.[32]

Byrne's *The Secret* created a cottage industry for books, pamphlets, newsletters, empowerment soundtracks, blog postings, and products related to the law of attraction and its promise of success. There are even personal life coaches available to share their energy talks in individualized formats, small seminars, conferences, and even on ship cruises to distant ports. One such example of this spinoff is the motivational author and lecturer Louise L. Hay (b. 1926), another frequent guest on *The Oprah Winfrey Show*. Considered by some of her fans to be the "mother" of the law of attraction, she is best known for *You Can Heal Your Life* (1984), which reportedly sold more than three million copies worldwide.

Growing up in Los Angeles, Hay lived the life of a troubled youth before moving to Chicago and then to New York, where she found employment as a fashion model. Following a failed marriage, she turned to transcendental meditation and Religious Science in the 1970s, where she learned the power of transformative thought. Examples of her books include *Heal Your Body: The Mental Causes for Physical Illness and the Metaphysical Way to Overcome Them* (1984), *The Power Within You* (1991), *Inner Wisdom: Meditations for the Heart and Soul* (2000), *The Adventures of Lulu: Three Stories to Help Build Self-Esteem and Courage in Children* (2005), and *You Can Create an Exceptional Life* (2011). Her publishing company handles not only her own books and tapes but also those of Deepak Chopra, Doreen Virtue, Esther Hicks, and Wayne Dyer.[33]

Winfrey's interest in meditation, self-guidance, intuition, and the law of attraction includes interviews with Meera Lester, author of *365 Ways to Live the Law of Attraction: Harness the Power of the Law of Attraction Every Day of the Year* (2009), who provides different perspectives from which to view the alignment of the individual with the universe. Whether it is a new car, a piece of jewelry, a romantic partner, happiness, a new career, or a well-paying job, Lester explains that anyone can have what they want. The law is unbiased and does not judge the value of the item desired, whether it is harmful or helpful, or whether the one desiring it is religious or not. What matters is simply what the individual feels about what he or she is thinking. "The law always responds to what you are focusing on in your thoughts," she wrote, "and the emotion generated in response to those thoughts." Lester notes that this ancient secret, possibly six or seven thousand years old, had been discovered in the late nineteenth century by Wallace Wattles, and later by Dr. Norman Vincent Peale, and later still by Esther and Jerry Hicks, the Canadian Michael Losier, and Byrne. Despite the fanfare of their proprietary "secrets" and "discoveries," they all referenced the energizing of one's desires using thoughts, emotion, and visual imagery.[34]

Lester urges readers to calm their minds, cultivate a positive mood, center their thoughts, and love what they are doing. Aligning oneself in harmony with these techniques brings one closer to the sources of health, wealth, and happiness. Just as the subtle energies (i.e., *prana, chi,* or life force) of the body can be trained and used in Reiki or therapeutic touch, so, too, the law of attraction works through thought energy with its inward and outward polarities to create or acquire something of desire. Her steps of alignment with the spirit follow a path well trodden by former and contemporary celebrities:

1. Clear the clutter, confusion, and negativity from your mind.
2. Set forth the intention to manifest something.
3. Be expectant. Be ready to receive. Believe you deserve it, and it is already yours.
4. Visualize yourself having it.
5. Feel and express gratitude for the blessings you already have, the gifts of the universe that the higher power makes available to you, and for the power that makes possible each manifestation.
6. Repeat these steps often each day.[35]

Mind/Body Healing

From pagan and Christian priests to the pastoral medicine of Unity and the Emmanuel Movement to the tactile, visual, silent, and verbal health-affirmation methods of today's secular gurus, there has been a convergence of learning, counsel, and suggestion to treat the sick and empower the soul. With the current interest of complementary and alternative medicine in parapsychology and psychosomatic drugs, and increased attention paid by biomedical physicians to the possibilities of the placebo effect, the proponents of New Thought have found numerous fellow travelers intent on pursuing the application of mental power in matters of health and self-discovery. While the chain of causation remains a question, even the great French Renaissance skeptic Michel de Montaigne recognized the fact that "the patients' belief should prepossess them with good hope and assurance of their effects and operation."[36]

For today's New Thought moguls, any physical condition due to pathogenic agents or functional abnormalities has its spiritual counterpart in some mental unhappiness or morbid idea or belief. The properties of matter are but ideas in the mind. The world is a mental picture and disease a manifestation of the lack of harmony existing in the mind. Disease, however explained, operates on the plane of the senses, which, by its very nature, is a region of deceptive appearances. To cure disease, one has only to elevate the mind above the plane of the senses where pain and disease cannot exist. The remedy is to be found in the region of the inner being where this state of dissatisfaction rests. Remove the idea and the object disappears. Disease is a form of unbelief that, when removed, causes its opposite to arise.

The names of cardiologist Herbert Benson (b. 1935), founder of the Body/Mind Institute at Massachusetts General Hospital in Boston and author of *The Relaxation Response* (1975); Norman Cousins (1915–90), whose famous *Anatomy of an Illness as Perceived by the Patient: Reflections on Healing* (1979) promoted the power of optimism in healing; physician Bernie Siegel (b. 1932), author of *Love, Medicine and Miracles* (1986); Texas physician Larry Dossey (b. 1940), author of *Healing Words* (1993); and physician Jeff Levin, author of *God, Faith and Health* (2001) come quickly to mind as representatives of the twentieth century's answer to the mind-cure movement of the nineteenth century. Each has reinforced a "religion" of healthy-mindedness that, for all intents and purposes, gives greater credence to hope and trust than acquiescence to life's many tragedies.[37]

Indian-born physician Deepak Chopra (b. 1946), author of more than sixty books, is exemplary of the celebrity spokespeople for mind/body healing today, having combined the traditions of New Thought with holistic science. Disenchanted with conventional medicine, Chopra established the Maharishi Ayurveda Health Center for Well Being in La Jolla, California, where he leads seminars based on a combination of biomedicine, transcendental meditation, Ayurveda, yoga, and other exercises that utilize positive thinking as the motive force to correct and maintain the patient's energy field. Having first achieved fame with his quantum healing techniques in the 1980s, he later combined them with the prosperity gospel in his *Unconditional Life—Discovering the Power to Fulfill Your Dreams* (1992) and *Creating Affluence—Wealth Consciousness in the Field of All Possibilities* (1993), a trend he has continued into recent times with titles such as *Spiritual Solutions: Answers to Life's Greatest Challenges* and *Super Brain: New Breakthroughs for Maximizing Health, Happiness, and Spiritual Well-Being,* both published in 2012. His entire catalog of books reflects an ongoing effort to merge the reductionist benefits of Western science with the spiritual insights of the East. In doing so, he claims to have arrived at a higher threshold of personal development and self-fulfillment. Like Larry Dossey, Andrew Weil, and Herbert Benson, Chopra serves as an example of how spirituality has impacted health and healing through a combination of Christian and Eastern metaphysical beliefs and practices.[38]

Another example is the medical intuitive and mystic Caroline Myss (b. 1952), who began her career as a journalist in Chicago in the early 1970s before pursuing a master's degree in theology, which she completed in 1979. Shortly thereafter, she began giving medical intuitive readings; co-founded Stillpoint Publishing in Walpole, New Hampshire; and began consulting with alternative and complementary healers. In collaboration with Dr. Norman Shealy, founder of the American Holistic Medical Association, Myss co-authored *Aids: Passageway to Transformation* (1987) and *The Creation of Health: the Emotional, Psychological, and Spiritual Responses that Promote Health and Healing* (1988). These were followed by *Anatomy of the Spirit: The Seven Stages of Power and*

Healing (1996); and *Why People Don't Heal and How They Can* (1998). Beginning around 2000, Myss expanded her repertoire from healing to more general topics of spirituality and mysticism. A few years later, she opened the Caroline Myss Educational Institute at Wisdom University in San Francisco. Her more recent books and audio tapes include *Sacred Contracts: Awakening Your Divine Potential* (2002); *Three Levels of Power and How to Use Them* (2004); *Invisible Acts of Power: Personal Choices that Create Miracles* (2004); *Spiritual Power, Spiritual Practice* (2004); *The Sacred Contract of America: Fulfilling the Vision of Our Mystic Founders* (2007); *Entering the Castle: An Inner Path to God and Your Soul* (2007); and *Defy Gravity: Healing Beyond the Bounds of Reason* (2009).[39]

Power Brokers

Taking the teachings of the prosperity gospel in an even more materially oriented direction are modern self-help gurus who ignore metaphysics entirely, promoting techniques for success in business and in life through a positive attitude. A typical formula for these books is a series of simple rules said to have been learned from successful entrepreneurs or executives, recalling the writings of Napoleon Hill decades earlier.

Epitomizing this trend is Stephen R. Covey (1932–2012), whose *The 7 Habits of Highly Effective People* (1990) brought him recognition as one of *Time* magazine's twenty-five most influential Americans. The book, which has sold over twenty-five million copies and led to numerous spin-offs, is centered around the idea of an "abundance mindset," in which there are enough resources for everyone involved to succeed, and therefore the best solution to any conflict is to seek a win-win scenario.

There is also the New Thought practitioner and dream interpreter Gayle M. V. Delaney (b. 1949), founding president of the Association for the Study of Dreams and director of the Delaney and Flowers Professional Dream Center in San Francisco. Delaney developed a career built around teaching people how to understand their dreams and using them for problem solving. Her book *Living Your Dreams: Using Sleep to Solve Problems and Enrich Your Life* (1979) became the basis for her dream consultation and training program, which offers sessions to individuals, groups, families, and couples. Her group sessions, which have included the American Bankers Association, Chevron, the Stanford School of Business, Safeway, Rotary, and the Association of General Contractors, teach that dreams not only provide understanding of emotional disorders but can be used for sophisticated and insightful problem assessment and problem solving.[40]

Other popular power brokers operating under the umbrella of New Thought and introduced to American audiences by television celebrities include Anthony Robbins (b. 1960), author of *Awaken the Giant Within: How to Take Immediate Control of Your Mental, Emotional, Physical, and Financial Destiny!* (1992); Brian Tracy (b. 1944), whose best-selling audiocassette programs include *The Psychology of Achievement* (1984) and *How to Start and Succeed in Your Own Business* (1987); and Dr. Spencer Johnson (b. 1940), author of *Who Moved My Cheese? An Amazing Way to Deal with Change in Your Work and in Your Life* (1998) and co-author, with Kenneth Blanchard, of *The One-Minute Manager* (1982).

Seeking Enlightenment

On the opposite end of the spectrum from those focused purely on mind-body healing or power brokering are the authors and speakers who promise the secret to spiritual understanding. While many of these authors could fall under the heading of New Age or even esotericism, others—including some of the most commercially successful—clearly reflect the principles of New Thought, even in cases where the authors themselves do not appear to have intended it.

One such celebrity was Thaddeus Stanley Golas (1924–97), who served in World War II and subsequently enrolled at Columbia University, where he earned a BA degree and published in *The Columbia Review*. After graduation, he worked for *Redbook* magazine and later Harper and Row before moving to San Francisco, where he self-published *The Lazy Man's Guide to Enlightenment* (1972), considered to be one of the classic books on spirituality. His thesis was quite simple: "Enlightenment doesn't care how you get there." As with a number of New Thought writers, he talked of spirituality using words and phrases drawn from quantum physics, general relativity, and chaos theory. He had little use for New Age philosophy, criticizing it for offering up notions of philosophical banality that had little relevance to conscious thinking.[41]

Similar to Golas was the Canadian New Thought author, lecturer, poet, musician, and composer Kenneth George Mills (1923–2004), who devoted a lifetime to metaphysical and philosophical speculation. His impromptu lectures, which he began in the 1960s, were an expression of his inner self that he called "unfoldment." Using poetry and spontaneous speaking, he claimed to express a plane of consciousness that awakened others to the possibility of living beyond themselves. His books, performances, and numerous recordings were intended to capture existential moments when the individual acted in harmony with the universe. His books included *Given to Praise! An Array of Provocative Metaphysical-Philosophical Utterances* (1976), *The Golden Nail* (1993), *Change Your Standpoint; Change Your World* (1996), and *The Cornucopia of Substance* (2004).[42]

A more recent popular example of this trend is *A Course in Miracles* (ACIM). According to "scribes" Helen Schucman (1909–1981) and William Thetford (1923–1933), the information contained in this self-study program was dictated to her between 1965 and 1972 by "the Voice," an entity she identified as Jesus. In 1972, Schucman and Thetford established the Foundation for Inner Peace to publish the material, which they did in 1975. The course emphasizes that God is one with all of creation and that the world we see around us is an illusion created by our false senses; our true selves, as created by God, are perfect and fully abundant, and only by union with Christ can we achieve a return to those selves. The course itself has reportedly sold two million copies and has inspired many teachers who have become popular authors in their own right.[43]

One such is the lecturer and "stand-up philosopher/comedian" Jon Mundy (aka Dr. Baba Jon Mundane) cofounder of the New Seminary in New York City and professor of philosophy at Marist College in Poughkeepsie, New York. Author of *Toward a Theology of Money* (1981), *Awaken to Your Own Call* (1994), *Listening to Your Inner Guide* (1995), *The Ten Laws of Happiness* (1998), and *What is Mysticism?* (2008),

Mundy promotes an awareness of each individual's inner guide (also called the *intelligent principle, inner genius, indwelling spirit, counselor, comforter, teacher,* and *conscience*), and the capacity of knowing "exactly the right decision you need to make, in each and every instance."[44]

Mundy explained his journey into spirituality as having begun early in his life when, at the age of eighteen, he served as a Methodist pastor for several rural churches in Missouri, an experience that led him progressively to the study of world religions, foreign travel, a fascination with meditation, Kirlian photography, and Rudolf Steiner's efforts to find a synthesis between science and mysticism in Anthroposophy. By the early 1970s, Mundy was active in the parapsychology community in New York City, where he met ACIM's Helen Schucman and William Thetford. Infatuated with the implications of the course, Mundy left the Methodist Church and, in 1989, he and the Reverend Diane Berke organized the Interfaith Fellowship in New York City and the magazine *On Course,* which advocates the philosophy of life based on *A Course in Miracles.* Explaining that the book represents "a Copernican revolution in Christianity," he and Berke offer a program for individuals to remove the "blocks to awareness" that separate them from their inner guide—a tool for replacing the siren call of the ego with truth coming from the inner spirit. Today, Mundy serves as executive director of All Faiths International Seminary in New York City and is publisher of *Miracles* magazine.[45]

Another dream weaver is the German-born spiritual lecturer Eckhart Tolle (b. 1948), who grew up among the bombed-out buildings in Lünen, Germany, before moving to Spain and then to England, where he taught German and Spanish. At the age of twenty-two, he enrolled at the University of London, where he studied philosophy, psychology, and literature, followed by graduate study at Cambridge University in 1977. It was in that year he experienced an "inner transformation" that seemed to change his life of existential uncertainty to one of inner peace. After exploring Buddhism and the writings of the German philosopher and mystic Eckhart von Hochheim, better known as Meister Eckhart (1260–1327), Tolle moved to Vancouver, British Columbia, where he became a spiritual teacher and author, writing *The Power of Now: A Guide to Spiritual Enlightenment* (1997), *Stillness Speaks* (2003), and *A New Earth* (2005), all of which sold several million copies each. Together with Oprah Winfrey, he hosted a series of web-based seminars and, in 2009, created Eckhart Tolle TV, a website designed to spread the transformative message of spiritual awakening. Although unaffiliated with any organized religion, his teachings cover a broad range of spiritual topics borrowed from the Tao Te Ching, the Bhagavad Gita, Buddhist scriptures, and the Old and New Testaments.[46]

Author and spiritual teacher Gary Zukav (b. 1942) left Harvard in 1960 to motor through Europe and the Middle East, volunteered for civil rights work in Mississippi, and in 1965 entered the US Army, where he participated in operations in both Vietnam and Laos. After completing his tour of duty in 1970, Zukav moved to San Francisco, where he lost himself in drugs and sex for about five years. Following an introduction to quantum physics, he emerged from his dissipations to write *The Dancing Wu Li Masters, An Overview of the New Physics* (1979), winning numerous awards. His second book, *The Seat of the Soul* (1989), made the *New York Times* best-seller list for thirty-one weeks. In 1998, he co-founded with is wife the Seat of the Soul Institute and proceeded to write other books, including *Soul Stories* (2000); *Thoughts from the Seat of the Soul: Meditations for Souls in Progress* (2001); *The Heart of the Soul: Emotional Awareness* (2002); *The Mind of the Soul: Responsible Choice* (2003); *Soul to Soul: Communications from the Heart* (2007), which he coauthored with his wife; and *Spiritual Partnership: The Journey to Authentic Power* (2010). Zukav stresses in his writings the need to align personality with soul, which, when accomplished, creates a transformative ability to grow spiritually, emotionally, and intuitively within the living, conscious Universe. The creation of this "authentic power" is the responsibility and challenge facing each individual. His objective is the realization of the "Universal Human," a concept strikingly similar to that of Swedenborg.[47]

Author, lecturer, and self-help advocate Wayne Walter Dyer (b. 1940) is another example of this trend. A native of Detroit, Michigan, he earned a doctorate in counseling from Wayne State University and worked as a high school guidance counselor before pursuing an academic career at St. John's University in New York. His motivational lectures at St. John's and his success in a private therapy practice brought him to the attention of a larger public audience that included talk-show celebrities such as Merv Griffin and Phil Donahue. Leaving his academic career, Dyer proceeded to build his reputation through lecture tours, video tapes, and a series of books that resonated with those in the New Thought movement. He was able to capitalize on his impoverished beginnings to promote concepts of self-actualization, higher consciousness, the emulation of Jesus, and more general aspects of spirituality. Dyer takes issue with organized religion, seeking instead to construct a definition of spirituality that involves being Christ-like rather than being Christian. His books and recordings include *Wisdom of the Ages: 60 Days to Enlightenment* (1998), *Your Sacred Self: Making the Decision to Be Free* (1995), *The Power of Intention* (2004), *Living the Wisdom of the Tao* (2008), *Excuses Begone! How to Change Lifelong, Self-Defeating Thinking Habits* (2009), and *Wishes Fulfilled: Mastering the Art of Manifesting* (2012).[48]

Church-Based Spiritual Teachers

While many of the popular teachers who embrace enlightenment keep a secular focus, others choose to utilize New Thought's religious heritage. Among the more popular church-based spiritual teachers of the New Thought movement in the twentieth century was Raymond Charles Barker (1911–88). Minister at the Unity Center in Rochester, New York, and later affiliated with the First Church of Religious Science in Manhattan, where he served for thirty-three years, Barker spoke at numerous congresses, lectured abroad, and authored the popular *Treat Yourself to Life* (1954), *The Science of Successful Living* (1957), *The Power of Decision* (1968), and *You Are Invisible: No One Has Seen Your Consciousness* (1973)—all considered classic representations of New Thought spirituality.[49] Along with Barker, author, lecturer, and former pastor of Manhattan's First Church of Religious Science Stuart Grayson (1923–2001) was very much a part of New Thought's public face. His books, which included *The Ten Demandments of Prosperity* (1986), *Collected Essays of Stuart Grayson* (1995), and *Spiritual Healing: A Simple Guide for the Healing of Body, Mind, and Spirit* (1997), explained how self-affirmation became the springboard to healthy-mindedness and prosperity.[50]

Among today's more popular New Thought teachers is the Unity Church minister, author, and activist Marianne Williamson (b. 1952), a former ACIM teacher. Her bestseller *A Return to Love: Reflections on the Principles of a Course in Miracles* (1992) is the source of a quote often misattributed to Nelson Mandela: "Our deepest fear is not that we are inadequate. Our deepest fear is that we are powerful beyond measure." Her other books include *The Gift of Change: Spiritual Guidance for Living Your Best Life* (2006); and *Everyday Grace: Having Hope, Finding Forgiveness, and Making Miracles* (2007).[51]

The Reverend Terry Cole-Whittaker (b. 1939), author of the *New York Times* bestseller *Every Saint Has a Past, Every Sinner a Future: Seven Steps to the Spiritual and Material Riches of Life* (2001), offers a message of hope, healing, and abundance to those in search of life's meaning. Ordained in the United Church of Religious Science in 1975, she became pastor of a New Thought church in La Jolla, California, and subsequently opened several teaching centers and a syndicated television program. In 1982, she founded the Terry Cole-Whittaker Ministries, drawing thousands to her services. As a preacher of empowerment and spiritual development, she employs autobiographical examples as well as heavy borrowing from Chopra's *The Seven Spiritual Laws of Success* (1994) to explain her own seven steps to self-fulfillment. *Every Saint Has a Past, Every Sinner a Future* has sold more than a million copies. Her other books and recordings include *How to Have More in a Have-Not World* (1983), *The Inner Path From Where You Are to Where You Want to Be* (1986), *Love and Power in a World Without Limits* (1989), *Dare to be Great: Seven Steps to Spiritual and Material Riches of Life* (2003), and *Live Your Bliss* (2009).[52]

Still another contemporary church-based New Thought spiritual leader is Matthew Fox (b. 1940), a former Dominican priest who taught at various universities before founding the Institute of Culture and Creation Spirituality at Chicago's Mundelein College in 1976. There he proceeded to develop programs in "art as meditation" and "body prayer" before finding himself at odds with Catholic orthodoxy as he sought to create a more visceral connection with the early church mystics. After moving his institute to Holy Names University in Oakland, California, his teachings came under the scrutiny of Cardinal Joseph Ratzinger (now Pope Benedict XVI), who was then prefect of the Congregation for the Doctrine of the Faith. Although exonerated by a panel of theologians, Fox's writings were judged negatively by Ratzinger, and he was ordered to desist from his lecture circuit. In 1993, Fox was expelled from the Dominican order, whereupon he turned to the Episcopal Church, which accepted him as a priest in 1994. Two years later, he founded the University of Creation Spirituality in Oakland (later renamed Wisdom University), offering degree programs in spirituality designed to attract young people to church worship.[53]

Fox's most popular book, *One River, Many Wells: Wisdom Springing from Global Faiths* (2000), draws heavily upon early mystics within the Catholic tradition as well as ecstatic experiences from other faiths. Noted for his "green" theology, Fox draws a relationship between humankind and nature that is best explained in his *The Coming of the Cosmic Christ: The Healing of Mother Earth and the Birth of a Global Renaissance* (1988). He also authored *Confessions: The Making of a Post-Denominational Priest* (1996), an autobiography that seeks to explain his problems with the Catholic church and his effort to understand true Christianity. His so-called "Techno Cosmic Mass" is intended to appeal to a younger generation with a combination of ritual, music, and ecstatic expression. Some of his other books include *Original Blessing: A Primer in Creation Spirituality* (1983); *Sheer Joy: Conversations with Thomas Aquinas on Creation Spirituality* (1992); and *Creativity: Where the Divine and the Human Meet* (2002).[54]

Word of Faith Movement

On the fringe of the New Thought movement is the Word of Faith, often called the epitome of the prosperity gospel, and which is arguably the fastest-growing segment of Christianity in Africa and other third-world regions. Within the family of Word of Faith or Faith churches, the basic doctrine preached is salvation through Jesus, and a salvation that can be achieved both in the spiritual kingdom and in the natural world. Its founder, Essek William Kenyon (1867–1948), a New England Bible teacher, preached a "guaranteed" covenant passed on by the apostle John (3 John 1:2), which pledged that God would bless their descendants with health and prosperity: "Beloved, I pray that all may go well with you and that you may be in good heath, just as it is with your soul."[56] Like the writer and spiritual teacher Ernest S. Holmes who, as founder of Religious Science, played a central role in the New Thought movement, Kenyon attended the Emerson School of Oratory in 1892. There he was influenced by its president, Christian Scientist Charles Emerson (1837–1908), as well as Ralph Waldo Trine and the Unitarian minister Minot J. Savage. Although Kenyon supposedly opposed these metaphysical religions, he nonetheless embraced many of their teachings, turning the Word of Faith movement into an apologist for many of their practices.

Generally speaking, Word of Faith is a religious movement whose beliefs lie somewhere between Pentecostal or evangelical Christianity and New Thought. Its views are (and have been) regularly expressed in the ministries such as the Lakewood Church of Joel (b. 1963) and Victoria (b. 1961) Osteen in Houston, Texas. Each week, Joel Osteen's Saturday and Sunday services draw upwards of forty thousand attendees and are broadcast to 210 markets, with an estimated seven million viewers. His seven-week program to achieve a fuller life involves seven steps:

1. Enlarging your vision
2. Developing a healthy self-image
3. Discovering the power of your thoughts and words
4. Letting go of the past
5. Finding strength through adversity
6. Living to give
7. Choosing to be happy.

His book, *Your Best Life Now: 7 Steps to Living at Your Full Potential* (2004), which has sold more than three million copies, makes one simple claim: "I believe God wants you to prosper. . . . God wants you to be a winner, not a whiner."[56]

The Rev. Creflo A. Dollar Jr. (b. 1962), pastor of the World Changers Church in New York, remains one of the more prominent prosperity preachers who play into the nation's self-help culture. A former college football player, Dollar started his church in an elementary school cafeteria in Atlanta in 1986 but later moved to New York City, where his church enjoys a broad television audience.

Other New York migrants include Frederick K. C. Price (b. 1932), who started the Crenshaw Christian Center East in Upper Manhattan and now preaches through his Ever Increasing Faith ministry broadcasts; the former commodities trader Dan Stratton, who with his wife, Ann, serves as pastor of the Faith Exchange Fellowship in Lower Manhattan; and the religious broadcaster Rev. Frederick J. Eikerenkoetter II (1935–2009), also known as "Reverend Ike." These charismatic pastors preach their messages using a cluster of anecdotal corroborations and vivid visionary encounters.[57]

Others who have preached in this vein are Kenneth (b. 1936) and Gloria Copeland of Kenneth Copeland Ministries of Newark, Texas; televangelist Marilyn Hickey (b. 1931); the Trinity Broadcasting Network of Paul (b. 1934) and Jan Crouch; Jim (b. 1940) and Tammy Faye (1942–2007) Bakker's PTL Club ministry in North Carolina; Benny Hinn's (b. 1952) World Healing Center Church in Grapevine, Texas; and Bishop Eddie L. Long (b. 1953) of New Birth Missionary Baptist Church in Lithonia, Georgia. Others include the Joyce Meyer (b. 1943) Ministries in Fenton, Missouri; televangelist Robert Gibson Tilton (b. 1946), whose television program *Success-N-Life* aired in the 1990's through BET and the Word Network; the Korean minister David Yonggi Cho (b. 1936), whose "law of incubation" drew a million members to his church in 2007; televangelist, faith healer, and motivational speaker John Avanzini (b. 1936), whose ministry is in Corpus Christi, Texas; and Paula White (b. 1966) Ministries in Tampa, Florida.

Whether it is fair to include the Word ministries under the category of New Thought is no doubt a subject of debate among friends and opponents alike. According to Daniel Ray McConnell of Oral Roberts University, Kenyon originally adopted the teachings of New Thought when he introduced the prosperity gospel into his Baptist ministry, a theme McConnell discusses in his exposé of the Word of Faith movement, *A Different Gospel* (1995). In the book he argues that Kenyon's teachings constituted a "Trojan horse" within Christianity.[58]

Other critics of Kenyon and his movement include Baptists Justin Peters, David Jones, and Russell S. Woodbridge, who tie the early proponents of the prosperity gospel directly to the unorthodox teachings of the New Thought movement and specifically to the writings of Swedenborg, Quimby, Evans, and Eddy.[59] What makes the Word ministries similar to those in the New Thought movement, explained another critic, Kevin Scott Smith, is their common embrace of metaphysical idealism and the "causative power of mind over matter," the identification of the mind with the Divine, the adoption of a "subjective epistemology by which one may distinguish between faulty external sensory evidence and inner spiritual Reality," the realization of one's spiritual identity, the defining of faith as "right thinking," and "verbal affirmation" of desired conditions.[60]

For those Word of Faith ministers aligned to the traditions of "low church" Protestantism, the most common feature in their delivery has been their preference for the "plain style" that begins with a quote from Scripture, followed by the reasons and meanings behind the quote, and concluding with its application to the lives of listeners. This formula eschews the rituals of "high church" and its embracing of an avowed Arminian belief in the individual's power to accept or reject God's grace for the sanctification of an individual wholly determined by God's sovereignty. By contrast, the majority of New Thought's celebrity ministers and secular lecturers have chosen to replace both formalities with personal narratives. Given that so many of the movement's more celebrated writers and lecturers have themselves experienced health and spiritual challenges in their younger years, the shift from doctrine to personal narrative (including storytelling, dreams, and visions) has become a pronounced characteristic of their homiletic style. This reflects a change from textual expositions and dogmatic preaching to secular and oftentimes highly personal accounts drawn from life.[61]

Like Christian Scientists and New Thoughters, those who self-identify as being part of either the Word of Faith movement or New Thought object to comparisons between the two. Nevertheless, the day-to-day practices of the two movements belie their differences. Distinguishing between the comforting words in Joel Osteen and those of Michael Beckwith makes for an interesting discussion, since both men closely align with mental self-discipline, affirmative prayer, symbolic interpretations of the Bible, an inspiring world vision, the presence of

God in each individual, and ideas that transcend all faiths. The simple fact is that the philosophical underpinnings of the New Thought movement have migrated into a host of contemporary religions and belief systems with or without their conscious awareness of it. In this age of global pluralism, movements are seldom idiosyncratic in their beliefs and practices.

* * *

For the most part, the term "New Thought" is curiously absent from present-day discussions of healing and spirituality—a term lost amid a myriad of labels and trademarks currently being marketed. Like psychotherapy, there has been a tendency in more recent years for healers and empowerment celebrities to affix their own trademark (i.e., Rick Warren's "Purpose Driven Life") to processes that are commonly held but selfishly garnered for personal gain. How else can one explain the hundreds of writers and lecturers whose terminology derives from (even plagiarizes) early New Thought writers but who adamantly resist being so labeled? As Deborah Whitehouse has documented in her article "New Age, New Thought, and Process Thought: A Psychological Perspective," both the denominations Unity and Religious Science, as well as the celebrities who preach the power of thought, remain in blissful and righteous denial of their historical lineage.[62]

Despite their trademark names and Internet sites, today's global ministries and secular celebrities for healing, self-discovery, and empowerment offer a "science" of cheer and discovery that transcends their differences. All cut across the socioeconomic layers of society to teach a nonaligned and trans-religious form of spirituality that promises a triumphal life combined with an unending supply of abundance, prosperity, blessedness, and health. Among the common components of their spirituality are themes dealing with angels, visualization, meditation, biofeedback, authenticity, and dream states—much of which feeds into the visual media. With a galaxy of charismatic and folksy preaching, these righteous weavers carry their messages to believers by way of mega-size meetings in stadiums and sports arenas, broadcasting networks, television audiences, DVDs, books, blogs, and Twitter feeds. Accompanying these methods of communication are a holistic grab bag of charms, prophetic words, self-healing lessons, call-in messaging, PayPal donations, and absent healing, to name but a few. With messaging that is asynchronous to any time of day or night via the Internet, they extol generous tidings of health, happiness, and prosperity to all. Championing fresh insights and new illuminations, they have been quick to dispose of Christian orthodoxy and its core teachings on sin and redemption for one crossbred with perfectionism, gnosticism, and other occult beliefs. The theme repeated by Word of Faith preacher Kenneth Hagin, "Say it; do it; receive it; tell it," reverberates across their respective media.[63]

The commodification of empowerment and self-discovery has been one of the characteristic elements of New Thought in American life and culture as it competes in the marketplace for audiences—a condition that has left its spokespeople indistinguishable on occasion from the crassest of hucksters. Utilizing oratory, salesmanship, pseudoscience, ritual, and entertainment to elevate the moral tone of their message, these dream weavers provide believers with much-needed assurances that they are the living legacies of the world's spiritual awakening and that the world is, indeed, their oyster. By playing down dogma, simplifying creeds, and offering oral and visual distractions rich in anecdote, they have won the loyalties of millions to their commercialized spirituality. It therefore seems irrelevant whether they are true believers, self-deluded sycophants, or conscious charlatans. Regardless of their motivation, and far from being understood to the point of reducing their ideas to a commonly understood law or principle, each accepts the proposition that the mind influences the body and vice versa. Strong mental suggestion—whether from fright, hope, faith, or imagination—marks their physical and psychical results.

10

A Retrospective

*Anyone can see that intending and not
acting when we can is not really intending, and loving and not doing good when
we can is not really loving.*

—Emanuel Swedenborg, *Heaven and Hell*

In an address delivered at the close of the summer session at Harvard's
School of Theology in 1909, President Charles W. Eliot (1834–1926)
identified several characterizations of future religions. First, they would
rely less upon authority—both organizational and literary—as a means
of ensuring their role in society. Second, there would be less adherence to the personifications of primitive forces such as mountains, fire,
and earthquakes as symbols of deities. Third, there would be less reliance on dead ancestors, teachers, and rulers. Fourth, future religious life
would not be constructed around personal welfare or safety. Fifth, religions would not be sacrificial or expiatory in nature. Sixth, they would
be less anthropomorphic in their representations of God. And seventh,
they would be less ascetic and gloomy. He also predicted that concepts
of God would adopt the language of modern physics by including such
descriptive terms as *energy, vital force, omnipresence,* and *infinite spirit.*
In addition, religion would be monotheistic, indwelling, and immanent
in all things, and reject any conception that humans or God might be
alienated from the world. Most important, humans would discover God
through self-consciousness. There is in each individual, Eliot observed,
"an animating, ruling, characteristic essence, or spirit, which is himself."

It was this personality or soul that rallied the body. The religions of the future would no longer approach evil or human pain and suffering as punishment or moral training but as a preventable evil. "Institutional Christianity as a rule condemned the mass of mankind to eternal torment," he noted. "The new religion will make no such pretensions, and will teach no such horrible and perverse doctrines." Instead of justice, the religions of the future would emphasize God's all-pervading love.[1]

Eliot's address was not just a prediction of religion and spirituality in the future, but an unusually prescient description of New Thought, which, by the start of the twentieth century, boasted some four hundred churches and centers serving approximately a million adherents. By the Second World War, its numbers had swelled to between fifteen and twenty million.[2] Today, estimates are difficult, since a large portion of New Thought's more secular literature is unattached to any specific church or organization. We may, in fact, be justified in calling New Thought a "secondary religion" whose churched and unchurched adherents profess teachings built on principles centered around healing, self-discovery, and empowerment.

The passage of American metaphysical thinking from Calvinism to New Thought took a circuitous route that began with sober orthodoxy and worked its way through a fashion spread of newly found sciences before turning sympathetically to the appeal of a dogma-free religion as conceived by Swedenborg and temporized by Emerson. Out of their inspiration emerged a school of thinking whose gifted teachers constructed an idealistic philosophy of free spirits searching for a pluralistic community of cooperating minds. Some of these teachers taught a science of mind using the empirical reality of the self to achieve personal and collective growth. For others, it was the more antiquated concept of the soul that asserted itself. In both, however, there was the acceptance of belief, however derived, as the basis for action. In this sense, New Thought became an expression of tolerance, of imagination, and of contentment with life, including its many paradoxes. Having fused together the faith of the seventeenth century, the reason of the eighteenth, and the feeling of the nineteenth, New Thought broke into the twentieth century with what one might call a genuine "Americanism"— a worship of the practical over the theoretical, of self-sufficiency over self-surrender, of instant over delayed gratification, and cash value as the measure of personal success.

The early devotees of New Thought endeavored to popularize Emerson's concept of self-reliance in a manner that best expressed the spiritual nature of the individual soul. "If one could read Emerson thoroughly and deeply," Horatio Dresser once wrote, "asking again and again how his wisdom is to be applied to actual life, one might easily dispense with a greater part of the literature of the New Thought, and be the gainer thereby, for many writers have simply restated clumsily what he had already put gracefully." Save for healing disease, Emerson provided much of the inspiration for New Thought's philosophy of mental life. Humans were neither wholly physical nor of the senses; rather, they were conjoined with a soul that was invisible, immortal, spiritual, and potentially self-reliant and free. New Thought accepted an idealistic theory of the universe where physical nature was a manifestation of the will of God and where the world was as large and as immediate as consciousness could make it. It represented a new application of wisdom drawn from the science of the West and the spiritual insight of the East.[3] The universe was a living organism complete with trials, errors, and "trivialities of finite life." Reality, explained Dresser, was "not a mere sea in which every drop is like the next drop; it is infinitely, minutely diverse."[4]

As intellectual descendents of Swedenborg, the earliest New Thoughters bred true in their writings by expounding a theology whose authority had, in their hands, undermined the drama of sin and salvation by substituting a tender and loving God. The innovations to Christian theology brought about by Swedenborg and his disciples induced people to discard the older legalisms and to experience for themselves the divine influx around them. It also brought them to the frontiers of psychology, pushing into the pre-, sub-, and unconscious while affirming free will, individuality, and a God whose benevolence accorded with human beings' highest wishes.

In assessing the history of New Thought in the first half of the twentieth century, one cannot ignore the fact that while its proponents were utilitarians who shared little or no interest in religious orthodoxy, they nevertheless explored many of the dark places of the soul. They were devotees of the scientific method who became highly suspect of Christian bibliolatry. New Thought's proponents did little to address the problems raised by biblical criticism. Instead, they took the Bible as they found it and chose to employ the portions they found most agreeable while ignoring others. They saw no reason why God would speak only through a Moses or Paul and not through someone like Whitman or Emerson. The same applied to the lessons learned from Buddhism, Hinduism, Islam, and Confucianism, which they considered as important as Scripture. Out of their writings emerged a respect for individual choice, opposition to textual literalists, rejection of any imposition on the mind and spirit of others, and an ever-present consciousness of the fragile space between individual freedom and the meaning of the One. God had to be approached through the heart, and it was an individual's benevolence toward Being that assured a harmony of purpose in his or her judgment and actions.[5]

Just as it is impossible to understand the nineteenth-century American psyche prior to the 1870s without seeing it within a Protestant/Puritan context, it is similarly impossible to fathom the twentieth-century psyche without touching upon science and its pervasive impact on Protestant evangelicalism, revivalism, voluntarism, personal identity, secularism, pluralism, reform, bigotry, and the spiritually inspired groups that dotted the landscape. During this transformative period in American culture, religion was forced to share the stage with technological, social, economic, intellectual, and political forces not of its own choosing. While there is ample evidence to suggest that the ubiquitous power of religion was sorely challenged, there is little reason to conclude that secularization, urbanization, and even bureaucratization were purposeful enough to hide the well-worn paths of religion in the post-industrial age. Perhaps a more reasonable explanation is to say that Americans moved away from their mainstream denominations to discover a more personal and nondenominational form of religious experience. Americans opened their ears to a plurality of voices, each offering social and spiritual comfort. Along with the Catholic/Protestant/Jew ecumenism documented by Will Herberg (1901–77), which replaced the old mainline Protestant denominations, Americans abandoned their dogmas and doctrines for a more palatable and undefined spirituality that recast religion into a social experience patterned on middle-class values and aspirations.[6] Secularization took a powerful hold on America in the post-industrial age, particularly among those professionals connected with science and the social sciences. Yet religion's resilience continued to shape the nation's politics, reminding citizens that America's power and destiny are intimately tied to its religious origins.[7]

Measured against European religiosity, early twentieth-century New Thought marked a triumph of voluntarism, a vindication of religious freedom, and scorn for all forms of authoritarian creeds. Having constituted a world within themselves, its proponents exalted the idea that the actions of the mind were stimulus enough for receiving the blessings of God.[8] Called upon in their forensic capacity to expound a worldview that argued for the welfare of the whole, but not at the expense of individual liberty, its various ministries served the status quo with the shibboleths of "healthy-mindedness," "unity," "wholeness," "harmony," and "prosperity"—virtues used against the threat of social levelism. Social stability became the qualification for happiness and economic freedom. The idea, inherited from the Puritans, was of a society rewarded for its virtues, but not at the expense of economic felicity. This confusion spoke of a tension in ideology between the functional power of inner grace and the spectacle of social irresponsibility in the rich, a tension that New Thought's representative leaders generally resolved by emphasizing the power of the moral individual over the state to correct immoral habits.

Described by historian and educator Alfred W. Griswold in 1934 as "a gnarled trunk and many branches," New Thoughters decried public service and projects intended to raise up the weaker elements of society. They assumed that their purpose was as instruments of self-discipline and self-reliance rather than jeremiads for charity, humility, and self-denial. These they considered the stigmata of outdated Christian beliefs. As a result, New Thought's proponents drifted easily into an ambivalence toward reform that left them embodying the principles of industrial and corporate capitalism with their defense of both the social order and the natural law. Before long, many among the multitude of New Thought writers and inspirational lecturers had transposed their own portion of the movement into little more than a get-rich formula, instructing neophytes on how to think their way to success. Long after New Thought's proponents had ceased to entertain the idea of communication with spirits, they created a distinctive intellectual tradition based on practical idealism intended to serve both the individual and society.[9]

No longer viewed as a predominantly Protestant nation, America emerged out of the Second World War with a secular religiosity best represented in Norman Vincent Peale's *The Power of Positive Thinking*. From the vantage point of Protestantism's religious elites and the theologies that once marked the American landscape, the New Thought movement had come to represent a reshaping of the normative assumptions about personal identity, choices, and prospects. Its new syncretism came loaded with elements derived from various non-Western spiritual and philosophical perspectives, along with new demographics showing the telling infusion of Catholics and Jews, and the prospect of an increasingly fragmented society. Rather than oppose such mixing, New Thought's writers, lecturers, and publishers celebrated America's pluralism as an unfinished creation, always evolving, with boundaries continually being redrawn to fit the circumstances. New Thought stood for peace of mind and personal success—a democratic religion whose oversimplification and commercial overtones appealed nicely to the nation's complacent yet optimistic culture.

While religious leaders within the New Thought movement moved quickly to broaden their reach with teachings that were transnational in scope, the movement's more secular leaders made little pretense to retaining religious affiliations. For them, religious sects, with their neat membership roles, failed to capture the multilayered nature of society. Unconcerned with whether they were communicating with Protestant evangelicals, Catholics, Christian Scientists, Jews, Mormons, Seventh-Day Adventists, or agnostics, they sought to teach a palatable list of human qualities that decried the hegemony of any single denomination or sect. As they stretched their imaginations, New Thought's secularists espoused a mystical communion of the individual with the universe; reclaimed what were formerly institutionally contained ecstatic experiences; challenged Enlightenment-driven rationality with a more intuitive experience; and cultivated the inner life through concentration, affirmation, visualization, and contemplation.[10]

Today, New Thought's writers, lecturers, and publishers offer a common set of ideas, dispositions, and attitudes that resonate across the American culture. Theirs is a pragmatic response to the challenges of the times, encouraging and reinforcing expressions of optimism in the future, the healthy-mindedness of self-affirmation, and commitment to the mores and ideals of a democratic culture. Whether belonging to New Thought's churched or unchurched elements, they share the belief that humanity should live morally and ethically in tune with a transcendent order and that the values and lifestyles of society should mesh with the prevailing views on individualism and the capitalist economy. Eschewing organized religion per se, they have chosen instead to celebrate the religious "experience" minus the anthropomorphic gods, doctrines, and dogmas used to explain them. Replacing theology with more metaphysical and scientific meanings, they have proceeded to formulate abstract statements of "forces" that either help or hinder self-realization.

When all is said and done, the contributors to New Thought's corpus of writings and media productions have been admitted into the canon of popular culture carrying reputations out of proportion to their achievements. For the most part, New Thought's plentitude of writers have merely drawn on the accumulated wisdom of their forbearers without adding much of their own save an expansion on the uses of self-discovery, healthy-mindedness, and empowerment. New Thought's celebrity spokespeople have clearly set out to cherry-pick those themes and attitudes that best fit America's comfort zone. In doing so, its multitude of celebrities have expressed themselves in almost caricature form, enjoining one and all to profit from their occupations and thank God for their gains. They offer glimpses of heaven in exchange for coin of the realm. Shorn of any pretense to piety, they have marketed God using the most modern business practices. Their metaphysically based "schools" and "universities" continue to cash in on the public's demand for spiritual instruction and revelation, offering access to the "secrets" and "keys" to success and self-healing; special "words" that evoke God's immediate response; and correspondence courses and printed lectures that open the soul to cosmic energies. Whether through the publishing houses or the lessons, degrees, and certificates offered through its online schools, New Thought's many media outlets promise the keys to health, wealth, and happiness.

Aside from the vast store of insightful ideas borrowed from ancient philosophies and religions by its early expositors, much of what currently passes as New Thought is an amalgam that even the eclectic Victor Cousin would not likely recognize. In this new metaphysical paradigm, religion and prosperity have been bound in an indissoluble union based on the self-serving premise that they represent the two things dearest to God and to humankind. Neither the avarice of the rich and successful nor the spreading power of corporate greed have done much to dampen New Thoughters' belief in a self-regulating society governed by moral individualism. New Thought's spokespeople have become the portrait painters of the American landscape, brushing over issues of class, race, and ethnicity with murals of economic life sanctioned by moral law. It seems manifestly obvious among New Thought's followers that personal health and happiness have become the equivalent to the soul's salvation.

We now know that New Thought was not a freestanding philosophy but rather an outgrowth of sources—both native and foreign—that were applied in novel new ways. As a metaphor, it stands for the discovery of a new freedom in which people not only reach their innermost selves but, in doing so, find God. New Thought's spokespeople have endowed the lives of their devotees with a self-reliant individualism, the avoidance of self-pity, a stoic's view of life's paradoxes, and a belief in the possible. In the American dream of money and power there is the potential for human realization and a sense of what life might be. The characteristic themes of its ministerial leaders coincide with the beliefs of its secular celebrities. Both are at home in America's budding popular culture—its rejection of biblical literalism, its toleration of a variety of different faiths, and its belief that people can make a better world building on the ethical ideals of Jesus and other spiritual leaders.

Although New Thought's legacy has been compromised time and again by its unsavory commercialism, it carries an unambiguous presence into the postmodern world, providing opportunities within and outside its churches and spiritual centers for direct engagement with other faiths, cultures, and issues. Initially driven by the discovery that physical healing was possible through the power of mind and spiritual awareness, it has unfolded into an appealing process of self-realization and grasping the power to remake the circumstances and conditions in one's personal life. Perhaps the meaning of New Thought is not to be found in any single fixed system of thought, philosophy, or religion, but rather as a growing, developing, progressive expression of American values—both good and bad—in a world made small by the Internet and other global media.

New Thought Denominations, Centers, and Institutes

As with most new religious movements in the United States, New Thought exists in a nearly constant state of flux. While the larger denominations have been stable over the long term, the history of New Thought has been marked by smaller groups forming, moving, renaming themselves, and, often, vanishing abruptly. Aside from the challenge of tracking and determining the status of these smaller organizations, there is the question of whether or not to include groups that share the beliefs of New Thought but do not identify themselves as such. The following represents a good-faith attempt to list the known New Thought denominations, centers, and institutes, while acknowledging that arriving at a completely accurate picture may be impossible.

Major Denominations, Associations, and Institutions

Affiliated New Thought Network, Pacific Grove, CA

Association for Global New Thought, Santa Barbara, CA

Association of Unity Churches, Lee's Summit, MO; operates the Unity Institute in the same location

Divine Science Federation International, St. Louis, MO

Divine Science School, Washington, DC

Emerson Theological Institute, Oakhurst, CA

International New Thought Alliance, Mesa, AZ

Seicho-No-Ie (United States headquarters), Gardena, CA

United Centers for Spiritual Living (also known as Religious Science International and the United Church of Religious Science), Golden CO; operates the Holmes Institute in Burbank, CA

Universal Foundation for Better Living, Miami Gardens, FL; operates the Johnnie Colemon Theological Seminary in the same location

Other Denominations, Associations, and Institutions (Current)

Abundant Life Center, Vancouver, WA

Agape International Spiritual Center, Culver City, CA

Center for Inner Awareness, Salem, OR

Christ Truth League, Fort Worth, TX

Church of Truth, Pasadena, CA; formerly operated the Albert Grier Ministerial School in the same location

College of Divine Metaphysics, Moab, Utah

Divine Unity Ministries, Cody, WY

First Church of Divine Science (formerly called the Church of the Healing Christ), New York, NY

Global Religious Science Ministries, Silver Spring, MD

Hillside International Chapel and Truth Center, Atlanta, GA

Home of Truth, Alameda, CA

Humanitarian New Thought Movement, Australia

Inner Light Ministries, Santa Cruz, CA

Institute of Mind Sciences, Karachi, Pakistan

International Metaphysical Ministry, Sedona, AZ

International Spiritual Truth Center, Stockton, CA

Life Changers International, Hoffman Estates, IL

Living Truth Center, East Cleveland, OH

Metropolitan Spiritual Churches of Christ, Kansas City, MO

New Thought Ministries, Glen Allen, VA

New Thought Ministries of Oregon, Wilsonville, OR

Noohra Foundation, Smyrna, GA

One Spirit Ministries (also known as God's Church), Cresco, PA

Piscean-Aquarian Ministry for New Thought (formerly the Aquarian Ministry), Asheville, NC

Real Life Today Church, Washington, DC

Society of Jewish Science, New York, NY

Society for the Study of Metaphysical Religion, Clearwater, FL

Southwestern College (formerly Quimby College), Santa Fe, NM

Spiritual Empowerment Center, Baltimore, MD

Teaching of the Inner Christ, El Cajon, CA

Understanding Principles for Better Living Church, Los Angeles, CA

United Church Schools, New York, NY; operates the Science of Living Institute

United Divine Science, Largo, MD; operates the United Divine Science Ministerial School

Universal Truth Center for Better Living, Miami Gardens, FL

Victoria Truth Center, British Columbia, Canada

Other Denominations, Associations, and Institutions (Defunct)

Altrurian Society, Birmingham, AL

Antioch Association of Metaphysical Science, Detroit, MI

Applied Power, Cedarville, MI

Association of Independent Ministries, Arcadia, CA

Brooks Divinity School (formerly Colorado College of Divine Science), Colorado

Christian Assembly, San Jose, CA

Church of the Divine Unity, Boston, MA

Church of Hakeem, Oakland, CA

Church of the Higher Life, Boston, MA

Church of Inner Wisdom, San Jose, CA

The Church and School of the New Civilization (also known as the New Civilization Church) Boston, MA

Church of the Trinity, Salem, OR

Crystal Silence League, Los Angeles, CA

Federation of Independent Religious Science Churches, Cresco, PA

Fillmore Theological College (also known as the Fillmore Seminary), various locations

Foundation for Divine Meditation, Santa Isabel, CA; operated the American School of Mentalvivology

Hisacres New Thought Center, Washington, DC; affiliated with the Church of the Fuller Concept

International Metaphysical League (became part of the International New Thought Alliance)

League for the Larger Life, New York, NY

Ligue Internationale de la Nouvelle Pensee, France

Living Enrichment Center, Scholls, OR

Metaphysical Club, Boston, MA (became part of the International New Thought Alliance)

National New Thought Alliance (became part of the International New Thought Alliance)

New Thought Federation, Chicago, IL

Procopeia Society, Boston, MA

Psychiana, Moscow, ID

Psychic Club, Chicago, IL

Radiant Center of Philosophy, Atlantic City, NJ

Sacred Center, New York, NY

School of Applied Metaphysics, Eliot, ME

School of the Builders, New York, NY

Society of Pragmatic Mysticism (also known as the Society of Religious Pragmatism), Vermont

Spiritual Enlightenment Alliance, Wylie, TX

World Federation of Practical Christianity (also known as the World Federation of Unity Churches and the Federation of Independent Unity Churches)

World New Thought Federation (became part of the International New Thought Alliance)

Appendix B

Sampling of
New Thought Authors

The following list includes not only representative authors associated with New Thought groups but those who have been associated with the prosperity gospel and the Word of Faith movement, as well as others whose writings clearly owe a debt to New Thought philosophy even when they do not identify themselves as such.

Addington, Jack
Allen, James
Andersen, Uell S.
Anderson, C. Alan
Atkinson, William Walker
Avanzini, John
Bach, Marcus
Bailes, Frederick
Bakker, Jim and Tammy Faye
Barker, Raymond Charles
Barton, Bruce
Beard, Rebecca
Beckwith, Michael
Behrend, Genevieve
Bendall, George
Beranger, Clara
Bixby, James Thompson
Bloodworth, Venice
Boehme, Kate Atkinson
Boyd, Thomas Parker
Bradbury, Harriet B.

Brande, Dorothea
Bristol, Claude M.
Brooks, Nona L.
Butterworth, Eric
Byrne, Rhonda
Cady, H. Emilie
Carnegie, Dale
Chesley, Egbert Morse
Cho, David Yonggi
Chopra, Deepak
Clark, Francis E.
Clark, Glenn
Clark, Susie C.
Cohen, Alan
Cole-Whittaker, Terry
Collier, Robert
Conlin, Claude Alexander
Conwell, Russell H.
Copeland, Kenneth and Gloria
Coué, Émile
Cramer, Malinda

Crane, Aaron Martin
Critchlow, Florence Tabor
Crouch, Paul and Jan
Curtis, Donald
Davis, Roy Eugene
Delaney, Gayle
DeWaters, Lillian
Dollar, Creflo
Dresser, Annetta
Dresser, Horatio W.
Dresser, Julius
Drummond, Henry
Dumont, Theron Q.
Duplantis, Jessie
Dyer, Ellen M.
Dyer, Wayne W.
Eddy, Mary Baker
Eikerenkoetter, Frederick J., II
Ellsworth, Paul
Emerson, Ralph Waldo
Evans, Warren Felt
Fallows, Samuel
Farmer, Sarah J.
Fillmore, Charles and Myrtle
Fiske, John
Foulks, Frances W.
Fox, Emmet
Freeman, James Dillet
Gaines, Edwene
Gates, Elmer
Gawain, Shakti
Gestefeld, Ursula
Goddard, Neville
Golas, Thaddeus Stanley
Goldsmith, Joel Solomon
Grayson, Stuart
Green, Joseph Perry
Grier, Albert C.
Haanel, Charles F.
Haddock, Frank Channing
Hagin, Kenneth

Hamblin, Henry T.
Hay, Louise L.
Hickey, Marilyn
Hicks, Esther
Hill, Napoleon
Hinn, Benny
Holmes, Ernest
Holmes, Fenwicke L.
Hopkins, Emma Curtis
Hopkins, Erastus Whitford
Hornaday, William
Houston, Jean
Howard, Vernon
Huckel, Oliver
Hudson, Thomson Jay
Ingalese, Richard
Jakes, T. D.
James, Fannie Brooks
James, George Wharton
Jordan, William G.
Katz, Michael
Kenyon, Essek William
Landone, Brown
Lanyon, Walter Clemow
Larson, Christian D.
Lathrop, John Howland
Lester, Meera
Lichtenstein, Morris
Long, Eddie
Long, Max Freedom
Losier, Michael
Macedo, Edir
Mandus, Brother
Mann, Charles H.
Mann, Mildred
Marden, Orison Swett
Markham, Edwin
Marston, Luther M.
Meyer, Joyce
Militz, Annie Rix
Mills, Anna W.

Mills, James Porter
Mills, Kenneth G.
Mitchell, Byron Kathleen
Mitchell, Stephen
Moody, Elinor S.
Morrissey, Edward
Morrissey, Mary Manin
Moses, Alfred G.
Mozumdar, Akhoy Kumar
Mulford, Prentice
Mundy, Jon
Murphy, Joseph
Murphy, Michael
Murray, W. John
Myss, Caroline
Nightingale, Earl
Osteen, Joel and Victoria
Palmer, Clara
Patterson, Charles Brodie
Peale, Norman Vincent
Ponder, Catherine
Popoff, Peter
Price, Frederick K.C.
Price, John Randolph
Prince, Joseph
Quimby, Phineas P.
Randall, Jr., John Herman
Redfield, James
Reese, Della
Robinson, Frank B.
Samuel, William
Sanford, Agnes
Schwartz, David J.
Seale, Ervin
Sears, F. W.
Sears, Julia Seton
Selby, John
Seward, Theodore F.
Shanklin, Imelda Octavia
Sheldon, Henry C.
Sheldon, Theodore

Shelton, Thomas J.
Sherman, Harold
Shinn, Florence Scovel
Small, Althea Brooks
Spinney, William Anthony
Sprague, Frank H.
Stone, W. Clement
Stratton, Dan and Ann
Tamaki, Brian
Taniguchi, Masaharu
Thurman, Howard
Tilton, Robert
Tolle, Eckhart
Towne, Elizabeth
Towne, William
Trine, Ralph Waldo
Troward, Thomas
Vanzant, Iyanla
Velarde, Mike
Vitale, Joe
Walsch, Neale Donald
Walters, Xelia M.
Wattles, Wallace D.
Weltmer, Sidney A.
Whipple, Leander Edmund
White, Paula
Whitehead, Alfred North
Whitehouse, Deb
Whiting, Lilian
Whitney, Frank C.
Wilcox, Ella Wheeler
Wilde, Stuart
Williamson, Marianne
Wilmans, Helen
Winkley, J. W.
Wood, Henry
Yarnall, Jane
Zukav, Gary

Notes

Foreword

1. Important accounts of the New Thought movement include William James, *The Varieties of Religious Experience* (Cambridge, MA: Harvard University Press, 1985); Horatio Dresser, *A History of the New Thought Movement* (New York: Thomas Crowell, 1919); Charles Braden, *Spirits in Rebellion : The Rise and Development of New Thought* (Dallas: Southern Methodist University Press, 1963); Donald Meyer, *The Positive Thinkers* (New York: Doubleday and Co., 1965): Sydney Ahlstrom, *A Religious History of the American People* (New Haven, CT: Yale University Press, 1972); Gail Thain Parker, *The History of Mind Cure in New England* (Hanover, NH: University Press of New England, 1973); Robert C. Fuller, *Mesmerism and the American Cure of Souls* (Philadelphia: The University of Pennsylvania Press, 1982); Roy Anker, *Self-Help and Popular Religion in Modern American Culture* (Westport, CN: Greenwood Press, 1999); Berryl Satter, *Each Mind a Kingdom: American Women, Sexual Purity, and the New Thought Movement, 1875–1920* (Berkeley: University of California Press, 2001); Catherine Albanese, *A Republic of Mind and Spirit* (New Haven, CT: Yale University Press, 2007); and Barbara Ehrenreich, *Bright-Sided: How the Relentless Promotion of Positive Thinking Has Undermined America* (New York: Metropolitan Books, 2009).

Introduction

1. Ralph Waldo Emerson, "Nature," in *The Conduct of Life and Other Essays* (New York: E. P. Dalton and Co., 1911), 4.

2. Sidney E. Ahlstrom, *A Religious History of the American People* (New Haven, CT: Yale University Press, 1972), 1019.

3. Robert N. Bellah, "Civil Religion in America," *Daedalus* 96 (1967), 1–21.

4. Egbert Morse Chesley, "The Law of the Good," in Horatio W. Dresser, ed., *The Spirit of the New Thought: Essays and Addresses by Representative Authors and Leaders* (New York: Thomas Y. Crowell Co., 1917), 239–40; John White Chadwick, *William Ellery Channing: Minister of Religion* (Boston: Houghton, Mifflin and Co., 1903), Chapter ll.

5. Ralph Waldo Emerson, "Graduation Address at the Recent Commencement of the Meadville Divinity School," quoted in John H. Lathrop, "Practical Idealism," *Practical Ideals* 6 (1903), 1.

6. Quoted in Horatio W. Dresser, *A History of the New Thought Movement* (New York: Thomas Y. Crowell Co., 1919), 153.

7. Stow Persons, *Free Religion; An American Faith* (Boston: Beacon Press, 1963 [1947]), 57.

8. Émile Coué, *My Method: Including American Impressions* (Garden City, NY: Doubleday, Page and Co., 1923), 112.

9. Napoleon Hill, et al., *The Prosperity Bible: The Greatest Writings of All Time on the Secrets of Wealth and Prosperity* (New York: Jeremy P. Tarcher/Penguin, 2007), 1271; "List of best-selling books," http://en.wikipedia.org/wiki/List_of_best-selling_books (accessed October 7, 2011).

10. Quoted in Jay Epstein, "Saul Bellow of Chicago," *New York Times Book Review*, May 9, 1971.

11. Richard Huber, *The American Idea of Success* (New York: McGraw-Hill, 1971), 125.

12. Henry C. Sheldon, *Theosophy and New Thought* (New York: Abingdon Press, 1916), 171.

13. Barbara Ehrenreich, *Bright-Sided: How the Relentless Promotion of Positive Thinking Has Undermined America* (New York: Metropolitan Books, 2009), 205.

14. Clifford Howard, "Trading in the Holy Spirit," in *The World's Work 1900–1932*, ed. Walter Hines Page, vol. 19 (New York: Doubleday, Page and Co., 1910), 12846–50.

Chapter 1: New Beginnings

1. See Victor Cousin, *Report on the State of Public Instruction in Prussia* (New York: Wiley and Long, 1835).

2. See Carl Bode, *The Half-World of American Culture: A Miscellany* (Carbondale: Southern Illinois University Press, 1965 [1923]); Carl Bode, *The American Lyceum: Town Meeting of the Mind* (Carbondale: Southern Illinois University Press, 1968); Carl Bode, *Antebellum Culture* (Carbondale: Southern Illinois University Press, 1970).

3. Oliver Wendell Holmes, *Ralph Waldo Emerson* (Boston: Houghton, Mifflin and Company, 1884), 412.

4. Ralph Waldo Emerson, "The Divinity School Address," in *The Complete Works of Ralph Waldo Emerson* (Boston: Houghton Mifflin, 1903–04), 3:117–51. See Also Thomas P. Joswick, "The Conversion Drama of 'Self-Reliance': A Logological Study," *American Literature* 55 (1983): 507–24.

5. Exemplary of this is T. A. Merrill, "How to Keep Young," *Practical Ideals* 6 (1903): 9–12.

6. Horatio W. Dresser, *Man and the Divine Order: Essays in the Philosophy of Religion and in Constructive Idealism* (New York and London: G. P. Putnam's Sons,

1903), 248, 257–8; E. Douglas Branch, *The Sentimental Years, 1836–1860* (New York: Hill and Wang, 1965 [1934]); Gilbert Seldes, *The Stammering Century* (New York: Harper and Row, 1965 [1928]).

7. See John S. Haller, Jr., *American Medicine in Transition, 1840–1910* (Urbana: University of Illinois Press, 1981), 192–217.

8. George Barton Cutten, *Three Thousand Years of Mental Healing* (New York: Charles Scribner's Sons, 1911), 250–54; Ernst Benz, *Theology and Electricity: On the Encounter and Explanation of Theology and Science in the 17th and 18th Centuries* (Allison Park, PA: Pickwick Publications, 1989), 5–23.

9. "Modern Faith Healing," *British Medical Journal* 2 (1911): 199–200; H. C. Erick Midelfort, *Exorcism and Enlightenment: Johann Joseph Gassner and the Demons of 18th Century Germany* (New Haven, CT: Yale University Press, 2005); Adam Crabtree, *From Mesmer to Freud: Magnetic Sleep and the Roots of Psychological Healing* (New Haven, CT: Yale University Press, 1993), 4–10.

10. Read Robert Darnton, *Mesmerism and the End of the Enlightenment in France* (Cambridge, MA: Harvard University Press, 1968); Margaret L. Goldsmith, *Franz Anton Mesmer: The History of an Idea* (London: A. Barker, 1934); Vincent Buranelli, *The Wizard from Vienna: Franz Anton Mesmer* (New York: Coward, McCann and Geoghegan, 1975), 20–21.

11. Cutten, *Three Thousand Years of Mental Healing*, 259; *Rapport des commissaries chargés par le Roi de l'examen du Magnétisme Animal* (Paris: De l'Imprimerie Royal, 1789); Benz, *Theology of Electricity*, 13–23.

12. Cutten, *Three Thousand Years of Mental Healing*, 264; J. P. F. Deluze, *Practical Instructions in Animal Magnetism*, 2nd ed. (New York: Samuel Wells, 1879).

13. Cutten, *Three Thousand Years of Mental Healing*, 261.

14. Ibid., 265.

15. Frank Podmore, *Modern Spiritualism: A History and a Criticism* (London: Methewn and Co., 1902), 1:109–10, 112–13.

16. Dr. John Elliotson, "Mesmeric Cure of Blindness of Twenty Years' Duration," *Journal of Man* 2 (1851): 213–18; Dr. John Elliotson, "Mesmerism and Surgery," *Journal of Man* 2 (1851): 218.

17. Podmore, *Modern Spiritualism*, 1:113–14.

18. Cutten, *Three Thousand Years of Mental Healing*, 267–68.

19. H. Addington Bruce, *Scientific Mental Healing* (Boston: Little Brown, 1911), 18–19.

20. Fred Kaplan, "The Mesmeric Mania: The Early Victorians and Animal Magnetism," *Journal of the History of Ideas* 35 (1974): 691–93; Ilza Veith, "From Mesmerism to Hypnotism," *Modern Medicine* (1959): 195–205; Cutten, *Three Thousand Years of Mental Healing*, 269; Ambrose A. Liébeault, *Du sommeil et des etats analogues* (Paris: Victor Masson et fils, 1866); Jean-Martin Charcot, *Lectures of Localization in Diseases of the Brain* (New York: William Wood, 1878); Jerome M. Schneck, "Jean-Martin Charcot and the History of Experimental Hypnosis," *Journal of the History of Medicine and Allied Sciences* 16 (1961): 297–300; Robert G. Hillman, "A

Scientific Study of Mystery: The Role of the Medical and Popular Press in the Nancy-Salpêtrière Controversy on Hypnotism," *Bulletin of the History of Medicine* 39 (1965): 163–82.

21. Podmore, *Modern Spiritualism*,1:95.

22. Ibid., 1:96–97. Also see Samuel Jackson, *Theory of Pneumatology* (London: Longman, Orme, Brown, Green, and Longman, 1834).

23. Warren Felt Evans, *The Mental-Cure, Illustrating the Influence of the Mind on the Body, Both in Health and Disease, and the Psychological Method of Treatment,* 8th ed. (Boston: Colby and Rich, 1886 [1869]), 95.

24. Podmore, *Modern Spiritualism*, 1:117–18. See James Braid, *Neurypnology; Or the Rationale of Nervous Sleep, Considered in Relation with Animal Magnetism* (London: Churchill, 1848); William Newnham, *Human Magnetism* (London: J. Churchill, 1845); Harriet Martineau, *Letters on Mesmerism* (London: Edward Moxon, 1845); and Karl von Reichenbach's *Psycho-Physiological Researches on Dynamides or Imponderables, Magnetism, Electricity, Heat, Light, Crystallization, and Chemical Attraction, in their Relation to Vital Force* (London: Taylor, Walton and Mabarly, 1850); "Researches of Baron Reichenbach on the 'Mesmeric,' Now Called the Odic Force," *The American Whig Review* 15 (1852): 485–501.

25. "Reichenbach's Researches on Magnetism," *Journal of Man* 1 (1849): 67–70.

26. T. M. Parssinen, "Popular Science and Society; The Phrenological Movement in Early Victorian Britain," *Journal of Social History* 8 (1974): 1–3; Stanley Finger, *Minds Behind the Brain; a History of the Pioneers and Their Discoveries* (New York: Oxford University Press, 2000), 119–36.

27. Joseph Rodes Buchanan, "Craniology and Cranioscopy," *Journal of Man* 1 (1849): 157. See also John van Wyhe, "The History of Phrenology: A Chronology," Victorian Web, accessed March 10, 2010, http://www.victorianweb.org/science/phrenology/chron.html.

28. Parssinen, "Popular Science and Society," 13; G. N. Cantor, "The Edinburgh Phrenology Debate: 1803–1828," *Annals of Science* 32 (1975): 197; Robert M. Young, "The Functions of the Brain: Gall to Ferrier (1808–1886)," *Isis* 59 (1968): 250–68; George Combe, *Notes on the United States of North America During a Phrenological Visit in 1838-1839-1840* (Philadelphia: Cary and Hart, 1841).

29. Podmore, *Modern Spiritualism*, 1:121; John Ashburner, *Notes and Studies on the Philosophy of Animal Magnetism and Spiritualism* (London: Baillière, 1867); "Animal Magnetism and Spiritualism," *The Spiritual Magazine* 2 (1867): 566–72.

30. Signe Toksvig, *Emanuel Swedenborg: Scientist and Mystic* (New York: Yale University Press, 1948), 32–40; Daniel Stempel, "Angels of Reason: Science and Myth in the Enlightenment," *Journal of the History of Ideas* 36 (1975), 63–78.

31. See Emanuel Swedenborg, *The Economy of the Animal Kingdom, Considered Anatomically, Physically, and Philosophically* (London: William Newbery, 1846); James John Garth Wilkinson, *Emanuel Swedenborg: a Biography* (London: William Newbery, 1849); Sigfried T. Synnestvedt, ed., *The Essential Swedenborg: Basic Teachings of Emanuel Swedenborg, Scientist, Philosopher, and Theologian* (New York: Twayne Publishers, 1970).

32. Read Marguerite Beck Block, *The New Church in the New World* (New York: Octagon Books, 1968).

33. John Weiss, ed., *Life and Correspondence of Theodore Parker* (London: Longman, Treen, 1863), 1:428.

34. Charles Poyen, *Progress of Animal Magnetism in New England* (New York: DeCapo Press, 1982 [1837].

35. Emma Hardinge, *Modern American Spiritualism: A Twenty Years' Record of the Communion Between Earth and the World of Spirits* (New York: The Author, 1870), 157–59.

36. James Rogers Newton, *Modern Bethesda, Or, the Gift of Healing Restored* (New York: Newton Publishing Co, 1879), 292–301; J. M. Buckley, *Faith-Healing, Christian Science and Kindred Phenomena* (New York: Century Company, 1887), 1–2.

37. Podmore, *Modern Spiritualism,* 1:154–55; John Bovee Dods, *The Philosophy of Electrical Psychology* (New York: S. R. Wells, 1870 [1850]), 123; Horatio W. Dresser, "A Forerunner of the Mental Cure," *Journal of Practical Metaphysics* (1897): 226–29; Theron Dumont, *Mental Therapeutics, Or, Just How to Heal Oneself and Others* (Chicago: Advanced Thought Publishing Co., 1916).

38. Joseph Rodes Buchanan, *Manual of Psychometry: The Dawn of a New Civilization* (Boston: Holman Brothers, 1885); Joseph Rodes Buchanan, *Therapeutic Sarcognomy: a Scientific Exposition of the Mysterious Union of Soul, Brain and Body* (Boston: J. G. Cupples, Co., 1884); Richard Ingalese, *The History and Power of Mind* (New York: The Occult Book Concern Publishers, 1902), 128.

39. Buchanan, *Manual of Psychometry,* 29, 48; Buchanan, *Therapeutic Sarcognomy,* 1–3, 10.

40. Joseph Rodes Buchanan, *Outlines of Lectures on the Neurological System of Anthropology* (Cincinnati: Journal of Man, 1854), 359–60.

41. Buchanan, *Therapeutic Sarcognomy,* 50.

42. Ibid., 64.

43. Joseph Rodes Buchanan, *Primitive Christianity, Containing the Lost Lives of Jesus Christ and the Apostles* (San Jose, CA: J. R. Buchanan, 1897), 106–8, 131.

44. La Roy Sunderland, *The Pathetism: With Practical Instructions* (New York: P. P. Good, 1847); R. Laurence Moore, *In Search of White Crows: Spiritualism, Parapsychology, and American Culture* (New York: Oxford University Press, 1977).

45. Robert W. Delp, "The Harmonial Philosopher: Andrew Jackson Davis and the Foundation of Modern Spiritualism" (unpublished PhD dissertation, George Washington University, 1965).

46. Podmore, *Modern Spiritualism,* 1:158.

47. Andrew Jackson Davis, *The Magic Staff: An Autobiography of Andrew Jackson Davis* (New York: A. J. Davis and Co., 1864); Andrew Jackson Davis, *The Principles of Nature, Her Divine Revelations, and a Voice to Mankind,* (London: John Chapman, 1847); Christopher G. White, "Minds Intensely Unsettled: Phrenology, Experience, and the American Pursuit of Spiritual Assurance, 1830–1860," *Religion and American Culture: A Journal of Interpretation* 16 (2006): 227–61.

48. Podmore, *Modern Spiritualism*, 1:170–71. See also George Bush and B. F. Barrett, *Davis' Revelations Revealed; Being a Critical Examination of the Character and Claims of that Work in Its Relations to the Teachings of Swedenborg* (New York: John Allen, 1847).

49. Robert W. Delp, "Andrew Jackson Davis: Prophet of American Spiritualism," *Journal of American History* 54 (1967): 54.

50. Renée Haynes, *The Society for Psychical Research, 1882–1982* (London: MacDonald and Co., 1982); Alan Gauld, *The Founders of Psychical Research* (London: Routledge and Kegan Paul, 1968).

51. Quoted in Bruce, *Scientific Mental Healing*, 195–207, 208–209.

52. Ibid., 212.

53. See White, "Minds Intensely Unsettled," 227–61; Nelson Sizer, *Forty Years in Phrenology: Embracing Recollections of History, Anecdote, and Experience* (New York: Fowler and Wells Co., 1888); James Freeman Clarke, *Autobiography, Diary, and Correspondence* (New York: Negro Universities Press, 1968).

54. Ralph Waldo Emerson, *Nature Addresses and Lectures* (Boston: Houghton Mifflin Co., 1876), 3.

Chapter 2: Christ Science

1. Horatio W. Dresser, ed., *The Quimby Manuscripts; Showing the Discovery of Spiritual Healing and the Origin of Christian Science* (New York: Thomas Y. Crowell, Co., 1921), 66–67; Ervin Seale, ed., *Phineas Parkhurst Quimby: The Complete Writings* (Marina del Rey, CA: Devorss and Co., 1988), 1:19–29; 369–70.

2. Dresser, *The Quimby Manuscripts,* 10.

3. The patents included: US patent no. 5650X (held jointly with Job White), dated 12 September 1829, for a "Circular Sawing Machine"; US patent no. 9679X (held by P. P. Quimby), dated 23 May 1836, for a "Permutation Lock"; and US patent no. 7197 (held by P. P. Quimby), dated 19 March 1850, for a "Steering Apparatus . . . a new and useful machine for Steering Ships and Steamboats." See "Phineas Quimby, Wikipedia, accessed May 22, 2012, http://en.wikipedia.org/wiki/Phineas_Quimby.

4. Quimby quoted in Dresser, *A History of the New Thought Movement,* 27–28.

5. Dresser, *The Quimby Manuscripts,* 10.

6. Robert H. Collyer, *Psychography, Or, The Embodiment of Thought; with an Analysis of Phrenomagnetism, "Neurology," and Mental Hallucination, including Rules to Govern and Produce the Magnetic State* (Boston: Redding, 1843).

7. Dresser, *The Quimby Manuscripts,* 30–31.

8. Annetta Gertrude Dresser, *The Philosophy of P. P. Quimby; With Selections from His Manuscripts and a Sketch of His Life* (Boston: George H. Ellis, 1895), 14.

9. Lucius Burkmar, *Lucius C. Burkmar's Private Journal,* Phineas Parkhurst Quimby Resource Center, accessed July 28, 2010, http://www.ppquimby.com/articles/journal.htm.

10. Dresser, *The Quimby Manuscripts,* 35, 47–48.

11. Quoted in Dresser, *A History of the New Thought Movement*, 31.

12. Dresser, *The Quimby Manuscripts*, 50; Seale, *The Complete Writings*, 3:40–41.

13. Dresser, *The Quimby Manuscripts*, 33.

14. Quoted in Horatio W. Dresser, *Health and the Inner Life: An Analytical and Historical Study of Spiritual Healing Theories, with an Account of the Life and Teachings of P. P. Quimby* (New York and London: G. P. Putnam's Sons, 1906), 31–32; Seale, *The Complete Writings*, 1:191–93.

15. Quoted in Dresser, *Health and the Inner Life*, 56, 75–78, 82; Seale, *The Complete Writings*, 3:306–17.

16. Dresser, *The Quimby Manuscripts*, 78, 188–89; Seale, *The Complete Writings*, 3:246–51.

17. Dresser, *The Philosophy of P. P. Quimby*, 58.

18. Dresser, *The Quimby Manuscripts*, 56, 58; Seale, *The Complete Writings*, 1:102–108; 426–29.

19. Dresser, *The Quimby Manuscripts*, 17; Seale, *The Complete Writings*, 1:53–58.

20. Dresser, *The Quimby Manuscripts*, 65, 68–69, 360; Seale, *The Complete Writings*, 1:377–80; 2:398–99.

21. Dresser, *The Quimby Manuscripts*, 141, 307–8; Seale, *The Complete Writings*, 2:282–83; 404.

22. Harriet B. Bradbury, *The New Philosophy of Health: A Study of the Science of Spiritual Healing and the Philosophy of Life* (Boston: The Philosophical Pub. Co., 1897), 22.

23. Bruce, *Scientific Mental Healing*, 27–28.

24. Dresser, *The Quimby Manuscripts*, 198, 201–2, 303; Seale, *The Complete Writings*, 2:207–10.

25. See, for example, Emanuel Swedenborg, *Secrets of Heaven*, vol. 2, trans. Lisa Hyatt Cooper (West Chester, PA: Swedenborg Foundation, 2011), §978. For a detailed discussion of Swedenborg's writings on the relationship between body and soul, particularly as interpreted and developed by his followers, see Douglas Taylor, *The Hidden Levels of the Mind* (West Chester, PA: Swedenborg Foundation, 2011).

26. Dresser, *The Quimby Manuscripts*, 17–18.

27. Quoted in Dresser, *Health and the Inner Life*, 64–67.

28. Dresser, *Health and the Inner Life*, 90–95; Seale, *The Complete Writings*, 1:352–55; 359–63.

29. Dresser, *The Quimby Manuscripts*, 215, 222; Seale, *The Complete Writings*, 3:54–56.

30. Dresser, *A History of the New Thought Movement*, 47, 49; Seale, *The Complete Writings*, 3:103–13; 163–65.

31. Dresser, *A History of the New Thought Movement*, 49–51; Seale, *The Complete Writings*, 3:325.

32. Seale, *The Complete Writings*, 2:36–40; Dresser, *The Quimby Manuscripts*, 193, 381, 383.

33. Charles B. Newcomb, *All's Right with the World* (Boston: Lee and Shepard, 1899), 122; Dresser, *Health and the Inner Life*, 104; Seale, *The Complete Writings*, 2:117–20.

34. Compare this with the idea of the "natural man" that appears widely in Swedenborgian writings. The term *homo naturalis* in Swedenborg's original Latin has been translated differently in various editions over the years, but in the English translations of the nineteenth century it was rendered *natural man,* and derivative works often used that term. For a description of the characteristics of a natural man, see Swedenborg's *Divine Love and Wisdom* §§248–255.

35. Dresser, *The Quimby Manuscripts*, 237–38, 241.

36. Dresser, *The Quimby Manuscripts*, 232; Seale, *The Complete Writings*, 3:348–49.

37. Dresser, *A History of the New Thought Movement*, 42–43, 45; Seale, *The Complete Writings*, 2:297–99.

38. Dresser, *A History of the New Thought Movement*, 52; Seale, *The Complete Writings*, 3:341–42.

39. Quoted in Dresser, *The Philosophy of P. P. Quimby*, 110.

40. Dresser, *The Quimby Manuscripts*, 69.

41. Catherine L. Albanese, "Physic and Metaphysic in 19th Century America: Medical Sectarians and Religious Healing," *Church History* 55 (1986): 498.

42. Dresser, *The Quimby Manuscripts*, 144.

43. Quoted in Dresser, *Health and the Inner Life*, 80.

44. Dresser, *The Quimby Manuscripts*, 70, 138.

45. Ibid., 56–57.

46. Ibid., 18, 425.

47. Dresser, *A History of the New Thought Movement*, 318.

48. Robert Peel, *Mary Baker Eddy: The Years of Discovery* (New York: Holt, Rinehart, and Winston, 1966), 162; Catherine L. Albanese, *A Republic of Mind and Spirit: A Cultural History of American Metaphysical Religion* (New Haven, CT: Yale University Press, 2007), 286–89.

49. Dresser, *The Quimby Manuscripts,*70, 102–3, 277.

50. Dresser, *A History of the New Thought Movement*, 43; Seale, *The Complete Writings*, 1:174–78; 307–13; 330–32; 392–407.

51. Dresser, *The Quimby Manuscripts*, 125–26, 140.

52. Ibid., 12. See also Thomas C. Johnsen, "Historical Consensus and Christian Science: The Career of a Manuscript Controversy," *New England Quarterly* 53 (1980), 3–22.

53. Dresser, *The Philosophy of P. P. Quimby*, 47–49.

54. Ibid., 45–48.

55. Annetta G. Dresser, "The Science of Life," in Horatio W. Dresser, ed., *The Spirit of the New Thought: Essays and Addresses by Representative Authors and Leaders* (New York: Thomas Y. Crowell Co., 1917), 201–3.

56. Dresser, *The Philosophy of P. P. Quimby*, 52.

57. Dresser, *Health and the Inner Life*, 123–27.

58. Dresser, *The Philosophy of P. P. Quimby*, 50; Willa Cather and Georgine Milmine, *The Life of Mary Baker G. Eddy and the History of Christian Science* (Nebraska: University of Nebraska Press, 1993), 92.

59. Julius A. Dresser, *The True History of Mental Science. A Lecture Delivered at the Church of the Divine Unity, Boston, Mass., on Sunday Evening, Feb. 6, 1887* (Boston: Alfred Mudge and Son, 1887), 5.

Chapter 3: Competing Sciences

1. C. Alan Anderson, *Healing Hypotheses; Horatio W. Dresser and the Philosophy of New Thought* (New York: Garland, 1993), 330. See Cather and Milmine, *The Life of Mary Baker G. Eddy*, 348.

2. Anderson, *Healing Hypotheses*, 331; William J. Leonard, "Warren Felt Evans, M.D.: An Account of His Life and Services as the First Author of the Metaphysical Healing Movement," *Practical Ideals* 10 (1905): 1–16; (1906): 10–26.

3. Warren Felt Evans, *The Primitive Mind-Cure: The Nature and Power of Faith; Or, Elementary Lessons in Christian Philosophy and Transcendental Medicines* (Boston: H. H. Carter and Karrick, 1884), 162.

4. Leonard, "Warren Felt Evans, M.D," 6, 10–26; Bruce, *Scientific Mental Healing*, 35–36. See also James F. Lawrence, "An Extraordinary Season in Prayer: Warren Felt Evans' Journey Into Scientific Spiritual Practice," *Studia Swedenborgiana* 12 (2002).

5. Warren Felt Evans, *The New Age and Its Messenger* (Boston: T. H. Carter and Co., 1864), 6, 9, 17, 87.

6. Ibid., 18, 21.

7. Dresser, *A History of the New Thought Movement*, 152.

8. Emanuel Swedenborg, *Arcana Coelestia*, trans. John Clowes (West Chester, PA: Swedenborg Foundation, 1998), 7:§5726. See also *Arcana Coelestia* 7:§5711–26; *Arcana Coelestia* 10:§8364; Emanuel Swedenborg, *Heaven and Hell*, trans. George F. Dole (West Chester, PA: Swedenborg Foundation, 2000), §569.

9. Evans, *The Mental Cure*, 38, 102.

10. Ibid., 71–72, 74–75.

11. Ibid., 135–6. See also William and Elizabeth M. F. Denton, *The Soul of Things; Or, Psychometric Researches and Discoveries* (Boston: Walker, Wise, and Co., 1863).

12. Evans, *The Mental Cure*, 300–4.

13. Horatio W. Dresser, *In Search of a Soul; A Series of Essays in Interpretation of the Higher Nature of Man* (New York and London: G. P. Putnam's Sons, 1899 [1897]), 3.

14. Evans, *The Mental Cure*, 63.

15. Dresser, *A History of the New Thought Movement*, 78.

16. Evans, *The Mental Cure*, 178.

17. Ibid., 202–4, 241.

18. Ibid., 167, 189, 191, 195–6.

19. Warren Felt Evans, *Healing by Faith; Or, Primitive Mind-Cure. Elementary Lessons in Christian Philosophy and Transcendental Medicine* (London: Reeves and Turner, 1885), 55, 82, 85–86.

20. Evans, *The Mental Cure*, 252, 255–56.

21. Evans, *Healing by Faith*, 142–7, 175–6.

22. Warren Felt Evans, *Mental Medicine: A Theoretical and Practical Treatise on Medical Psychology*, 6th ed. (Boston: Colby and Rich, 1881 [1872]), 154–5, 160–5.

23. Evans, *The Mental Cure*, 261–74.

24. Evans, *Mental Medicine*, 12, 14. See also Midelfort, *Exorcism and Enlightenment*.

25. Evans, *Mental Medicine*, 17, 26.

26. Ibid., 42, 48.

27. Ibid., 49–50, 182–3.

28. Warren Felt Evans, *The Divine Law of Cure* (Boston: H. H. Carter and Co., 1884), 9, 204, 256.

29. Evans, *Healing by Faith*, iv–v, 7.

30. Warren Felt Evans, *Esoteric Christianity and Mental Therapeutics* (Boston: H. H. Carter and Karrick, Publishers, 1886), 1–8, 15, 18, 19, 28–29.

31. Ibid., 137, 149, 152.

32. Evans quoted in Dresser, *A History of the New Thought Movement*, 84–85.

33. Dresser, *The Philosophy of P. P. Quimby*, 50; Ernest Bates and John V. Dittemore, *Mary Baker Eddy: The Truth and the Tradition* (New York: Alfred A. Knopf, 1932), 88.

34. Dresser, *The Quimby Manuscripts*, 160–1.

35. Dresser, *A History of the New Thought Movement*, 104–5. See Also Rennie B. Schoepflin, *Christian Science on Trial: Religious Healing in America* (Madison: University of Wisconsin Press, 2003).

36. Mary Baker Eddy, *Message to the Mother Church, Boston, Massachusetts, June 1901*(Boston: The Christian Science Publishing Society, 1901), 17.

37. Cather and Milmine, *The Life of Mary Baker G. Eddy*, 76–80; Dresser, *A History of the New Thought Movement*, 113. Later, in her *Retrospection and Introspection* (Boston: Allison V. Steward, 1909 [1891]), Mary Baker Eddy dates her experiments in mind-healing to 1866.

38. Mary Baker G. Eddy, "Mind-Healing History," *Christian Science Journal* 5 (1887): 111.

39. Mary Baker Eddy, *Historical Sketch or Christian Science Mind-Healing* (Boston: Published by the Author, 1888), 6.

40. Eddy, *Retrospection and Introspection*, 24.

41. Ibid., 24, 43.

42. Dresser, *Health and the Inner Life*, 239; Lyman P. Powell, *Christian Science: the Faith and Its Founder* (New York: G. P. Putnam's Sons, 1908), 231.

43. Eddy, *Historical Sketch or Christian Science Mind-Healing*, 6–8, 11.

44. Dresser, *The Quimby Manuscripts*, 22, 25. According to Dresser, Mrs. Eddy had seen only the first volume of Quimby's writings (written in 1859) that had been loaned to her by his father. See Dresser, *A History of the New Thought Movement*, 113. For alternative point of view, read Johnsen, "Historical Consensus and Christian Science: the Career of a Manuscript Controversy," 3–22. The complete writings of Quimby are found in Ervin Seale, ed., *Phineas Parkhurst Quimby: The Complete Writings* (Marina del Rey, CA: Devorss and Co., 1988).

45. Mary Baker Eddy, *Miscellaneous Writings, 1883–1896* (Boston: Trustees Under the Will of Mary Baker G. Eddy, 1924); Mary Baker Eddy, *Science and Health with Key to the Scriptures* (Boston: Trustees Under the Will of Mary Baker G. Eddy, 1906), 441.

46. Mary Baker Eddy, *Christian Science: No and Yes* (Boston: Published by the Author, 1887), 20.

47. Quoted in Margaret Beecher White, "Beecher and Christian Science," *Cosmopolitan* 45 (1908): 320.

48. Mary Baker Eddy, *Science and Health*, 71, 77–79, 109.

49. Eddy, *Message to the Mother Church*, 4–5.

50. Eddy, *Science of Health*, 268–9, 280–3.

51. Eddy, *Christian Science: No and Yes*, 23; Mary Baker Eddy, *Christian Science Versus Pantheism* (Boston: The Christian Science Publishing Society, 1898), 3–4, 8, 12–13.

52. Mary Baker Eddy, *Christian Healing: a Sermon Delivered at Boston* (Boston: The Christian Science Publishing Society, 1886), 11.

53. Eddy, *Science and Health*, 365–6, 379.

54. Eddy, *Historical Sketch or Christian Science Mind-Healing*, 5.

55. Eddy, *Christian Healing: A Sermon Delivered at Boston*, 13.

56. Eddy, *Science and Health*, 156–7.

57. Ibid., 398.

58. Mary Baker Eddy, *The People's Idea of God: Its Effect on Health and Christianity: A Sermon Delivered at Boston* (Boston: The First church of Christ, Scientist, 1886), 4.

59. Eddy, *Science and Health*, 415–18.

60. Ibid., 184–85.

61. Ibid., 402.

62. Charles E. Heitman, "Christian Science and Couéism," *North American Review* 216 (1922): 718.

63. Eddy, *Science and Health*, 14–15.

64. Eddy, *Christian Science: No and Yes*, 43–44.

65. Eddy, *Science and Health*, 427–28.

66. Ibid., 291.

67. Eddy, *Retrospection and Introspection*, 14–16, 17–19. See also Stephen J. Stein, "Retrospection and Introspection: The Gospel According to Mary Baker Eddy," *Harvard Theological Review* 75 (1982): 97–116.

68. Eddy, *Retrospection and Introspection,* 36–39.

69. Ibid., 50–52, 55.

70. Ibid., 90.

71. Ibid., 101–30.

72. Schoepflin, *Christian Science on Trial,* 7–8, 34; Bates and Dittemore, *Mary Baker Eddy: The Truth and the Tradition;* Mary Farrell Bednarowski, "Outside the Mainstream: Women's Religion and Women Religious Leaders in 19th Century America," *Journal of the American Academy of Religion* 48 (1980): 207–31; Ann Braude, *Radical Spirits: Spiritualism and Women's Rights in 19th Century America* (Boston: Beacon Press, 1989). Due to a lack of clarification in the public statutes of Massachusetts, a number of quasi-medical schools organized at the time. These included Joseph Rodes Buchanan's American University of Boston, the New England University of Arts and Sciences, the Bellevue Medical College of Massachusetts, the First Medical College of the American Health Society, and Excelsior Medical College. Each opened storefront operations intended to subvert the state's intent and caused the Massachusetts Medical Society to seek stricter regulation of the practice of medicine.

73. "Massachusetts Medical College," Wikipedia, accessed November 26, 2011, http://en.wikipedia.org/wiki/Massachusetts_Metaphysical_College.

74. Rosemary R. Hicks, "Religion and Remedies Reunited: Rethinking Christian Science," *Journal of Feminist Studies in Religion* 29 (2004): 51.

75. Frank Podmore, *Mesmer to Christian Science: A Short History of Mental Healing* (Philadelphia: George W. Jacobs and Co., 1909), 279; Bednarowski, "Outside the Mainstream," 207–31.

76. Eddy, *Historical Sketch or Christian Science Mind-Healing,* 15–16.

77. Cather and Milmine, *The Life of Mary Baker G. Eddy,* 480.

78. Raymond J. Cunningham, "The Impact of Christian Science on the American Churches, 1880–1910," *The American Historical Review* 72 (1967): 890, 893.

79. Read Margret M. Poloma, "A Comparison of Christian Science and Mainline Christian Healing Ideologies and Practices," *Review of Religious Research* 32 (1991): 337–50; Christian Science Publishing Society, *Christian Science: A Sourcebook of Contemporary Materials* (Boston: The Christian Science Publishing Society, 1990); Stephen Gottschalk, *The Emergence of Christian Science in American Religious Life* (Berkeley: University of California Press, 1973); Morton T. Kelsey, *Psychology, Medicine and Christian Healing* (San Francisco: Harper and Row Publishers, 1988); Robert Peel, *Spiritual Healing in a Scientific Age* (San Francisco: Harper and Row Publishers, 1987).

80. Abel Leighton Allen, *The Message of New Thought* (New York: Thomas Y. Crowell Co., 1914), 89–90, 94–95.

81. Ibid., 118–19.

82. Henry Wood, *The New Thought Simplified: How to Gain Harmony and Health* (Boston: Lee and Shepard, 1903), 148–50.

83. John F. Teahan, "Warren Felt Evans and Mental Healing: Romantic Idealism and Practical Mysticism in Nineteenth Century America," *Church History* 48 (1979): 69.

84. James H. Leuba, "Psychotherapic Cults: Christian Science, Mind Cure, New Thought," *The Monist* 22 (1912): 348.

Chapter 4: Metropolitan Religions

1. L. M. Marston, *Essentials of Mental Healing: The Theory and Practice* (Boston: Published by the Author, 1887 [1886]), 10–15, 20–21, 36.

2. Gail M. Harley, *Emma Curtis Hopkins: Forgotten Founder of New Thought* (New York: Syracuse University Press, 2002), 1–14.

3. "Emma Curtis Hopkins: 'Teacher of Teachers,'" accessed January 14, 2012, http://emmacurtishopkins.wwwhubs.com.

4. Read Beryl Satter, *Each Mind a Kingdom: American Women, Sexual Purity, and the New Thought Movement, 1875–1920* (Berkeley: University of California Press, 1999) and a critique from Patricia R. Hill, "Rethinking New Thought," *Reviews in American History* 29 (2001): 85–92.

5. James D. Freeman, *The Household of Faith* (Lee's Summit, MO: Unity School of Christianity, 1956), 75–76; "H. Emilie Cady: Author of the Unity Textbook 'Lessons in Truth,'" accessed January 15, 2012, http://hemiliecady.wwwhubs.com.

6. Eleve, *Spiritual Law in the Natural World* (Chicago: Purdy Publishing Co., 1894), 1, 15.

7. Ibid., 45.

8. Ibid., 20, 53.

9. Ibid., 60.

10. Ibid., 24, 34, 42.

11. Ibid., 87.

12. Ibid.,147.

13. Ibid., 173–74.

14. Ibid., 175, 176, 179, 181.

15. Ibid., 188.

16. Emma Curtis Hopkins, *Scientific Christian Mental Practice* (Cornwall Bridge, CN: High Watch Fellowship, 1958), chapter 1.

17. See Harley, *Emma Curtis Hopkins: Forgotten Founder of New Thought*; Schoepflin, *Christian Science on Trial*, 86–92; Buckley, *Faith-Healing, Christian Science, and Kindred Phenomena*, 242, 247. See also Catherine Tumber, *American Feminism and the Birth of New Age Spirituality: Searching for the Higher Self, 1875–1915* (Maryland: Rowman and Littlefield Publishing Co., 2002).

18. "Emma Curtis Hopkins," New Thought Library, accessed January 11, 2012, http://newthoughtlibrary.com/hopkinsEmmaCurtis/bio_Emma.htm.

19. "Announcement," *Unity* 19 (1903): frontispiece.

20. "Publishers Department," *Unity* 14 (1901): 93.

21. "Society of Silent Unity," *Unity* 14 (1901): 26.

22. "What We Believe" and "Frequently Asked Questions," Unity website, accessed November 21, 2011, http://unity.org/aboutunity/whatWeBelieve/index.html; Charles Fillmore, *Jesus Christ Heals* (Unity Village, MO: Unity School of Christianity, 1939), 9–35; Neal Vahle, *The Unity Movement: Its Evolution and Spiritual Teachings* (Philadelphia: Templeton Foundation Press, 2002); Rosemary Fillmore Rhea, "Unity in the Twenty-First Century," *Unity Magazine* (Sept.–Oct. 2004): 32–34; Jim Rosemergy, "No More Dogmas, No More Creeds," *Unity Magazine* (March–April 2003): 17; Charles Fillmore, *Talks on Truth* (Kansas City, MO: Unity School of Christianity, 1934), 7–13; Steve Baherman, "Unity: The Healing Edge of Christianity," *Unity Magazine* (Jan.-Feb. 2008): 20–22.

23. Rosemergy, "No More Dogmas, No More Creeds," 17; Mike Oberg, "The Five Basic Beliefs of Unity," Yahoo! Voices, accessed January 18, 2011, http://www.associatedcontent.com/article/5477648/the_five_basic_beliefs_of_unity.html.

24. H. Emilie Cady, *Lessons in Truth: A Course of Twelve Lessons in Practical Christianity* (Kansas City, MO: Unity School of Christianity, 1919), 98, 149, 157.

25. Charles Fillmore, *Christian Healing: The Science of Being* (Kansas City, MO: Unity School of Christianity, 1917), 4.

26. Ibid., 244–45.

27. Ibid., 248.

28. Ibid., 102.

29. Ibid., 139-40.

30. "Malinda Cramer," Wikipedia, accessed October 26, 2011, http://en.wikipedia.org/wiki/Malinda_Cramer.

31. Malinda E. Cramer, *Divine Science and Healing: A Text-book for the Study of Divine Science, Its Application in Healing, and for the Well-being of Each Individual* (San Francisco: The Home College of Divine Science, 1905), advertisement.

32. Ibid., 15–20.

33. Ibid., 24, 27, 39–41, 49.

34. Ibid., 40–41.

35. Ibid., 173–75.

36. Ibid., 134.

37. Ibid., 205–10.

38. Ibid., 212.

39. Satter, *Each Mind a Kingdom*.

40. "Nona L. Brooks," Wikipedia, accessed October 26, 2011, http://en.wikipedia.org/wiki/Nona_L._Brooks.

41. "Nona L. Brooks: Co-Founder of Divine Science," accessed October 27, 2011, http://nonabrooks.wwwhubs.com.

42. Dresser, *A History of the New Thought Movement*, 192–94.

43. "An Introduction to Science of Mind," DivinceScience.com, accessed January 19, 2012, http://divinescience.com/beliefs/rs_an_introduction.htm;

"Frederick Bailes: Science of Mind Teacher," accessed January 19, 2012, http://frederickbailes.wwwhubs.com.

44. "Ernest Holmes," Wikipedia, accessed October 27, 20100, http://en.wikipedia.org/wiki/Ernest_Holmes . See also R.C. Armor, R. Llast, and A. Vergara, *That Was Ernest: The Story of Ernest Holmes and the Religious Science Movement* (Marina del Rey, CA: DeVorss Publications, 2000).

45. Read Fenwicke L. Holmes, *Ernest Holmes: His Life and Times* (New York: Dodd, Mead, 1970).

46. Ernest Holmes, "What We Believe," DivineScience.com, accessed January 19, 2011, http://divinescience.com/beliefs/whatwebelievebyEH.htm.

47. Ibid.

48. "Fenwicke Holmes," Wikipedia, accessed October 27, 2011, http://en.wikipedia.org/wiki/Fenwicke_Holmes.

49. Read Annie Rix Militz, *Primary Lessons in Christian Living and Healing* (Los Angeles: Master Mind Press, 1904).

50. Ibid., 27, 32–33, 56–57, 100, 116, 133, 156.

51. Annie Rix Militz, *The Renewal of the Body* (Holyoke, MA: The Elizabeth Towne Co., 1914), 120–21.

52. Annie Rix Militz, *Concentration* (Los Angeles: The Master Mind Publishing Co., 1918), 12.

53. Ibid., 17, 21, 24–25, 30.

54. Ibid., 60, 78.

55. Annie Rix Militz, *All Things Are Possible to Them That Believe* (Los Angeles: The Master Mind Publishing Co., 1905), 3, 15.

56. "Home of Truth Statement of Principles," Home of Truth Spiritual Center, accessed January 19, 2012, http://thehomeoftruth.org.

57. Annie Rix Militz, *The Way to Heal As Taught by Jesus Christ* (Los Angeles: The Master Mind Publishing Co., 1918), 5, 12, 20, 21–23.

58. "Annie Rix Militz," Wikipedia, accessed October 29, 2011, http://en.wikipedia.org/wiki/Annie_Rix_Militz.

59. John K. Simmons, "The Forgotten Contributions of Annie Rix Militz to the Unity School of Christianity," *Nova Religio: The Journal of Alternative and Emergent Religions* 2 (1998): 76–92.

60. "Cult Head Buried as Disciples Give up Hope of Return," newspaper clipping found in Militz, *Primary Lessons in Christian Living and Healing,* frontispiece.

61. One of the speakers at the Parliament was Swami Vivekananda, whose subsequent popularity led to the establishment of Vedanta Societies in various cities. See Charles S. Braden, *These Also Believe: A Study of Modern American Cults and Minority Religious Movements* (New York: Macmillan Co., 1949), 473; John Henry Barrows, ed., *The World's Parliament of Religions* (Chicago: The Parliament Publishing Co., 1893).

62. Mary Hanford Ford, "Under the Pines at Green Acre," *Practical Ideals* 6 (1903): 17–21.

63. Quoted in Dresser, *A History of the New Thought Movement*, 171, 182, 195; Barrows, *The World's Parliament of Religion*; Tumber, *American Feminism and the Birth of a New Age Spirituality*, 122–34.

64. Dresser, *A History of the New Thought Movement*, 200.

65. Ibid., 211.

66. Ibid., 175–76.

67. Ibid., 155–56.

68. "The Metaphysical Movement," in Dresser, *The Spirit of the New Thought*, 222–24, 243–44.

69. Read L. A. Fealy, *Mind Powers* (Birmingham, AL: Altrurian Society, 1914).

70. Read Frank B. Robinson, *The Strange Autobiography of Frank B. Robinson* (Moscow, ID: Psychiana, Inc., 1941). See also Braden, *These Also Believe*.

Chapter 5: The Psychologies of Healthy-Mindedness

1. William James, *Essays, Reviews and Comments* (Cambridge, MA: Harvard University Press, 1987), 62.

2. Ibid., 657–58.

3. William James, *The Varieties of Religious Experience: A Study in Human Nature* (New York: Modern Library, 1902), 94.

4. Ibid., 77–78, 79.

5. Walt Whitman, "Song of Myself," in *Leaves of Grass* (Philadelphia: Rees Welsh and Co., 1882), 32.

6. James, *The Varieties of Religious Experience*, 92–93.

7. Read Henry Wood, *Ideal Suggestion Through Mental Photography* (Boston: Lea and Shepard, 1893); Horatio W. Dresser, *Voices of Freedom and Studies in the Philosophy of Individuality* (New York: G. P. Putnam's Sons, 1899); Ralph Waldo Trine, *In Tune With the Infinite: Fullness of Peace, Power and Plenty* (London: Thorsons/ Harper-Collins, 1899).

8. James, *The Varieties of Religious Experience*, 118.

9. Ibid., 104, 106.

10. John H. Noble, "Psychology on the 'New Thought' Movement," *The Monist* 14 (1904): 418.

11. Read Cushing Strout, "The Pluralistic Identity of William James: a Psycho-Historical Reading of 'The Varieties of Religious Experience,'" *American Quarterly* 23 (1971): 135–52.

12. Julius Seelye Bixler, "Mysticism and the Philosophy of William James," *International Journal of Ethics* 36 (1925): 71–85.

13. James, *The Varieties of Religious Experience*, 87.

14. William James, "The Energies of Men," *The Philosophical Review* 16 (1907): 1–20; for an online version, see Classics in the History of Psychology, accessed December 20, 2011, http://psychclassics.yorku.ca/James/energies.htm.

15. See "Dresser's Letter to Mrs. Browne on Extrasensory Perception, February 8, 1943," in Anderson, *Healing Hypotheses,* 344–54. Horatio's brother Jean Paul (1877–1935) became a minister in the Church of the New Jerusalem, and Philip Seabury (1885–1960) became a popular writer of New Thought ideas. See also "Mary Baker Eddy," New World Encyclopedia, accessed February 14, 2011, http://www.newworldencyclopedia.org/entry/Mary_Baker_Eddy.

16. Horatio W. Dresser, *The Immanent God: An Essay* (Boston: Published by the Author, 1895), 17, 25.

17. Quoted in "Horatio Dresser," The Secrets of The Secret, accessed August 26, 2010, http://secretsofthesecret.com/horatio-dresser.htm.

18. For examples see Horatio W. Dresser, "The Method of Emerson," *Unity* 19 (1903): 3–11; and Horatio W. Dresser, "Plato's *Republic,*" *Unity* 19 (1903): 131–35.

19. Anderson, *Healing Hypotheses,* 99–100.

20. Dresser, *In Search of a Soul,* 74.

21. Horatio W. Dresser, *The Religion of the Spirit in Modern Life* (New York: G.P. Putnam's Sons, 1914), ix–x.

22. Timothy C. Dowling, ed., *The African-American Experience in World War I* (Santa Barbara, CA: ABC-CLIO, Inc., 2006), 235–36.

23. Horatio W. Dresser, *The Power of Silence: A Study of the Values and Ideals of the Inner Life* (New York and London: G. P. Putnam's Sons, 1906 [1895]), 184–87, 311.

24. Ibid., 26.

25. Ibid., 30.

26. Ibid., 12.

27. Ibid., 262.

28. Ibid., 272.

29. Ibid., 324.

30. Ibid., 16, 125.

31. Dresser, *In Search of a Soul,* l, 42, 46.

32. Ibid., 26–28, 35–37, 75–77, 83, 90.

33. Ibid., 127–28, 132, 180–82.

34. Ibid., 171.

35. Ibid., 127, 140, 147–48.

36. Dresser, *Voices of Freedom,* 158, 171–96, 199.

37. Ibid., iii–v.

38. Ibid., 6.

39. Dresser, *Health and the Inner Life,* 171, 176–77.

40. Ibid., 179–82, 184.

41. Ibid., 185–92, 195–200, 222.

42. Ibid., 227.

43. Horatio W. Dresser, "The Psychology and Philosophy of Emanuel Swedenborg" (unpublished manuscript, Swedenborgian House of Studies, Berkeley, CA, n.d.), iv.

44. Ibid., vi.

45. Ibid., ix.

46. Ibid., ch. 1, p. 9.

47. Ibid., ch. 2, p. 7. Swedenborg quote taken from *The Economy of the Animal Kingdom: Considered Anatomically, Physically, and Philosophically,* trans. Augustus Clissold (New York: The New Church Press, n.d.), 2:5.

48. Ibid., ch. 2, pp. 13–14.

49. Ibid., ch. 2, pp. 15–16; ch. 3, pp. 1–2.

50. Ibid., ch. 3, p. 5.

51. Ibid., ch. 6, p. 5.

52. Ibid., ch. 6, p. 4.

53. Ibid., ch. 11, p. 2.

54. Ibid., ch. 11, p. 4.

55. Ibid., ch. 11, p. 6.

56. Ibid., ch. 39, pp. 2–3.

57. Ibid., iii.

58. Ibid., ch. 52, pg. 6. See also Emanuel Swedenborg, *Secrets of Heaven* (West Chester, PA: Swedenborg Foundation, 2008), 1:§687.

59. Dresser, "The Psychology and Philosophy of Emanuel Swedenborg," ch. 2, pp. 9, 15.

60. Ibid., ch. 7, p. 5.

61. Ibid., ch. 10, p. 6; 263.

62. Ibid., ch. 32, p. 2.

63. Ibid., 262; Francis G. Gosling, *Before Freud: Neurasthenia and the American Medical Community, 1870–1910* (Urbana: University of Illinois Press, 1987); Henry A. Bunker, "From Beard to Freud: A Brief History of the Concept of Neurasthenia," *Medical Review of Reviews* 36 (1930): 108–14.

64. Anderson, *Healing Hypotheses,* 108–9. See also "John Howland Lathrop," Dictionary of Unitarian & Universalist Biography, accessed January 17, 2011, http://www25.uua.org/uuhs/duub/articles/johnhlathrop.html.

65. Bruce, *Scientific Mental Healing,* 43.

66. Sanford Gifford, "Medical Psychotherapy and the Emmanuel Movement in Boston, 1904–1912," in George E. Gifford, Jr., ed., *Psychoanalysis, Psychotherapy and the New England Medical Scene, 1894–1944* (New York: Science History Publications, 1978), 106–18; James Hoopes, *Consciousness in New England: From Puritanism and Ideas to Psychoanalysis and Semiotics* (Baltimore: Johns Hopkins University Press, 1989).

67. Raymond Joseph Cunningham, "The Emmanuel Movement: a Variety of American Religious Experience," *American Quarterly* 14 (1962): 48–63; Horatio W. Dresser, *A Message to the Well And Other Essays and Letters on the Art of Health* (New York and London: G. P. Putnam's Sons, 1910), 70–73.

68. Stow Persons, *American Minds: A History of Ideas* (New York; Holt, Rinehart and Winston, 1958), 423; Robert Bruce Mullin, "The Debate Over Religion and Healing in the Episcopal Church: 1870–1930," *Anglican and Episcopal History* 60 (1991): 213–34; Eric Caplan, *Mind Games: American Culture and the Birth of Psychotherapy* (Berkeley: University of California Press, 1998), 118.

69. Dresser, *A Message to the Well*, 73–76.

70. Nathan G. Hale, Jr., *The Rise and Crisis of Psychoanalysis in the United States: Freud and the Americans, 1917-1985* (New York: Oxford University Press, 1995); Dresser, *A Message to the Well*, 78–79.

71. Elwood Worcester and Samuel McComb, *The Christian Religion as a Healing Power: A Defense and Exposition of the Emmanuel Movement* (New York: Moffat, Yard and Co., 1909), 11–13.

72. Ibid., 27–28.

73. Ibid., 2–5, 17–18.

74. Elwood Worcester, Samuel McComb, and Isador H. Coriat, *Religion and Medicine: the Moral Control of Nervous Disorders* (New York: Moffat, Yard and Co., 1908), 7–8.

75. Worcester and McComb, *The Christian Religion as a Healing Power,* 91, 95–96.

76. Ibid., 99, 103, 117–18.

77. Dresser, *A Message to the Well*, 130.

78. Worcester, McComb, and Coriat, *Religion and Medicine*, 67: Elwood Worcester, *The Living Word* (New York: Moffat, Yard and Co., 1908).

79. Worcester and McComb, *The Christian Religion as a Healing Power*, 20, 46–47; Samuel McComb, *The Healing Ministry of the Church* (Boston: Emmanuel Church, 1908).

80. Worcester, McComb, and Coriat, *Religion and Medicine*, 11–12.

81. Samuel Fallows, *Health and Happiness; Or, Religious Therapeutics and Right Living* (Chicago: A. C. McClurg and Co., 1908), x–xvii.

82. Oliver Huckel, *Mental Medicine: Some Practical Suggestions from a Spiritual Standpoint* (New York: Thomas Y. Crowell and Co., 1909), xiii–xv; John K. Mitchell, "The Emmanuel Movement: Its Pretensions, Its Practice, Its Dangers," *American Journal of the Medical Sciences* (1909): 781–93.

83. Huckel, *Mental Medicine*, xviii–xx. Note the three articles by Lightner Witmer in *Psychological Clinic,* which, while commending the social work of participants in the Emmanuel Movement, took exception to the use of hypnotism.

84. Dresser, *A Message to the Well*, 21.

85. Andrew R. Heinze, "Jews and American Popular Psychology: Reconsidering the Protestant Paradigm of Popular Thought," *Journal of American History* 88 (2001): 950. See also Donald Meyer, *The Positive Thinkers: A Study of the American Quest for*

Health, Wealth, and Personal Power from Mary Baker Eddy to Norman Vincent Peale (New York: Doubleday, 1965); Laura Fermi, *Illustrious Immigrants: The Intellectual Migration from Europe, 1930-41* (Chicago: University of Chicago Press, 1968); and Lewis A. Coser, *Refuge Scholars in America: Their Impact and their Experiences* (New Haven, CT: Yale University Press, 1984.

86. Martin Seligman, "The Presidential Address," *APA 1998 Annual Report,* accessed December 20, 2011, http://www.positive psychology.org/aparep98htm; James O. Pawelski, "William James, Positive Psychology, and Healthy-Mindedness," *Journal of Speculative Philosophy* 17 (2003): 58–61.

87. Martin Seligman, and Mihaly Csikszentmihalyi, "Positive Psychology: An Introduction," *American Psychologist* 55 (2000): 5–14; Martin Seligman, *Authentic Happiness: Using the New Positive Psychology to Realize Your Potential for Lasting Fulfillment* (New York: Simon and Schuster, 2002).

88. Seligman and Csikszentmihalyi, "Positive Psychology: An Introduction," 5. See also Ken Sheldon, Barbara Frederickson, Kevin Rathunke, Mihaly Csikszentmihalyi, and Jonathan Haidt, "Positive Psychology Manifesto," Positive Psychology Center, University of Pennsylvania, accessed January 1, 2012, http://www.ppc.sas.upenn.edu/akumalmanifesto.htm.

89. Martin E. P. Seligman, "Positive Psychology, Positive Prevention, and Positive Therapy," accessed December 21, 2011 at http://uqu.edu.sa/files2/tiny_mce/plugins/filemanager/files/4281464/positiev%20psychology.pdf. See also M. W. Fordyce, "A Program to Increase Happiness: Further Studies," *Journal of Counseling Psychology* 30 (1983): 483–98.

90. Seligman, "Positive Psychology, Positive Prevention, and Positive Therapy."

91. The six virtues are wisdom and knowledge, courage, humanity, justice, temperance, and transcendence. Within these virtues are the character strengths of creativity, curiosity, open-mindedness, love of learning, perspective, authenticity, bravery, persistence, zest, kindness, love, social intelligence, fairness, leadership, teamwork, forgiveness, modesty, prudence, appreciation of beauty and excellence, gratitude, hope, humor, and religiousness. See C. Peterson, and M. E. P. Seligman, *Character Strengths and Virtues: A Handbook and Classification* (Washington, DC: American Psychological Association, 2004).

92. Claudia Wallis, "The New Science of Happiness," *Time Magazine,* published in 2004, accessed December 21, 2011 at http://s.psych.uiuc.edu/~ediener/Documents/Time-Happiness.pdf.

93. Quoted in Claudia Wallis, "The Science of Happiness Turns Ten. What Has It Taught?" *Time Magazine,* published July 8, 2009, accessed December 21, 2011 at http://www.time.com/time/health/article/0,8599,1908173,00.html. See also Eugene Taylor, "Positive Psychology and Humanistic Psychology: A Reply to Seligman," *Journal of Humanistic Psychology* 41 (2001): 13–29.

94. Dresser, *A History of the New Thought Movement,* 158–63.

Chapter 6: Evolution's Divine Plan

1. Dresser, *The Spirit of the New Thought,* 249–51, 263–65.

2. Persons, *Free Religion,* 57.

3. D. H. Meyer, "American Intellectuals and the Victorian Crisis of Faith," *American Quarterly* 27 (1975): 586.

4. Allen, *The Message of New Thought,* 58.

5. Henry Wood, *God's Image in Man: Some Intuitive Perceptions of Truth* (Boston: Lee and Shepard Publishers, 1892), 240–44.

6. Dresser, *The Power of Silence,* 1, 29–30.

7. Ibid., 30, 42–43.

8. Dresser, *Man and the Divine Order,* 354, 363.

9. Dresser, *Voices of Freedom,* 86–87.

10. Dresser, *The Spirit of the New Thought,* 12.

11. Peter J. Bowler, *Evolution: the History of an Idea* (Berkeley: University of California Press, 1984), 81–82, 237–39, 251–53.

12. Charles Darwin, *The Origin of Species and the Descent of Man* (New York: The Modern Library, n.d.), 494–95.

13. Quoted in Allen, *The Message of New Thought,* 136–38, 146–47.

14. Elizabeth Towne, *Fifteen Lessons in New Thought, Or Lessons in Living* (Holyoke, MA: The Elizabeth Towne Co., 1921 [1910]), 49, 51–52.

15. Allen, *The Message of New Thought,* 15, 21.

16. James Bixby, *The New World and the New Thought* (New York: Thomas Whittaker, 1902); John Wesley Conley, *Evolution and Man, Here and Hereafter* (Chicago: Fleming H. Revel Co., 1902).

17. Bixby, *The New World and the New Thought,* 14, 19.

18. Ibid., 25. Compare to Emanuel Swedenborg, *Life on Other Planets,* trans. John Chadwick (West Chester, PA: Swedenborg Foundation, 2006).

19. Ibid., 26–27.

20. Ibid., 24, 34–37, 53.

21. Ibid., 118, 129.

22. See Joseph Le Conte, "The Factors of Evolution," *The Monist* 1 (1892): 321–35.

23. Joseph Le Conte, *Evolution: Its Nature, Its Evidences, and Its Relation to Religious Thought* (New York: D. Appleton and Co., 1891), 301.

24. Joseph Le Conte, "Man's Place in Nature," *Princeton Review* 54 (1878): 775–803.

25. Le Conte, *Evolution,* 361–62.

26. Herbert W. Schneider, *A History of American Philosophy,* 2nd ed. (New York and London: Columbia University Press, 1963), 313.

27. Allen, *The Message of New Thought,* 155.

28. John Hamlin Dewey, *The Pathway of the Spirit. A Guide to Inspiration, Illumination and Divine Realization on Earth* (New York: Frank F. Lovell and Co., 1890), 112–17, 234–35.

29. Ibid.,135–37, 182–83.

30. Wood, *God's Image in Man,* 55, 64. See also Henry Wood, *Edward Burton* (Boston: Lee and Shepard Publishers, 1890); and Henry Wood, *Victor Serenus; A Story of the Pauline Era* (Boston: Lee and Shepard Publishers, 1898).

31. Wood, *God's Image in Man,* 212, 214; James, *The Varieties of Religious Experience,* 94.

32. Wood, *God's Image in Man,* 221–22.

33. Trine, *In Tune with the Infinite,* 16.

34. Fillmore, *Christian Healing,* 11–12.

35. Thomas Troward, *The Edinburgh Lectures on Mental Science* (New York: Robert M. McBride and Co., 1922), 72–73.

36. Ibid., 105.

37. Ibid., 124.

38. Horatio Dresser, *The Christ Ideal: A Study of the Spiritual Teachings of Jesus* (New York: G. P. Putnam's Sons, 1904), 135–38, 142.

39. Wood, *God's Image in Man,* 91–93, 164–67.

40. Wood, *The New Thought Simplified,* 95–96, 155–57.

41. Henry Ward Beecher, *Plymouth Pulpit: Sermons Preached in Plymouth Church, Brooklyn* (Boston: The Pilgrim Press, 1875), 4:463.

42. Andrew Carnegie, "Wealth," *North American Review* 148 (1889): 653–64.

43. Read Francis G. Peabody, *Jesus Christ and the Social Question* (New York: Macmillan Co., 1900); Sidney E. Mead, "American Protestantism since the Civil War. II. From Americanism to Christianity," *The Journal of Religion* 36 (1956): 67–89.

44. James Allen, *The Mastery of Destiny* (New York: G. P. Putnam's Sons, 1909), iii, 61.

45. James Allen, *From Poverty to Power; Or, the Realization of Prosperity and Peace,* 3rd ed. (Illinois: The Sheldon University Press, 1908 [1901]), 13, 38, 40.

46. James Allen, "As a Man Thinketh," in Napoleon Hill, et al., *The Prosperity Bible,* 224.

47. Ingalese, *The History and Power of Mind,* 263–64, 283.

48. Wood, *The New Thought Simplified,* 93–94.

49. Theodore F. Seward, *Spiritual Knowing or Bible Sunshine: The Spiritual Gospel of Jesus the Christ* (New York and London: Funk and Wagnalls Co., 1901 [1900]).

50. Newcomb, *All's Right with the World,* 5, 11.

51. Ibid., 25–26.

52. Ibid., 43–46.

53. Ibid., 112–13.

54. Martin E. Marty, *Righteous Empire* (New York: Deal Press, 1970), 211.

55. Read Alison Bashford and Philippa Levine, eds., *The Oxford Handbook of the History of Eugenics* (New York: Oxford University Press, 2010).

56. Newcomb, *All's Right with the World*, 78–79, 92.

57. Richard Maurice Bucke, *Cosmic Consciousness: A Study in the Evolution of the Human Mind* (Philadelphia: Innes and Sons, 1901), 8; P. D. Ouspensky, *The Cosmic Consciousness of Dr. Richard M. Bucke* (Montana: Kessinger Publishing, 2005).

58. Read Meyer, "American Intellectuals and the Victorian Crisis of Faith," 585–603.

59. Dewey, *The Pathway of the Spirit*, 112–17, 234–35.

Chapter 7: The Marketplace of Healing

1. Read George Gordon Dawson, *Healing: Pagan and Christian* (London: Society for Promoting Christian Knowledge, 1935).

2. Read A. J. Gayner Banks, *The Healing Evangel* (Milwaukee, WI: Morehouse, 1925).

3. Cather and Milmine, *The Life of Mary Baker G. Eddy*, 380–81.

4. Wood, *The New Thought Simplified*, 150, 160–62.

5. Julia Anderson Root, *Healing Power of Mind. A Treatise on Mind-Cure, with Original Views on the Subject, and Complete Instructions for Practice, and Self-Improvement* (San Francisco: Women's Cooperative Printing Office, 1884), 56, 64, 68–72.

6. Leander Edmund Whipple, *The Philosophy of Mental Healing: A Practical Exposition of Natural Restorative Power* (New York: The Metaphysical Publishing Co., 1893), 136, 138; Wood, *Ideal Suggestion Through Mental Photography*, 36.

7. Ursula N. Gestefeld, *How We Master Our Fate* (New York: The Alliance Publishing Co., 1899), 56–57; Tumber, *American Feminism and the Birth of New Age Spirituality*, 50–57.

8. Charles Brodie Patterson, *In the Sunlight of Health* (New York: Funk and Wagnalls Co., 1913), 62.

9. Charles Brodie Patterson, *What is New Thought? The Living Way* (New York: T.Y. Crowell, 1913), 74.

10. Helen Bigelow Merriman, *What Shall Make Us Whole? Or, Thoughts in the Direction of Man's Spiritual and Physical Integrity* (Boston: De. Wolfe, Fiske and Co., 1890 [1888]), 107.

11. M. J. Barnett, *Practical Metaphysics; Or, the True Method of Healing* (Boston: H. H. Carter and Karrick, 1889), 72–75.

12. Ingalese, *The History and Power of Mind*, 195.

13. Wood, *Ideal Suggestion Through Mental Photography*, 108–109.

14. Dewey, *The Pathway of the Spirit*, 164, 166–68; S. E. D. Short, "Physicians and Psychics: The Anglo-American Response to Spiritualism, 1870-1890," *Journal of the History of Medicine and Allied Sciences* 39 (1984): 339–55; Edward M. Brown, "Neurol-

ogy and Spiritualism in the 1870s," *Bulletin of the History of Medicine* 57 (1983): 563–77. As a gender issue, spiritual healing was much more a woman's choice because of her perceived intuitive capabilities. Men, on the other hand, were thought to be less intuitive, tending more toward scholastic and traditional forms of wisdom. See Wood, *Ideal Suggestion Through Mental Photography*, 24–26.

15. Read Michael F. Brown, *The Channeling Zone: American Spirituality in an Anxious Age* (Oxford: Harvard university Press, 1997).

16. W. J. Colville, *The Spiritual Science of Health and Healing; Considered in Twelve Lectures, Delivered Inspirationally* (Chicago: Garden City Publishing Co., 1888 [1887]), 230–31.

17. John Hamlin Dewey, *The Way, the Truth, and the Life; A Handbook of Christian Theosophy, Healing and Psychic Culture, a New Education Based on the Ideal and Method of the Christ*, 3rd ed. (New York: Frank F. Lovell and Co., 1888), 322.

18. Jane W. Yarnall, *Practical Healing for Mind and Body. A Complete Treatise on the Principles and Practice of Healing by a Knowledge of Divine Law* (Chicago: E. M. Harley Publishing Co., 1893 [1891]), 93–94.

19. Catherine Ponder, *Pray and Grow Rich* (West Nyack, NY: Parker Publishing Co., Inc., 1968), x.

20. Ibid., 76–77.

21. Colville, *The Spiritual Science of Health and Healing*, 5–6, 8–13, 34.

22. Ibid., 36–37, 58.

23. See Julian H. Miller, *Can a Jew Be a Jew and a Christian Scientist at One and the Same Time?* (Chattanooga, TN: Mizpah Congregation, 1909).

24. Michael A. Meyer, *Response to Modernity: A History of the Reform Movement in Judaism* (New York: Oxford University Press, 1988), 314; Joseph Jastrow, "Christian Science," *Popular Science Monthly* 58 (1901): 551.

25. Read Ellen M. Umansky, *From Christian Science to Jewish Science: Spiritual Healing and American Jews* (New York: Oxford University Press, 2005).

26. Alfred G. Moses, *Jewish Science: Divine Healing in Judaism, With Special Reference to the Jewish Scriptures and Prayer Book* (Mobile, AL: Alfred G. Moses, 1916), 7–12.

27. Ibid., 22.

28. Ibid., 42.

29. Ibid., 48.

30. Ibid., 19.

31. Ibid., 32–33.

32. Ibid., Chapters 1–4.

33. "Morris Lichtenstein," Wikipedia, accessed October 28, 2011, http://en. wikipedia.org/wiki/Morris_Lichtenstein.

34. "Jewish Science," Wikipedia, accessed October 29, 2011, http://en.wikipedia. org/wiki/Jewish_Science.

35. Rabbi Morris Lichtenstein, *Cures for Minds in Distress* (New York: Jewish Science Publishing Co., 1936), 12.

36. Ibid., 15.

37. Ibid., 20–23.

38. Ibid., 62.

39. Ibid., 71.

40. Ibid., 75.

41. Ibid., 86.

42. Ibid., 97.

43. "Rabbi Morris Lichtenstein," Jewish Science California, accessed January 16, 2012, http://www.irenedanon.com/Rabbi.htm.

44. Helena Blavatsky, *The Secret Doctrine: The Synthesis of Science, Religion, and Philosophy* (London: Theosophical Publishing Society, 1893).

45. William Quan Judge, "Replanting Diseases for Future Use," in H. P. Blavatsky and William Quan Judge, *The Laws of Healing: Physical and Metaphysical* (Los Angeles: Theosophy Co., 1937), 9–11.

46. Henry Steel Olcott, *Old Diary Leaves: The True Story of the Theosophical Society* (New York: G. P. Putnam's Sons, 1895), vii.

47. Helena Blavatsky, *The Key to Theosophy* (London: Theosophical Publishing Company, 1889); Blavatsky, *The Secret Doctrine.*

48. Rudolf Steiner, *Autobiography: Chapters in the Course of My Life: 1861–1907* (Great Barrington, MA: Anthroposophic Press, 2006); Rudolf Steiner, *The Story of My Life* (New York: Anthroposophic Press, 1928); Corinna Treitel, *A Science for the Soul: Occultism and the Genesis of the German Modern* (Baltimore: Johns Hopkins University Press, 2004).

49. Towne, *Fifteen Lessons in New Thought, Or Lessons in Living,* 180, 183–85.

50. Newcomb, *All's Right with the World,* 132–33.

51. Read Dale Riepe, *The Philosophy of India and Its Impact on American Thought* (Springfield, IL: Charles C. Thomas, 1970); and Hal Bridges, *American Mysticism: From William James to Zen* (New York; Harper and Row, 1970).

52. Charles Brodie Patterson, *The Measure of a Man* (New York: Funk and Wagnalls Co., 1904), 123.

53. Sheldon, *Theosophy and New Thought,*158–63, 169–70.

54. Dewey, *The Way, the Truth, and the Life,* 45–46, 50–51, 71.

55. Dewey, *The Pathway of the Spirit,* 41–42.

56. Ibid., 150, 157.

57. Ibid., 157–58. Compare with Swedenborg: "Even while we are living in our bodies, each one of us is in a community with spirits as to our own spirits even though we are unaware of it. Good people are in angelic communities by means of [their spirits] and evil people are in hellish communities." Emanuel Swedenborg, *Heaven and Hell,* trans. George F. Dole (West Chester, PA: Swedenborg Foundation, 2000), §438.

58. Dewey, *The Way, the Truth, and the Life,* 15–20.

59. Ibid., 115.

60. Ibid., 120–21.

61. Ibid., 138–40.

62. Ibid., 287–90, 316.

63. Barnett, *Practical Metaphysics,* 7–9.

Chapter 8: The Prophet Margin

1. Huber, *The American Idea of Success,* 124.

2. Kemper Fullerton, "Calvinism and Capitalism," *Harvard Theological Review* 21 (1928): 163–95.

3. Anna W. Mills, *Practical Metaphysics for Healing and Self Culture; Or, the Way to Save Both Soul and Body Now* (Chicago: Universal Truth Publishing Co., 1896), 4–8, 45–49, 54, 59.

4. Militz, *Concentration,* 25–31.

5. Militz, *All Things are Possible to Them that Believe,* 2–3.

6. Charles Fillmore, "Prosperity," in Napoleon Hill, et al., *The Prosperity Bible,* 409–10.

7. Fillmore, "Prosperity," 449, 462.

8. Ralph Waldo Trine, *What All the World's A-Seeking; Or, the Vital Law of True Life, True Greatness, Power, and Happiness* (New York: Thomas Y. Crowell and Co., 1896), 71, 112.

9. Russell H. Conwell, *"Gleams of Grace." Eight Sermons. To which is added the Chautauqua Report of His Celebrated Popular Lecture, "Acres of Diamonds"* (Philadelphia: J. B. Lippincott Co., 1887), 84–85.

10. Newcomb, *All's Right with the World,* 199–201, 204.

11. Ibid., 212, 217, 220.

12. Ibid., 60, 64.

13. Helen Wilmans, "The Conquest of Poverty," in Napoleon Hill, et al., *The Prosperity Bible,* 1009.

14. Elizabeth Towne, "How to Grow Success," in Napoleon Hill, et al., *The Prosperity Bible,* 1207.

15. Towne, "How to Grow Success," 1214–15.

16. Orison Swett Marden, *The Miracle of Right Thought* (New York: Thomas Y. Crowell and Co., 1910), vii–viii, 7.

17. Ibid., 30, 33–34.

18. Ibid., 40, 64, 86.

19. Paul Ellsworth, *Direct Healing* (Holyoke, MA: The Elizabeth Towne Co., 1916 [1914]), 5–6, 13.

20. Ibid., 25–26.

21. Ibid., 102.

22. Ibid., 106–7.

23. "William Walker Atkinson: Prolific New Thought Writer," accessed October 26, 2011, http://williamwalkeratkinson.wwwhubs.com.

24. William Walker Atkinson, *The Law of the New Thought: A Study of Fundamental Principles and Their Application* (Chicago: The Psychic Research Company, 1902), 11.

25. John S. Haller, Jr., and Robin M. Haller, *The Physician and Sexuality in Victorian America* (Urbana: University of Illinois Press, 1974), 191–234.

26. William Walker Atkinson, *Thought Vibration; Or, the Law of Attraction in the Thought World* (Chicago: The Library Shelf, 1908 [1906]), xxvii–ix. Atkinson's law of attraction was also prominent in the works of Napoleon Hill, Wallace Wattles, Norman Vincent Peale, and Dale Carnegie, to name just a few.

27. William Walker Atkinson, *Thought-Force in Business and Everyday Life* (Chicago: The Psychic Research Co., 1901), 42, 57–58.

28. Ibid., 5, 8–14.

29. William Walker Atkinson, *Mind-Power: The Secret of Mental Magic* (Chicago: Advanced Thought Publishing Co., 1907), 123.

30. Atkinson, *Thought-Force in Business and Everyday Life,* 54.

31. Ibid., 64.

32. Atkinson, *Mind-Power,* 200–238.

33. Ibid., 202.

34. Theron Q. Dumont, *The Master Mind; Or, the Key to Mental Power, Development and Efficiency* (Chicago: Advanced Thought Publishing Co., 1918) 123–25, 178–79. Theron Q. Dumont was one of Atkinson's pseudonyms.

35. William Walker Atkinson, *The Inner Consciousness: A Course of Lessons on the Inner Planes of the Mind, Intuition, Instinct, Automatic Mentation, and Other Wonderful Phases of Mental Phenomena* (Chicago: Advanced Thought Publishing Co., 1908), 38.

36. Ibid., 40.

37. Atkinson, *Thought Vibration,* 39; Franklin D. Roosevelt, "First Inaugural Address" (1932), accessed December 7, 2011 at http://historymatters.gmu.edu/d/5057.

38. Atkinson, *Thought Vibration,* xxiv.

39. Ingalese, *The History and Power of Mind,* 155, 159.

40. Ibid., 161, 166.

41. Ibid., 155, 159, 161, 166.

42. John S. Haller, Jr., "Neurasthenia: Medical Profession and Urban 'Blahs,'" *New York State Journal of Medicine* 70 (October 1, 1970): 2489–97; John S. Haller, Jr., "Neurasthenia: The Medical Profession and the 'New Women' of the Late 19th Century," *New York State Journal of Medicine* 71 (February 15, 1971): 472–82.

43. H. L. Mencken, *Prejudices: First Series* (New York: Alfred A. Knopf, 1919), 194.

44. Quoted in Dresser, *A History of the New Thought Movement*, 279.

45. "Making the World 'Safe for Democracy': Woodrow Wilson Asks for War," accessed December 27, 2011, at http://historymatters.gmu.edu/d/4943.

46. Dresser, *A History of the New Thought Movement*, 284.

47. See Tom Zender, *God Goes to Work: New Thought Paths to Prosperity and Profits* (Hoboken, NJ: John Wiley and Sons, 2010).

48. Quoted in Myer S. Reed, Jr., "After the Alliance: The Sociology of Religion in the United States from 1925 to 1949," *Sociological Analysis* 543 (1982): 190.

49. Reed Bain, "Editor's Note—Science, Values and Sociology," *American Sociological Review* 4 (1939): 564.

50. James, *The Varieties of Religious Experience*, 36.

51. Charles F. Haanel, "The Master Key System," in Napoleon Hill, et al., *The Prosperity Bible*, 600.

52. Ibid., 609, 656–57.

53. Alfred Whitney Griswold, "New Thought: A Cult of Success," *American Journal of Sociology* 40 (1934): 316.

54. Frank Channing Haddock, *Business Power: A Practical Manual in Financial Ability* (Alhambra, CA: The Power-Book Co., 1911), v, 40.

55. Read Richard M. Fried, *The Man Everybody Knew: Bruce Barton and the Making of Modern America* (Chicago: Ivan R. Dee, 2005).

56. Bruce Barton, *The Man Nobody Knows* (Indianapolis: Bobbs-Merrill, 1925), iv.

57. Alice Payne Hackett, *Sixty Years of Best Sellers: Advertising, 1895-1955* (New York: R. R. Bowker, 1956), 139–41.

58. See James A. Neuchterlein, "Bruce Barton and the Business Ethos of the 1920s," *South Atlantic Quarterly* 77 (1977): 293–308; Huber, *The American Idea of Success*; Lawrence Chenoweth, *The American Dream of Success: The Search for the Self in the Twentieth Century* (North Scituate, MA: Duxbury Press, 1974); and John G. Cawelti, *Apostles of the Self-Made Man* (Chicago: University of Chicago Press, 1965).

59. Read Bouck White, *The Call of the Carpenter* (Garden City, NY: Doubleday, 1911); Reinhold Niebuhr, "What Are the Churches Advertising?" *Christian Century* 41 (1924): 532–33.

60. William T. Doherty, "The Impact of Business on Protestantism, 1900–29," *The Business History Review* 28 (1954), 151.

61. Leo P. Ribuffo, "Jesus Christ as Business Statesman: Bruce Barton and the Selling of Corporate Capitalism," *American Quarterly* 33 (1981): 206–31; David Greenberg, "The Forgotten Imagemeister," *Washington Monthly*, uploaded April 2006, accessed November 3, 2011, http://www.washingtonmonthly.com/features/2006/0604.greenberg.html.

62. Robert Collier, "The Secret of the Ages," in Napoleon Hill, et al., *The Prosperity Bible*, 840–41.

63. Ibid., 852.

64. Ibid., 892–93.

65. Ibid., 894–95.

66. "Robert Collier: One of America's Original Success Authors," accessed January 21, 2012 at http://robertcollier.wwwhubs.com.

67. "Napoleon Hill," Wikipedia, accessed October 27, 2011, http://en.wikipedia. org/wiki/Napoleon_Hill. The businessman, philanthropist and New Thought author W. Clement Stone (1902–2002) built the Combined Insurance Company of America in 1919 and, by 1930, had agents in all parts of the country selling insurance. An admirer of Napoleon Hill's *Think and Grow Rich*, he distributed thousands of copies as a means of inspiring the author's principles. His own *The Success System that Never Fails* told multiple examples of rags-to-riches stories in the tradition of Horatio Alger. The author's copy of Hill's book was part of a shipment sent to Harry H. Woodward, Jr., director of Correctional Programs in Chicago and distributed widely to its employees. See Napoleon Hill, *Think and Grow Rich* (New York: Hawthorn Books, Inc., 1967); also, W. Clement Stone, *The Success System that Never Fails* (Englewood, NJ: PrenticeHall, 1962).

68. "Publisher's Note," in Hill, *Think and Grow Rich*, 6; "Grow Rich Author Dies," *Milwaukee Sentinel,* November 10, 1970.

69. Hill, *Think and Grow Rich*, 9, 190, 246–47.

70. Gail Thain Parker, "How to Win Friends and Influence People: Dale Carnegie and the Problem of Sincerity," *American Quarterly* 29 (1977): 508.

71. "Dale Carnegie," Wikipedia, accessed January 21, 2012, http://en.wikipedia. org/wiki/Dale_Carnegie.

72. Huber, *The American Idea of Success*, 454–55.

73. "Norman Vincent Peale," Wikipedia, accessed November 19, 2011, http://en. wikipedia.org/wiki/Norman_Vincent-Peale.

74. Donald Meyer, "Confidence Man," *New Republic,* July 11, 1955: 8–10; R. C. Murphy, "Think Right: Reverend Peale's Panacea," *The Nation*, May 7, 1955, 398–400; "Norman Vincent Peale," Wikipedia.

75. Quoted in "Norman Vincent Peale," Wikipedia.

Chapter 9: Dream Weavers and Money Changers

1. Read Tona J. Hangen, *Redeeming the Dial: Radio, Religion, and Popular Culture in America* (Chapel Hill: University of North Carolina Press, 2002); Steve Bruce, *Pray TV: Televangelism in America* (London: Routledge, 1990); Coleen McDannel, *Material Christianity: Religion and Popular Culture in America* (New Haven, CT: Yale University Press, 1996); Leigh Eric Schmidt, *Consumer Rites: The Buying and Selling of American Holidays* (Princeton, NJ: Princeton University Press, 1995); David Morgan, *Protestants and Pictures: Religion, Visual Culture, and the Age of American Mass Production* (New York: Oxford University Press, 1999).

2. See Wouter J. Hanegraaff, "New Age Religion and Secularization," *Numen* 47 (2000): 288–312.

3. A full list of New Thought churches and affiliated organizations can be found in appendix A.

4. The Daily Word: A Unity Publication, accessed May 22, 2012, http://www.dailyword.com.

5. See the estimates compiled on Adherents.com, accessed May 24, 2012, http://www.adherents.com/Na/Na_653.html.

6. "Johnnie Colemon," Gale Contemporary Black Biographies, accessed May 22, 2012, via http://www.answers.com/topic/johnnie-colemon; see also the Universal Foundation for Better Living website at http://ufbl.org.

7. "Della Reese," The Internet Movie Database, accessed May 22, 2012, http://www.imdb.com/name/nm0005343/bio; see also the Understanding Principles for Better Living home page, accessed May 22, 2012, at http://www.upchurch.org.

8. For the number of active centers, see the list on the UFBL website, accessed May 22, 2012, http://ufbl.org/churches.

9. One Spirit Ministries, accessed November 21, 2011, http://www.1-spirit.net.

10. The number of centers is based on a count from the United Centers for Spiritual Living website, accessed May 22, 2012, http://www.unitedcentersforspiritual-living.org/Find_A_Community/center.php.

11. "Dr. Michael Bernard Beckwith," Agape Live, accessed February 3, 2012, http://agapelive.com/index.php?page=3.

12. See the ANTN membership roster, accessed May 16, 2012, at http://www.newthought.org/antn-members/antn-complete-roster.html.

13. Emerson Institute, accessed November 21, 2011, http://emersoninstitute.edu.

14. "About ANTN," accessed November 21, 2011, http://www.newthought.org/about-antn.html.

15. See the list of Divine Science centers, Divine Science Federation, accessed May 22, 2012, http://www.divinesciencefederation.org/what-we-offer/ministries.

16. See J. Gordon Melton, ed., *The Encyclopedia of American Religions: Religious Creeds* (Detroit: Gale Research Co., 1988).

17. "About Us," Church of Truth, accessed November 21, 2011, http://churchoftruth.org/about.html.

18. Hans A. Baer, "The Metropolitan Spiritual Churches of Christ: The Socio-Religious Evolution of the Largest of the Black Spiritual Associations," *Review of Religious Research* 30 (1988): 140–50.

19. Read Hans A. Baer, *The Black Spiritual Movement: A Religious Response to Racism* (Knoxville: University of Tennessee Press, 1984).

20. Robert Ellwood, "New Religions in Japan," in Mircea Eliade, ed., *The Encyclopedia of Religion* (New York: Macmillan Co., 1987), 10:410–14.

21. "Our Mission," Seicho-No-Ie US Missionary Headquarters, accessed November 21, 2011, http://www.snitruth.org/teachings.html.

22. "Centers," Seicho-No-Ie US Missionary Headquarters, accessed May 22, 2012, http://www.snitruth.org/centers.html.

23. "Association for Global New Thought," Wiser.org, accessed February 3, 2012, http://www.wiserearth.org/organization/view/828e01082302d4a10977396e88d11a47.

24. Quoted in Dresser, *A History of the New Thought Movement*, 215.

25. Leona Feathers, "The Third Congress of the International New Thought Alliance," *Master Mind Magazine* 15 (1918): 62.

26. James R. Lewis and J. Gordon Melton, eds., *Perspectives on the New Age* (Albany, NY: State University of New York Press, 1992), 16–18.

27. "About INTA," International New Thought Alliance, accessed November 1, 2011, http://www.newthoughtalliance.org/about.html.

28. C. Alan Anderson and Deborah G. Whitehouse, *New Thought: A Practical American Spirituality* (New York: Crossroad Publishing Co., 2002); Wood, *New Thought Simplified*.

29. Read Trysh Travis, "'It Will Change the World If Everybody Reads This Book': New Thought Religion in Oprah's Book Club," *American Quarterly* 59 (2007): 1017–41; Cecilia Konchar Farr, *Reading Oprah: How Oprah's Book Club Changed the Way America Reads* (Albany: State University of New York Press, 2004); Kathleen Rooney, *Reading with Oprah: The Book Club that Changed America* (Fayetteville: University of Arkansas Press, 2005); Wade Clark Roof, *A Generation of Seekers: The Spiritual Journeys of the Baby Boom Generation* (San Francisco: HarperSanFrancisco, 1993).

30. Andy Kaiser, "Book Review of 'The Secret,' by Rhonda Byrne: A skeptical review of a subjective reality," Digital Bits Skeptic, posted February 18, 2008, accessed November 1, 2011, http://www.dbskeptic.com/2008/02/18/book-review-of-the-secret-by-rhonda-byrne-a-skeptical-review-of-a-subjective-reality.

31. "Esther Hicks and the Law of Attraction," Oprah.com, accessed May 2, 2012, http://www.oprah.com/oprahradio/Esther-Hicks-and-the-Law-of-Attraction.

32. "Official website for the film," accessed December 8, 2011, http://www.thesecret.tv; "Website about the Secret," accessed December 8, 2011, http://secret4 lifenet; Rhonda Byrne, *The Secret* (Hillsboro, OR: Beyond Words, 2006); Alexandra Bruce, *Beyond the Secret: The Definitive Unauthorized Guide to the Secret* (New York: The Disinformation Co., 2007); Richard Giuilliat, "The Secret of Rhonda's Success," The Australian, posted August 23, 2008, accessed November 1, 2011, http://www.theaustralian.com.au/news/features/the-secret-of-rhondas-success/story-e6frg8h6-1111117271174. See also Kathlyn and Gay Hendricks, "What Can We Learn From the Lawsuit Against Rhonda Byrne and The Secret?" Huffington Post, accessed November 1, 2011, http://www.huffingtonpost.com/kathlyn-and-gay-hendricks/what-can-we-learn-from-th_b_198995.html.

33. Eugene Cheung, "Louise Hay Appeared on the Oprah Winfrey Show," EugeneCheung.com, posted July 3, 2008, accessed May 2, 2012, http://eugenecheung.com/blog/2008/louise-hay-appeared-on-the-oprah-winfrey-show.

34. Meera Lester, *365 Ways to Live the Law of Attraction* (Avon, MA: Adams Media, 2009), vi–vii, 8.

35. Ibid., 21–22.

36. William Hazlitt, ed., *The Complete Works of Michael de Montaigne* (London: John Templeman, 1892), 356.

37. Read L. Dossey, *Healing Words: The Power of Prayer and the Practice of Medicine* (New York: HarperCollins, 1993); Norman Cousins, *Head First: The Biology of Hope and the Healing Power of the Human Spirit* (New York: Penguin Books, 1990); H. Benson with M. Z. Klipper, *The Relaxation Response* (New York: Avon Books, 1976); H. Benson with M. Stark, *Timeless Healing: The Power and Biology of Belief* (New York: Simon and Schuster, 1997); B. S. Siegel, *Love, Medicine and Miracles: Lessons Learned About Self-Healing From a Surgeon's Experience with Exceptional Patients* (New York: Harper and Row, 1986); J. Levin, *God, Faith, and Health: Exploring the Spirituality-Healing Connection* (New York: John Wiley and Sons, 2001).

38. Deepak Chopra, *Ageless Body, Timeless Mind: The Quantum Alternative to Growing Old* (New York: Harmony Books, 1993); Deepak Chopra, *Quantum Healing: Discovering the Power to Fulfill Your Dreams* (New York: Bantam, 1991); Deepak Chopra, *Creating Affluence: Wealth Consciousness in the Field of All Possibilities* (San Rafael, CA: New World Library, 1993); Deepak Chopra, *Unconditional Life: Discovering the Power to Fulfill Your Dreams* (New York: Bantam Books, 1992. See also Joseph Waligore, "Deepak Chopra," Spiritual Critiques, posted in 2009, accessed May 12, 2012, http://www.spiritualcritiques.com/author-criticisms/deepak-chopra.

39. Carolyn Myss, accessed May 3, 2012, http://www.myss.com.

40. Gayle M. V. Delaney, *Living Your Dreams: Using Sleep to Solve Problems and Enrich Your Life* (San Francisco: HarperSanFrancisco, 1988), ix–xiv.

41. Thaddeus Golas, *The Lazy Man's Guide to Enlightenment* (Palo Alto, CA: Seed Center, 1972); The Thaddeus Golas Café, accessed May 3, 2012, http://www.thaddeusgolas.com.

42. The Kenneth G. Mills Foundation, accessed May 3, 2012, http://www.kgmfoundation.org; "Kenneth George Mills: Obituary," TC Palm, posted November 5, 2011, accessed May 3, 2012, http://www.legacy.com/obituaries/tcpalm/obituary.aspx?n=kenneth-george-mills&pid=154463598.

43. See the A Course in Miracles website, http://acim.org, for the early history of the project; for sales figures, "A Course in Miracles," Wikipedia, accessed May 23, 2012, http://en.wikipedia.org/wiki/A_Course_in_Miracles .

44. Jon Mundy, *Listening to Your Inner Guide* (New York: The Crossroad Publishing Co., 1995), 15.

45. Ibid., 23.

46. Eckhart Teachings, accessed May 3, 2012, http://www.eckharttolle.com.

47. "About Gary," Seat of the Soul Institute, accessed May 3, 2012, http://seatofthesoul.com/about/gary-zukav.

48. Dr. Wayne W. Dyer (website), accessed May 3, 2012, http://www.drwayne-dyer.com.

49. "Raymond Charles Barker, Church Founder, 77," The New York Times, Obituaries, published February 3, 1988, accessed May 3, 2012, http://www.nytimes.com/1988/02/03/obituaries/raymond-charles-barker-church-founder-77.html;

"Raymond Charles Barker: An Influential New Thought Lecturer and Author," accessed May 3, 2012, http://raymondcharlesbarker.wwwhubs.com.

50. "Stuart Grayson: Science of Mind Teacher," accessed May 3, 2012, "Dr. Stuart Grayson (In Memory) on The Woman's Connection," video posted January 13, 2011, accessed May 3, 2012, http://www.youtube.com/watch?v=V3310dNq7-s.

51. Marianne Williamson (website), accessed May 22, 2012, http://www.marianne.com.

52. Terry Cole-Whittaker (website), accessed May 3, 2012, http://www.terrycolewhittaker.com; "Abrupt Exit: The Rev. Terry Cole-Whittaker," *Time Magazine,* published April 22, 1985, accessed May 3, 2012, http://www.time.com/time/magazine/article/0,9171,966843,00.html.

53. Matthew Fox (website), accessed May 3, 2012, http://www.matthewfox.org.

54. Matthew Fox, "One River, Many Wells," lecture at the Earth & Spirit Council, video uploaded September 24, 2012, accessed May 3, 2012, http://www.youtube.com/watch?v=l9J9AZ7vJ-Y.

55. See 3 John 1:2, New Revised Standard Version; "Word of Faith," Wikipedia, accessed November 18, 2011, http://en.wikipedia.org/wiki/Word_of_Faith.

56. Joel Osteen, *Your Best Life Now: Seven Steps to Living at Your Full Potential* (New York: Warner Faith Publishers, 2004); Ralph Blumenthal, "Joel Osteen's Credo: Eliminate the Negative, Accentuate Prosperity," *The New York Times,* Books section, posted March 30, 2006, accessed February 4, 2012, http://www.nytimes.com/2006/03/30/books/30oste.html?pagewanted=all.

57. Michael Luo, "Preaching a Gospel of Wealth in a Glittery Market, New York," The New York Times, posted January 15, 2006, accessed November 27, 2011, http://www.nytimes.com/2006/01/15/nyregion/15prosperity.html?sq=prosperity.

58. D. R. McConnell, *A Different Gospel: A Historical and Biblical Analysis of the Modern Faith Movement* (Peabody, MA: Hendrickson Publishers, 1988).

59. David Jones and Russell S. Woodbridge, *Health, Wealth and Happiness: Has the Prosperity Gospel Overshadowed the Gospel of Christ?* (Grand Rapids, MI: Kregel Publications, 2011), 20–22; 25–31; "Exposing the Word of Faith Prosperity Gospel: Justin Peters/SO4J," video uploaded September 28, 2011, accessed February 2, 2012, http://bibleapologetic.blogspot.com/2011/09/exposing-word-of-faith-prosperity.html.

60. Kevin Scott Smith, "Mind, Might, and Mastery: Human Potential in Metaphysical Religion and E. W. Kenyon" (unpublished master's thesis, Liberty University Graduate School of Religion, 1995), 76.

61. See David S. Reynolds, "From Doctrine to Narrative: The Rise of Pulpit Storytelling in America," *American Quarterly* 32 (1980): 479–98. The exception to this use of the narrative is Christian Science which has banned such "ministerial personalism" and insists on only sermons approved by the Mother Church.

62. Deb Whitehouse, "New Age, New Thought, and Process Thought: A Psychological Perspective," http://websyte.com/alan/psychper.html (accessed November 23, 2011).

63. Kenneth E. Hagin, "Step One: Say It," Life Changing Truth, accessed February 4, 2012, http://www.lifechangingtruth.org/English/ArticlesEng/KennethHagin/Step1SayIt.htm; William K. Kay and Anne E. Dyer, eds., *Pentecostal and Charismatic Studies: A Reader* (London: SCM Press, 2004).

Chapter 10: A Retrospective

1. Charles W. Eliot, "The Religion of the Future," *Harvard Theological Review* 2 (1909): 396, 401.

2. Huber, *The American Idea of Success*, 125.

3. Dresser, *Voices of Freedom*, 25–26, 29–30.

4. Ibid., 48–49, 137–38.

5. Sheldon, *Theosophy and New Thought*, 137–38.

6. Read Will Herberg, *Protestant, Catholic, Jew: An Essay in American Religious Sociology* (Garden City, NY: Doubleday, 1955).

7. David A. Hollinger, *Science, Jews, and Secular Culture: Studies in Mid-Twentieth-Century American Intellectual History* (Princeton; Princeton University Press, 1996); George M. Marsden, *The Soul of the American University: From Protestant Establishment to Established Nonbelief* (New York: Oxford University Press, 1994); Christian Smith, ed., *The Secular Revolution: Power, Interests, and Conflict in the Secularization of American Life* (Berkeley: University of California Press, 2003); Jon Butler, *Awash in a Sea of Faith: Christianizing the American People* (Cambridge, MA: Harvard University Press, 1990).

8. Rodney Stark, William S. Bainbridge, and Daniel P. Doyle, "Cults of America: A Reconnaissance in Space and Time," *Sociological Analysis* 40 (1979): 347–59.

9. Alfred Whitney Griswold, "New Thought: A Cult of Success," *American Journal of Sociology* 40 (1934): 309.

10. See Thomas A. Tweed, ed., *Rethinking U. S. Religious History* (Berkeley: University of California Press, 1997); David A. Hollinger, *Postethnic America* (New York: Basic Books, 1995); Stewart M. Hoover and Knut Lundby, *Rethinking Media, Religion, and Culture* (Thousand Oaks, CA: Sage, 1997); R. Laurence Moore, *Religious Outsiders and the Making of Americans* (New York: Oxford University Press, 1986); and Marianna Torgovnick, *Primitive Passions: Men, Women, and the Quest for Ecstasy* (New York: Alfred A. Knopf, 1997).

Bibliography

Journals and Magazines

Advanced Thought
American Historical Review
American Journal of the Medical Sciences
American Literature
American Journal of Education
American Psychologist
American Sociological Review
American Quarterly
American Whig Review
Anglican and Episcopal History
Annals of Science
Arena
British Medical Journal
Bulletin of the History of Medicine
Business History Review
Christian Century
Christian Metaphysician
Christian Science Journal
Church History
Cosmopolitan
Creative Thought Magazine
Daedalus
Daily Word
Das Wort
Eleanor Kirk's Idea
The Essene
Eternal Progress
Exodus
The Gleaner
Harmony

Harvard Theological Review
Hill's Golden Rule
Immortality
Jewish Science Interpreter
Journal of American History
Journal of Counseling Psychology
Journal of Feminist Studies in Religion
Journal of Humanistic Psychology
Journal of Man
Journal of Practical Metaphysics
Journal of Social History
Journal of Speculative Philosophy
Journal of the American Academy
    of Religion
Journal of the History of Ideas
Journal of the History of Medicine
    and Allied Sciences
The Life
The Master Mind
Mental Healing Monthly
Mental Science Magazine
Merchants' Magazine
Metaphysical Magazine
Milwaukee Sentinel
Modern Thought
The Monist
Nation
National Christian Crusader
Nautilus
New England Quarterly

New Republic
New Thought
New Thought Magazine
New York State Journal of Medicine
New York Times Book Review
North American Review
Nova Religio
Now
Numen
Pharmacy in History
Philosophical Review
Phreno-Magnet
Popular Science Monthly
Power
Practical Ideals
Religion and American Culture: A Journal
of Interpretation
Review of Religious Research
Reviews in American History

Science of Mind Magazine
Scientific Christian
Sociological Analysis
South Atlantic Quarterly
Spirit Walk-Daily Reflection
Spiritual Philosopher
Studia Swedenborgiana
Success Magazine
Suggestion
Thought
Time Magazine
Unity Magazine
Universal Truth
Uplift Magazine
Wayside Lights
Wee Wisdom's Way
Wilman's Express
The World's Advance Thought
The Zoist, A Journal of Cerebral
Physiology and Mesmerism

Books

Abbott, Lyman. *The Theology of an Evolutionist.* Boston: Houghton Mifflin, 1897.

Adams, Grace and Edward Hutter. *The Mad Forties.* New York: Harper and Brothers, 1942.

Adams, Myron. *The Continuous Creation.* Boston: Houghton, Mifflin, 1889.

Adams, William. *The Elements of Christian Science; A Treatise Upon Moral Philosophy and Practice.* Philadelphia: H. Hooker, 1850.

Addington, Jack Ensign. *Psychogenesis: Everything Begins in Mind.* New York: Dodd, 1971.

Ahlstrom, Sidney E. *A Religious History of the American People.* New Haven, CT: Yale University Press, 1972.

Albanese, Catherine L. *America, Religions and Religion.* Belmont, CA: Wadsworth Publishing Co., 1981.

———. *Corresponding Motion: Transcendental Religion and the New America.* Philadelphia: Temple University Press, 1977.

———. "Physic and Metaphysic in 19th Century America: Medical Sectarians and Religious Healing." *Church History* 55 (1986): 498.

———. *A Republic of Mind and Spirit: A Cultural History of American Metaphysical Religion.* New Haven, CT: Yale University Press, 2007.

Alexander, Colin. *The Inner Secrets of Psychology.* 2 vols. Los Angeles: C. Alexander Publishing Co., 1924.

———. *Personal Lessons, Codes, and Instructions for Members of the Crystal Silence League: A Concise and Comprehensive Treatise Embracing Proper Care of the Body* and Development of the Inner or Mental Powers. Los Angeles: C. Alexander Publishing Co., 1921.

Alexander, Rolf. *The Doctor Alone Can't Cure You.* St. Paul, MN: Macalester Park Publishing Co., 1949.

Allen, Abel Leighton. *The Message of New Thought.* New York: Thomas Y. Crowell Co., 1914.

Allen, James. *Above Life's Turmoil.* New York: G. P. Putnam's Sons, 1910.

———. *All These Things Added.* London: s.n., 1903.

———. *As a Man Thinketh.* Westwood, NJ: Revell, 1957 [1900].

———. *The Divine Companion.* London: Fowler, 1919.

———. *The Eight Pillars of Prosperity.* New York: Thomas Y. Crowell Co., 1911.

———. *Foundation Stones to Happiness and Success.* New York: Thomas Y. Crowell Co., 1913.

———. *From Poverty to Power: Or, the Realization of Prosperity and Peace.* Chicago: The Science Press, 1906.

———. *The Life Triumphant.* Libertyville, IL: Sheldon University Press, 1908.

———. *The Mastery of Destiny.* New York: G. P. Putnam's Sons, 1909.

———. *The Path of Prosperity.* New York: R. F. Fenno and Co., 1907.

———. *Selected Teachings of James Allen.* Radford, VA: Wilder, 2007.

Anderson, C. Alan. *Healing Hypotheses; Horatio W. Dresser and the Philosophy of New Thought.* New York: Garland, 1993.

Anderson, C. Alan, and Deborah G. Whitehouse. *New Thought: A Practical American Spirituality.* New York: Crossroad Publishing Co., 2002.

Anderson, John Benjamin. *New Thought, Its Lights and Shadows; An Appreciation and a Criticism.* Boston: Sherman French and Co., 1911.

Anderson, Uell Stanley. *The Magic in Your Mind.* North Hollywood, CA: Wilshire Book Co., 1975.

———. *Three Magic Words: the Key to Power, Peace and Plenty.* North Hollywood, CA: Wilshire Book Co., 1974.

Anker, Roy M. *Self-Help and Popular Religion in Early American Culture: An Interpretive Guide.* Westport, CN: Greenwood Press, 1999.

Anthony, Robert. *Beyond Positive Thinking.* Newport News, VA: Morgan James, 2004.

Appel, Joseph H. *Living the Creative Life.* New York: R. M. McBride and Co., 1918.

Apple, Rima D., ed. *Women, Health, and Medicine in America: A Historical Handbook.* New York: Garland, 1990.

Armor, Reginald C., Robin Llast, and Arthur Vergara. *That was Ernest: The Story of Ernest Holmes and the Religious Science Movement.* Marina del Rey, CA: DeVorss Publications, 1999.

Ashburner, John. *Notes and Studies on the Philosophy of Animal Magnetism and Spiritualism.* London: Baillière, 1867.

Atkins, Gaius Glenn. *Modern Religious Cults and Movements.* New York: Fleming H. Revell Co., 1923.

Atkinson, Henry G. and Harriet Martineau. *Letters on the Laws of Man's Nature and Development.* Boston: Josiah P. Mendum, 1889 [1851].

Atkinson, William Walker. *Dynamic Thought or the Law of Vibrant Energy*. Los Angeles: The Senogram Publishing Co., 1906.

———. *How to Read Human Nature: Its Inner States and Outer Forms*. Holyoke, MA: The Elizabeth Towne Co., 1913.

———. *The Inner Consciousness: A Course of Lessons on the Inner Planes of the Mind, Intuition, Instinct, Automatic Mentation, and Other Wonderful Phases of Mental Phenomena*. Chicago: Advanced Thought Publishing Co., 1908.

———. *The Law of the New Thought: A Study of Fundamental Principles and Their Application*. Chicago: The Psychic Research Company, 1902.

———. *Mastery of Being: A Study of the Ultimate Principle of Reality and the Practical Application Thereof*. Holyoke, MA: The Elizabeth Towne Co., 1911.

———. *Memory Culture: The Science of Observing, Remembering and Recalling*. Chicago: Psychic Research Co., 1903.

———. *Memory: How to Develop, Train, and Use It*. Holyoke, MA: The Elizabeth Towne Co., 1911.

———. *Mental Fascination*. Chicago: Fiduciary Press, 1907.

———. *Mind and Body or Mental States and Physical Conditions*. Chicago: The Progress Co., 1910.

———. *The Mind Building of a Child*. Chicago: The Library Shelf, 1907.

———. *Mind Power; The Secret of Mental Magic*. Chicago: Advanced Thought Publishing Co., 1912; 1940.

———. *New Psychology, Its Message, Principles and Practice*. Chicago: The Progress Co., 1909.

———. *New Thought, Its History and Principles; Or, The Message of the New Thought: A Condensed History of its Real Origin with Statement of Its Basic Principles and True Aims*. Holyoke, MA: Elizabeth Towne, 1915.

———. *Nuggets of the New Thought: Several Things That Have Helped People*. Chicago: The Psychic Research Co., 1902.

———. *Practical Mental Influence*. Chicago, IL: Advanced Thought Publishing Co., 1908.

———. *Practical New Thought; Several Things that Have Helped People*. Chicago: A.C. McClurg and Co., 1911.

———. *The Psychology of Salesmanship*. Holyoke, MA: E. Towne, 1912.

———. *Psychomancy and Crystal Gazing, a Course of Lessons on the Psychic Phenomena of Distant Sensing, Clairvoyance, Psychometry, Crystal Gazing, etc.* Chicago: Advanced Thought Publishing Co., 1907.

———. *Reincarnation and the Law of Karma: A Study of the Old-New World-Doctrine of Rebirth, and Spiritual Cause and Effect*. 1908.

———. *Secret of Success*. Chicago: Advanced Thought Publishing Co., 1908.

———. *Self-Healing by Thought Force*. Chicago: The Library Shelf, 1907.

———. *Subconscious and Superconscious Planes of Mind*. Chicago: The Progress Co., 1909.

———. *Suggestion and Auto-Suggestion*. Chicago: The Progress Press, 1909.

———. *Telepathy: Its Theory, Facts and Proof*. Chicago: New Thought Publishing Co., 1910.

————. *Thought-Force in Business and Everyday Life.* Chicago: The Psychic Research Company, 1901.

————. *Thought Vibration or the Law of Attraction in the Thought World.* Chicago: New Thought Publishing Co., 1906.

————. *The Will: Its Nature, Power and Development.* London: Fowler, 1915.

————. *Your Mind and How to Use It: A Manual of Practical Psychology.* Holyoke, MA: The Elizabeth Towne Co., 1911.

———— (as Magus Incognito). *The Secret Doctrines of the Rosicrucians.* New York: Barnes and Noble, 1993.

———— (as Swami Bhakta Vishita). *A Course of Lessons in Practical Yoga.* Chicago: Advanced Thought Publishing Co., 1900.

———— (as Swami Bhakta Vishita). *The Development of Seership: The Science of Knowing the Future; Hindoo and Oriental Methods.* Chicago: Advanced Thought Publishing Co., 1915.

———— (as Swami Bhakta Vishita). *Genuine Mediumship or the Invisible Powers.* Chicago: Advanced Thought Publishing Co., 1919.

———— (as Swami Bhakta Vishita). *The Mystic Sixth Sense.* Whitefish, MT: Kessinger Publishers, 2005.

———— (as Swami Panchadasi). *The Astral World: Its Scenes, Dwellers, and Phenomena.* Chicago: Advanced Thought Publishing Co., 1915.

———— (as Swami Panchadasi). *A Course of Advanced Lessons in Clairvoyance and Occult Powers.* Chicago: Advanced Thought Publishing Co., 1916.

———— (as Swami Panchadasi). *The Human Aura; Astral Colors and Thought Forms.* Des Plaines, IL: Yoga Publication Society, 1940.

———— (as Theodore Sheldon). *Vim Culture.* Holyoke, MA: The Elizabeth Towne Company, 1913.

———— (as Theron Q. Dumont). *The Advanced Course in Personal Magnetism: The Secrets of Mental Fascination.* Chicago: Advanced Thought Publishing Co., 1914.

———— (as Theron Q. Dumont). *The Master Mind or the Key to Mental Power Development and Efficiency.* Chicago: Advanced Thought Publishing Co., 1918.

———— (as Theron Q. Dumont). *Mental Therapeutics, or Just How to Heal Oneself and Others.* Chicago: Advanced Thought Publishing Co., 1916.

———— (as Theron Q. Dumont). *The Power of Concentration.* Chicago: Advanced Thought Publishing Co., 1918.

———— (as Theron Q. Dumont). *Practical Memory Training.* Chicago: Advanced Thought Publishing Co., 1916.

———— (as Theron Q. Dumont). *The Psychology of Personal Magnetism.* Philadelphia: Domino Publishing Co., n.d.

———— (as Theron Q. Dumont). *The Solar Plexus or Abdominal Brain.* N.P.: 1920.

———— (as Theron Q. Dumont). *Successful Salesmanship.* Chicago: Advanced Thought Publishing Co., 1917.

———— (as The Three Initiates). *The Kybalion: A Study of the Hermetic Philosophy of Ancient Egypt and Greece.* Chicago: Yogi Publication Society, 1940.

———— (as Yogi Ramacharaka). *Advanced Course in Yogi Philosophy.* N.P.: Yogi Publication Society, 1905.

——— (as Yogi Ramacharaka). *Fourteen Lessons in Yogi Philosophy and Oriental Occultism*. Chicago: The Yogi Publication Society, 1931.

——— (as Yogi Ramacharaka). *The Hindu-Yogi Science of Breath*. Chicago: Yogi Publication Society, 1903.

——— (as Yogi Ramacharaka). *The Hindu-Yogi System of Practical Water Cure, as Practiced in India and Other Oriental Countries*. Chicago: The Yogi Publication Society, 1909.

——— (as Yogi Ramacharaka). *Life Beyond Death*. Des Plaines, IL: Yogi Publishing Society, 1937.

——— (as Yogi Ramacharaka). *Mystic Christianity, Or, the Inner Teachings of the Master*. Chicago: Yogi Publication Society, 1908.

——— (as Yogi Ramacharaka). *The Science of Psychic Healing: A Sequel to Hatha-Yoga*. Chicago: Yogi Publication Society, 1906.

——— (Anonymous). *The Arcane Formulas, or Mental Alchemy*. Chicago: Arcane Book Concern, 1909.

——— (Anonymous). *Cosmic Law*. Chicago: McClurg, 1911.

——— (Anonymous). *The Mystery of Sex, or Sex Polarity*. Chicago: McClurg, 1909.

——— (Anonymous). *The One and the Many*. Chicago: McClurg, 1911.

——— (Anonymous). *The Psychic Planes*. Chicago: McClurg, 1911.

——— (Anonymous). *Vril, or Vital Magnetism*. Chicago: McClurg, 1909.

Atkinson, William Walker, and Edward Beals. *Personal Power Books*. 12 vols. London: L. N. Fowler, 1922.

Atkinson, William Walker, and L. W. De Laurence. *Practical Psychomancy and Crystal Gazing: A Course of Lessons on the Psychic Phenomena of Distant Sensing, Clairvoyance, Psychometry, Crystal Gazing, etc*. Chicago: Advanced Thought Publishing Co., 1908.

Baer, Hans. A. *Biomedicine and Alternative Healing Systems in America: Issues of Class, Race, Ethnicity, and Gender*. Madison: University of Wisconsin Press, 2001.

———. *The Black Spiritual Movement: A Religious Response to Racism*. Knoxville: University of Tennessee Press, 1984.

———. "The Metropolitan Spiritual Churches of Christ: The Socio-Religious Evolution of the Largest of the Black Spiritual Associations." *Review of Religious Research* 30 (1988): 140–50.

Bailes, Frederick. *Hidden Power for Human Problems, Your Mind Can Heal You*. Englewood Cliffs, NJ: Prentice-Hall, 1957.

Baldwin, Mark. *Mental Development in the Child and the Race*. New York: Macmillan, 1895.

Banks, A. J. Gayner. *The Healing Evangel*. Milwaukee, WI: Morehouse, 1925.

Barker, Raymond Charles. *Money is God in Action*. Marina del Rey, CA: DeVorss, 1984.

———. *The Power of Decision*. New York: Dodd, Mead, 1968.

———. *Treat Yourself to Life*. New York: Dodd, Mead, 1954.

———. *The Science of Successful Living*. New York: Dodd, Mead, 1957.

Barnett, M. J. *Practical Metaphysics; Or, the True Method of Healing*. Boston: H. H. Carter and Karrick, 1889.

Barrows, Charles Mason. *Bread Pills: A Study of Mind-Cure*. Boston: Deland and Barta, 1885.

———. *Christian Science is not Pantheism*. Boston: Deland and Barta, 1885.

———. *Facts and Fictions of Mental Healing*. Boston: H. H. Carter and Carrick, 1887.

Barrows, John H., ed. *The World's Parliament of Religions*. Vol. 1. Chicago: The Parliament Publishing Co., 1893.

Bartol, Rev. C. A. *Mind in Medicine*. Boston: H. H. Carter and Kerrick, 1886.

Barton, Bruce. *The Man Nobody Knows*. Indianapolis: Bobbs-Merrill, 1925.

Bashford, Alison, and Philippa Levine, eds. *The Oxford Handbook of the History of Eugenics*. New York: Oxford University Press, 2010.

Bates, Ernest B. and John V. Dittemore. *Mary Baker Eddy: The Truth and the Tradition*. New York: Alfred A. Knopf, 1932.

Bauan, Z. *Life in Fragments: Essays in Postmodern Morality*. Oxford: Blackwell, 1995.

Baughman, John Lee. *The Bible as the Story of You: A Journey Into Light*. Marina del Rey, CA: DeVorss and Co., 1980.

Beals, Edward E. *The Inner Secret or That Something Within*. New York: R. F. Fenno and Co., 1922.

———. *The Law of Financial Success*. Chicago: Fiduciary Press, 1907.

———. *Regenerative Power or Vital Rejuvenation*. N.P.: Gardners Books, 2007.

———. *Subconscious Power or Your Secret Forces*. N.P.: Gardners Books, 2007.

Beard, George M. *American Nervousness, Its Causes and Consequences*. New York: G. P. Putnam's Sons, 1881.

Beard, Rebecca. *Everyman's Goal, the Expanded Consciousness*. Wells, VT: Merrybrook Press, 1951.

———. *Everyman's Mission, the Development of the Christ-self*. Bala Cynwyd, PA: Merrybrook Press, 1952.

———. *Everyman's Search*. Wells, VT: Merrybrook Press, 1950.

Beckwith, Michael Bernard. *The Answer is You*. Los Angeles: Agape Media International, 2009.

———. *Forty Day Mind Fast Soul Feast*. Culver City, CA: Agape Publishers, 2000.

———. *Inspirations of the Heart*. Los Angeles: Agape Global Ventures, 2004.

———. *Life Visioning*. Boulder, CO: Sounds True, 2008.

———. *Living From the Overflow: A Practical Guide to a Life of Plenitude*. Louisville, CO: Sounds True, 2010.

———. *Spiritual Liberation: Fulfilling Your Soul's Potential*. New York: Atria Books/ Beyond Words, 2008.

———. *True Abundance Practices for Living from the Overflow*. Boulder, CO: Sounds True, 2010.

———. *Your Soul's Evolution*. Boulder, CO: Sounds True, 2009.

Bednarowski, Mary Farrell. *New Religions and the Theological Imagination in America*. Bloomington: Indiana University Press, 1989.

———. "Outside the Mainstream: Women's Religion and Women Religious Leaders in 19th Century America." *Journal of the Academy of Religion* 48 (1980): 207–31.

Beebe, Tom. *Who's Who in New Thought*. Lakewood, GA: CSA Press, 1977.

Beecher, Henry Ward. *Evolution and Religion*. New York: Fords, Howard and Hulbert, 1885.

———. *Plymouth Pulpit: Sermons Preached in Plymouth Church, Brooklyn*. Boston: Pilgrim Press, 1875.

Behrend, Genevieve. *Your Invisible Power; Working Principles and Concrete Examples in Applied Mental Science*. New York: The School of the Builders, Inc., 1921.

Behrend, Genevieve, and Joe Vitale, *How to Attain Your Desires by Letting Your Subconscious Mind Work for You*. Newport News, VA: Morgan James Publisher, 2005.

Bellah, Robert N. "Civil Religion in America." *Daedalus* 96 (1967): 1–21.

Bellah, R.N., R. Madsen, W. M. Sullivan, A. Swidler, and S. M. Tipton. *Habits of the Heart: Individualism and Commitment in American Life*. Berkeley, CA: University of California Press, 1985.

Bellamy, Edward. *Equality*. New York: D. Appleton and Co., 1897.

———. *Looking Backward*. Boston: Ticknor and Co., 1888.

Bellwald, A. M. *Christian Science and the Catholic Faith, Including a Brief Account of New Thought and Other Modern Mental Healing Movements*. New York: Macmillan, 1922.

Benson, H., and M. Z. Klipper. *The Relaxation Response*. New York: Avon Books, 1976.

Benson, H., and M. Stark. *Timeless Healing: the Power and Biology of Belief*. New York: Simon and Schuster, 1997.

Benz, Ernst. *Theology and Electricity: On the Encounter and Explanation of Theology and Science in the 17th and 18th Centuries*. Allison Park, PA: Pickwick Publishers, 1989.

Bernard, Clinton E., and Jeffrey Fischer. *The Charles Fillmore Concordance: An Expanded Index to the Writings of Charles Fillmore*. Unity Village, MO: Unity Books, 1975.

Besant, Annie. *Thought Power: Its Control and Culture*. London and Benares: The Theosophical Publishing Co., 1901.

Bixby, James Thomson. *The New World and the New Thought*. Boston: The Beacon Press, 1915 [1902].

Bixler, Julius Seelye. "Mysticism and the Philosophy of William James." *International Journal of Ethics* 36 (1925): 71–85.

Blaikie, John S. *How to Get Strong and How to Stay So*. New York: Harper, 1879.

Blanton, Smiley. *Faith is the Answer; A Psychiatrist and a Pastor Discuss Your Problems*. New York: Abingdon-Cokebury Press, 1940.

Blavatsky, Helena. *Isis Unveiled: A Master Key to the Mysteries of Ancient and Modern Science and Theology*. Pasadena, CA: Theosophical University Press, 1972 [1877].

———. *The Key to Theosophy*. London: Theosophical Publishing Co., 1889.

———. *The Secret Doctrine: The Synthesis of Science, Religion and Philosophy*. 2 vols. London: Theosophical Publishing Society, 1893.

Blavatsky, Helena, and William Quan Judge. *The Laws of Healing: Physical and Metaphysical*. Los Angeles: Theosophy Co., 1937.

Block, Marguerite Beck. *The New Church in the New World.* New York: Octagon Books, 1968.

Bloodworth, Venice. *The Key to Yourself.* Marina del Rey, CA: DeVorss, 1981.

Bode, Carl. *The American Lyceum: Town Meeting of the Mind.* Carbondale: Southern Illinois University Press, 1968.

———. *Antebellum Culture.* Carbondale: Southern Illinois University Press, 1970.

———. *The Half-World of American Culture: A Miscellany.* Carbondale: Southern Illinois University Press, 1965 [1923].

Boehme, Kate Atkinson. *The Attainment of Happiness.* Niagara-on-the-Lake, Ontario: Anglo-American Book Co., 1909.

———. *Mental Healing Made Plain.* Washington, D.C.: National Publishing Company, 1902.

———. *New Thought Healing Made Plain.* Holyoke, MA: The Elizabeth Towne Co., 1916.

———. *The Radiant Path to Achievement: How a Miracle of Healing Was Done.* Holyoke, MA: Elizabeth Towne Co., 1917.

———. *Realization Made Easy, for Health, Wealth, Supply, Self-Direction.* Holyoke, MA: The Elizabeth Towne Co., 1916.

———. *Thinking in the Heart; Ten Lessons in Realization.* London: The Power-Book Co., 1912.

Bowler, Peter J. *Evolution: The History of an Idea.* Berkeley: University of California Press, 1984.

Bradbury, Harriet B. *The New Philosophy of Health: A Study of the Science of Spiritual Healing and the Philosophy of Life.* Boston: The Philosophical Publishing Co., 1897.

Braden, Charles S. *Christian Science Today: Power, Policy, Practice.* Dallas: Southern Methodist Press, 1958.

———. *Spirits in Rebellion: The Rise and Development of New Thought.* Dallas: Southern Methodist University Press, 1963.

———. *These Also Believe: A Study of Modern American Cults and Minority Religious Movements.* New York: Macmillan, 1949.

Braden, Gregg. *The Divine Matrix: Bridging Time, Space, Miracles, and Belief.* Carlsbad, CA: Hay House, 2007.

———. *The God Code: the Secret of our Past, the Promise of Our Future.* Carlsbad, CA: Hay House, 2004.

———. *Fractal Time: The Secret of 2012 and a New World Age.* Carlsbad, CA: Hay House, 2009.

———. *The Science of Miracles: The Quantum Language of Healing, Peace, Feeling and Belief.* U.S.: Hun House, 2007.

———. *Secrets of the Lost Mode of Prayer: The Hidden Power of Beauty, Blessing, Wisdom, and Hurt.* London: Hay House, 2006.

———. *The Spontaneous Healing of Belief: Shattering the Paradigm of False Limits.* Carlsbad, CA: Hay House, 2008.

———. *Walking Between the Worlds: The Science of Compassion.* Bellevue, WA: Radio Bookstore Press, 1997.

Braid, James. *Neurypnology; Or, the Rationale of Nervous Sleep, Considered in Relation with Animal Magnetism.* London: Churchill, 1848.

Branch, E. Douglas. *The Sentimental Years, 1836-1860.* New York: Hill and Wang, 1965 [1934].

Bramwell, J. Milne. *Hypnotism, Its History, Practice and Theory.* London: Moring, 1906.

Brande, Dorothea. *Wake Up and Live!* New York: Simon and Schuster, 1936.

Braude, Ann. *Radical Spirits: Spiritualism and Women's Rights in 19th Century America.* Boston: Beacon Press, 1989.

Brent, Charles Henry. *The Sixth Sense: Its Cultivation and Use.* New York: B. W. Huebsch, 1911.

Bridgers, Lynn. *Contemporary Varieties of Religious Experience.* Lanham, MD: Rowman and Littfield, 2005.

Bridges, Hal. *American Mysticism: From William James to Zen.* New York: Harper and Row, 1970.

Brinton, Daniel Garrison. *The Religious Sentiment, Its Source and Aim.* New York: Holt, 1876.

Brisbane, Albert. *The Social Destiny of Man, Or, The Theory of the Four Movements.* New York: Robert M. Dewitt, 1857.

Britten, Emma Hardinge. *Modern American Spiritualism.* New York: published by the author, 1870.

Brock, Erland J. *Swedenborg and His Influence.* Bryn Athyn, PA: Academy of the New Church, 1988.

Bronstein, Jamie. *Land Reform and Working-Class Experience in Britain and the United States.* Stanford, CA: Stanford University Press, 1992.

Brooks, Nona. *Basic Truths: Omnipresence, Omnipotence, Omniscience; Three Addresses.* Denver, CO: n. p., 1921.

———. *In the Light of Healing: Sermons.* Denver, CO: First Divine Science Church, 1986.

———. *Mysteries.* Denver, CO: Welch-Haffner Printing Co., 1924.

———. *The Prayer that Never Fails.* Denver, CO: Divine Science Federation International, 1959.

———. *Short Lessons in Divine Science.* Denver, CO: N. L. Brooks, 1928.

———. *Studies in Health.* Denver, CO: N. L. Brooks, 1925.

———. *The Training of Children: Based Upon the Practical Principles of Life.* Denver, CO: Power Publishing Co., 1900.

———. *What is Real and What Illusion?* Denver, CO: n. p., 1925.

Broomell, Clyde W. *Divine Healing: the Origin and Cure of Disease as Taught in the Bible and Explained by Emanuel Swedenborg.* Boston: George H. Ellis Co., 1907.

Brown, Charles R. *Faith and Health.* New York: T. Y. Crowell and Co., 1910.

———. *The Healing Power of Suggestion.* New York: T. Y. Crowell, 1910.

Brown, Edward M. "Neurology and Spiritualism in the 1870s." *Bulletin of the History of Medicine* 57 (1983): 563–77.

Brown, Henry Harrison. *Concentration: The Road to Success: A Lesson in Soul Culture.* Denver, CO: The Balance, 1907.

———. *New Thought Primer, Origin, History and Principles of the Movement; A Lesson in Soul Culture.* San Francisco: Now Folk, 1903.

Brown, Michael F. *The Channeling Zone: American Spirituality in an Anxious Age.* Cambridge, MA: Harvard University Press, 1997.

Brownell, George B. *Reincarnation.* Santa Barbara, CA: Aquarian Ministry, 1946.

Brownell, Louise Brightman. *Life Abundant for You.* Santa Barbara, CA: Aquarian Ministry, 1936.

Bruce, Alexandra. *Beyond the Secret: The Definitive Unauthorized Guide to the Secret.* New York: The Disinformation Co., 2007.

Bruce, H. Addington. *Scientific Mental Healing.* Boston: Little Brown, 1911.

Bruce, Steve. *Pray TV: Televangelism in America.* London: Routledge, 1990.

Buchanan, Joseph Rodes. "Craniology and Cranioscopy." *Journal of Man* 1 (1849): 157.

———. *Manual of Psychometry: The Dawn of a New Civilization.* Boston: Holman Brothers, 1885.

———. *Outlines of Lectures on the Neurological System of Anthropology.* Cincinnati: Journal of Man, 1854.

———. *Primitive Christianity.* San Jose, CA: Joseph Rodes Buchanan, 1897–98.

———. *Therapeutic Sarcognomy: A Scientific Exposition of the Mysterious Union of Soul, Brain and Body.* Boston: J. G. Cupples Co., 1891.

Buchanan, Uriel. *The Mind's Attainment; A Study of Laws and Methods for Obtaining Individual Happiness, Success and Power Through the Silent Force of Thought.* Chicago: Psychic Research Co., 1902.

Bucke, Richard Maurice. *Cosmic Consciousness: A Study in the Evolution of the Human Mind.* Philadelphia: Innes and Sons, 1905.

Buckley, J. M. *Faith Healing, Christian Science, and Kindred Phenomena.* New York: Century Co., 1887.

Bunker, A. "From Beard to Freud: A Brief History of the Concept of Neurasthenia." *Medical Review of Reviews* 36 (1930): 108–14.

Buranelli, Vincent. *The Wizard from Vienna: Franz Anton Mesmer.* New York: Coward, McCann and Geoghegan, 1975.

Burkmar, Lucius C. *Lucius C. Burkmar's Private Journal.* The Phineas Parkhurst Quimby Resource Center, accessed January 9, 2011. http://www.ppquimby.com/articles/journal.htm.

Burnham, John C. *How Superstition Won and Science Lost: Popularizing Science and Health in the United States.* New Brunswick: Rutgers University Press, 1987.

———. *Paths Into American Culture: Psychology, Medicine, and Morals.* Philadelphia: Temple University Press, 1988.

Bush, David B. *Practical Helps for Health, Poise, Power: Being Selected Articles from Mind Power Plus.* Chicago: D. V. Bush, 1928.

Bush, George and B. F. Barrett. *Davis' Revelations Revealed; Being a Critical Examination of the Character and Claims of That Work in Its Relations to the Teachings of Swedenborg.* New York: John Allen, 1847.

Butler, Jon. *Awash in a Sea of Faith: Christianizing the American People.* Cambridge, MA: Harvard University Press, 1990.

Butler-Bowden, Tom. *50 Prosperity Classics: Attract It, Create It, Manage It, Share It: Wisdom from the Best Books on Wealth Creation and Abundance.* London: Brealy Publishing, 2008.

Butterworth, Eric. *Chicken Soup for the Soul: 101 Stories to Open the Heart and Rekindle the Spirit.* Deerfield Beach, FL: Health Communications, 1993.

———. *Life is for Loving.* New York: Harper and Row, 1973.

Byrne, Rhonda. *The Power.* New York: Atria Books, 2010.

———. *The Secret.* New York: Atria Books, 2006.

———. *The Secret Gratitude Book.* New York: Atria Books, 2007.

Cabot, Richard C. *Psychotherapy and Its Relation to Medicine.* Boston: Emmanuel Church, 1908.

Cady, H. Emilie. *Finding the Christ in Ourselves.* Kansas City, MO: Unity Book Co., 1891.

———. *God a Present Help.* Lee's Summit, MO: Unity Books, 1938.

———. *How I Used the Truth.* Kansas City, MO: Unity School of Christianity, 1916.

———. *Lessons in Truth: A Course of Twelve Lessons in Practical Christianity.* Unity Village, MO: Unity Books, 1995 [1896].

Caine, Ken Winston. *The Positive Bible: From Genesis to Revelation: Scripture that Inspires, Nurtures, and Heals.* Thorndike, ME: G.K. Hall, 1998.

———. *Prayer, Faith and Healing: Cure Your Body, Heal Your Mind, and Restore Your Soul.* Emmaus, PA: Rodale Press, 1999.

Call, Annie Payson. *Power Through Repose.* Boston: Little, Brown and Co., 1900.

Campbell, James Mann. *New Thought Christianized.* New York: T. Y. Crowell, 1917.

Campbell, Nicol C. *My Path of Truth.* Johannesburg, SA: School of Truth, 1953.

Cantor, G. N. "The Edinburgh Phrenology Debate: 1803–1828." *Annals of Science* 32 (1975).

Caplan, Eric. *Mind Games: American Culture and the Birth of Psychotherapy.* Berkeley: University of California Press, 1998.

Carman, Bliss. *The Making of Personality.* Boston: L. C. Page, 1908.

Carnegie, Andrew. "Wealth." *North American Review* 148 (1889): 653–64.

Carnegie, Dale. *How to Win Friends and Influence People.* New York: Simon and Schuster, 1937 [1936].

Carpenter, William B. *Principles of Mental Physiology.* New York: D. Appleton and Co., 1874.

Carter, Crain. *How to Use the Power of Mind in Everyday Life.* Los Angeles: Science of Mind Publications, 1976.

Castberg, Biarne. *The Way That Wins: Principles of Pragmatic Psychology and Applied Christianity for Every-Day Use.* Los Angeles: Divine Power Publishing Co., 1928.

Cather, Willa, and Georgine Milmine. *The Life of Mary Baker Eddy and the History of Christian Science.* Lincoln: University of Nebraska Press, 1993 [1909].

The Catholic Encyclopedia. New York: The Encyclopedia Press, 1922.

Cawelti, John G. *Apostles of the Self-Made Man.* Chicago: University of Chicago Press, 1965.

Chadwick, John White. *William Ellery Channing: Minister of Religion.* Boston: Houghton, Mifflin and Co., 1903.

Chambers, Rev. Arthur. *Our Self After Death.* Philadelphia: G. W. Jacobs, 1916.

Chambers, Robert. *Vestiges of the Natural History of Creation.* London: John Churchill, 1844.

Charcot, Jean-Martin. *Lectures of Localization in Diseases of the Brain.* New York: William Wood, 1878.

Chenoweth, Lawrence. *The American Dream of Success: The Search for the Self in the Twentieth Century.* North Scituate, MA: Duxbury Press, 1974.

Choate, Clara E. *True Christianity: The Basis of Healing with Mind.* Boston: H. H. Carter and Karrick, 1886.

———. *The Unfolding; Or, Mind Understood, the Healing Power.* Boston: Carter, 1883.

Chopra, Deepak. *Ageless Body, Timeless Mind: The Quantum Alternative to Growing Old.* New York: Harmony Books, 1993.

———. *Creating Affluence: Wealth Consciousness in the Field of All Possibilities.* San Rafael, CA: New World Library, 1993.

———. *Quantum Healing: Discovering the Power to Fulfill Your Dreams.* New York: Bantam, 1991.

———. *Unconditional Life: Discovering the Power to Fulfill Your Dreams.* New York: Bantam Books, 1992.

Choquette, Sonia. *Diary of a Psychic: Shattering the Myths.* Carlsbad, CA: Hay House, 2003.

———. *The Psychic Pathway: A Workbook for Reawakening the Voice of Your Soul.* New York: Carol Trade Paperbacks, 1995.

———. *Soul Lessons and Soul Purpose: A Channeled Guide to Why You Are Here.* Carlsbad, CA: Hay House, 2007.

———. *Trust Your Vibes: Secret Tools for Six-Sensory Living.* Carlsbad, CA: Hay House, 2004.

———. *Your Heart's Desire: Instructions for Creating the Life You Really Want.* New York: Three Rivers Press, 1997.

Christian Science Publishing Society. *Christian Science: A Sourcebook of Contemporary Materials.* Boston: The Christian Science Publishing Society, 1990.

Clark, Elmer T. *The Small Sects of America.* Nashville: Abingdon Press, 1949.

Clark, Mason A. *The Healing Wisdom of Dr. P. P. Quimby.* Los Altos, CA: Frontal Lobe, 1982.

Clarke, James Freeman. *Autobiography, Diary, and Correspondence.* New York: Negro Universities Press, 1968.

Chryssides, George D. *Exploring New Religions.* New York: Cassell, 1999.

Cobb, Rev. W. F. *Spiritual Healing.* London: G. Bell and Sons, 1914.

Cocroft, Susanna. *Growth in Silence, Know Thyself.* Chicago: Physical Culture Extension Society, 1905.

Coe, George A. *The Spiritual Life.* New York: Eaton and Mains, 1900.

Cole-Whittaker, Terry. *Dare to be Great: Seven Steps to Spiritual and Material Riches of Life.* New York: Jeremy P. Tarcher/Penguin, 2003.

———. *Every Saint Has a Past, Every Sinner a Future: Seven Steps to the Spiritual and Material Riches of Life.* New York: Jeremy P. Tarcher/Putnam, 2001.

———. *How to Have More in a Have-not World.* New York: Rawson Associates, 1983.

———. *Live Your Bliss: Practices that Produce Happiness and Prosperity.* Novato, CA: New World Library, 2009.

———. *Love and Power in a World Without Limits: A Woman's Guide to the Goddess Within.* San Francisco: Harper and Row, 1989.

Collier, Robert. *Be Rich! The Science of Getting What You Want.* Tarrytown, NY: Book of Gold, 1949.

———. *Book of Life.* New York: R. Collier, 1925.

———. *The Law of the Higher Potential.* Tarrytown, NY: The Book of Gold, 1947.

———. *The Life Magnet.* New York: Jeremy P. Tarcher/Penguin, 2010.

———. *Riches Within Your Reach: The Law of the Higher Potential.* Indialantic, FL: Robert Collier Publications, 1947.

Collyer, Robert H. *Psychography, Or, the Embodiment of Thought; With an Analysis of Phrenomagnetism, "Neurology," and Mental Hallucination, Including Rules to Govern and Produce the Magnetic State.* Boston: Redding, 1843.

Colville, W. J. *Life and Power from Within.* NY: Alliance Publications Co., 1900.

———. *Metaphysical Queries.* Cambridgeport, MA: s.n., 1898.

———.*The Spiritual Science of Health and Healing; Considered in Twelve Lectures, Delivered Inspirationally.* Chicago: Garden City Publishing Co., 1888 [1887].

Combe, George. *The Constitution of Man Considered in Relation to External Objects.* Edinburgh: John Anderson, 1828.

———. *Notes on the United States of North America During a Phrenological Visit in 1838–1839–1840.* Philadelphia: Cary and Hart, 1841.

Conley, John Wesley. *Evolution and Man, Here and Hereafter.* Chicago: Fleming H. Revel Co., 1902.

Conwell, Russell Herman. *"Gleams of Grace." Eight Sermons. To which is added the Chautauqua Report of His Celebrated popular lecture, "Acres of Diamonds."* Uhrichsville, OH: Barbour and Co., 1993.

Coolidge, Herbert. *Mother's Might, How to Use It.* Holyoke, MA: Elizabeth Towne, 1920.

Copeland, Gloria. *God's Will is Prosperity.* Tulsa, OK: Harrison House, 1978.

Coser, Lewis A. *Refuge Scholars in America: Their Impact and Their Experiences.* New Haven, CT: Yale University Press, 1984.

Coué, Émile. *Better and Better Every Day; Two Classic Texts on the Healing Power of the Mind.* London: Allen and Unwin, 1961.

———. *My Method: Including American Impressions.* Garden City, NY: Doubleday, Page and Co., 1923.

———. *Self Mastery Through Conscious Autosuggestion.* New York: American Library Service, 1922.

Courtenay, Rev. Charles. *The Empire of Silence.* New York: Sturgis and Walton, 1916.

Cousin, Victor. *Course of the History of Modern Philosophy.* 2 vols.; New York: D. Appleton and Co., 1852.

———. *Report on the State of Public Instruction in Prussia.* New York: Wiley and Long, 1835.

Cousins, Norman. *Anatomy of an Illness as Perceived by the Patient: Reflections on Healing and Regeneration.* New York: Norton, 1979.

———. *Head First: The Biology of Hope and the Healing Power of the Human Spirit.* New York: Penguin Books, 1990.

Covey, Steven. *The Seven Habits of Highly Effective People*. Melbourne: Business Library, 1989.

Crabtree, Adam. *From Mesmer to Freud: Magnetic Sleep and the Roots of Psychological Healing*. New Haven: Yale University Press, 1993.

Cramer, Malinda. *Basic Statements and Health Treatment of Truth*. San Francisco: M. E. Cramer, 1895.

———. *Divine Science and Healing: A Text-book for the Study of Divine Science, Its Application in Healing, and for the Well-being of Each Individual*. San Francisco: Home College of Divine Science, 1902.

———. *Lessons in the Science of Infinite Spirit, and the Christ Method of Healing*. San Francisco: C.W. Gordon Printer, 1890.

———. *The Unity of Life, and the Methods of Arriving at Truth*. San Francisco; M.E. Cramer, 1888.

Crane, Aaron M. *Right and Wrong Thinking, and their Results; the Undreamed-of Possibilities Which Man May Achieve Through His Own Mental Control*. Boston: Lothrop, 1905.

Curtis, Donald. *Your Thoughts Can Change Your Life*. Englewood Cliffs, NJ: Prentice-Hall, 1961.

Cunningham, Raymond J. "The Emmanuel Movement: A Variety of American Religious Experience." *American Quarterly* 14 (1962): 48–63.

———. "The Impact of Christian Science on the American Churches, 1880–1910." *The American Historical Review* 72 (1967).

Cutten, George Barton. *The Psychological Phenomena of Christianity*. New York: C. Scribner's Sons, 1908.

———. *Three Thousand Years of Mental Healing*. New York: Charles Scribner's Sons, 1911.

Dale, George LeRoy. *Special Methods for Attaining Spiritual Mastery*. Lee's Summit, MO: Unity School of Christianity, 1956.

D'Andrade, Hugh. *Charles Fillmore: Herald of the New Age*. New York: Harper and Row, 1974.

Darnton, Robert. *Mesmerism and the End of the Enlightenment in France*. Cambridge, MA: Harvard University Press, 1968.

Darwin, Charles. *The Origin of Species and the Descent of Man*. New York: The Modern Library, n.d.

Davies, John D. *Phrenology—Fad and Science: A Nineteenth-Century American Crusade*. New Haven: Yale University Press, 1955.

Davis, Andrew Jackson. *The Great Harmonia: Being a Philosophical Revelation of the Natural, Spiritual, and Celestial Universe*. 5 vols.; Boston: Benjamin B. Massey and Co., 1851–66.

———. *The Magic Staff: An Autobiography of Andrew Jackson Davis*. New York: A. J. Davis and Co., 1864.

———. *Penetralia: Being Harmonial Answers to Important Questions*. Boston: Bela Marsh, 1856.

———. *The Present Age and Inner Life; Ancient and Modern Spirit Mysteries Classified and Explained*. Boston: William White and Co., 1870.

———. *The Principles of Nature, Her Divine Revelations, and a Voice to Mankind.* 2 vols.; London: John Chapman, 1847.

Dawson, George Gordon. *Healing: Pagan and Christian.* London: Society for Promoting Christian Knowledge, 1935.

Decker, James A. *Unity's Seventy Years of Faith and Works.* Lee's Summit, MO: Unity School of Christianity, 1959.

Del Mar, Eugene. *Spiritual and Material Attraction; A Conception of Unity.* Denver, CO: The Smith-Brooks Printing Co., 1901.

Delaney, Gayle M. V. *Living Your Dreams: Using Sleep to Solve Problems and Enrich Your Life.* San Francisco: HarperSanFrancisco, 1988.

Delp, Robert W. "Andrew Jackson Davis: Prophet of American Spiritualism." *Journal of American History* 54 (1967): 54.

———. "The Harmonial Philosopher: Andrew Jackson Davis and the Foundation of Modern Spiritualism." Washington, D.C.: Unpublished PhD dissertation, George Washington University, 1965.

Deluze, J. P. F. *Practical Instructions in Animal Magnetism.* 2nd ed. New York: Samuel Wells, 1879.

Denton, William and Elizabeth M. F. *The Soul of Things; Or, Psychometric Researches and Discoveries.* 2 vols. Boston: Walker, Wiso, and Co., 1863.

De Waters, Lillian. *The Christ Within: A Study of the Absolute.* Stamford, CT: L. De Waters, 1925.

———. *Glad Tidings.* Boston: Davis and Bond, 1909.

———. *The Finished Kingdom, A Study of the Absolute.* Stamford, CT: L. De Waters, 1924.

———. *Journeying Onward.* Stamford, CT: Lillian De Waters, 1908.

———. *Thinking Heavenward.* Mt. Vernon, NY: Mrs. Lillan De Waters, 1908.

Dewey, John Hamlin. *The Pathway of the Spirit. A Guide to Inspiration, Illumination and Divine Realization on Earth.* New York: Frank F. Lovell and Co., 1890.

———. *The Way, the Truth, and the Life; A Handbook of Christian Theosophy, Healing and Psychic Culture, a New Education Based on the Ideal and Method of the Christ.* 3rd ed. New York: Frank. F. Lovell and Co., 1888.

Dey, Frederick Van Rensselaer. *The Magic Story.* Auckland, N.Z.: Floating Press, 2008.

Diaz, Mrs. Abby Morton. *The Law of Perfection.* Belmont, MA: s.n., 1886.

———. *Spirit as a Power.* Belmont, MA: s.n., 1886.

Dobbs, Heather Andrews, Valerie Thompson, and Thomas Troward Society. *New Light on Thomas Troward.* London: Thomas Troward Society, 1990.

Dods, John Bovee. *The Philosophy of Electrical Psychology.* New York: S. R. Wells, 1870.

———. *Six Lectures on the Philosophy of Mesmerism.* New York: Fowler and Wells, 1847.

Doherty, William T. "The Impact of Business on Protestantism, 1900–29." *The Business History Review* 28 (1954).

Dolbear, Amos E. *Matter, Ether, and Motion.* London: Society for Promoting Christian Knowledge, 1903.

———. *Science and Theism.* Boston: Universalist Publishing House, 1897.

Dooley, Mike. *Infinite Possibilities: The Art of Living Your Dreams.* New York: Atria Books, 2009.

Dossey, Larry. *Healing Words: The Power of Prayer and the Practice of Medicine.* New York: HarperCollins, 1993.

Dowling, Timothy C., ed. *The African-American Experience in World War.* Santa Barbara, CA: ABC-CLIO, Inc., 2006.

Dresser, Annetta G. *The Philosophy of P. P. Quimby, With Selections from His Manuscripts and a Sketch of His Life.* Boston: G. H. Ellis, 1895.

Dresser, Horatio. *The Christ Ideal: A Study of the Spiritual Teachings of Jesus.* New York: G. P. Putman's Sons, 1904.

———. *Handbook of the New Thought.* New York: G. P. Putnam, 1917.

———. *Health and the Inner Life: An Analytical and Historical Study of Spiritual Healing Theories, With an Account of the Life and Teachings of P. P. Quimby.* New York and London: G. P. Putnam's Sons, 1906.

———. *The Heart of It.* Boston: George Ellis, 1897.

———. *A History of Ancient and Medieval Philosophy.* New York: Thomas Y. Crowell, 1926.

———. *A History of Modern Philosophy.* New York: Thomas Y. Crowell Co., 1928.

———. *A History of the New Thought Movement.* New York: T. Y. Crowell, Co., 1919.

———. *The Immanent God: An Essay.* Boston: Printed by the Author, 1895.

———. *Man and the Divine Order: Essays in the Philosophy of Religion and in Constructive Idealism.* New York and London: G. P. Putnam's Sons, 1903.

———. *A Message to the Well and Other Essays and Letters on the Art of Health.* New York and London: G. P. Putnam's Sons, 1910.

———. *Methods and Problems of Spiritual Healing.* New York: G. P. Putnam's Sons, 1899.

———. *Outlines of the Psychology of Religion.* New York: Crowell, 1929.

———. *The Perfect Whole: An Essay on the Conduct and Meaning of Life.* Boston: G. H. Ellis, 1896.

———. *The Power of Silence: A Study of the Values and Ideals of the Inner Life.* New York and London: G. P Putnam's Sons, 1906 [1895].

———. "The Psychology and Philosophy of Emanuel Swedenborg." Unpublished manuscript, Swedenborg House and Study Library and Archives, Pacific School of Religion, Berkeley, CA.

———. *Psychology in Theory and Application.* New York: Thomas Y. Crowell Co., 1924.

———, ed. *The Quimby Manuscripts; Showing the Discovery of Spiritual Healing and the Origin of Christian Science.* New York: Thomas Y. Crowell, Co., 1921.

———. *The Religion of the Spirit in Modern Life.* New York: G. P. Putnam's Sons, 1914.

———. *In Search of a Soul; A Series of Essays in Interpretation of the Higher Nature of Man.* New York and London: G. P. Putnam's Sons, 1899 [1897].

———, ed. *The Spirit of the New Thought: Essays and Addresses by Representative Authors and Leaders.* New York: Thomas Y. Crowell Co., 1917.

———. *Spiritual Health and Healing.* New York: Thomas Y. Crowell Co., 1922.

—————. *Voices of Freedom: And Studies in the Philosophy of Individuality.* New York and London: G. P. Putnam's Sons, 1899.

Dresser, Julius A. *The True History of Mental Science; the Facts Concerning the Discovery of Mental Healing.* Boston: Ellis, 1899.

Drummond, Henry. *The Changed Life.* New York: James Pott & Co., 1891

—————. *The City Without a Church.* New York: J. Pott, 1893.

—————. *The Greatest Thing in the World.* Mount Vernon, NY: Peter Pauper Press, 1950.

—————. *The Ideal Life.* London: Hodder and Stoughton, 1897.

—————. *A Life for a Life and Other Essays.* Grand Rapids, MI: Christian Classics Ethereal Library, 1990.

—————. *The Lowell Lectures on the Ascent of Man.* New York: J. Pott and Co., 1894.

—————. *Natural Law in the Spiritual World.* New York: J. Pott and Co., 1884.

—————. *The New Evangelism and Other Papers.* New York: Dodd, Mead and Co., 1899.

—————. *Pax Vobiscum.* New York: J. Pott, 1890.

—————. *The Programme of Christianity.* New York: J. Potts and Co., 1892.

—————. *Stones Rolled Away and Other Addresses to Young Men, Delivered in America.* New York: J. Pott and Co., 1899.

DuBois, P. *The Psychic Treatment of Nervous Disorders.* New York: Funk and Wagnalls Co., 1907.

Duff, E. M., and Thomas G. Allen. *Psychic Research and Gospel Miracles.* New York: Thomas Whittaker, 1902.

Dunes, Jackson. *Pug At the Beach, An Island Dog's Reflections on Life.* Keene, NH: AIA Press, 2004.

Dyer, Wayne. *Change Your Thoughts, Change Your Life.* Carlsbad, CA: Hay House, 2007.

—————. *There's a Spiritual Solution to Every Problem.* New York: HarperCollins, 2001.

Eddy, Mary Baker. *Christian Healing; A Sermon Delivered at Boston.* Boston: Trustees of M. B. Eddy, 1914.

—————. *Christian Science: No and Yes.* Boston: Published by the Author, 1887.

—————. *Christian Science Versus Pantheism.* Boston: The Christian Science Publishing Society, 1898.

—————. *Historical Sketch or Christian Science Mind-Healing.* Boston: Published by the Author, 1885.

—————. *Message to the Mother Church, Boston, Massachusetts, June 1901.* Boston: The Christian Science Publishing Society, 1901.

—————. *Miscellaneous Writings, 1883–1896.* Boston: Trustees Under the Will of Mary Baker G. Eddy, 1924.

—————. *The People's Idea of God: Its Effects on Health and Christianity: A Sermon Delivered at Boston.* Boston: The First Church of Christ, Scientist, 1886.

—————. *Retrospection and Introspection.* Boston: Allison V. Steward, 1909 [1891].

—————. *Science and Health with Key to the Scriptures.* Boston: Trustees Under the Will of Mary Baker Eddy, 1906 [1875].

Ehrenreich, Barbara. *Bright-Sided: How the Relentless Promotion of Positive Thinking Has Undermined America.* New York: Metropolitan Books, 2009.

Eleve, *Spiritual Law in the Natural World*. Chicago: Purdy Publishing Co., 1894.

Eliade, Mircea, ed. *The Encyclopedia of Religion*. 15 vols. New York: Macmillan Co., 1987.

Eliot, Charles W. "The Religion of the Future." *Harvard Theological Review* 2 (1909).

Ellenberger, Henri. *The Discovery of the Unconscious: The History and Evolution of Dynamic Psychiatry*. New York: Basic Books, 1970.

Ellis, Havelock. *The Dance of Life*. Boston: Houghton Mifflin Co., 1923.

Ellsworth, Paul. *Direct Healing*. Holyoke, MA: Elizabeth Towne Co., 1916 [1914].

———. *Health and Power Through Creation*. Holyoke, MA: The Elizabeth Towne Co., 1915.

———. *Mind Magnet: How to Unify and Intensify Your Natural Faculties for Efficiency, Health and Success*. Holyoke, MA: The Elizabeth Towne Co., 1924.

Ellwood, Robert S. *The Fifties Spiritual Marketplace: American Religion in a Decade of Conflict*. New Jersey: Rutgers University Press, 1997.

———. *Religious and Spiritual Groups in Modern America*. Englewood Cliffs, N.J.: Prentice-Hall, 1973.

Ellwood, Robert S. and G. D. Alles. *The Encyclopedia of World Religions*. New York: Infobase Publishing, 2007.

Emerson, Ralph Waldo. *The Complete Works of Ralph Waldo Emerson*. 12 vols. Boston: Houghton Mifflin, 1903–1904.

———. *The Conduct of Life and Other Essays*. New York: E. P. Dalton and Co., 1911.

———. *Nature Addresses and Lectures*. Boston: Houghton Mifflin Co., 1876.

Esdaile, James. *Mesmerism in India and its Practical Application in Surgery and Medicine*. New York: Arno Press, 1976 [1846].

Estes, Joseph R. *The Unity School of Christianity*. Atlanta, GA: Home Mission Board SBC, 1968.

Evans, Warren Felt. *The Celestial Dawn; Or, Connection of Earth and Heaven*. Boston: T. H. Carter, 1862.

———. *The Divine Law of Cure*. Boston: H. H. Carter and Co., 1884.

———. *Divine Order in the Process of Full Salvation*. Boston: Henry V. Degen and Son, 1860.

———. *Esoteric Christianity and Mental Therapeutics*. Boston: H. H. Carter and Karrick Publishers, 1886.

———. *Happy Islands, Or, Paradise Restored*. Boston: Henry. V. Degen and Son, 1860.

———. *Healing by Faith; Or, Primitive Mind-Cure. Elementary Lessons in Christian Philosophy and Transcendental Medicine*. London: Reeves and Turner, 1885.

———. *The Mental-Cure, Illustrating the Influence of the Mind on the Body, Both in Health and Disease, and the Psychological Method of Treatment*. 8th ed. Boston: Colby and Rich, 1886 [1869].

———. *Mental Medicine: A Theoretical and Practical Treatise on Medical Psychology*. 6th ed. Boston: Colby and Rich, 1881 [1872].

———. *The New Age and Its Messenger*. Boston: T. H. Carter and Co., 1864.

———. *The Primitive Mind-Cure: The Nature and Power of Faith; Or, Elementary Lessons in Christian Philosophy and Transcendental Medicine*. Boston: H. H. Carter and Karrick, 1884.

———. *Soul and Body; Or, The Spiritual Science of Health and Disease*. Boston: Carter, 1876.

Fallows, Samuel. *Health and Happiness; Or, Religious Therapeutics and Right Living.* Chicago: A. C. McClurg and Co., 1909.

Farr, Cecilia Konchar. *Reading Oprah: How Oprah's Book Club Changed the Way America Reads.* Albany: State University of New York Press, 2004.

Farwell, William. *Be Thou a Blessing.* San Jose, CA: First Christian Assembly, 1936.

Fee, Gordon. *The Disease of the Health and Wealth Gospels.* Vancouver, BC: Regent Publishing, 1985.

Fermi, Laura. *Illustrious Immigrants: The Intellectual Migration from Europe, 1930–41.* Chicago: University of Chicago Press, 1968.

Fillmore, Charles. *Atom-Smashing Power of Mind.* Unity Village, MO: Unity Books, 1949.

———. *Christian Healing.* Unity Village, MO: Unity School of Christianity, 1917.

———. *Dynamics for Living.* Unity Village, MO: Unity Books, 1967.

———. *Jesus Christ Heals.* Unity Village, MO: Unity School of Christianity, 1939 [1936].

———. *Keep a True Lent.* Lee's Summit, MO: Unity School of Christianity, 1953.

———. *Mysteries of Genesis.* Kansas City, MO: Unity School of Christianity, 1936.

———. *Mysteries of John.* Kansas City, MO: Unity School of Christianity, 1946.

———. *Prosperity.* New York: Jeremy P. Tarcher/Penguin, 2008.

———. *The Revealing Word.* Lee's Summit, MO: Unity School of Christianity, 1959.

———. *Talks on Truth.* Kansas City, MO: Unity School of Christianity, 1934.

———. *Teach Us to Pray.* Kansas City, MO: Unity School of Christianity, 1941.

———. *The Twelve Powers of Man.* Lee's Summit, MO: Unity School of Christianity, 1930.

Fillmore, Cora. *Christ Enthroned in Man: Or, The Glorification of the Twelve.* Kansas City, MO: Unity School of Christianity, 1937.

———. *The Twelve Powers.* Unity Village, MO: Unity Books, 1999.

Fillmore, Lowell. *The Prayer Way to Health, Wealth, and Happiness.* Lee's Summit, MO: Unity School of Christianity, 1964.

———. *Things to Be Remembered.* Lee's Summit, MO: Unity School of Christianity, 1952.

———. *The Unity Treasure Chest; A Selection of the Best of Unity Writing.* New York: Hawthorn Books, 1956.

Fillmore, Myrtle. *How to Let God Help You.* Lee's Summit, MO: Unity School of Christianity, 1956.

———. *Letters of Myrtle Fillmore.* Kansas City, MO: Unity School of Christianity, 1936.

———. *Myrtle Fillmore's Healing Letters.* Unity Village, MO: Unity Books, 1981. Finger, Stanley. *Minds Behind the Brain: A History of the Pioneers and Their Discoveries.* New York: Oxford University Press, 2000.

Fiske, John. *The Idea of God as Affected by Modern Knowledge.* Boston: Houghton, Mifflin, 1885.

———. *Outlines of Cosmic Philosophy; Based on the Doctrine of Evolution, with Criticisms on the Positive Philosophy.* Boston: Houghton, Mifflin and Co., 1902 [1875].

Fletcher, Horace. *Menticulture; Or, the A-B-C of True Living.* Chicago: A. C. McClurg and Co., 1895.

Flower, Sydney. *The New Thought System of Dietetics*. Chicago: New Thought Book Department, 1921.

———. *A Study of Hypnotism*. Chicago: Psychic Publishers, 1896.

Fordyce, M. W. "A Program to Increase Happiness: Further Studies." *Journal of Counseling Psychology* 30 (1983): 483–93.

Fothergill, John Milner. *The Will Power: Its Range in Action*. London: Hodder and Stroughton, 1885.

Foulks, Frances W. *All Things Made New; Meditations for Practical Use*. Kansas City, MO: Unity School of Christianity, 1931.

———. *Effectual Prayer*. Holyoke, MA: Elizabeth Towne Co., 1928.

———. *The Secret of Demonstration*. Los Angeles: DeVoress and Co., 1935.

———. *Steps in Spiritual Unfoldment*. London: Fowler, 1929.

Fox, Emmet. *Power Through Constructive Thinking*. New York: Harper and Brothers, 1940.

———. *The Sermon on the Mount: A General Introduction to Scientific Christianity*. New York: Harper and Row, 1938.

Freeman, James Dillet. *The Case for Optimism*. New York: Harper and Row, 1971.

———. *The Household of Faith*. Lee's Summit, MO: Unity School of Christianity, 1956.

———. *Prayer, the Master Key*. Garden City, NY: Doubleday, 1968.

———. *The Story of Unity*. Lee's Summit, MO: Unity School of Christianity, 1954.

Fried, Richard M. *The Man Everybody Knew: Bruce Barton and the Making of Modern America*. Chicago: Ivan R. Dee, 2005.

Frohock, Fred M. *Healing Powers: Alternative Medicine, Spiritual Communities, and the State*. Chicago: University of Chicago Press, 1992.

Frothingham, Octavius Brooks. *Transcendentalism in New England*. New York: Harper and Brothers, 1959 [1876].

Fuller, Robert C. *Alternative Medicine and American Religious Life*. New York: Oxford University Press, 1989.

———. *Americans and the Unconscious*. New York: Oxford University Press, 1986.

———. *Mesmerism and the American Cure of Souls*. Philadelphia: University of Pennsylvania Press, 1982.

Gaines, Edwene. *The Four Spiritual Laws of Prosperity a Simple Guide to Unlimited Abundance*. N.P.: Rodale, 2005.

———. *Prosperity Plus*. Solon, OH: Playaway Digital Audio, 2007.

Gaines, Thomas Robert. *Higher Mental Action*. Milwaukee, WI: Interstate Press, 1936.

Gall, Franz Joseph, and J. G. Spurzheim. *Anatomie et physiologie due système nerveux en general, et du cerveau en particulier*. Paris: Chez F. Schoell, 1810–19.

Gallagher, Eugene V., and W. Michael Ashcraft. *Introduction to New and Alternative Religions in America*. Westport, CT: Greenwood Press, 2006.

Gardner, Martin. *The Healing Revelations of Mary Baker Eddy: The Rise and Fall of Christian Science*. Buffalo, NY: Prometheus Books, 1993.

———. *When You Were a Tadpole and I Was a Fish: And Other Speculations About This and That*. New York: Hill and Wang, 2009.

Gauld, Alan. *The Founders of Psychical Research*. London: Routledge and Kegan Paul, 1968.

George, Carol. V. R. *God's Salesman: Norman Vincent Peale and the Power of Positive Thinking*. New York: Oxford University Press, 1993.

George, Henry. *Progress and Poverty*. San Francisco: W.M. Hinton and Co., 1879

Gestefeld, Ursula N. *The Builder and the Plan; A Textbook of the Science of Being*. Pelham, NY: Gestefeld, 1901.

———. *A Chicago Bible Class*. New York: United States Book Co., 1891.

———. *How We Master Our Fate*. New York: Gestefeld Publishing Co., 1897.

———. *Jesuitism in Christian Science*. Chicago: n.p., 1988.

———. *Reincarnation or Immortality*. New York: Alliance Publishing Co, 1899.

———. *Ursula N. Gestefeld's Statement of Christian Science*. Chicago: Ursula N. Gestefeld, 1888.

———. *What is Christian Science?* Chicago: Published by the Author, 1886.

Gibran, Khalil. *The Prophet*. New York: Knopf, 1942.

Gifford, Elmer M. *New Thought Defined*. Milwaukee, WI: Elmer M. Gifford, 1948.

Gifford, Jr., George E., ed. *Psychoanalysis, Psychotherapy and the New England Medical Scene, 1894–1944*. New York: Science History Publications, 1978.

Gifford, Stanford. *The Emmanuel Movement (Boston, 1904–1929): The Origins of Group Therapy and the Assault on Lay Psychotherapy*. Boston: Frances Countway Library of Medicine, 1996.

Gill, William I. *Philosophical Realism*. Boston: Index Association, 1886.

Glock, Charles Y. *The New Religious Consciousness*. Berkeley: University of California Press, 1976.

Goddard, Neville. *The Power of Awareness*. N.P.: Pacific Pub. Studio, 2010.

Golas, Thaddeus. *The Lazy Man's Guide to Enlightenment*. Palo Alto, CA: Seed Center, 1972.

Gold, August. *The Prayer Chest: A Novel About Receiving All of Life's Riches*. New York: Doubleday, 2007.

———. *Thank You, God, for Everything*. New York: G. P. Putnam's Sons, 2009.

Goldberg, Phillip. *American Veda: From Emerson and the Beatles to Yoga and Meditation. How Indian Spirituality Changed the West*. New York: Harmony Books, 2010.

Goldsmith, Joel S. *The Art of Spiritual Healing*. New York: Harper and Row, 1959.

———. *The Infinite Way*. Marina del Rey, CA: DeVorss, 1983.

———. *The Invisible Supply: Finding the Gifts of the Spirit Within*. San Francisco: HarperCollins, 1994.

———. *Living the Infinite Way*. New York: Harper and Row, 1961.

———. *Practicing the Presence: The Inspirational Guide to Regaining Meaning and a Sense of Purpose in Your Life*. San Francisco: HarperSanFrancisco, 1958.

Goldsmith, Margaret L. *Franz Anton Mesmer: The History of an Idea*. London: A. Barker, 1934.

Goldwag, Arthur. *Isms and Ologies: All the Movements, Ideologies and Doctrines That Have Shaped Our World*. New York: Vintage Books, 2007.

Goodrick-Clarke, Nicholas. *The Western Esoteric Traditions: A Historical Introduction*. New York: Oxford University Press, 2004.

Gosling, Francis G. *Before Freud: Neurasthenia and the American Medical Community, 1870–1919*. Urbana: University of Illinois Press, 1987.

Gottschalk, Stephen. *The Emergence of Christian Science in American Religious Life.* Berkeley: University of California Press, 1973.

Greenbaum, Leon. *Mind and Money, a Text-Book on Spiritual Economics; Or, the Cosmic Laws of Wealth and Success.* Los Angeles: The Open Vision School of Truth, 1923.

Greenland, Cyril, and John Robert Colombo, eds. *The New Consciousness: Selected Papers of Richard Maurice Bucke.* N.P.: Colombo and Co., 1997.

Grier, Albert C. *Truth and Life.* New York: E.P. Dutton and Co., 1921.

Griffith, Ruth Marie. *Born Again Bodies: Flesh and Spirit in American Christianity.* Berkeley: University of California Press, 2004.

Grimké, Sarah Stanley. *Personified Unthinkables, An Argument Against Physical Causation.* Ann Arbor: Register Printing and Publishing House, 1884.

Griswold, Alfred Whitney. "New Thought: A Cult of Success." *American Journal of Sociology* 40 (1934).

Gulick, Luther H. *Mind and Work.* New York: Doubleday and Page, 1909.

Gruss, Edmond C. *Cults and the Occult.* New Jersey: P. and R. Publishers, 1994.

Haanel, Charles F. *The Master Key System.* Hillsboro, OR: Beyond Words Pub., 2008.

———. *The Secret to Getting Rich Trilogy: The Ultimate Law of Attraction Classics.* Berkeley, CA: Ulysses Press, 2008.

Hackett, Alice Payne. *Sixty Years of Best Sellers: Advertising, 1895–1955.* New York: R. R. Bowker, 1956.

Haddock, Frank Channing. *Business Power: A Practical Manual in Financial Ability.* Meriden, CT: Pelton Publishing Co., 1919.

———. *Creative Personality.* Meriden, CT: The Pelton Publishing Co., 1916.

———. *The Culture of Courage: A Practical Companion-Book for Unfoldment of Fearless Personality.* Meriden, CT: Pelton Publishing Co., 1919.

———. *Power for Success Through Culture of Vibrant Magnetism.* Meriden, CT: Pelton Publishing Co., 1918.

———. *Power of Will: A Practical Companion Book for Unfoldment of the Powers of Mind.* Meriden, CT: Pelton Publishing Co., 1916.

Haeckel, Ernst. *The History of Creation.* New York: D. Appleton, 1876.

Hagin, Kenneth. *How to Write Your Own Ticket with God.* Tulsa, OK: K. Hagin Ministries, 1979.

Hale, Jr., Nathan G. *Freud and the Americans: The Beginnings of Psychoanalysis in the United States, 1876–1917.* New York: Oxford University Press, 1971.

———. *The Rise and Crisis of Psychoanalysis in the United States: Freud and the Americans, 1917–1985.* New York: Oxford University Press, 1995.

Haller, Jr., John S. *American Medicine in Transition, 1840–1910.* Urbana: University of Illinois Press, 1981.

———. *The History of American Homeopathy: The Academic Years, 1820–1935.* New York: Haworth Press, 2005.

———. *Medical Protestants: the Eclectics in American Medicine, 1825–1939.* Carbondale: Southern Illinois University Press, 1994.

———. *Swedenborg, Mesmer, and the Mind/Body Connection: The Roots of Complementary Medicine.* West Chester, PA: Swedenborg Foundation, 2010.

Haller, Jr., John S., and Robin M. Haller. *The Physician and Sexuality in Victorian America*. Urbana: University of Illinois Press, 1974.

Hamblin, Henry Thomas. *Right Thinking*. N.P.: Chichester, 1927.

——. *Science of Thought Text Books*. N.P.: Chichester, 1924.

——. *Simple Talks on Science of Thought*. N.P.: Chichester, 1928.

Hanegraaff, Hank. *Bible Answer Book*. Nashville: J. Countryman, 2004.

Hanegraaff, Wouter J. "New Age Religion and Secularization." *Numen* 47 (2000): 288–312.

——. *New Age Religion and Western Culture: Esotericism in the Mirror of Secular*. Albany, NY: State University of New York Press, 1996.

Hangen, Tona J. *Redeeming the Dial: Radio, Religion, and Popular Culture in America*. Chapel Hill: University of North Carolina Press, 2002.

Hanson, Julia. *Awakening to Your Creation*. Huntsville, AR: Ozark Mountain Pub., 2009.

Hardinge, Emma. *Modern American Spiritualism: A Twenty Years' Record of the Communion Between Earth and the World of Spirits*. New York: Published by the Author, 1870.

Hardman, Harvey. *Making Your Self the Master*. Denver: Hardman, 1935.

——. *Mental Power Leaks and How to Stop Them*. Denver: Divine Science College, 1930.

——. *The Silent Partner: Making Our Two Minds Pull Together*. Denver: Colorado College of Divine Science, 1933.

Harley, Gail M. *Emma Curtis Hopkins: Forgotten Founder of New Thought*. Syracuse, NY: Syracuse University Press, 2002.

Hartmann, Edouard Von. *The Philosophy of the Unconscious*. New York: Harcourt, Brace and Co., 1931.

Hawkins, Rev. Chauncey R. *The Quest of Health and Happiness*. Boston: Pilgrim Press, 1908.

Hay, Louise. *You Can Heal Your Life*. Santa Monica, CA: Hay House, 1987.

Haynes, Renée. *The Society for Psychical Research, 1882–1982*. London: Macdonald and Co., 1982.

Heinze, Andrew R. "Jews and American Popular Psychology: Reconsidering the Protestant Paradigm of Popular Thought." *Journal of American History* 88 (2001).

Hepher, Cyril. *The Fellowship of Silence; Being Experiences in the Common Use of Prayer Without Words*. London: Macmillan, 1915.

Herberg, Will. *Protestant, Catholic, Jew: An Essay in American Religious Sociology*. Garden City, NY: Doubleday, 1955.

Herndl, Diane Price. *Invalid Women: Figuring Feminine Illness in American Fiction and Culture, 1840–1940*. Chapel Hill: University of North Carolina Press, 1993.

Herring, Daniel Boone. *Arise and Walk: Or, Jesus the Man, Christ the God*. Los Angeles: DeVorss and Co., 1930.

Hexham, Irving, and Karla O. Poewe. *New Religions as Global Cultures: Making the Human Sacred*. Boulder, CO: Westview Press, 1997.

Hexham, Irving, Stephen Rost, and John W. Morehead II. *Encountering New Religious Movements: A Holistic Evangelical Approach*. Grand Rapids, MI: Kregel Academic and Professional, 2004.

Hickey, Marilyn. *Make Your Faith effectual: Speak the Word*. Denver, CO: Life for Laymen, 1980.

Hicks, Esther, and J. Hicks. *Ask and It is Given: Learning to Manifest Your Desires*. Carlsbad, CA: Hay House, Inc., 2004.

———. *Money, and the Law of Attraction: Learning to Attract Wealth, Health, and Happiness*. Carlsbad, CA: Hay House, 2008.

Hicks, Rosemary R. "Religion and Remedies Reunited: Rethinking Christian Science." *Journal of Feminist Studies in Religion* 29 (2004).

Hill, Napoleon. *The Law of Success*. New York: Jeremy P. Tarcher/Peguin, 2008.

———. *Napoleon Hill's Keys to Success: the Seventeen Principles of Personal Achievement*. New York: Dutton, 1994.

———. *Success Through a Positive Mental Attitude*. Englewood Cliffs, NJ: Prentice-Hall, 1960.

———. *Think and Grow Rich*. New York: Fawcett Columbine, 1991.

Hill, Napoleon, et al. *The Prosperity Bible: The Greatest Writings of All Time on the Secrets to Wealth and Prosperity*. New York: Jeremy P. Tarcher, 2007.

Hill, Patricia R. "Rethinking New Thought." *Reviews in American History* 29 (2001): 85–92.

Hillman, Robert G. "A Scientific Study of Mystery: The Role of the Medical and Popular Press in the Nancy-Salpêtrière Controversy on Hypnotism." *Bulletin of the History of Medicine* 39 (1965): 163–82.

Hitchcock, A. W. *The Psychology of Jesus*. Boston: Pilgrim Press, 1907.

Hoffman, Frank S. *Psychology and Common Life*. New York: G. P. Putnam's Sons, 1907.

Holcombe, William H. *Condensed Thoughts on Christian Science*. Chicago: Purdy Publishing Co., 1887.

Holifield, E. Brooks. *A History of Pastoral Care in America: From Salvation to Self-Realization*. Nashville: Abingdon Press, 1983.

Holland, Jack H. *Man's Victorious Spirit: How to Release the Victory With You*. Monterey, CA: Hudson-Cohan Publishing Co., 1971.

Hollen, Aura May. *Consciousness and Its Purpose*. Hollywood, CA: The Keats Publications, 1931.

Hollinger, David A. *Postethnic America*. New York: Basic Books, 1995.

———. *Science, Jews, and Secular Culture: Studies in Mid-Twentieth Century American Intellectual History*. Princeton: Princeton University Press, 1996.

Holmes, Ernest. *Creative Mind and Success*. New York: Penguin Group, 2004 [1919].

———. *Discover a Richer Life*. New York: Jeremy P. Tarcher/Penguin, 2010.

———. *How to Change Your Life*. Deerfield Beach, FL: Health Communications, 1999.

———. *How to Use the Science of Mind*. New York: Dodd Mead, 1950.

———. *It's Up to You*. New York: Jeremy P. Tarcher/Penguin, 2010.

———. *Mind Remakes Your World*. Chicago: Dodd, Mead and Co., 1941.

———. *New Thought Terms and Their Meanings*. Los Angeles: Institute of Religious Science and Philosophy, 1953.

———. *Living Without Fear*. New York: Jeremy P. Tarcher/Penguin, 2010.

———. *Science of Mind*. New York: Dodd, Mead, 1938 [1926].

———. *Think Your Troubles Away*. New York: Jeremy P. Tarcher/Penguin, 2010.

———. *Thoughts are Things: The Things in Your Life and the Thoughts That are Behind Them*. Deerfield Beach, FL: Health Communications, 1999.

Holmes, Fenwicke L. *Being and Becoming*. New York: R. M. McBride and Co., 1920.

———. *Ernest Holmes: His Life and Times*. New York: Dodd, Mead, 1970.

———. *Healing Treatments in Verse*. Los Angeles: DeVorss, 1943.

———. *How to Develop Faith that Heals*. New York: R. M. McBride and Co., 1919.

———. *The Law of Mind in Action; Daily Lessons and Treatments in Mental and Spiritual Science*. New York: R.M. McBride and Co., 1919.

———. *Practical Healing*. Los Angeles: J. F. Rowny Press, 1921.

———. *Religion and Mental Science*. New York: R. M. McBride, 1929.

———. *Songs of the Silence and Other Poems*. New York: R. M. McBride and Co., 1923.

———. *Text Book of Practical Healing*. Chatsworth, CA: F.L. Holmes, 1943.

———. *The Twenty Secrets of Success*. New York: R. M. McBride and Co., 1927.

———. *The Unfailing Formula*. Los Angeles: Uplift, n.d.

———. *Visualization and Concentration, and How to Choose a Career*. New York: R. M. McBride and Co., 1927.

Holmes, Oliver Wendell. *Ralph Waldo Emerson*. Boston: Houghton, Mifflin and Co., 1894.

Hoolihan, Christopher, and Edward C. Atwater. *An Annotated Catalogue of the Edward C. Atwater Collection*. 3 vols. Rochester, NY: University of Rochester Press, 2001–2008.

Hoopes, James. *Consciousness in New England: From Puritanism and Ideas to Psychoanalysis and Semiotics*. Baltimore: Johns Hopkins University Press, 1989.

Hoover, Stewart M., and Knut Lundby. *Rethinking Media, Religion, and Culture*. Thousand Oaks, CA: Sage, 1997.

Hopkins, Emma Curtis. *All is Divine Order*. Pittsfield, MA: Sun Printing, 1925.

———. *Bible Interpretations*. Cornwall Bridge, CT: Emma Curtis Hopkins Fund, 1892.

———. *Class Lessons, 1888*. Marina del Rey, CA: DeVorss, 1977.

———. *High Mysticism*. New York: Cosimo Classics, 2007 [1888].

———. *Scientific Christian Mental Science*. Santa Monica, CA: DeVorss, 1958.

———. *Self Treatment*. Roseville, CA: High Watch Fellowship, 1900.

———. *Spiritual Law in the Natural World*. Chicago: Purdy Publishing Co., 1894.

———. *The Statement of Being*. Seattle: Metaphysical News, 1930.

Hopkins, Jane Hanford, and Charles Henry Hopkins. *Applied Power*. Cedarville, MI: Published by the Authors, 1926.

Hornaday, William. *Tales From Nature's Wonderlands*. New York: C. Scribner's Sons, 1924.

Hornaday, William, and Harlan Ware. *The Inner Light, An Informal Portrait of a Philosopher*. New York: Dodd, Mead, 1964.

Horowitz, Mitch. *Occult America: The Secret History of How Mysticism Shaped Our Nation.* S.I.: Random House Digital, Inc., 2009.

House, Jeanne M. *Peak Vitality: Raising the Threshold of Abundance in Our Material, Spiritual and Emotional Lives.* Santa Rosa, CA: Elite Books, 2008.

Houston, Jean. *A Mythic Life: Learning to Live Our Greater Story.* San Francisco: HarperSanFrancisco, 1996.

———. *A Passion for the Possible: A Guide to Realizing Your True Potential.* San Francisco: HarperSanFrancisco, 1997.

Howard, Vernon. *Mystic Path to Cosmic Power.* West Nyack, NY: Parker Publishing Co., 1967.

———. *The Power of Your Supermind.* Englewood Cliffs, NJ: Prentice Hall, 1975.

Howison, George Holmes. *The Limits of Evolution and Other Essays Illustrating the Metaphysical Theory of Personal Idealism.* New York: Macmillan, 1905.

Huber, Richard. *The American Idea of Success.* New York: McGraw-Hill, 1971.

Huckel, Oliver. *Mental Medicine: Some Practical Suggestions from a Spiritual Standpoint.* New York: Thomas Y. Crowell and Co., 1909.

Hudson, Thomas J. *The Law of Psychic Phenomena.* Chicago: A. C. McClurg and Co., 1897.

———. *Scientific Demonstration of the Future Life.* Chicago: A. C. McClurg and Co., 1895.

Humphrey, Lucius. *It Shall Be Done Unto You: A Technique of Thinking.* London: Methuen and Co., 1937.

Hunting, Gardner. *Prove Me Now.* Lee's Summit, MO: Unity School of Christianity, 1953.

———. *Working With God.* Unity Village, MO: Unity Books, 1976.

Hyde, John. *Emanuel Swedenborg; A Lecture.* London: Speirs, 1889.

Ingalese, Richard. *The History and Power of Mind.* New York: The Occult Book Concern, 1902.

Ingalese, Richard, and Isabella Ingalese. *The Greater Mysteries.* New York: Dodd, Mead and Co., 1923.

Jackson, Samuel. *Theory of Pneumatology.* London: Longman, Orme, Brown, Green, and Longman, 1834.

James, Fannie Brooks. *Divine Science: New Light Upon Old Truths, To All Who Seek More Light.* Denver: Barkhausen and Lester, 1896.

———. *Truth and Health: Science of the Perfect Mind and the Law of Its Expression.* Denver: Divine Science College, 1942.

James, William. *Essays, Reviews and Comments.* Cambridge, MA: Harvard University Press, 1987.

———. *The Meaning of Truth.* Cambridge, MA: Harvard University Press, 1975 [1909].

———. *The Principles of Psychology.* New York: Dover Publications. 1950 [1890].

———. *The Varieties of Religious Experience: A Study in Human Nature.* New York: Modern Library, 1902.

———. *The Will to Believe, and Other Essays in Popular Psychology, and Human Immortality.* New York: Dover Publishers, 1960 [1899].

———. *Writings, 1902–1910.* New York: Literary Classics, 1987.

Jarrett, R. H. *The Meaning of the Mark; The Miracle Mark of Omar, Adopted as His Guide to Health, Wealth and Happiness; in Three Versions.* Chicago: Larger Life Library, 1931.

Jastrow, Joseph. "Christian Science." *Popular Science Monthly* 58 (1901).

———. *On the Trail of the Subconscious.* S.I.: S.N., 1908.

Jastrow, Morris. *The Study of Religion.* London: W. Scott, 1901.

Jeffrey, H. B. *Coordination of Spirit, Soul and Body.* Fort Worth: Christ Truth League, 1948.

Johnsen, Thomas C. "Historical Consensus and Christian Science: The Career of a Manuscript Controversy." *New England Quarterly* 53 (1980): 3–22.

Jones, David, and Russell S. Woodbridge. *Health, Wealth and Happiness: Has the Prosperity Gospel Overshadowed the Gospel of Christ?* Grand Rapids, MI: Kregel Publications, 2011.

Jones, Ernest. *Papers on Psycho-Analysis.* New York: William Wood and Co., 1913.

Joswich, Thomas P. "The Conversion Drama of 'Self-Reliance': A Logological Study." *American Literature* 55 (1983): 507–24.

Judah, J. Stillson. *The History and Philosophy of the Metaphysical Movements in America.* Philadelphia: Westminster Press, 1967.

Jung, Johann Heinrich. *Theorie der Geister-Kunde.* P.A.: n.p., 1816.

Kaplan, Fred. "The Mesmeric Mania: The Early Victorians and Animal Magnetism." *Journal of the History of Ideas* 35 (1974): 691–693.

Kassem, Suzy. *Rise Up and Salute the Sun: The Writings of Suzy Kassem.* Boston: Awakened Press, 2011.

Katie, Byron, and Stephen Mitchell. *Loving What Is: Four Questions that Can Change Your Life.* New York: Harmony Books, 2001.

Kay, William K., and Anne E. Dyer, eds. *Pentecostal and Charismatic Studies: A Reader.* London: SCM Press, 2004.

Keeler, W. Frederic. *The Self Superlative.* London: L. N. Fowler, 1912.

Kelsey, Morton T. *Psychology, Medicine and Christian Healing.* San Francisco: Harper and Row Publishers, 1988.

Kenilworth, Walter Winston. *The Life of the Soul.* New York: R. F. Fenno and Co., 1911.

Kerr, Howard and Charles L. Crow, eds. *The Occult in America: New Historical Perspectives.* Urbana: University of Illinois Press, 1983.

King, Henry Churchill. *Rational Living; Some Practical Inferences from Modern Psychology.* New York: Macmillan, 1905.

Kleinman, Arthur. *Patients and Healers in the Contest of Culture: An Exploration of the Borderland Between Anthropology, Medicine, and Psychiatry.* Berkeley: University of California Press, 1980.

Knee, Stuart. *Christian Science in the Age of Mary Baker Eddy.* Westport, CT: Greenwood, 1994.

Kraepelin, Emil. *Lectures on Clinical Psychiatry.* New York: Hafner Publishing Co., 1968 [1904].

Kyle, Charles Wesley. *Concentration, the Key to Constructive Thought.* San Francisco, CA: C. W. Kyle, Co., 1916.

Lanyon, Walter C. *2 A.M.* Los Angeles: DeVorss and Co., 1944.

―――. *Impressions of a Nomad*. New York: T. Gaus' Sons, 1930.

―――. *A Lamp Unto My Feet*. Los Angeles: Bookhaven Press, 1941.

―――. *Life More Abundant*. Los Angeles: Kellaway-Ide Co., 1943.

―――. *Out of the Clouds*. Los Angeles: Bookhaven Press, 1941.

Larsen, Robin, ed. *Emanuel Swedenborg: A Continuing Vision*. New York: Swedenborg Foundation, 1988.

Larson, Christian D. *Business Psychology*. New York: Thomas Y. Crowell, 1912.

―――. *The Great Within*. Chicago: Progress Co., 1908.

―――. *The Ideal Made Real; Or, Applied Metaphysics for Beginners*. Chicago: Progress Co., 1909.

―――. *Mastery of Fate*. Chicago: The Progress Co., 1908.

―――. *The Mind Cure*. Los Angeles: The New Literature Publishing Co., 1912.

―――. *Practical Self-Help; Or, How to Make Full and Effective Use of the Greatest and Best That Is in You*. New York: Thomas Y. Crowell Co., 1922.

―――. *Thinking for Results*. Los Angeles: New Literature, 1912.

―――. *What Is Truth*. Los Angeles: New Literature Publishing Co., 1912.

―――. *Your Forces and How to Use Them*. New York: T. Y. Crowell, 1912.

Larson, Martin Alfred. *New Thought; Or, A Modern Religious Approach*. New York: Philosophical Library, 1985.

Lause, Mark. *Young America*. Urbana: University of Illinois Press, 2005.

Lawrence, James F. "An Extraordinary Season in Prayer: Warren Felt Evans' Journey into Scientific Spiritual Practice." *Studia Swedenborgiana* 12 (2002).

Lawson, Agnes. *Hints to Bible Study*. Denver, CO: Colorado College of Divine Science, 1920.

Leavitt, Sheldon. *Paths to the Heights*. New York: T. Y. Crowell and Co., 1908.

Le Conte, Joseph. *Evolution: Its Nature, Its Evidences, and Its Relation to Religious Thought*. New York: D. Appleton and Co., 1897.

Lester, Meera. *365 Ways to Live the Law of Attraction*. Avon, MA: Adams Media, 2009.

Leuba, James Henry. *The Belief in God and Immortality*. Boston: Sherman, French and Co., 1916.

―――. "Psychotherapic Cults: Christian Science, Mind Cure, New Thought." *The Monist* 22 (1912).

Levin, J. *God, Faith, and Health: Exploring the Spirituality-Healing Connection*. New York: John Wiley and Sons, 2001.

Levinson, Henry S. *The Religious Investigations of William James*. Chapel Hill: University of North Carolina Press, 1981.

Lewis, James R. *The Encyclopedia of Cults, Sects, and New Religions*. Amherst, NY: Prometheus Press, 1998.

―――. *The Encyclopedic Sourcebook of New Age Religions*. Amherst, NY: Prometheus Press, 2004.

Lewis, James R. and J. Gordon Melton. *Perspectives on the New Age*. Albany: State University of New York Press, 1992.

Lichtenstein, Morris. *The Conquest of Fear: A Jewish Science View Point*. New York: Society of Jewish Science, 1922.

―――. *Cures for Minds in Distress*. New York: Jewish Science Publishing Co., 1936.

———. *How to Live: Jewish Science Essays*. New York: Jewish Science Publishing Co., 1928.

———. *Jewish Science and Health*. New York: Jewish Science Publishing Co., 1925.

———. *Joy of Life: Jewish Science Essays*. New York: Jewish Science Publishing Co., 1938.

———. *Peace of Mind: Jewish Science Essays*. New York: Jewish Science Publishing Co., 1927.

Liébeault, Ambrose A. *Du sommeil et des etats analogues*. Paris: Victor Masson et fils, 1866.

Lloyd, Henry Demarest. *Wealth Against Commonwealth*. New York: Harper and Brothers, 1894.

Lofton, Ksyjtum. *Oprah: The Gospel of an Icon*. Berkeley, CA: University of California Press, 2011.

Long, Max Freedom. *The Secret Science Behind Miracles*. Los Angeles: Kosmon Press, 1948.

Lynch, Gordon. *The New Spirituality: An Introduction to Progressive Belief in the Twenty-first Century*. London: I. B. Tauris, 2007.

Lynch, Richard. *Know Thyself*. Unity Village, MO: Unity Books, 1935.

———. *The Secret of Health*. Unity Village, MO: Unity Books, 1996.

Mack, Gwynne Dresser. *Talking With God: The Healing Power of Prayer*. Pound Ridge, NY: New-Church Prayer Fellowship, 1960.

MacDonald, Robert. *Mind, Religion and Health, With an Appreciation of the Emmanuel Movement*. New York: Funk and Wagnalls, 1909.

MacLelland, Bruce. *The Law of Success*. New York: R. F. Fenno, 1916.

———. *Prosperity Through Thought Force*. Holyoke, MA: E. Towne, 1907.

McComb, Samuel. *The Healing Ministry of the Church*. Boston: Emmanuel Church, 1908.

McConnell, D. R. *A Different Gospel: A Historical and Biblical Analysis of the Modern Faith Movement*. Peabody, MA: Hendrickson, 1988.

McDannel, Colleen, *Material Christianity: Religion and Popular Culture in America*. New Haven, CT: Yale University Press, 1995.

McWilliams, Peter. *You Can't Afford the Luxury of Negative Thought*. Los Angeles: Prelude Press, 1989.

McWilliams, Peter, and John Roger. *Do It! Let's Get Off Our Buts*. Los Angeles, Prelude Press, 1991.

Mann, Charles H. *Psychiasis: Healing Through the Soul*. Boston: Massachusetts New Church Union, 1900.

Mann, Mildred. *How to Find Your Real Self*. New York: Society of Pragmatic Mysticism, 1952.

———. *Mind and Consciousness*. New York: Society of Pragmatic Mysticism, 1978.

Mann, Stella Terrill. *Change Your Life Through Prayer*. New York: Dodd Mead and Co., 1945.

Marden, Orison Swett. *Ambition and Success*. New York: Thomas Y. Crowell, 1919.

———. *Architects of Fate, or Steps to Success and Power*. Boston: Houghton Mifflin, 1895.

———. *Be Good to Yourself*. New York: T. Y. Crowell and Co., 1910.

———. *Character: The Grandest Thing in the World.* New York: Crowell, 1899.

———. *Cheerfulness as a Life Power.* Boston: T. Y. Crowell and Co., 1899.

———. *Choosing a Career.* Indianapolis: The Bobbs-Merrill Co., 1905.

———. *The Conquest of Worry.* New York: Thomas Y. Crowell Co., 1924.

———. *The Crime of Silence.* New York: Physical Culture Publishing Co., 1915.

———. *Do It To a Finish.* New York: T. Y. Crowell, 1909.

———. *Economy: The Self Denying Depositor and Prudent Paymaster at the Bank of Thrift.* New York: T.Y. Crowell and Co., 1901.

———. *Everybody Ahead, or Getting the Most Out of Life.* New York: F.E. Morrison, 1916.

———. *Every Man a King.* New York: T. Y. Crowell and Co., 1906.

———. *The Exceptional Employee.* New York: Thomas Y. Crowell Co., 1913.

———. *Friendship.* Lexington, KY: Successful Achievement, Inc., 1971.

———. *Getting On.* New York: N. Y. Crowell and Co., 1910.

———. *Good Manners: A Passport to Success.* New York: T. Y. Crowell and Co., 1900.

———. *He Can Who Thinks He Can.* New York. T. Y. Crowell and Co., 1908.

———. *Heading for Victory, or Getting the Most Out of Life.* New York: Success Magazine Corporation, 1922.

———. *The Hour of Opportunity.* New York: T. Y. Crowell and Co., 1900.

———. *How They Succeeded.* Boston: Lothrop Publishing Co., 1901.

———. *How To Get What You Want.* New York: Thomas Y. Crowell Co., 1917.

———. *How to Succeed, or Stepping Stones to Fame and Fortune.* New York: Christian Herald, 1896.

———. *I Had a Friend.* New York: Thomas Y. Crowell Co., 1914.

———. *An Iron Will.* New York: Crowell, 1901.

———. *The Joys of Living.* New York: Thomas Y. Crowell Co., 1913.

———. *Keeping Fit.* New York: Thomas Y. Crowell Co., 1914.

———. *Little Visits With Great Americans, Or, Success, Ideals, and How to Attain Them.* New York: Success Co., 1905.

———. *Love's Way.* New York: Thomas Y. Crowell Co., 1918.

———. *The Masterful Personality.* New York: Thomas Y. Crowell Co., 1921.

———. *Making Life a Masterpiece.* New York: Thomas Y. Crowell Co., 1916.

———. *The Miracle of Right Thought and the Divinity of Desire.* New York: T. Y. Crowell and Co., 1910.

———. *Not the Salary But the Opportunity.* Santa Fe: Sun Publishing Co., 1999.

———. *The Optimistic Life, Or, In the Cheering-up Business.* New York: T. Y. Crowell, 1907.

———. *Peace, Power, and Plenty.* New York: T.Y. Crowell and Co., 1909.

———. *The Power of Personality.* New York: T. Y. Crowell and Co., 1906.

———. *Prosperity: How to Attract It.* New York: Success Magazine, 1922.

———. *Pushing to the Front.* Toledo, NY: The Success Company's Branch Offices, 1911.

———. *Rising in the World, or Architects of Fate.* New York: Crowell, 1897.

———. *Round Pegs in Square Holes.* New York: Thomas Y. Crowell Co., 1922.

———. *The Secret of Achievement.* New York: T. Y. Crowell and Co., 1898.

———. *Self-Discovery or Why Remain a Dwarf.* New York: Thomas Y. Crowell Co., 1922.

———. *Self-Investment*. New York: Thomas Y. Crowell Co., 1911.

———. *Selling Things*. New York: Thomas Y. Crowell, 1916.

———. *Stories from Life, A Book for Young People*. New York: American Book Co., 1904.

———. *Success: A Book of Ideals, Helps, and Examples for All Desiring to Make the Most of Life*. Boston: W. A. Wild and Co., 1897.

———. *Success Fundamentals*. New York: Thomas Y. Crowell Co., 1920.

———. *Success Nuggets*. New York: T. Y. Crowell, 1906.

———. *Thoughts About Character*. New York: Thomas Y. Crowell, 1910.

———. *Thrift*. New York: Thomas Y. Crowell Co., 1918.

———. *Training for Efficiency*. New York: Thomas Y. Crowell Co., 1913.

———. *The Uplift Book of Child Culture*. Philadelphia: Uplift Publishing Co., 1913.

———. *The Victorious Attitude*. New York: Thomas Y. Crowell Co., 1916.

———. *Why Grow Old?* New York: T. Y. Crowell and Co., 1909.

———. *Winning Out*. Boston: Lothrop Publishing Co., 1900.

———. *Woman and Home*. New York: T. Y. Crowell, 1915.

———. *You Can, But Will You?* New York: Thomas Y. Crowell Co., 1920.

———. *The Young Man Entering Business*. New York: T. Y. Crowell, 1903.

Marsden, George M. *The Soul of the American University: From Protestant Establishment to Established Nonbelief*. New York: Oxford University Press, 1994.

Marshall, Henry Rutgers. *Instinct and Reason*. New York: Macmillan Co., 1898.

Marston, L. M. *Essentials of Mental Healing: The Theory and Practice*. Boston: Published by the Author, 1887.

Martin, Alfred W. *Psychic Tendencies of To-Day an Exposition and Critique of New Thought, Christian Science, Spiritualism, Psychical Research, and Modern Materialism in Relation to Immortality*. New York: D. Appleton, 1918.

Martin, Walter R. *The Christian and the Cults: Answering the Cultist from the Bible*. Grand Rapids, MI: Zondervan Publishing Co., 1956.

———. *The Kingdom of the Cults: An Analysis of the Major Cult Systems in the Present Christian Era*. Minneapolis, MI: Bethany Fellowship, 1969.

Martineau, Harriet. *Letters on Mesmerism*. London: Edward Moxon, 1845.

Marty, Martin E. *Righteous Empire*. New York: Deal Press, 1970.

Mason, Osgood. *Telepathy and the Subliminal Self*. New York: Henry Holt and Co., 1899.

Mather, George A., and Larry A. Nichols. *Dictionary of Cults, Sects, Religions, and the Occult*. Grand Rapids, MI: Zondervan Publishing House, 1993.

Mathison, Richard. *Faiths, Cults and Sects of America from Atheism to Zen*. Indianapolis: Bobbs-Merrill Co., 1960.

Matthews, Walter. *Human Life from Many Angles; Teaches You the Law, the Way, the Means, the Methods, to Health, Happiness and Prosperity*. Cincinnati, OH: Goodwill Publishing Co., 1922.

Maxon, J. R. *ReBecoming: the Way of Opportunity*. Anna Maria, FL: Dassana Press, 2009.

Mead, Frank Spencer. *Handbook of Denominations in the United States*. Nashville, TN: Abingdon Press, 1979.

Mead, Sydney E. "American Protestantism since the Civil War. II. From Americanism to Christianity." *The Journal of Religion* 36 (1956): 67–89.

Melton, J. Gordon. *Biographical Dictionary of American Cult and Sect Leaders.* New York: Garland Publishing, Inc., 1986.

———, ed. *The Encyclopedia of American Religions.* 2 vols.; Wilmington, NC: McGrath Publishing Co., 1978.

———. *Religious Leaders of America: A Bibliographical Guide to Founders and Leaders.* Detroit, MI: Gale Research, 1991.

Mencken Henry. *Prejudices: First Series.* New York: Alfred A. Knopf, 1919.

Merrill, T. A. "How to Keep Young." *Practical Ideals* 6 (1903): 9–12.

Merriman, Helen Bigelow. *What Shall Make Us Whole? Or, Thoughts in the Direction of Man's Spiritual and Physical Integrity.* Boston: De. Wolfe, Fisk and Co., 1890 [1888].

Meyer, Donald. "American Intellectuals and the Victorian Crisis of Faith." *American Quarterly* 27 (1975).

———. *The Positive Thinkers; a Study of the American Quest for Health, Wealth and Personal Power from Mary Baker Eddy to Norman Vincent Peale.* Garden City, NY: Doubleday, 1965.

Meyer, Louis E., and Unity School of Christianity. *As You Tithe So You Prosper. A Series of Four Lessons in Tithing.* Kansas City, MO: Unity School of Christianity, 1944.

Meyer, Michael A. *Response to Modernity: A History of the Reform Movement in Judaism.* New York: Oxford University Press, 1988.

Milburn, Maude Frances. *The Gold Mine in You.* Los Angeles: Pacific Envelope and Printing Co., 1924.

Midelfort, H. C. Erik. *Exorcism and Enlightenment: Johann Joseph Gassner and the Demons of 18th Century Germany.* New Haven, CT: Yale University Press, 2005.

Militz, Annie Rix. *All Things Are Possible to Them That Believe.* Los Angeles: The Master Mind Publishing Co., 1905.

———. *Both Honor and Riches, Formerly Prosperity.* Kansas City, MO: Unity School of Christianity, 1945.

———. *Concentration.* New York: The Absolute Press, 1910.

———. *Primary Lessons in Christian Healing and Living and Healing; a Textbook of Healing by the Power of Truth as Taught and Demonstrated by the Master Lord Jesus Christ.* New York: Absolute Press, 1904.

———. *The Renewal of the Body.* Holyoke, MA: The Elizabeth Towne Co., 1914.

———. *Spiritual Housekeeping; A Study in Concentration in the Busy Life.* New York: The Absolute Press, 1910.

———. *The Way to Heal as Taught by Jesus Christ.* Los Angeles: The Master Mind Publishing Co., 1918.

Miller, Julian H. *Can a Jew Be a Jew and a Christian Scientist at One and the Same Time?* Chattanooga, TN: Mizpah Congregation, 1909.

Miller, Timothy. *America's Alternative Religions.* Albany: State University of New York Press, 1995.

Mills, Anna W. *Practical Metaphysics for Healing and Self Culture; Or, the Way to Save Both Soul and Body Now.* Chicago: Universal Truth Publishing Co., 1896.

Mills, Kenneth G. *Change Your Standpoint, Change Your World.* Toronto: Sun-Scape Publishers, 1994.

———. *The Key: Identity; Change Your Standpoint, Change Your World*. Stamford, CT: Sun-Scape Publications, 1994.

Mitchell, John K. "The Emmanuel Movement: Its Pretensions, Its Practice, Its Dangers." *American Journal of the Medical Sciences* (1909): 781–93.

———. *Self-Help for Nervous Women*. Philadelphia: J. P. Lippincott, 1909.

Mitchell, Silas Weir. *Doctor and Patient*. New York: Arno Press, 1972 [1888].

"Modern Faith Healing." *British Medical Journal* 2 (1911): 199–200.

Moody, Elinor S. *How to Remake Yourself Through Applied Psychology*. Holyoke, MA: Elizabeth Towne Co., 1924.

Moore, Laurence. *Religious Outsiders and the Making of Americans*. New York: Oxford University Press, 1986.

———. *In Search of White Crows: Spiritualism, Parapsychology, and American Culture*. New York: Oxford University Press, 1977.

Morgan, David. *Protestants and Pictures: Religion, Visual Culture, and the Age of American Mass Production*. New York: Oxford University Press, 1999.

Morrissey, Mary Manin. *New Thought: A Practical Spirituality*. New York: Jeremy P. Tarcher/Putnam, 2002.

Moses, Alfred G. *Jewish Science: Divine Healing in Judaism, With Special Reference to the Jewish Scriptures and Prayer Book*. Mobile, AL: A.G. Moses, 1916.

———. *Jewish Science; Psychology of Health, Joy and Success; Or, The Applied Psychology of Judaism*. New Orleans: Searcy and Pfaff, 1920.

———. *Universalism and Nationalism in the Prophets*. Unpublished Dissertation, HUC-JIR, 1901.

Moskowitz, Eva S. *In Therapy We Trust: America's Obsession with Self Fulfillment*. Baltimore: Johns Hopkins University Press, 2001.

Mosley, Glenn. *New Thought, Ancient Wisdom: The History and Future of the New Thought Movement*. Philadelphia: Templeton Foundation Press, 2006.

Mozumdar, Akhoy Kuman. *The Commanding Life*. Hollywood, CA: A.K. Mozumdar, 1933.

———. *The Triumphant Spirit: Lesson Book of the Ages, the Christ Message of Today; Convincing, Dynamic, Practical and Spiritual*. Marina del Rey, CA: DeVorss and Co., 1943.

Mulford, Prentice. *The God in You; A Selections from the Essays of Prentice Mulford*. London: William Rider and Son, 1917.

———. *Thoughts Are Things*. Radford, VA: Wilder Publications, 2007.

Mullin, Robert Bruce. "The Debate Over Religion and Healing in the Episcopal Church: 1870–1930." *Anglican and Episcopal History* 60 (1991): 213–34.

———. *Miracles and the Modern Religious Imagination*. New Haven, CT: Yale University Press, 1996.

Mundy, Jon. *Listening to Your Inner Guide*. New York: The Crossroad Publishing Co., 1995.

Munsterberg, Hugo. *Psychotherapy*. New York: Moffat, Yard, 1909.

Murray, William John. *The Astor Lectures on Predestination*. Whitefish, MT: Kessinger Publishers, 2007.

———. *Mental Medicine*. New York: Divine Science Publishing Association, 1923.

———. *The Necessity of Law*. Kila, MT: Kessinger, 1998.

Myss, Caroline. *Anatomy of the Spirit: The Seven Stages of Power and Healing.* New York: Harmony Books, 1996.

———. *Entering the Castle: An Inner Path to God and Your Soul.* New York: Free Press, 2007.

———. *Invisible Acts of Power: Personal Choices that Create Miracles.* New York: Free Press, 2004.

———. *On Life After Death.* Berkeley, CA: Celestial Arts, 2008.

———. *Sacred Contracts: Awakening Your Divine Potential.* New York: Harmony Books, 2001.

———. *Why People Don't Heal and How They Can.* New York: Harmony Books, 1997.

Neuchterlein, James A. "Bruce Barton and the Business Ethos of the 1920s." *South Atlantic Quarterly* 77 (1977): 293–308.

Newcomb, Charles B. *All's Right with the World.* Boston: Lee and Shepard, 1899.

Newman, Mrs. A. B. *Trust in the Infinite.* Boston: T. W. Ripley, 1886.

Newnham, William. *Human Magnetism.* London: J. Churchill, 1845.

Newton, James Rogers. *The Modern Bethesda, Or, the Gift of Healing Restored.* New York: Newton Publishing Co., 1879.

Nightingale, Earl. *Earl Nightingale's Greatest Discovery: "The Strangest Secret— Revisited."* New York: Dodd, Mead, 1987.

———. *The Strangest Secret.* Chicago: Nightingale-Conant Corp., 1988.

Noble, John H. "Psychology on the 'New Thought' Movement." *The Monist* 14 (1904).

Nordhoff, Charles. *The Communist Societies of the United States.* New York: Hillary House Publishers, 1961.

Olston, Albert B. *Mind Power and Privileges.* New York: T. Y. Crowell and Co., 1902.

Osteen, Joel. *Your Best Life Now: Seven Steps to Living at Your Full Potential.* New York: Warner Books, 2004.

Ostrander, Rick. *The Life of Prayer in a World of Science: Protestants, Prayer, and American Culture, 1870–1930.* New York: Oxford University Press, 2000.

O'Sullivan, Michael. *Harmony of Worlds: Spiritualism and the Quest for Community in 19th Century America.* New York: N.P., 1981.

Ouspensky, P. D. *The Cosmic Consciousness of Dr. Richard M. Bucke.* N. P.: Kessinger Publishing Co., 2005.

Page, Walter Hines, ed. *The World's Work 1900–1932.* 6 vols. New York: Doubleday, Page and Co., 1900–32.

Paley, William. *A View of the Evidences of Christianity.* London: Printed for R. Faulder, 1794.

Palmer, Clara, and the Unity School of Christianity. *You Can Be Healed.* Kansas City, MO: Unity School of Christianity, 1937.

Parker, Gail Thain. "How to Win Friends and Influence People: Dale Carnegie and the Problem of Sincerity." *American Quarterly* 29 (1977).

———. *Mind Cure in New England: From the Civil War to World War I.* Hanover, NH: University Press of New England, 1873.

Parker, Merle E. *Instant Healing Now!* Santa Isabel, CA: Foundation for Divine Meditation, 1955.

———. *The Mentalvivology Story*. Thornfield, MO: Published by the Author, 1969.

Parssinen, T. M. "Popular Science and Society; The Phrenological Movement in Early Victorian Britain." *Journal of Social History* 8 (1974): 1–3.

Partlow, Francis. *Training of Children in the New Thought*. N.P.: Sun Books, 1993.

Patterson, Charles Brodie. *The Measure of Man*. New York: Funk and Wagnalls Co., 1904.

———. *New Thought Essays*. New York: Alliance Publishing Co., 1898.

———. *In the Sunlight of Health*. New York: Funk and Wagnalls Co., 1913.

———. *What is New Thought? The Living Way*. New York: Alliance Publishing Co., 1901.

———. *The Will to be Well*. New York: Alliance Publishers, 1901.

Pawelski, James O. "William James, Positive Psychology, and Healthy-Mindedness." *Journal of Speculative Philosophy* 17 (2003): 58–61.

Payot, Jules. *The Education of the Will: The Theory and Practice of Self-Culture*. New York: Funk and Wagnalls, 1910.

Peabody, Francis G. *Jesus Christ and the Social Question*. New York: Macmillan, 1900.

Peale, Norman Vincent. *The Power of Positive Thinking*. New York: Prentice-Hall, 1952.

Peck, Paul Lachlan. *Freeway to Health*. North Granby, CT: Harmony Press, 1982.

———. *Freeway to Human Love*. North Granby, CT: Harmony Press, 1982.

———. *Freeway to Personal Growth*. North Granby, CT: Harmony Press, 1982.

———. *Freeway to Work and Wealth*. North Granby, CT: Harmony Press, 1982.

———. *Inherit the Kingdom*. North Granby, CT: Harmony Press, 1982.

———. *Your Dreams Count: A Layman's Approach to Dream Analysis*. New York: iUniverse, 2005.

Peel, Robert. *Christian Science: Its Encounter with American Culture*. New York: Holt, 1958.

———. *Mary Baker Eddy: The Years of Discovery*. New York: Holt, Rinehart, and Winston, 1966.

———. *Spiritual Healing in a Scientific Age*. San Francisco: Harper and Row Publishers, 1987.

Pelton, Albert Lewis. *The Creed of the Conquering Chief: An Experiment in Psychology Written Down*. Meriden, CT: Pelton Publishing Co., 1915.

Persons, Stow. *American Minds: A History of Ideas*. New York: Holt, Rinehart and Winston, 1958.

———. *Free Religion: An American Faith*. Boston: Beacon Press, 1963 [1947].

Peterson, C., and M. E. P. Seligman. *Character Strengths and Virtues: A Handbook and Classification*. Washington, D.C.: American Psychological Association, 2004.

Pettigrew, Thomas J. *Superstitions Connected with the History and Practices of|Medicine and Surgery*. London: John Churchill, 1844.

Pfister, Joel and Nancy Schnog, eds. *Inventing the Psychological: Toward a Cultural History of Emotional Life in America*. New Haven: Yale University Press, 1997.

Pike, Sarah M. *New Age and Neopagan Religions in America*. New York: Columbia University Press, 2004.

Podmore, Frank. *Mesmer to Christian Science: A Short History of Mental Healing.* Philadelphia: George W. Jacobs and Co., 1909.

———. *Modern Spiritualism: A History and a Criticism.* 2 vols.; London: Methuen and Company, 1902.

Poloma, Margret M. "A Comparison of Christian Science and Mainline Christian Healing Ideologies and Practices." *Review of Religious Research* 32 (1991): 337–50.

Pomeroy, Ella. *Powers of the Soul and How to Use Them.* New York: Island Press, 1948.

Ponder, Catherine. *The Dynamic Laws of Healing.* Marina del Rey, CA: DeVorss, 1985.

———. *The Dynamic Laws of Prayer.* Marina del Rey, CA: DeVorss, 1987.

———. *The Dynamic Laws of Prosperity; Forces that Bring Riches to You.* Marina del Rey, CA: DeVorss, 1985.

———. *Pray and Grow Rich.* West Nyack, NY: Parker Publishing Co., 1968.

———. *The Prosperity Secrets of the Ages.* Marina del Rey, CA: DeVorss and Co., 1986.

Pounders, Margaret. *Finding Your Inner Harmony.* Unity Village, MO: Unity, 1993.

———. *Laws of Love.* Unity Village, MO: Unity Books, 1979.

Powell, Edward Payson. *Our Heredity from God.* New York: D. Appleton, 1887.

Powell, Lyman P. *Christian Science: The Faith and Its Founder.* New York: G. P. Putnam's Sons, 1908.

———. *The Emmanuel Movement in a New England Town.* New York: G. P. Putnam's Sons, 1909.

Poyen, Charles. *Progress of Animal Magnetism in New England.* New York: DeCapo Press, 1982 [1837].

Pratt, James Bissett. *The Religious Consciousness: A Psychological Study.* New York: Macmillan, 1920.

Proctor, Bob. *You Were Born Rich: Now You Can Discover and Develop Those Riches.* Cartersville, GA: LifeSuccess Productions, 1997.

Quimby, Phineas Parkhurst. *The Complete Writings.* Ed. Ervin Seale. 3 vols. Marina del Rey, CA: DeVorss, 1988.

———. *The Quimby Manuscripts: Showing the Discovery of Spiritual Healing and the Origin of Christian Science.* Ed. Horatio Dresser. New York: T. Y. Crowell Co., 1921.

Randall, John Herman. *Man's Undeveloped Powers. Awakening Latent Mental Powers. The Achievement of Character.* New York: H. M. Calwell, 1909.

———. *A New Philosophy of Life.* New York: Dodge Publishing Co., 1911.

———. *The Rebirth of Religion: Spiritual Consciousness. The Rediscovery of Jesus.* Boston: H. M. Caldwell, Co., 1909.

———. *The Spirit of the New Philosophy.* New York: Brentano's, 1919.

Rapport des commissaries chargés par le Roy de l'examen du Magnétisme Animal. Paris: De l'Imprimerie Royal, 1789.

Raschke, Carl A. *The Interruption of Eternity: Modern Gnosticism and the Origins of the New Religious Consciousness.* Chicago: Nelson-Hall, 1980.

Rawson, F. L. *Life Understood from a Scientific and Religious Point of View, and the Practical Method of Destroying Sin, Disease, and Death.* London: The Crystal Press, 1912.

Redfield, James. *The Celestine Prophecy: An Adventure.* New York: Warner Books, 1993.

———. *The Celestine Vision: Living the New Spiritual Awareness.* New York: Warner Books, 1997.

———. *The Tenth Insight: Holding the Vision.* New York: Warner Books, 1996.

Reed, Jr., Myer S. "After the Alliance: The Sociology of Religion in the United States from 1925 to 1949." *Sociological Analysis* 543 (1982).

Reese, Della. *Angels Along the Way: My Life with Help from Above.* New York: G. P. Putnam's Sons, 1997.

———. *God Inside of Me.* New York: Hyperion Books for Children, 1999.

Reichenbach, Karl von. *Psycho-Physiological Researches on Dynamides or Imponderables, Magnetism, Electricity, Heat, Light, Crystallization, and Chemical Attraction, in Their Relation to Vital Force.* London: Taylor, Walton and Mabarly, 1850.

"Reichenbach's Researches on Magnetism." *Journal of Man* 1 (1849): 67–70.

Riepe, Dale. *The Philosophy of India and Its Impact on American Thought.* Springfield, IL: Charles C. Thomas, 1970.

"Researches of Baron Reichenbach on the 'Mesmeric,' Now Called the Odic Force." *The American Whig Review* 15 (1852): 485–501.

Reynolds, David S. "From Doctrine to Narrative: The Rise of Pulpit Storytelling in America." *American Quarterly* 32 (1980): 479–98.

Ribuffo, Leo P. "Jesus Christ as Business Statesman: Bruce Barton and the Selling of Corporate Capitalism." *American Quarterly* 33 (1981): 206–31.

Riley, Woodbridge. *American Thought from Puritanism to Pragmatism.* Cloucester, MA: Peter Smith, 1959 [1915].

Risse, Guenter B., Roland L. Numbers, and Judith Walzer Leavitt, eds. *Medicine Without Doctors: Home Health Care in American History.* New York: Science History Publications, 1977.

Rix, Harriet. *The Christ Mind.* Los Angeles: Home of Truth Publishing Co., 1925.

———. *Christian Mind Healing, A Course of Lessons in the Fundamentals of New Thought.* Los Angeles: Master Mind Publishing Co. 1914.

———. *The Rich Mentality.* Los Angeles: The Master Mind Publishing Co., 1916.

Rhodes-Wallace, Helen. *Sleep as the Great Opportunity: Or, Psychcoma.* Holyoke, MA: Elizabeth Towne, 1918 [1908].

———. *Religious Education for New Thought Children.* New York: The London Book Concern, 1911.

Robinson, Frank B. *The Psychiana, the Teaching that is Bringing New Life to a Spiritually Dead World. Lessons.* Moscow, ID: Psychiana, 1949–51.

———. *The Strange Autobiography of Frank B. Robinson: Founder of "Psychiana," Moscow, Idaho.* Moscow, ID: Psychiana Inc., 1941.

Rogers, D. T. *The Work Ethic in Industrial America, 1850–1920.* Chicago: University of Chicago Press, 1979.

Roof, Wade Clark. *A Generation of Seekers: the Spiritual Journeys of the Baby Boom Generation.* San Francisco: HarperSanFrancisco, 1993.

Rooney, Kathleen. *Reading with Oprah: The Book Club that Changed America.* Fayetteville: University of Arkansas Press, 2005.

Root, Julia Anderson. *Healing Power of Mind. A Treatise on Mind-Cure, with Original Views on the Subject, and Complete Instructions for Practice, and Self Improvement.* San Francisco: Women's Cooperative Printing House, 1884.

Rosemergy, Jim. *A Closer Walk with God.* Lakewood, CO: Awakening, Acropolis Books, 1997.

———. *Living the Mystical Life Today.* Lee's Summit, MO: Inner Journey, 1987.

———. *The Transcendent Life: Understanding the Nature of True Power.* Lakewood, CO: Acropolis Books, 1998.

———. *The Quest for Meaning: Living a Life of Purpose.* Unity Village, MO: Unity Books, 1999.

Roth, Charles. *Mind, the Master Power.* Unity Village, MO: Unity Books, 1974.

Royce, Josiah. *Outlines of Psychology.* New York: Macmillan, 1903.

———. *The Religious Aspect of Philosophy.* New York: Harper, 1958.

Russell, Robert A. *Getting Better Results from Spiritual Practice.* Denver, CO: Guild of Religious Science, 1939.

Sadler, William S. *The Physiology of Faith and Fear.* Chicago: A. C. McClurg, 1912.

Satter, Beryl. *Each Mind a Kingdom: American Women, Sexual Purity, and the New Thought Movement, 1875–1920.* Berkeley: University of California Press, 1999.

Savelle, Jerry. *Victory and Success Are Yours!* Tulsa, OK: Harrison House, 1982.

Schenck, Ruthanna, and Unity School of Christianity. *Be Ye Prospered.* Kansas City, MO: United School of Christianity, 1929.

Schmidt, Leigh Eric. *Consumer Rites: The Buying and Selling of American Holidays.* Princeton, NJ: Princeton University Press, 1995.

Schneck, Jerome M. "Jean-Martin Charcot and the History of Experimental Hypnosis," *Journal of the History of Medicine and Allied Sciences* 16 (1961): 297–300.

Schneider, Herbert W. *A History of American Philosophy.* New York: Columbia University Press, 1946.

Schobert, Theodosia DeWitt, and Unity School of Christianity. *Divine Remedies; A Textbook on Christian Healing.* Kansas City, MO: Unity School of Christianity, 1945.

Schoepflin, Rennie B. *Christian Science on Trial: Religious Healing in America.* Baltimore: Johns Hopkins University Press, 2003.

Schofield, Alfred T. *The Force of Mind; Or, the Mental Factor in Medicine.* New York: Funk and Wagnalls, 1908.

———. *Modern Spiritism; Its Science and Religion.* Philadelphia: P. Blakiston, 1920.

———. *The Unconscious Mind.* New York: Funk and Wagnalls Co., 1901.

Schuller, Robert H. *Move Ahead with Possibility Thinking.* Old Tappan, NY: Revell, 1967.

Scolastico, Ron. *Doorway to the Soul: How to Have a Profound Spiritual Experience.* New York: Scribner, 1995.

———. *Healing the Heart, Healing the Body: A Spiritual Perspective on Emotional, Mental, and Physical Health.* Carson, CA: Hay House, 1992.

Seldes, Gilbert. *The Stammering Century.* New York: Harper and Row, 1965 [1928].

Seligman, Martin. *Authentic Happiness: Using the New Positive Psychology to Realize Your Potential for Lasting Fulfillment.* New York: Simon and Schuster, 2002.

Seton, Julia. *Concentration, the Secret of Success.* New York: E. J. Clode, 1912.

———. *Fundamental Principles of the New Civilization, New Thought; Student's Manual.* New York: E. J. Clode, 1916.

———. *The Key to Health, Wealth, and Love.* New York: E. J. Clode, 1917.

Severn, Elizabeth. *Psychotherapy: Its Doctrines and Practices.* Philadelphia: McKay, 1914.

Seward, Theodore F. *The Don't Worry Philosophy.* New York: Crowell, 1894.

———. *Spiritual Knowing or Bible Sunshine: The Spiritual Gospel of Jesus the Christ.* New York and London: Funk and Wagnalls Co., 1901 [1900].

Sheldon, Ellen H. *Direction for Health on a Metaphysical Basis.* Washington, D.C.: Rufus H. Darby, 1887.

Sheldon, Henry C. *Theosophy and New Thought.* New York and Cincinnati: The Abingdon Press, 1916.

Sheldon, Theodore. *Vim Culture.* Holyoke, MA: Elizabeth Towne Co., 1913.

Shepard, Leslie. *Encyclopedia of Occultism and Parapsychology.* Detroit, MI: Gale Research Co., 1984.

Shinn, Florence Scovel. *The Game of Life and How to Play It.* Marina del Rey, CA: DeVorss, 1925.

———. *How to Prosper in Hard Times.* New York: Jeremy P. Tarcher/Penguin, 2009.

———. *The Power of the Spoken Word.* Marina del Rey, CA: DeVorss, 1978.

———. *The Secret Door to Success.* Saffron Walden: C. W. Daniel, 1999.

———. *Your Word Is Your Wand.* Saffron Walden: C. W. Daniel, 1999.

Short, S. E. D. "Physicians and Psychics: The Anglo-American Response to Spiritualism, 1870–1890." *Journal of the History of Medicine and Allied Sciences* 39 (1984): 339–55.

Shultz, J. Kennedy. *A Legacy of Truth: Your Mind, Great Minds, One Mind.* Atlanta: Brob House, 1993.

———. *Questions Jesus Asked.* Marina del Rey, CA: DeVorss, 1982.

———. *You Are the Power: A Guide to Personal Greatness.* Carson, CA: Hay House, 1993.

Shumsky, Susan G. *Miracle Prayers: Nine Steps to Creating Prayers that Get Results.* Berkeley, CA: Celestial Arts, 2006.

Sidis, Boris. *Multiple Personality.* New York: Greenwood Press, 1968 [1904].

Siegel, B. S. *Love, Medicine and Miracles: Lessons Learned About Self-Healing From a Surgeon's Experience with Exceptional Patients.* New York: Harper and Row, 1986.

Simmons, Dale H. *E. W. Kenyon and the Postbellum Pursuit of Peace, Power, and Plenty.* Lanham, MD: Scarecrow Press, 1997.

Simmons, John Kent. "The Ascension of Annie Rix Militz and the Homes of Truth: Perfection Meets Paradise in Early 20th Century Los Angeles." Unpublished PhD thesis, University of California Santa Barbara, 1987.

———. "The Forgotten Contributions of Annie Rix Militz to the Unity School of Christianity." *Nova Religio: The Journal of Alternative and Emergent Religions* 2 (1998): 76–92.

Sizer, Nelson. *Forty Years in Phrenology: Embracing Recollections of History, Anecdote, and Experience.* New York: Fowler and Wells Co., 1888.

Smiles, Samuel. *Self-Help the Art of Achievement, Illustrated by Accounts of the Lives of Great Men.* Champaign, IL: Project Gutenberg, 1990.

———. *Self-Help; With Illustrations of Conduct and Perseverance.* London: J. Murray, 1958.

Smith, Arthur Preston. "The Power of Thought to Heal: An Ontology of Personal Faith." Unpublished PhD dissertation, Claremont Graduate University, 1998.

Smith, Christian, ed. *The Secular Revolution: Power, Interests, and Conflict in the Secularization of American Life.* Berkeley: University of California Press, 2003.

Smith, Eldridge. *In His Image.* S.I.: E. Smith, 1887.

Smith, H. *Rethinking America.* New York: Random House, 1995.

Smith, Kevin Scott. "Mind, Might, and Mastery: Human Potential in Metaphysical Religion and E. W. Kenyon." Unpublished master's thesis, Liberty University Graduate School of Religion, 1995.

Smyth, Julian, and William F. Wunsch. *The Gist of Swedenborg.* Philadelphia: J. P. Lippincott Company, 1920.

Spalding, John Howard. *Introduction to Swedenborg's Religious Thought.* New York: Swedenborg Publishing Association, 1977.

Spinney, William Anthony. *Health Through Self-Control in Thinking, Breathing, Eating.* Boston: Lothrop, Lee and Shepard Co., 1906.

Sprague, Frank H. *Spiritual Consciousness.* Wollaston, MA: F. H. Sprague, 1898.

Spurzheim. J. G. *Phrenology in Connexion with the Study of Physiognomy.* Boston: Marsh, Capen and Lyon, 1826.

St. John, Noah. *Permission to Succeed.* Deerfield Beach, FL: Health Communications, 1999.

———. *The Secret Code of Success: 7 Hidden Steps to More Wealth and Happiness.* New York: HarperCollins Publishers, 2009.

Stark, Rodney, William S. Bainbridge, and Daniel P. Doyle. "Cults of America: A Reconnaissance in Space and Time." *Sociological Analysis* 40 (1979): 347–59.

Starker, Stephen. *The American Preoccupation With Self-Help Books.* New Jersey: Transaction Publishers, 2002.

Stein, Stephen J. "Retrospection and Introspection: The Gospel According to Mary Baker Eddy." *Harvard Theological Review* 75 (1982): 97–116.

Steiner, Rudolph. *Autobiography: Chapters in the Course of My Life: 1861–1907.* MA: Anthroposophic Press, 2006.

———. *The Story of My Life.* NY: Anthroposophic Press, 1928.

Stempel, Daniel. "Angels of Reason: Science and Myth in Enlightenment," *Journal of the History of Ideas* 36 (1975): 63–78.

Stern, Madeleine B. *Heads and Headlines: The Phrenological Fowlers.* Norman: University of Oklahoma Press, 1971.

Stevens, Lucie Beckham. *The Progressive Life and Its Requirements: Or, the Beneficence of Nature's Laws.* Los Angeles: Concord Publishing Co., 1907.

Stevens, Margaret. *Prosperity is God's Idea.* Marina del Rey, CA: DeVorss and Co., 1978.

Stokes, Allison. *Ministry After Freud.* New York: Pilgrim, 1985.

Stone, W. Clement. *The Success System that Never Fails.* Englewood, NJ: Prentice-Hall, 1962.

Strout, Cushing. "The Pluralistic Identity of William James: A Psycho-Historical Reading of 'The Varieties of Religious Experience.'" *American Quarterly* 23 (1971): 135–52.

Stuart, Mrs. E. G. *Healing Power of Thought*. Hyde Park, MA: E. G. Stuart, 1887.

Suess, Jenean B. *The Science of Practical Christianity*. Oakland, CA: J. B. Suess, 1894.

Sunderland, La Roy. *The Pathetism: With Practical Instructions*. New York: P. P. Good, 1847.

———. *The Trance and Correlative Phenomena*. Chicago: J. Walker, 1868.

Swank, Scott Trego. "The Unfettered Conscience: A Study of Sectarianism, Spiritualism, and Social Reform in the New Jerusalem Church, 1840–1870." Unpublished PhD thesis, University of Pennsylvania, 1970.

Sweaney, James E. *Practical Christianity for You*. Lee's Summit, MO: Unity Books, 1956.

Swedenborg, Emanuel. *A Compendium of the Theological Writings of Emanuel Swedenborg*. New York: Swedenborg Foundation, 1974.

———. *The Economy of the Animal Kingdom, Considered Anatomically, Physically, and Philosophically*. London: William Newbery, 1846.

———. *Divine Love and Wisdom*. Trans. George F. Dole. West Chester, PA: Swedenborg Foundation, 2003.

———. *Heaven and Hell*. Trans. George F. Dole. West Chester, PA: Swedenborg Foundation, 2000.

———. *Secrets of Heaven*. Trans. Lisa Hyatt Cooper. 2 vols. West Chester, PA: Swedenborg Foundation, 2008–2011.

Synnestvedt, Sigfried T., ed. *The Essential Swedenborg: Basic Teachings of Emanuel Swedenborg, Scientist, Philosopher, and Theologian*. New York: Twayne Publishers, 1970.

Taniguchi, Masaharu. *Divine Education and Spiritual Training of Mankind*. Tokyo: Divine Publication Department, 1956.

———. *Recovery from All Diseases: Seicho-no-Ie's Method of Psychoanalysis*. Tokyo: Divine Publication Department, 1963.

Taves, Ann. *Fits, Trances, and Visions: Experiencing Religion and Explaining Experience from Wesley to James*. Princeton: Princeton University Press, 1999.

Taylor, Douglas. *The Hidden Levels of the Mind*. West Chester, PA: Swedenborg Foundation, 2011.

Taylor, Eugene. "Positive Psychology and Humanistic Psychology: A Reply to Seligman." *Journal of Humanistic Psychology* 41 (2001): 13–29.

———. *Shadow Culture: Psychology and Spirituality in America*. Washington, D.C.: Counterpoint, 1999.

Teahan, John F. "Warren Felt Evans and Mental Healing: Romantic Idealism and Practical Mysticism in Nineteenth Century America." *Church History* 48 (1979).

Teener, James Woodruff. "The Unity School of Christianity." Unpublished PhD thesis, University of Chicago Divinity School, 1939.

Thompson, L. Buckland. *Exact Science of Christianity; Or, Mystery of the Subconscious Mind Revealed, Immortality a Fact*. Garden City, NY: Country Life Press, 1916.

Toksvig, Signe. *Emanuel Swedenborg: Scientist and Mystic*. New Haven, CT: Yale University Press, 1948.

Torgovnick, Marianna. *Primitive Passions: Men, Women, and the Quest for Ecstasy.* New York: Alfred A. Knopf, 1997.

Towne, Elizabeth Jones. *Experiences in Self-Healing.* Holyoke, MA: E. Towne, 1905.

———. *Fifteen Lessons in New Thought, Or Lessons in Living.* SI: Gardner Books, 2007 [1910].

———. *Happiness and Marriage.* Holyoke, MA: E. Towne, 1904.

———. *How to Grow Success.* Holyoke, MA: E. Towne, 1903.

———. *How to Use New Thought in Home Life.* Holyoke, MA: E. Towne Co., 1915.

———. *Lessons in Living.* Holyoke, MA: E. Towne, 1911.

———. *The Life Power and How to Use It.* Holyoke, MA: E. Towne, 1906.

———. *Joy Philosophy.* New York: S. Flower, 1903.

———. *Just How to Concentrate.* Holyoke, MA: E. Towne, 1904.

———. *Practical Methods for Self-Development, Spiritual—Mental—Physical.* Holyoke, MA: E. Towne, 1904.

———. *You and Your Forces: Or, the Constitution of Man.* Holyoke, MA: E. Towne, 1926.

Towne, Elizabeth Jones, and Wallace Wattles. *Health Through New Thought and Fasting.* Holyoke, MA: E. Towne, 1907.

Towne, William E. *Health and Wealth from Within.* U.S.: Gardner Books, 1986.

———. *The Way to Perfect Healing. The Power of the Word in Ancient and Modern Spiritual Healing. How to Apply this Power in Self-Healing. How to Train the Mind to Realize Health.* Holyoke, MA: William E. Towne, 1910.

Tracy, Brian. *Create Your Own Future.* Hoboken, NJ: Wiley, 2002.

Travis, Trysh. "'It Will Change the World if Everybody Reads This Book': New Thought Religion in Oprah's Book Club." *American Quarterly* 59 (2007): 1017–41.

Treitel, Corinna. *A Science for the Soul: Occultism and the Genesis of the German Modern.* Baltimore: Johns Hopkins University Press, 2004.

Triem, Paul Ellsworth. *Direct Healing.* Holyoke, MA: The Elizabeth Towne Co., 1916.

———. *The Mind Magnet; How to Unify and Intensify Your Natural Faculties for Efficiency, Health and Success.* Holyoke, MA: The Elizabeth Towne Co., 1924.

Trine, Ralph Waldo. *Character Building Thought Power.* Regio Park, NY: Gildan Media Corp., 2005.

———. *The Greatest Thing Ever Known.* New York: Thomas Y. Crowell and Co., 1898.

———. *The Man Who Knew; How He Brought the Good News that the Kingdom of God Is Within Us, and We May Put Ourselves in Tune with the Centre of Life.* Indianapolis: The Bobs-Merrill Co., 1936.

———. *In Tune With the Infinite.* New York: T. Y. Crowell, 1897.

———. *The Wayfarer on the Open Road.* London: G. Bell and Sons, 1919.

———. *What All the World's A-Seeking: Or, the Vital Law of True Life, True Greatness, Power, and Happiness.* New York: Crowell, 1899.

Troward, Thomas. *The Creative Process in the Individual.* New York: McBride, Nast and Co., 1915.

———. *The Dore Lectures on Mental Science.* New York: Roger Brothers, 1909.

———. *The Edinburgh Lectures on Mental Science.* New York: Dodd, Mead and Co., 1909.

———. *The Hidden Power And Other Papers on Mental Science.* New York: Dodd, Mead, 1921.

———. *The Law and the Word.* New York: Dodd, Mead and Co., 1950 [1917].

Tuke, Daniel H. *The Influence of the Mind Upon the Body in Health and Disease.* Philadelphia: Henry C. Lea's Son and Co., 1884.

Tumber, Catherine. *American Feminism and the Birth of New Age Spirituality: Searching for the Higher Self, 1875–1915.* Lanham, MD: Rowman and Littlefield, 2002.

Turley, David. *American Religion: Literary Sources and Documents.* The Banks, Mountfield, U.K.: Helm Information, 1998.

Tuttle, Joseph Erwin. *Prosperity Through Thought Force.* Holyoke, MA: E. Towne, 1907.

Tweed, Thomas. *The American Encounter with Buddhism, 1844–1912: Victorian Culture and the Limits of Dissent.* Chapel Hill, NC: University of North Carolina Press, 1992.

———, ed. *Rethinking U.S. Religious History.* Berkeley: University of California Press, 1997.

Ullman, Dana. *The Homeopathic Revolution: Why Famous People and Cultural Heroes Choose Homeopathy.* Berkeley, CA: North Atlantic Books, 2007.

Umansky, Ellen M. *From Christian Science to Jewish Science: Spiritual Healing and American Jews.* New York: Oxford University Press, 2005.

Vahle, Neal. *The Spiritual Journey of Charles Fillmore: Discovering the Power Within.* Philadelphia: Templeton Foundation Press, 2008.

———. *The Unity Movement: Its Evolution and Spiritual Teachings.* Philadelphia: Templeton Foundation Press, 2002.

Van-Anderson, Helen. *Journal of a Live Woman.* Boston: G.H. Wright, 1895.

———. *The Mystic Scroll, a Book of Revelation.* New York: New York Magazine, 1906.

———. *The Right Knock.* Chicago: H. Van Anderson, 1889.

Vanzant, Iyanla. *One Day My Soul Just Opened Up: 40 Days and 40 Nights Toward Spiritual Strength and Personal Growth.* New York: Fireside, 1998.

———. *Tapping the Power Within: A Path to Self-Empowerment for Women.* London: Hay House, Inc., 2008.

Versluis, Arthur. *Magic and Mysticism; An Introduction to Western Esotericism.* Lanham, MD: Rowman and Littlefield Publishers, 2007.

Veith, Ilza. "From Mesmerism to Hypnotism." *Modern Medicine* (1959): 195–205.

Waldstein, Louis. *The Subconscious Self and Its Relation to Education and Health.* New York: C. Scribner's Sons, 1897.

Walker, Edward. *Thoughts Are Things.* Chicago: The Progress, 1909.

Wallace, Helen Kelsey. *How to Enter the Silence.* London: L. N. Fowler, 1920.

Wallis, J. *The Soul of Politics.* New York: New Press, 1994.

Walsh, Mary Roth. *"Doctors Wanted, No Women Need Apply": Sexual Barriers in the Medical Profession, 1835–1975.* New Haven, CT: Yale University Press, 1977.

Warman, Edward B. *Psychic Science Made Plain.* 2 vols. Holyoke, MA: The Elizabeth Towne Co., 1914.

Warner, Frances Larimer. *Our Invisible Supply.* Chicago: The Library Shelf, 1907.

Wattles, Wallace. *Making the Man Who Can.* Holyoke, MA: E. Towne, 1909.

———. *The Science of Being Great.* New York: Jeremy P. Tarcher/Penguin, 2007.

———. *Science of Being Well*. Largo, FL: Top of the Mountain Publishers, 1993.

———. *The Science of Getting Rich*. New York: Atria Books, 2007 [1910].

Weatherhead, Leslie D. *Psychology, Religion and Healing*. New York: Abingdon Press, 1952.

Webb, James. *The Occult Establishment*. La Salle, IL: Open Court Publishing Co., 1976.

Weber, Francis J. *The Religious Heritage of Southern California: a Bicentennial Survey*. Los Angeles: Interreligious Council of Southern California, 1976.

Weiss, John, ed. *Life and Correspondence of Theodore Parker. Vol. 1*. London: Longman, Treen, 1863.

Weiss, Richard. *The American Myth of Success: From Horatio Alger to Norman Vincent Peale*. New York: Basic Books, 1969.

Welsh, Frank Manington, and Frances Lillian Gordon. *Thinking Success into Business*. Chicago: Weldon Press, 1932.

Werkmeister, W. H. *A History of Philosophical Ideas in America*. New York: Ronald Press Co., 1949.

West, Georgiana Tree. *Prosperity's Ten Commandments*. Kansas City, MO: Unity School of Christianity, 1946.

Whalen, William Joseph. *Faith for the Few: A Study of Minority Religions*. Milwaukee, WI: Bruce Publishing Co., 1963.

Whaley, Harold. "The Collection and Preservation of the Materials of the New Thought Movement, to Which is Appended a Bibliography of New Thought Literature from 1875 to the Present." Unpublished master's thesis, University of Missouri, Columbia, 1973.

Whipple, Leander Edmund. *The Philosophy of Mental Healing: a Practical Exposition of Natural Restorative Power*. New York: The Metaphysical Publishing Co., 1893.

White, Andrew D. *History of the Warfare of Science with Theology in Christendom*. 2 vols. New York: D. Appleton and Co., 1898.

White, Bouck. *The Call of the Carpenter*. Garden City, NY: Doubleday, 1911.

White, Christopher G. "Minds Intensely Unsettled: Phrenology, Experience, and the American Pursuit of Spiritual Assurance, 1830–1860." *Religion and American Culture: A Journal of Interpretation* 16 (2006): 227–61.

Whitehead, John. *The Illusions of Christian Science, Its Philosophy Rationally Examined*. Boston: The Garden Press, 1907.

Whitehouse, Deborah G. *Practicing the Presence of God for Practical Purposes*. Bloomington, IN: 1st Books, 2000.

Whiting, Lilian. *The Land of Enchantment from Pike's Peak to the Pacific*. Boston: Little, Brown and Co., 1906.

———. *The World Beautiful*. Boston: Roberts Brothers, 1897.

Whitman, Walt. *Leaves of Grass*. Philadelphia: Rees Welsh and Co., 1882 [1855].

Whitney, Frank B. *Be of Good Courage*. Lee's Summit, MO: Unity School of Christianity, 1953.

———. *Beginning Again: A Guide to Taking a New Hold on Life*. Kansas City, MO: Unity School of Christianity, 1943.

Wilcox, Ella Wheeler. *The Heart of the New Thought*. Chicago: The Psychic Research Company, 1902.

———. *Poems of Power*. Chicago: W. B. Conkey Co., 1901.

———. *Poems of Progress; and New Thought Pastels*. Chicago: Albert Whitman and Co., 1909.

———. *Sonnets of Sorrow and Triumph*. New York: George H. Doran Co., 1918.

Wilkinson, James John Garth. *Emanuel Swedenborg: A Biography*. London: William Newbery, 1849.

Williamson, Marianne. *A Return to Love: Reflections on the Principles of a Course in Miracles*. New York: HarperCollins, 1996.

Wilmans, Helen. *Blossom of the Century*. Atlanta, GA: The Foote and Davies Co., 1893.

———. *Conquest of Death*. London: Ernest Bell, 1902.

———. *Conquest of Poverty*. Sea Breeze, FL: International Scientific Association, 1899.

———. *Home Course in Mental Science*. London: G. Bell, 1914.

———. *Second Birth: A Practical Treatise on Mental Healing*. Douglasville, GA: H. Wilmans, 1888.

Wilson, Ernest Charles. *The Great Physician: Master Class Lessons*. Kansas City, MO: Unity School of Christianity, 1956.

Wilson, Floyd B. *Man Limitless*. New York: R. F. Fenno and Co., 1905.

———. *Paths to Power*. New York: R. F. Fenno and Co., 1901.

Winkley, J. W. *First Lessons in the New Thought; Or, the Way to the Ideal Life*. Boston: James H. West Co., 1904.

Winslow, Forbes. *On the Obscure Diseases of the Brain and Disorders of the Mind*. New York: Arno Press, 1976 [1860].

Witherspoon, Thomas E. *Myrtle Fillmore: Mother of Unity*. Unity Village, MO: Unity Books, 1984.

Wood, Henry. *Edward Burton*. Boston: Lee and Shepard Publishers, 1890.

———. *God's Image in Man: Some Intuitive Perceptions of Truth*. Boston: Lee and Shepard Publishers, 1892.

———. *Ideal Suggestion Through Mental Photography: A Restorative System for Home and Private Use Preceded by a Study of the Laws of Mental Healing*. Boston: Lee and Shepard Publishers, 1893.

———. *Natural Law in the Business World*. Boston: Lee and Shepard, 1887.

———. *The New Thought Simplified: How to Gain Harmony and Health*. Boston: Lee and Shepard, 1903.

———. *Victor Serenus: A Story of the Pauline Era*. Boston: Lee and Shepard Publishers, 1898.

Woofenden, William Ross. *Swedenborg Explorer's Guidebook: A Research Manual for Inquiring New Readers, Seekers of Spiritual Ideas, and Writers of Swedenborgian Treatises*. Revised 2nd ed. West Chester, PA: Swedenborg Foundation, 2008.

Worcester, Elwood. *Allies of Religion*. Boston: Marshall Jones, 1929.

———. *The Living Word*. New York: Moffat, Yard and Co., 1908.

Worcester, Elwood, and Samuel McComb. *Body, Mind and Spirit*. Boston: Marshall Jones, 1931.

———. *The Christian Religion as a Healing Power*. New York: Moffat, Yard, 1909.

Worcester, Elwood, Samuel McComb, and Isador Coriat. *Religion and Medicine: The Moral Control of Nervous Disorders*. New York: Moffat, Yard, 1908.

Wuthnow, R. *Sharing the Journey: Support Groups and America's New Quest for Community*. New York: Free Press, 1994.

Wyckoff, Albert Clarke. *The Non-Sense of Christian Science*. New York: Fleming H. Revell Co., 1921.

Yarnall, Jane W. *Practical Healing for Mind and Body. A Complete Treatise on the Principles and Practice of Healing by a Knowledge of Divine Law*. Chicago: E. M. Harley Publishing Co., 1893 [1891].

York, Michael. *The Emerging Network: A Sociology of the New Age and Neo-Pagan Movements*. Lanham, MD: Rowman and Littlefield, 1995.

———. *Historical Dictionary of New Age Movements*. Lanham, MD: Scarecrow Press, 2004.

Young, Caroline, and Cyndie Koopsen. *Spirituality, Health, and Healing: An Integrative Approach*. Sudbury, MA: Jones and Bartlett, 2005.

Young, Robert M. "The Functions of the Brain: Gall to Ferrier (1808–1886)." *Isis* 59 (1968): 250–68.

Zender, Tom. *God Goes to Work: New Thought Paths to Prosperity and Profits*. Hoboken, NJ: John Wiley and Sons, 2010.

Zukav, Gary. *The Seat of the Soul*. New York: Simon and Schuster, 1989.

Zweig, Stefan. *Mental Healers; Anton Mesmer, Mary Baker Eddy, Sigmund Freud*. New York: Garden City, 1932.

Index

Buckley, James Monroe, 35–36
Bulwer-Lytton, Edward, 213
Burkmar, Lucius, 46–48
Burnham, John, 155
Bush, Dr. George, 40
business ethos, 235, 236
Byrne, Rhonda, vii–viii, 244; on law of
attraction, 255–56, 257, 258

C
Cabot, Dr. Richard C., 123, 149
Cady, Dr. Harriet Emilie, 103, 223; on
Unity, 99, 105–6
Caldwell, Dr. Charles, 36
Canfield, Jack, 256
Carlyle, Thomas, 118
Carnegie, Andrew, 179, 224, 234, 238
Carnegie, Dale B., 14, 217, 238–40
Carus, Paul, 209
Cather, Willa, 66
Cayce, Edgar, 12, 197
Center for Awakening Consciousness,
248
channeling, 197–98, 256
Channing, William Ellery, 10
character ethic, 122, 216–17, 218, 240
Character Strengths and Virtues Scale,
156–57, 310n91
Charcot, Jean-Martin, 28, 123, 147
charisma, 228; and personality ethic,
254, 269–70, 271
charity, 177, 179, 184–85. See also social
gospel
Charles, George and Lizzie, 97
Chasidic movement, 201–2
Chenevix, Richard, 27
Chesley, Egbert Morse, 79
Cho, David Yonggi, 270
chochmoh, 200
Chopra, Deepak, 13, 244, 257, 260, 267
Christ. See Jesus
Christian and Missionary Alliance, 105
Christian Assembly, 219
"Christian Science" ("Christ Science")
(term), 4, 54, 55, 82, 95, 122

Christian Science, 7, 63, 191, 205, 206;
as absolute idealism, 94–95; colleges
of, 90–91; on death, 88; defections
from, 92, 97–103; divine principles of,
83–84; differs from other religions,
87–88, 92–93; Eddy claims to
discover, 80, 81–82, 84; Emmanuel
Movement compared to, 152–53;
Evans on, 95; healing in, 85, 93; on
illness as evil, 93; influence of, 104,
108, 109; James on, 126, 128; on Jesus's
role, 88; and Jews, 199–201; journal of,
91, 98; as pantheism, 84; on prayer,
93; Quimby's, 54, 55–56, 64, 82, 122;
Theosophy compared to, 84; women
attracted to, 90, 91; Wood on, 94, 254
Christian Science Association, 90, 91
Christian Science Journal, 91, 98
Christian Science Theological
Seminary, 99
Christian Yoga, 114–15
Christ ideal, 138, 172, 173
Christ Universal Temple, 246
Church and School of the New
Civilization, 120–21
Church of Christ, Scientist (Eddy's), 89,
90, 92
Church of Divine Science, 8, 113. *See also*
Divine Science
Church of Religious Science, 111. *See
also* Religious Science
Church of the Divine Unity, 63
Church of the Higher Life, 99, 120
Church of the New Jerusalem, 9, 34, 58,
66, 67
Church of Truth, 248
clairvoyance, 27, 29, 41, 211, 238;
criticized, 83, 131; Davis uses, 39–40;
in diagnosis, 35, 40; Quimby uses, 45,
47–49, 50
Cobbs, Rev. Clarence H., 248
Cogswell, Joseph G., 21
Cohen, Morris Raphael, 125
Cohen, Sheldon, 157
Coleman, Rev. Johnnie, 246

Quimby on, 49, 50, 212; Swedenborg on, 69; Theosophy on, 207, 210. *See also* healing

Divine Science, 103, 108–11; churches of, 8, 99, 113; colleges of, 108–9, 110; healing in, 109, 110; journal of, 108

Divine Science Church of the Healing Christ, 113

Divine Science College 108, 110

Divine Science Federation International, 248

divinity, 105, 173–74; aspiring to, 122, 124; science proves, 32–33, 34. *See also* God

Dods, John Bovee, 36, 51

Doherty, William T., 236

Dolbear, Amos E., 119

Dollar, Rev. Creflo A. Jr., 269–70

Dossey, Larry, 259, 260

Dowie, John Alexander, 191

dream: disease as, 100–101; interpretation, 203, 261–62

Dresser, Alice Mae (Reed), 132

Dresser, Annetta Seabury, 54, 61–63, 82, 131

Dresser, Horatio Willis, ix, 62, 111, 119, 126, 130–46, 148, 153; on affirmation, 158; on body's role, 145; on brain's role, 145; on Christ-ideal, 138; on clairvoyance, 131; on democracy, 231–32; on disease, 140, 146, 154; on Emerson, 276; on Emmanuel Movement, 154; on evolution, 131, 164–65; on freedom, 138–39; on God, 131, 133, 136, 137–38, 163–64; idealism of, 133; interprets Swedenborg, 141–45; on Jesus, 177; journals of, 131–32; on mediumship, 131; on mind, 134, 136; optimism of, 231–32; on power of suggestion, 139; on practicality, 135, 138; psychology and, 136, 141–45, 146; on Quimby, 59, 60, 83, 134; on receptivity, 139–40; on self-reliance, 137–38; on self-knowledge, 136, 143; on silence, 134–40; on sin, 140; on

the soul, 137–38, 143, 145; "Spiritual Science" of, 62–63; writings of, 131, 132–33, 134–40

Dresser, Julius, ix, 54, 61, 63, 131

drug therapy, 193, 206, 259

Drummond, Henry, 161

Dumont, Theron Q., 226. *See also* William Walker Atkinson

Dyer, Wayne Walter, 257, 265–66

E

Eddy, Asa Gilbert, 80, 89

Eddy, Mary Baker, 54, 80–92, 205; allays fear in patients, 86–87; on animal magnetism, 81, 88, 92, 95; as authoritarian, 93–94, 95; autobiography of, 88–90; Bible interpreted by, 83; claims to found Christian Science, 80, 81–82, 84; on clairvoyance, 83; college of, 90–91, 98; compares herself to Jesus, 89, 90; defections from beliefs of, 97, 117, 194; on divine mind, 84, 87–88, 90; Divine Principles of, 83–85; on early Christian healing, 85; Evans's system compared to, 94, 95–96; on faith, 86; on God, 84; on healing by Jesus, 82, 84; on healing as mental, 65, 81, 82, 86, 87–88; heard voices, 88–89; on homeopathy, 85–86, 89; on hydropathy, 89; on hypnosis, 87, 88; idealism of, 93, 94, 95, 117; influence/legacy of, 94, 98, 99, 100, 104, 109, 111, 152, 194, 200, 201, 271; on materialistic healing, 85–86, 89; on mediumship, 85; on mesmerism, 83, 88; mother church of, 89, 90, 92; occultism of, 65; as pantheist, 94; on phrenology, 85; on Quimby, 80, 81; as Quimby's disciple, 61, 64, 65, 67, 80, 81, 89, 95; Quimby's writings as basis for hers, 64, 82, 83; *Science and Health* of, 67, 82, 83, 87, 88, 89, 90, 93, 152, 201; on Spiritualism, 83, 85; on suggestion, 87; treatment techniques of, 86–87; on theism, 84; on Theosophy, 84

Edwards, Jonathan, 225
Eikerenkoetter, Rev. Frederick (Rev.
  Ike), 270
electricity, 36
electro-biology, 36
Eliot, Charles W., 274–75
Elliotson, Dr. John, 27–28, 32, 35
Ellis, Havelock, 130
Ellsworth, Paul, 13, 223, 224–26
Emerson, Charles Wesley, 220, 269
Emerson, Ralph Waldo, 5, 21, 43; on
  conversion, 18, 23, 65; on God, 5;
  influence of, 7, 12–13, 23, 37, 63, 100,
  105, 111, 118, 127, 132, 133, 182, 217, 275;
  on lyceum circuit, 22; optimism
  of, 5, 231; "Over-Soul," 9, 12, 84, 131;
  on religion, 23–24; on self-reliant
  individual, 22–23, 137, 187, 230,
  233, 276; on Swedenborg, 141, 144;
  transcendentalism of, 10–11, 126;
  as transparent eyeball, 5, 22; on
  Universal Soul, 24; wisdom of, 276
Emerson School of Oratory, 220, 269
Emerson Theological Institute, 8, 246,
  247
Emma Hopkins College of
  Metaphysical Science, 99, 113
Emmanuel Movement, 146, 147–55,
  258; biomedicine used by, 192;
  compared to Christian Science,
  152–53; on God's role in healing,
  151–52; hypnosis used by, 152, 154;
  imitated, 153, 154; suggestion used by,
  151; treated functional, not organic,
  diseases, 150, 152
Engledue, W. C., 32
enlightenment, sought, 232, 262–68
Esdaile, James, 28
ether, 73–74
etherium, 36
eugenics, 184
Evans, George Henry, 20
Evans, M. Charlotte Tinker, 66
Evans, Warren Felt, 54, 59–60, 66–79,
  139; anticipated Eddy, 82; anticipated

Freud, 79; on auras, 69–70, 71; on
  biomedicine, 78, 96; "Christian
  Science" (term) used by, 95; on disease,
  65, 71, 79; Eddy's system compared to,
  94–96; on faith, 76–77, 79; on God's
  immanence, 69; healing system of, 66–
  67, 68, 72, 73, 76–78, 86, 97; idealism
  of, 76, 79, 94; influence of, 67–68, 79,
  95–96, 134, 212, 271; on interior man,
  69, 71, 79; on Jesus's healing, 72, 73–74,
  78–79; on law of correspondences, 68,
  71; on mesmerism, 66–67, 75; mind-
  cure system (phrenopathy) of, 72, 73,
  74, 76–78, 93; on phrenology, 69; on
  prayer, 74, 96; as Quimby's disciple,
  61, 64, 65, 66, 67, 68–69, 77, 93, 95,
  96; on religion, 78; on silence, 134;
  as Spiritualist, 66–67, 97; suggestion
  used by, 67, 75, 78; Swedenborg
  influences, 66, 67, 68–69, 71, 74, 77, 96,
  140; thought-transference used by 73,
  77–78; Universal Life Principle of, 96;
  writings of, 67–68, 76–77
Everett, Edward, 21
evolution/evolutionary theory, 8–9,
  160–89, 221; acceptance of, 176–78; as
  anti-materialistic, 161; Bible's authority
  threatened by, 163, 174; Christ-ideal
  reached by, 172, 173; Darwin's, 8, 160,
  161, 162, 166; Dewey on, 173; Dresser
  on, 131, 164–65; as God's design, 164,
  166, 168, 169–70, 171, 172, 173, 188–89; of
  ideas, 181-83; Le Conte on, 172; man's
  role in, 166, 169, 173, 175, 186–87; in
  mind cure, 126, 160–61, 166; morality
  in, 171; natural selection in, 8, 164, 165;
  optimism in, 126, 162; as progress/
  growth, 160, 164–65, 166–67, 169,
  173–75, 207; as purposeful, 173, 176,
  221; religion confirmed by, 174; and
  social reform, 178–79; Spencer on,
  141; in success, 180–81; as theistic, 169,
  175–76; Theosophy on, 207; Wood on,
  173–75
expression, law of, 109

Home College of Divine Science, 108–9
Home of Truth, 8, 99, 103, 113–17, 219,
   248; principles of, 115, 116
homeopathy, 85–86, 89, 91, 195, 227
Hopkins, Emma Curtis, 98–103; as anti-
   materialistic, 99–100; on God, 101–2;
   on gospel of "The Good", 102, 109,
   218; influence of, 104, 105, 108, 110,
   111, 113, 248; on prayer, 102; spiritual
   healing by, 98, 100–2; seminary of, 99,
   113; writings of, 98, 99–100
Hopkins, George Irving, 98
Howard, Clifford, 16
Howe, Julia Ward, 119
Howison, George Holmes, 161
Hubbard, Barbara Marx, 247
Hubbard, Elbert, 217
Huber, Richard, 14, 216–17, 240
Huckel, Oliver, 153–54
Hudson, W. J., 148
Hufeland, Christoph Wilhelm von, 29
Hunt, Freeman, 217
Hunting, Gardner, 108
Hurd, Dr. Henry M., 154
Huxley, Thomas, 170, 175
hydropathy, 89, 91
hypnosis/hypnotism, 27, 49, 57, 73, 126,
   139, 206; concerns about, 41, 87, 88,
   107, 147–48, 196; used in healing, 28,
   47–48, 147, 152, 154
hypochondria, 150
Hyslop, James Hervey, 42
hysteria, 147, 150, 202

I

idealism, 6, 133, 271, 276; Berkeley's, 100,
   126; Eddy's, 93, 94, 95, 117; Evans's,
   76, 79, 94; practical, x, 16, 278–79; in
   phrenopathy, 76; scarred by World
   War I, 230–32
illumination, 199, 211
individual, 158, 176, 241–42; power
   of, 210–11, 227, 230–31, 233, 278;
   responsibility, 103, 182, 183–84,
   187–88, 189, 214, 216, 218, 222, 236;

rights of, 250, 276, 277; self-reliant,
   22–23, 137–38, 187, 215, 230, 233, 276;
   self-made, 241; as work in progress,
   209–10
influx, divine, 4, 37, 98, 276; Christian
   Theosophy on, 213; Emerson's
   belief in, 22; Evans on, 68, 71, 73;
   Swedenborg on, 33–34, 69, 140, 143–
   45, 162; Trine on, 175
Ingalese, Richard, 180–81, 196, 230
Institute of Culture and Creation
   Spirituality, 267
Institute of Religious Science and
   School of Philosophy, 111, 113
intelligence, 164, 176
International College of Mental
   Science, 113
International Divine Science
   Association, 99, 108, 110
International Metaphysical League,
   119, 131
International New Thought Alliance
   (INTA), 8, 110, 116, 231; principles of,
   250–53; purpose of, 119–20
intuition, 4–5, 161, 238; Carnegie on, 238;
   Emerson on, 22–23; James on, 129;
   Quimby's, 51, 55; Theosophy on, 207;
   Troward on, 176
isolationism, 231, 232

J

James, Fannie Brooks, 99, 110, 108
James, Henry Jr. and Sr., 124
James, William, x, 12, 41, 124–30, 132,
   137, 148, 149, 151, 161, 174, 186, 220,
   234; on Christian Science, 126, 128;
   on conventional medicine, 125, 126,
   129; on existence of God, 128; on
   healthy-mindedness, ix, 125, 126,
   127–28, 155–56; on hypnosis, 126; on
   mind cure, 125, 126, 127–28, 129, 130;
   optimism of, 127, 129, 130; on the
   practical, 130, 138; on psychology, 127;
   on relationship of God and soul, 133;
   on religion and happiness, 126; on

the "sick soul", 124, 125, 128–29; on Spiritualism, 125–26; on subliminal consciousness, 128; on suggestion, 126; *The Varieties of Religious Experience* of, 123, 125, 126, 127, 128, 233

Janet, Pierre, 123, 124–25, 129

Jastrow, Joseph, 41

Jastrow, Morris, 123

Jeans, Sir James, 159

Jesus: Christian Science on, 88; divinity of, 104–5; Eddy compares herself to, 89, 90; as healer, 53, 54–55, 72, 73–74, 77, 78–79, 82, 100, 109, 150–51; love of, 72; salvation through, 268; as scientific man, 46, 53; social gospel of, 177, 181–82, 211; success of, 235–36

Jews: in Christian Science, 199–200, 201; faith healing/mind cure by (Jewish science), 199–205; psychology by, 155

Johns Hopkins School of Medicine, 154

Johnson, Dr. Spencer, 262

Jones, David, 270

Jordan, Dr. David Starr, 238

Judge, William Quan, 207

Jung, Carl Gustav, 146, 203

Jung, Johann Heinrich (Jung-Stilling), 29–30

K

Kant, Immanuel, 162

Kardec, Allan, 197

Katie, Byron, 244

Keim, Karl Theodor, 149

Kenyon, Essek William, 268–69, 270–71

Kimball, Edward A., 91

King, Larry, 256

Kluge, Karl A. F., 29

Knight, Judy Zebra, 197

knowledge, 4, 100; self-, 222–23

Krishnamurti, Jiddu, 208

Kuh, Dr. Sidney, 153

L

LaFontaine, Charles, 28

Lakewood Church, 269

Lamarck, Jean-Baptiste, 160

Lamarckianism, 165

Larkin, Dr. E., 35

Lathrop, John H., 146

Larson, Christian D., 111, 113

Lauer, Matt, 256

Lavoisier, Antoine-Laurent, 26

League for the Larger Life, 113, 121

Le Conte, Joseph, 161, 171–72, 174

Lee, Mother Ann, 20, 91, 190–91

Lester, Meera, 257–58

Leuba, James Henry, 96, 123

Levin, Jeff, 259

Levingston, William, 39

Lewis, Clarence I., 125

Lichtenstein, Morris, 202–5

Liébeault, Ambroise-Auguste, 28, 147

Life Visioning Process, 247

Lindy, J. W., 118

Lloyd, Henry Demarest, 183, 184

Lodge, Sir Oliver, 41

Lombroso, Cesare, 41

London Dialectical Society, 41

Long, Bishop Eddie L., 270

Longfellow, Henry W., 21

Losier, Michael, 258

love: divine, 6, 114, 115, 131, 142–43, 145–46, 275, 276; of money, 219–20; Swedenborg on, 72, 140, 142

Luhan, Mabel Dodge, 103

lyceum movement, 3, 22, 43

Lynch, Richard, 108

M

Mabie, Hamilton Wright, 119

McComb, Samuel, 148, 150, 151, 152

McConnell, Daniel Ray, 270

Macdonald, L. B., 118

McElroy, Margaret, 198

McFadden, Cynthia, 256

McGuffey, William H., 14, 217, 240

magnetism, 39, 228. *See also* animal magnetism

Magus Incognitus, 226. *See also* William Walker Atkinson

healing by, 60; Dresser on, 59, 60, 83, 134; Eddy's science based on, 64, 82, 83; on healer-patient relationship, 61, 62; healing by, 44, 47–49, 53, 54, 55, 57–58, 59, 60, 61, 62; on hypnosis, 47–49, 57; on inner mind, 57; on Jesus 46, 53, 54–55, 56; on medical profession, 49–50; as mesmerist, 44–45, 46–49, 51, 81; on mesmerism, 57, 75, 196; mind cure of, 48, 122; on natural vs. scientific man, 52, 53, 56, 58, 60; patents of, 45; on phrenology 50; on power of mind, 49, 50–51; practice of, 59, 60; psychotherapy of, 48–49; and religion, 53, 56; on science as wisdom, 55–56, 58; Science of Health of, 45, 51–60; silent method of, 45, 52–53; Spiritualism of, 50, 59; on suggestion, 48–49, 51–52; on thought-transference, 52, 53; treatment techniques of, 49, 86; writings of, 82–83

R
Raja-Yoga School and Theosophical University, 208
Ramacharaka, Yogi, 226. See also William Walker Atkinson
Rapp, Johann George, 20
Ratzinger, Cardinal Joseph (Pope Benedict XVI), 267–68
Rauschenbusch, Walter, 183
Ray, James Arthur, 256
Redfield, James, vii–viii, 244
Reed, Frederick, 117, 118, 132
Reese, Della, 246
Reichenbach, Baron Karl von, 30–31, 41, 75, 213
Reiki, 258
reincarnation, 103, 207, 208, 209
relaxation treatment, 127, 128
religion, 149, 274–75; practical, 275–76; psychology in, 123–24, 149–50; science impacts, 163, 174, 207, 209, 277–78
Religious Science, 8, 103, 111, 246, 247, 257, 269, 272; principles of, 112–13

religious therapeutics. See Emmanuel Movement
Renan, Ernest, 149
right thinking, 85, 100, 108, 181–82, 202, 271
Rix, Harriet Hale, 114, 248
Robbins, Anthony, 262
Roberts, Jane, 197
Robinson, Frank Bruce, 121
Rockefeller, John D., 224, 238
Romanes, George, 170
Roosevelt, Franklin D., 229, 238
Roosevelt, Theodore, 224, 238
Root, Julia Anderson, 193
Royce, Josiah, 41, 132, 133, 137

S
salvation, 214–15, 218, 281
Santayana, George, 125
sarcognomy, 36, 37, 43
Savage, Minot Judson, 119, 269
Schirmer, David, 256
Schlatter, Francis, 191
Schneider, Herbert W., 172
School of Applied Metaphysics, 8
Schucman, Helen, 263, 264
Schuller, Robert H., 13
science, 52, 53, 60; biomedicine tied to, 194–95; holistic, 260; religion impacted by, 163, 174, 207, 209, 277–78; spiritual, 200; as wisdom, 55–56, 58
Science of Being, 90, 194
Science of Health, 45, 51–60
Science of Mind, 111–13
Scoresby, William, 28
Seabury, Annetta. See Dresser, Annetta
Seat of the Soul Institute, 265
secularism, 278, 279–80
Seicho-No-Ie, 249–50
self: -culture, 219; -discipline, 238; -discovery, 167, 243–44; -healing, 76–77, 106, 253; -help, 91, 155, 180, 235, 261–62; inner, 74, 136, 159, 236, 263; -interest, 232; -knowledge, 136,

Unity Village, 246
Universal Foundation for Better Living, 246
University of Christ, 116
utopians, 20

V
Vail, Dr. William, 80
Van-Anderson, Rev. Helen, 99, 120
van Helmont, Jan Baptista, 25
Vedanta Societies, 118, 121, 305n61
Virtue, Doreen, 257
virtue: nature of changes, 217–18; success as, 215, 216, 276, 279
visualization, 230, 238–39
vitalism, 213
Vivekananda, Swami, 12, 113–14, 305n61
volation, 227
voluntarism, 92, 277, 278

W
Waitley, Denis, 256
Wallace, Alfred R., 170
Walters, Zelia M., 108, 223
Wanamaker, John, 238
Ware, Judge Ashur, 61
Ware, Emma, 54, 60, 61
Ware, Sarah, 54, 60, 61
Warren, Rick, 272
Wattles, Wallace D., 13, 223, 238, 256, 258
Weeks, Dr. E. B., 104
Weil, Andrew, 260
Welch, Dr. William H., 154
Wells, Samuel Robert, 32
Weiss, Richard, 155
Wesley, John, 190
West Coast Metaphysical Bureau, 114
Whipple, Leander Edmund, 193
White, Andrew D., 41
White, Ellen G., 20
White, Paula, 270
Whitehouse, Deborah, 254, 272
Whitell, Evelyn, 108
Whitman, Walt, 12, 21, 127
Whitney, Frank B., 107–8, 223

Wienholt, Arnold, 29
Wilcox, Ella Wheeler, 11, 99
Williams, Montel, 256
Williamson, Marianne, 267
Wilmans, Helen, 99, 222–23
Wilson, Ernest C., 108
Wilson, Woodrow, 231, 238
Winfrey, Oprah, 247, 255–58, 265
Winkley, Jonathan W., 119
Wisdom University, 268
Wolfe, Walter B., 155
Wood, Henry, 11, 126, 148; on Christian Science, 94, 254; on evolution, 173–75; Ideal Suggestion of, 196–97; on regular medicine, 192–93; on silence, 196; on socialism, 177–78
Woodbridge, Russell S., 270
Woodbury, Josephine Curtis, 97
Worcester, Elwood, 148, 149–53; on angels, 152; on Christ as physician, 150–52; on Christian Science, 152–53; on psychology in religion, 149–50; on subconscious, 151
Worcester Medical School, 66
Word of Faith movement, 268–72
World Parliament of Religions, 118, 133, 209
World War I, 230–31
Wright, Chauncey, 125
Wrigley, William Jr., 238
Wundt, Wilhelm, 149, 151

Y, Z
Yarnall, Jane W., 199
yoga, 114–15, 219, 247, 260
Yogananda, Paramhansa, 12
Zukav, Gary, 265